Charles L. Hutchins

A Hymnal and Service-Book

For Sunday schools, day schools, guilds, brotherhoods

Charles L. Hutchins

A Hymnal and Service-Book
For Sunday schools, day schools, guilds, brotherhoods

ISBN/EAN: 9783337083038

Printed in Europe, USA, Canada, Australia, Japan

Cover: Foto ©Thomas Meinert / pixelio.de

More available books at **www.hansebooks.com**

A

Hymnal and Service - Book

for

Sunday Schools

Day Schools, Guilds, Brotherhoods, etc.

Edited by the

Rev. Charles L. Hutchins

Two Hundred and Forty-fifth Thousand

𝔈𝔡𝔦𝔱𝔦𝔬𝔫 𝔄

Parish Choir
Boston

Prefatory Note.

THE revision of the Book of Common Prayer has rendered desirable, if not necessary, a revision of the Liturgical portions of the Sunday-School Hymnal taken from that Book. The editor has availed himself of the opportunity thus afforded him to add a considerable number of hymns and carols, and trusts that the revision and additions thus made may increase the usefulness of this Hymnal and Service-Book among the children of the Church.

WHITSUNTIDE, 1893.

Contents.

The Choral Service.

(TALLIS'S FESTIVAL.)

FOR MORNING AND EVENING PRAYER.

[If preferred, the Service may be taken on any note in monotone as far as to the Responses after the Lord's Prayer.]

The Minister shall begin by reading one or more of the following Sentences of Scripture:
Those marked with an * are for Evening Prayer.

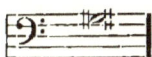

THE Lord is in his holy temple: let all the earth keep silence before him. *Hab.* ii. 20.

I was glad when they said unto me, We will go into the house of the LORD. *Psalm* cxxii. 1.

Let the words of my mouth, and the meditation of my heart, be alway acceptable in thy sight, O LORD, my strength and my redeemer. *Psalm* xix. 14, 15.

Grace be unto you, and peace, from God our Father, and from the Lord Jesus Christ. *Phil.* i. 2.

*Lord, I have loved the habitation of thy house, and the place where thine honour dwelleth. *Psalm* xxvi. 8.

*Let my prayer be set forth in thy sight as the incense; and let the lifting up of my hands be an evening sacrifice. *Psalm* cxli. 2.

*O worship the Lord in the beauty of holiness; let the whole earth stand in awe of him. *Psalm* xcvi. 9. '

Repent ye, for the Kingdom of Heaven is at hand. *St. Matt.* iii. 2. **Advent.**

Prepare ye the way of the LORD, make straight in the desert a highway for our God. *Isaiah.* xl. 3.

*Watch ye, for ye know not when the master of the house cometh, at even, or at midnight, or at the cock-crowing, or in the morning: lest coming suddenly he find you sleeping. *St. Mark* xiii. 35, 36.

Behold, I bring you good tidings of great joy, which shall be to all people. For unto you is born this day in the city of David a Saviour, which is **Christmas.** Christ the Lord. *St. Luke* ii. 10, 11.

*Behold, the tabernacle of God is with men, and he will dwell with them, and they shall be his people, and God himself shall be with them, and be their God. *Rev.* xxi. 3.

From the rising of the sun even unto the going down of the same my Name shall be great among the Gentiles; and in every place incense shall be offered **Epiphany.** unto my Name, and a pure offering: for my Name shall be great among the heathen, saith the LORD of hosts. *Mal.* i. 11.

Awake, awake; put on thy strength, put on thy beautiful garments, O Jerusalem. *Isaiah* lii. 1.

*Come ye, and let us walk in the light of the LORD. And he will teach us of his ways, and we will walk in his paths. *Isaiah* ii. 5, 3. (3)

Is it nothing to you, all ye that pass by? behold, and see if there be any sorrow like unto my sorrow which is done unto me, wherewith the Lord hath afflicted me. *Lam.* i. 12.

Good Friday.

*He hath made him to be sin for us, who knew no sin; that we might be made the righteousness of God in him. 2 *Cor.* v. 21.

*In whom we have redemption through his blood, the forgiveness of sins, according to the riches of his grace. *Eph.* i. 7.

Easter. He is risen. The Lord is risen indeed. *St. Mark.* xvi. 6. *St. Luke* xxiv. 34.

This is the day which the Lord hath made; we will rejoice and be glad in it. *Psalm* cxviii. 24.

*If ye then be risen with Christ, seek those things which are above, where Christ sitteth on the right hand of God. *Col.* iii. 1.

Seeing that we have a great High Priest, that is passed into the heavens, Jesus the Son of God, let us come boldly unto the throne of grace, that we may obtain mercy, and find grace to help in time of need. *Heb.* iv. 14, 16.

Ascension.

*Christ is not entered into the holy places made with hands, which are the figures of the true; but into heaven itself, now to appear in the presence of God for us. *Heb.* ix. 24.

Whitsun- day. Because ye are sons, God hath sent forth the Spirit of His Son into your hearts, crying, Abba, Father. *Gal.* iv. 6.

There is a river, the streams whereof shall make glad the city of God, the holy place of the tabernacles of the Most High. *Psalm* xlvi. 4.

The hour cometh, and now is, when the true worshippers shall worship the Father in spirit and in truth. *St. John* iv. 23.

*The Spirit and the bride say, Come. And let him that heareth say, Come. And let him that is athirst come. And whosoever will, let him take the water of life freely. *Rev.* xxii. 17.

*O send out thy light and thy truth, that they may lead me, and bring me unto thy holy hill, and to thy dwelling. *Psalm* xliii. 3.

Holy, holy, holy, Lord God Almighty, which was, and is, and is to come. *Rev.* iv. 8.

Trinity- Sunday. *Holy, holy, holy, is the LORD of hosts: the whole earth is full of His glory. *Isaiah* vi. 3.

When the wicked man turneth away from his wickedness that he hath committed, and doeth that which is lawful and right, he shall save his soul alive. *Ezek.* xviii. 27.

I acknowledge my transgressions: and my sin is ever before me. *Psalm* li. 3.

Hide thy face from my sins, and blot out all mine iniquities. *Psalm* li. 9.

The sacrifices of God are a broken spirit: a broken and a contrite heart, O God, thou wilt not despise. *Psalm* li. 17.

Rend your heart, and not your garments, and turn unto the LORD your God: for he is gracious and merciful, slow to anger, and of great kindness, and repenteth him of the evil. *Joel* ii. 13.

To the Lord our God belong mercies and forgivenesses, though we have rebelled against him; neither have we obeyed the voice of the LORD our God, to walk in his laws which he set before us. *Dan.* ix. 9, 10.

O LORD, correct me, but with judgment; not in thine anger, lest thou bring me to nothing. *Jer.* x. 24. *Psalm* vi. 1.

I will arise and go to my father, and will say unto him, Father, I have sinned against heaven, and before thee, and am no more worthy to be called thy son. *St. Luke* xv. 18, 19.

Enter not into judgment with thy servant, O LORD; for in thy sight shall no man living be justified. *Psalm* cxliii. 2.

If we say that we have no sin, we deceive ourselves, and the truth is not in us; but if we confess our sins, God is faithful and just to forgive us our sins, and to cleanse us from all unrighteousness. 1 *St. John* i. 8, 9.

At Evening Prayer the Minister may say:
Let us humbly confess our sins unto Almighty God.—
And pass to the General Confession below.

¶ *Or else he shall say:*

DEARLY beloved brethren, the Scripture moveth us, in sundry places, to acknowledge and confess our manifold sins and wickedness; and that we should not dissemble nor cloak them before the face of Almighty God our heavenly Father; but confess them with an humble, lowly, penitent, and obedient heart; to the end that we may obtain forgiveness of the same, by his infinite goodness and mercy. And although we ought, at all times, humbly to acknowledge our sins before God; yet ought we chiefly so to do, when we assemble and meet together to render thanks for the great benefits that we have received at his hands, to set forth his most worthy praise, to hear his most holy Word, and to ask those things which are requisite and necessary, as well for the body as the soul. Wherefore I pray and beseech you, as many as are here present, to accompany me with a pure heart, and humble voice, unto the throne of the heavenly grace, say - ing,—

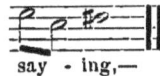

A GENERAL CONFESSION, *to be said by all kneeling.*

Almighty and most merciful Father; We have erred and strayed from Thy ways like lost sheep.

We have followed too much the devices and desires of our own hearts.
We have offended against thy holy laws.
We have left undone those things which we ought to have done;
And we have done those things which we ought not to have done;
And there is no health in us.
But thou, O Lord, have mercy upon us, miserable offenders.
Spare thou those, O God, who confess their faults.
Restore thou those who are penitent;

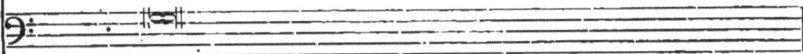

According to thy promises declared unto mankind in Christ Je - sus our Lord.

And grant, O most merciful Father, for his sake;

2 trebles.

That we may ⎱
hereafter live a ⎰ godly, righteous, and sober life, To the glory of thy ⎱
⎰ ho - ly Name. A-MEN.

¶ *The Declaration of Absolution, or Remission of Sins; to be made by the Priest alone, standing; the People still kneeling.*

ALMIGHTY God, the Father of our Lord Jesus Christ, who desireth not the death of a sinner, but rather that he may turn from his wickedness and live, hath given power, and commandment, to his Ministers, to declare and pronounce to his people, being penitent, the Absolution and Remission of their sins. He pardoneth and absolveth all those who truly repent, and unfeignedly believe his holy Gospel. Wherefore let us beseech him to grant us true repentance, and his Holy Spirit, that those things may please him which we do at this present; and that the rest of our life hereafter may be pure and holy; so that at the last we may come to his eternal joy; through Jesus Christ our Lord.

A - men.

¶ *Or this.*

ALMIGHTY God, our heavenly Father, who of his great mercy hath promised forgiveness of sins to all those who, with hearty repentance and true faith, turn unto him; have mercy upon you; pardon and deliver you from all your sins; confirm and strengthen you in all goodness; and bring you to everlasting life; through Jesus Christ our Lord.

A - men.

¶ *Then the Minister shall kneel, and say the Lord's Prayer; the People still kneeling, and repeating it with him.*

Our Father, who art in heaven,

Hallowed be thy Name. Thy kingdom come. Thy will be done on earth, As it is in heaven. Give us this day our daily bread. And forgive us our trespasses, As we forgive those who trespass against us. And lead us not into temptation; But deliver us from evil; For thine is the kingdom, and the power, and the glory, for ever and ever.

A - MEN.

¶ *Then likewise he shall say.*

MINISTER.

ORG.
O Lord, open thou our lips.

ANSWER.

p
And our mouth shall show forth . thy praise.

All standing.

MINISTER.

Glory be to the Father, and to the Son, and to the Holy Ghost;

ANSWER.

f
As . . it was in the beginning, is now, and ever shall be, world without end. A-MEN.

ORG.   ORG.

MINISTER.

Praise ye the Lord.

ANSWER.

f
The Lord's Name be prais - ed.

ORG.

¶ *Then, if the Service be* MORNING PRAYER, *shall be sung the* VENITE (*page 42*), *except on those days for which other Anthems are appointed,* (*page 54, etc.*) *After which shall follow one of the* PSALMS (*page 56, etc.*)

But if the Service be EVENING PRAYER, *then shall follow one of the* PSALMS, (*page 56, etc.*)

¶ AFTER *the* PSALM, *shall be read the* FIRST LESSON. *After which, if the Service be* MORNING PRAYER, *shall be sung the* TE DEUM (*page* 43), *or the* BENEDICITE (*page* 44).

But if the Service be EVENING PRAYER, *there shall be sung the* MAGNIFICAT (*page* 48): *or the* CANTATE DOMINO (*page* 49), *or the* BONUM EST (*page* 50).

¶ *Then shall be read the* SECOND LESSON. *After which, if the Service be* MORNING PRAYER, *shall be sung the* BENEDICTUS (*page* 45), *or the* JUBILATE DEO, (*page* 46).

But if the Service be EVENING PRAYER, *there shall be sung the* NUNC DIMITTIS (*page* 51), *or the* DEUS MISEREATUR (*page* 52), *or the* BENEDIC, ANIMA MEA (*page* 53).

¶ *Then shall be said by the Minister and the People, standing, the* APOSTLES' CREED, *or the* NICENE CREED, *as followeth.*

APOSTLES' CREED.

in God the Father Almighty, Maker of heaven and earth: And in Jesus Christ his only Son our Lord: Who was conceived by the Holy Ghost, Born of the Virgin Mary: Suffered under Pontius Pilate, Was crucified, dead, and buried: He descended into hell; The third day he rose again from the dead: He ascended into heaven, And sitteth on the right hand of God the Father Almighty: From thence he shall come to judge the quick and the dead.

I believe in the Holy Ghost: The holy Catholic Church; The Communion of Saints: the Forgiveness of sins: the Resurrection of the body: And the Life everlasting.

NICENE CREED.

I BELIEVE in one God the Father Almighty, Maker of heaven and earth, And of all things visible and invisible:

And in one Lord Jesus Christ, the only begotten Son of God: Begotten of his Father before all worlds, God of God, Light of Light, Very God of very God; Begotten, not made; Being of one substance with the Father; By whom all things were made: Who for us men and for our salvation came down from heaven, And was incarnate by the Holy Ghost of the Virgin Mary, And was made man: And was crucified also for us under Pontius Pilate; He suffered and was buried: And the third day he rose again according to the Scriptures: and ascended into heaven, And sitteth on the right hand of the Father: And he shall come again, with glory, to judge both the quick and the dead; Whose kingdom shall have no end.

And I believe in the Holy Ghost, the Lord, and Giver of Life, Who proceedeth from the Father and the Son; Who with the Father and the Son together is worshipped and glorified; Who spake by the Prophets: And I believe one Catholic and Apostolic Church: I acknowledge one Baptism for the remission of sins: And I look for the Resurrection of the dead: And the Life of the world to come. Amen.

¶ *And after that, these Prayers following, all devoutly kneeling; the Minister first pronouncing,*

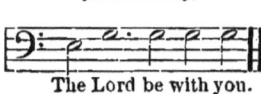

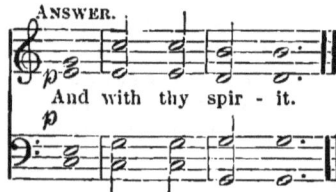

The Lord be with you.

ANSWER. And with thy spir-it.

MINISTER. Let us pray.

MINISTER.

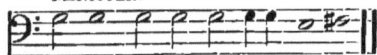

O Lord, show thy mer-cy up-on us.

ANSWER.

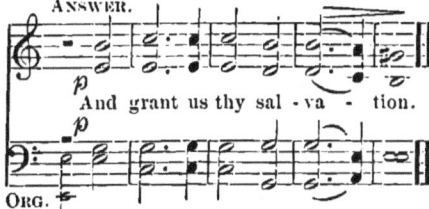

p
And grant us thy sal - va - tion.

p

ORG.

The next four Versicles and Responses are to be used only at Evening Prayer.

MINISTER.

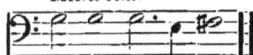

O Lord, save the State.

ANSWER.

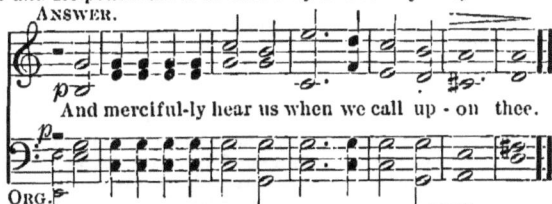

p
And merciful-ly hear us when we call up - on thee.

p

ORG.

MINISTER.

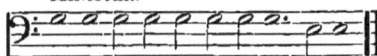

Endue thy min-is-ters with righteousness.

ANSWER.

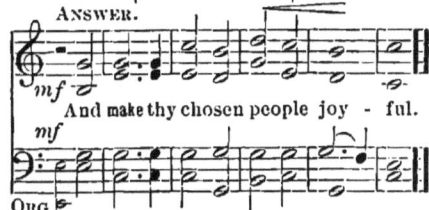

mf
And make thy chosen people joy - ful.

mf

ORG.

MINISTER.

O Lord, save thy peo - ple.

ANSWER.

p
And bless thine in - he - ri - tance.

p

ORG.

MINISTER.

Give peace in our time, O Lord.

ANSWER.

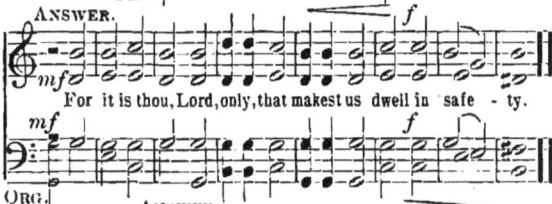

mf
For it is thou, Lord, only, that makest us dwell in safe - ty.

mf *f*

ORG.

MINISTER.

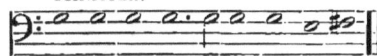

O God, make clean our hearts within us.

ANSWER.

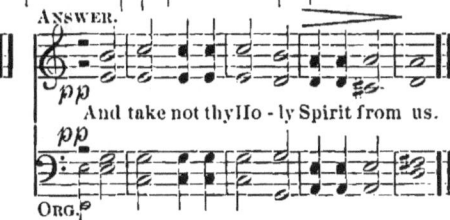

pp
And take not thy Ho - ly Spirit from us.

pp

ORG.

¶ *Then shall follow the* COLLECT FOR THE DAY *(page 28, etc.), except when the Communion Service is read; and after that, the Collects and Prayers following.*

But NOTE, *that if the Service be* MORNING PRAYER, *the* FOURTH, FIFTH AND SIXTH *of the* FOLLOWING COLLECTS *are to be* OMITTED, *and the* LITANY *(page 10), is to be said in its proper place on the appointed days.*

If the Service be EVENING PRAYER, *the* FIRST THREE COLLECTS *are to be* OMITTED.

A COLLECT FOR PEACE. (ONLY IN MORNING.)

O GOD, who art the author of peace and lover of concord, in knowledge of whom standeth our eternal life, whose service is perfect freedom; Defend us thy humble servants in all assaults of our enemies; that we, surely trusting in thy defence, may not fear the power of any adversaries, through the might of Jesus Christ our Lord.

A-MEN.

A COLLECT FOR GRACE. (ONLY IN MORNING.)

O LORD, our heavenly Father, Almighty and everlasting God, who hast safely brought us to the beginning of this day; Defend us in the same with thy mighty power; and grant that this day we fall into no sin, neither run into any kind of danger; but that all our doings, being ordered by thy governance, may be righteous in thy sight; through Jesus Christ our Lord. *Amen.*

A PRAYER FOR THE PRESIDENT OF THE UNITED STATES, AND ALL IN CIVIL AUTHORITY. (ONLY IN MORNING.)

O LORD, our heavenly Father, the high and mighty Ruler of the universe, who dost from thy throne behold all the dwellers upon earth; Most heartily we beseech thee, with thy favour to behold and bless thy servant THE PRESIDENT OF THE UNITED STATES, and all others in authority; and so replenish them with the grace of thy Holy Spirit, that they may always incline to thy will, and walk in thy way. Endue them plenteously with heavenly gifts; grant them in health and prosperity long to live; and finally, after this life, to attain everlasting joy and felicity; through Jesus Christ our Lord. *Amen.*

A COLLECT FOR PEACE. (ONLY IN EVENING.)

O GOD, from whom all holy desires, all good counsels, and all just works do proceed; Give unto thy servants that peace which the world cannot give; that our hearts may be set to obey thy commandments, and also that by thee, we, being defended from the fear of our enemies, may pass our time in rest and quietness; through the merits of Jesus Christ our Saviour. *Amen.*

A COLLECT FOR AID AGAINST PERILS. (ONLY IN EVENING.)

L IGHTEN our darkness, we beseech thee, O Lord; and by thy great mercy defend us from all perils and dangers of this night; for the love of thy only Son, our Saviour, Jesus Christ. *Amen.*

Evening Prayer may end here.

A PRAYER FOR THE PRESIDENT OF THE UNITED STATES, AND ALL IN CIVIL AUTHORTY. (ONLY IN EVENING.)

A LMIGHTY God, whose kingdom is everlasting and power infinite, Have mercy upon this whole land; and so rule the hearts of thy servants THE PRESIDENT OF THE UNITED STATES, *the Governor of this State,* and all others in authority, that they, knowing whose ministers they are, may above all things seek thy honour and glory; and that we and all the People, duly considering whose authority they bear, may faithfully and obediently honour them, in thee, and for thee, according to thy blessed Word and ordinance; through Jesus Christ our Lord, who with thee and the Holy Ghost liveth and reigneth ever, one God, world without end. *Amen.*

¶ *The following Prayers shall be omitted here when the Litany is said.*

A PRAYER FOR THE CLERGY AND PEOPLE.

ALMIGHTY and everlasting God, from whom cometh every good and perfect gift; Send down upon our Bishops, and other Clergy, and upon the Congregations committed to their charge, the healthful Spirit of thy grace; and, that they may truly please thee, pour upon them the continual dew of thy blessing. Grant this, O Lord, for the honour of our Advocate and Mediator, Jesus Christ. *Amen.*

A PRAYER FOR ALL CONDITIONS OF MEN.

O GOD, the Creator and Preserver of all mankind, we humbly beseech thee for all sorts and conditions of men; that thou wouldest be pleased to make thy ways known unto them, thy saving health unto all nations. More especially we pray for thy holy Church universal; that it may be so guided and governed by Thy good Spirit, that all who profess and call themselves Christians may be led into the way of truth, and hold the faith in unity of spirit, in the bond of peace, and in righteousness of life. Finally, we commend to thy fatherly goodness all those who are any ways afflicted, or distressed, in mind, body, or estate; [* *especial-* | * *This may be said when any* *ly those for whom our prayers are desired,*] that it may please thee to | *desire the* comfort and relieve them, according to their several necessities; giv- | *Prayers of the* ing them patience under their sufferings, and a happy issue out of all | *Congregation.* their afflictions. And this we beg for Jesus Christ's sake. *Amen.*

A GENERAL THANKSGIVING.

ALMIGHTY God, Father of all mercies, we, thine unworthy servants, do give thee most humble and hearty thanks for all thy goodness and loving-kindness to us, and to all men; [* *particularly to those who desire now to offer up* | * *This may be* *their praises and thanksgivings for thy late mercies vouchsafed unto them.*] | *used when any* | *desire to return* We bless thee for our creation, preservation, and all the blessings of | *thanks for mer-* this life; but above all, for thine inestimable love in the redemption | *cies vouchsafed* of the world by our Lord Jesus Christ; for the means of grace, and | *to them.* for the hope of glory. And, we beseech thee, give us that due sense of all thy mercies that our hearts may be unfeignedly thankful, and that we show forth thy praise, not only with our lips, but in our lives, by giving up our selves to thy service, and by walking before thee in holiness and righteousness all our days; through Jesus Christ our Lord, to whom, with thee and the Holy Ghost, be all honour and glory, world without end. *Amen.*

A PRAYER OF ST. CHRYSOSTOM.

ALMIGHTY God, who hast given us grace at this time with one accord to make our common supplications unto thee; and dost promise that when two or three are gathered together in thy Name thou wilt grant their requests; Fulfil now, O Lord, the desires and petitions of thy servants, as may be most expedient for them; granting us in this world knowledge of thy truth, and in the world to come life everlasting. *Amen.*

2 *Cor.* xiii. 14.

THE grace of our Lord Jesus Christ, and the love of God, and the fellowship of the Holy Ghost, be with us all evermore.

A - men.

The Litany.
(TALLIS.)

MINISTER.

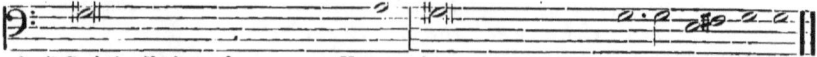

1. O God the Father of   Heaven : have mercy upon us mis-er - a-ble sinners.
2. O God the Son, Redeemer of the   world : have mercy upon us mis-er - a-ble sinners.
3. O God the Holy Ghost, proceed- } Son : have mercy upou us mis-er - a-ble sinners.
     ing from the Father and the
4. O holy, blessed, and glorious } God : have mercy upou us mis-er - a-ble sinners.
     Trinity, three Persons and one

ANSWER.

1. *O God the Father of*   *Heaven : have mercy upon us mis-er - a - ble sin - ners.*
2. *O God the Son, Redeemer of the*   *world : have mercy upon us mis-er - a - ble sin - ners.*
3. *O God the Holy Ghost, proceed-* } *Son : have mercy upon us mis-er - a - ble sin - ners.*
    ing from the Father and the
4. *O holy, blessed, and glorious* } *God : have mercy upon us mis-er - a - ble sin - ners.*
    Trinity, three Persons and one

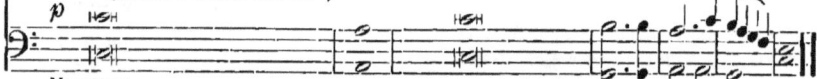

MINISTER.

Remember not, Lord, our offences, nor
the offences of our forefathers ; neither take thou vengeance of our
sins : spare us, good Lord, spare thy
people, whom thou hast redeemed
with thy most precious blood, and be
not angry with . . . . us for ev - er.

ANSWER.

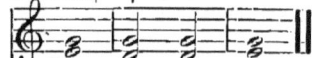

Spare us, good Lord.

MINISTER.

From all evil and mischief ;
from sin ; from the crafts
and assaults of the devil ;
from thy wrath, and from
everlast - - - ing dam-na-tion,

ANSWER.

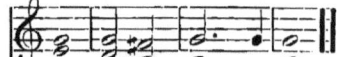

Good Lord, de - liv - er us.

From all blindness of heart ; from pride, vain-glory, and hypocrisy ; from envy, hatred,
    and malice, and all unchari | ta-ble-ness,   *Good Lord, deliver us.*
From all inordinate and sinful affections ; and from all the deceits of the world, the
    flesh, | and the devil,   *Good Lord, deliver us.*
From lightning and tempest ; from plague, pestilence, and famine ; from battle and
    murder, and from | sudden death,   *Good Lord, deliver us.*
From all sedition, privy conspiracy, and rebellion ; from all false doctrine, heresy,
    and schism ; from hardness of heart, and contempt of thy Word | and Command-
    ment,   *Good Lord, deliver us.*
By the mystery of thy holy Incarnation ; by thy holy Nativity and Circumcision ; by
    thy Baptism, Fasting, | and Temptation,   *Good Lord, deliver us.*
By thine Agony and Bloody Sweat ; By thy Cross and Passion ; by thy precious
    Death and Burial ; by thy glorious Resurrection and Ascension ; and by the coming
    of the | Holy Ghost,   *Good Lord, deliver us.*
In all time of our tribulation ; in all time of our prosperity ; in the hour of death, and
    in the | day of judgment,   *Good Lord, deliver us.*

MINISTER.   **ANSWER.**

We sinners do beseech
thee to hear us, O Lord
God; and that it may
please thee to rule
and govern thy holy
Church universal in the right way;

We be-seech thee to hear us, good Lord.

That it may please thee to bless and preserve all Christian Rulers, and Magistrates, giving them grace to execute justice, and to | main-tain truth;
We beseech thee to hear us, good Lord.

That it may please thee to illuminate all Bishops, Priests, and Deacons, with true knowledge and understanding of thy Word; and that both by their preaching and living they may set it forth, and show | it ac-cordingly;
We beseech thee to hear us, good Lord.

That it may please thee to send forth labourers | into thy harvest;
We beseech thee to hear us, good Lord.

That it may please thee to bless and keep | all thy people;
We beseech thee to hear us, good Lord.

That it may please thee to give to all nations unity, | peace, and concord;
We beseech thee to hear us, good Lord.

That it may please thee to give us an heart to love and fear thee, and diligently to live after | thy com-mandments; *We beseech thee to hear us, good Lord.*

That it may please thee to give to all thy people increase of grace to hear meekly thy Word, and to receive it with pure affection, and to bring forth the fruits | of the Spirit; *We beseech thee to hear us, good Lord.*

That it may please thee to bring into the way of truth all such as have erred, and | are de-ceived; *We beseech thee to hear us, good Lord.*

That it may please thee to strengthen such as do stand; and to comfort and help the weak-hearted; and to raise up those who fall; and finally to beat down Satan | under our feet; *We beseech thee to hear us, good Lord.*

That it may please thee to succour, help, and comfort, all who are in danger, necessity, and | tri-bu-lation; *We beseech thee to hear us, good Lord.*

That it may please thee to preserve all who travel by land or by water, all women in the perils of child-birth, all sick persons, and young children; and to show thy pity upon all prison- | ers and captives;
We beseech thee to hear us, good Lord.

That it may please thee to defend, and provide for, the fatherless children, and widows, and all who are desolate | and oppressed;
We beseech thee to hear us, good Lord.

That it may please thee to have mercy up- | on all men;
We beseech thee to hear us, good Lord.

That it may please thee to forgive our enemies, persecutors, and slanderers, and to | turn their hearts; *We beseech thee to hear us, good Lord.*

That it may please thee to give and preserve to our use the kindly fruits of the earth, so that in due time we | may en-joy them;
We beseech thee to hear us, good Lord.

That it may please thee to give us true repentance; to forgive us all our sins, negligences, and ignorances; and to endue us with the grace of thy Holy Spirit to amend our lives according to thy | ho-ly Word;
We beseech thee to hear us, good Lord.

MINISTER.   **ANSWER.**

Son of God; we beseech thee to hear us.   Son of God, we be-seech thee to hear us.

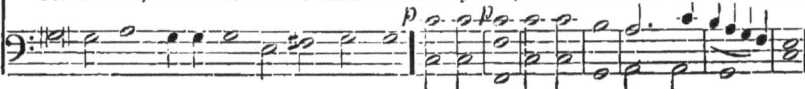

MINISTER.

ANSWER.

O Lamb of God, who takest away the sins of the world; Grant us thy peace.

MINISTER.

ANSWER.

O Lamb of God, who takest away the } sins of the world; Have mer-cy up-on us, have mercy up-on us.

¶ *The Minister may, at his discretion, omit all that followeth, to the Prayer, "We humbly beseech thee, O Father," etc.*

MINISTER.

ANSWER.

O CHRIST, hear us. O Christ, hear us.

MINISTER.

ANSWER.

Lord, have mer-cy up-on us. Lord, have mer-cy up - on us.
Christ, have mer-cy up-on us. Christ, have mer-cy up - on us.

MINISTER.

ANSWER.

LORD, have mer-cy up-on us. Lord, have mer-cy up-on . . . . us.

Minister and People.

Our Father, Who art in heaven, Hallowed be thy Name. Thy kingdom come. Thy will be done on earth, As it is in heaven. Give us this day our daily bread. And forgive us our trespasses, as we forgive those who trespass against us. And lead us not into temptation; But deliver us from evil.

A MEN.

Minister.   **Answer.**

O Lord, deal not with us according to } our sins. Neither reward us according to our in - i - qui - ties.

Minister.   **Minister.**

Let us pray.   O God, merciful Father, who despisest not the sighing of a contrite heart, nor the desire of such as are sorrowful; Mercifully assist our prayers which we make before thee in all our troubles and adversities, whensoever they oppress us; and graciously hear us, that those evils which the craft and subtilty of the devil or man worketh against us, may, by thy good providence, be brought to nought; that we thy servants, being hurt by no persecutions, may evermore give thanks unto thee in thy holy Church; through Jesus Christ our Lord.

Answer.

O Lord, a - rise, help us, and de - li - ver us for thy Name's sake.

Minister.

O God, we have heard with our ears, and our fathers have } declared unto us, the noble works that thou didst in their } be - fore them. days, and in the old time . . . . }

Answer.

O Lord, a - rise, help us, and de - li - ver us for thine hon - our.

MINISTER.

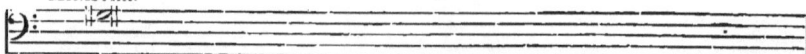

Glory be to the Father, and to the Son, and to the Holy Ghost;

ANSWER.

As it was in the beginning, is now, and ever shall be, world without end. A-MEN.

ORG.   ORG.

MINISTER.   ANSWER.

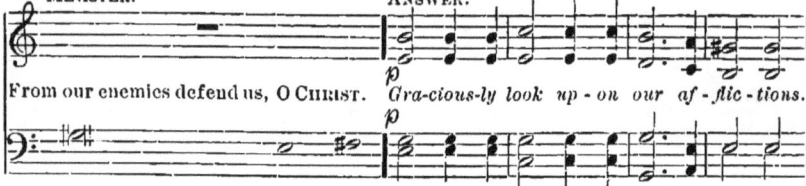

From our enemies defend us, O CHRIST. *Gra-cious-ly look up-on our af-flic-tions.*

MINISTER.   ANSWER.

With pity behold } of our hearts. *Mer-ci-ful-ly forgive the sins of thy peo-ple.*
the sorrows

MINISTER.   ANSWER.

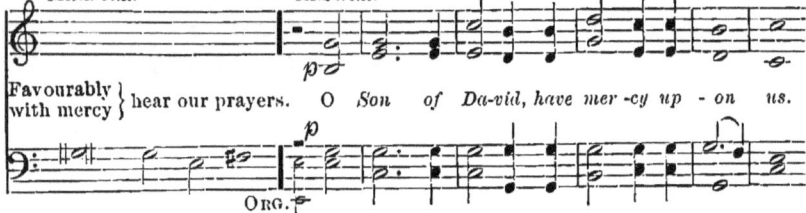

Favourably } hear our prayers. *O Son of Da-vid, have mer-cy up-on us.*
with mercy

ORG.

MINISTER.   ANSWER.

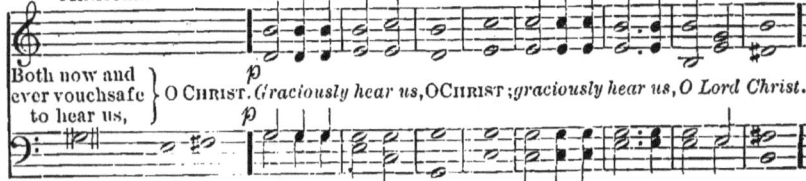

Both now and }
ever vouchsafe } O CHRIST. *Graciously hear us, O CHRIST; graciously hear us, O Lord Christ.*
to hear us, }

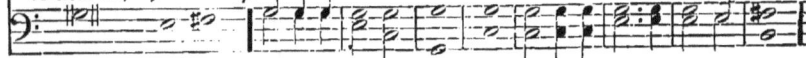

MINISTER. ANSWER. MINISTER.

O LORD, let thy mercy be showed up- } on us; As we do put our trust in thee. Let us pray.

ORG.

MINISTER.

WE humbly beseech thee, O Father, mercifully to look upon our infirmities; and, for the glory of thy Name, turn from us all those evils that we most justly have deserved; and grant, that in all our troubles we may put our whole trust and confidence in thy mercy, and evermore serve thee in holiness and pureness of living, to thy honour and glory; through our only Mediator and Advocate, Jesus Christ our Lord. *Amen.*

A GENERAL THANKSGIVING.

ALMIGHTY God, Father of all mercies, we, thine unworthy servants, do give thee most humble and hearty thanks for all thy goodness and loving-kindness to us, and to all men; [* *Particularly to those who desire now to offer up their praises and thanksgivings for thy late mercies vouchsafed unto them*]. We bless thee for our creation, preservation, and all the blessings of this life; but above all, for thine inestimable love in the redemption of the world by our Lord Jesus Christ; for the means of grace, and for the hope of glory. And, we beseech thee, give us that due sense of all thy mercies, that our hearts may be unfeignedly thankful; and that we show forth thy praise, not only with our lips, but in our lives, by giving up ourselves to thy service, and by walking before thee in holiness and righteousness all our days; through Jesus Christ our Lord, to whom, with thee and the Holy Ghost, be all honour and glory, world without end. *Amen.*

* This may be said when any desire to return thanks for mercies vouchsafed to them.

A PRAYER OF ST. CHRYSOSTOM.

ALMIGHTY God, who hast given us grace at this time with one accord to make our common supplications unto thee; and dost promise that when two or three are gathered together in thy Name thou wilt grant their requests; Fulfil now, O Lord, the desires and petitions of thy servants, as may be most expedient for them; granting us in this world knowledge of thy truth, and in the world to come life everlasting. *Amen.*

2 Cor. xiii. 14.

THE GRACE of our Lord Jesus Christ, and the love of God, and the fellowship of the Holy Ghost, be with us all evermore. *Amen.*

No. 1. No. 2. No. 3.

A - men. A - men. A - men.

HERE ENDETH THE LITANY,

Short Services for Sunday Schools.

First Service.

OPENING OF THE SCHOOL.

[*All standing, the Minister or Superintendent shall say:*]

In the Name of the FATHER, and of the SON, and of the HOLY GHOST. *Amen.*

Versicle. — Come ye, and let us walk in the light of the LORD.

Response. — *And He will teach us of His ways, and we will walk in His paths.*

V. — The path of the just is as the shining light.

R. — *That shineth more and more unto the perfect day.*

V. — While ye have light, believe in the light.

R. — *That ye may be the children of the light.*

V. — Let us pray.

[*All kneeling.*]

OUR FATHER, who art in heaven, Hallowed be thy Name. Thy kingdom come. Thy will be done on earth, As it is in heaven. Give us this day our daily bread. And forgive us our trespasses, As we forgive those who trespass against us. And lead us not into temptation; But deliver us from evil: For thine is the kingdom, and the power, and the glory, for ever and ever. *Amen.*

V. — O LORD, open Thou our lips,

R. — *And our mouth shall show forth Thy praise.*

V. — O GOD, make speed to save us.

R. — *O Lord, make haste to help us.*

[*All standing.*]

V. — GLORY be to the FATHER, and to the SON, and to the HOLY GHOST;

R. — *As it was in the beginning, is now, and ever shall be, world without end.* *Amen.*

V. — This is the day which the LORD hath made.

R. — *Let us rejoice and be glad in it.*

[*Then may follow a Lesson, which may be the Gospel or the Epistle for the Day, or any other brief passage of Holy Scripture.*]

[*Then may be sung a Psalm, or a Hymn.*]

[*All standing.*]

I BELIEVE in God the Father Almighty, Maker of heaven and earth: And in Jesus Christ his only SON our LORD: Who was conceived by the Holy Ghost, Born of the Virgin Mary: Suffered under Pontius Pilate, Was crucified, dead, and buried: He descended into hell; The third day he rose again from the dead: He ascended into heaven, And sitteth on the right hand of God the Father Almighty: From thence he shall come to judge the quick and the dead.

I believe in the Holy Ghost: The Holy Catholic Church; The Communion of Saints: The Forgiveness of sins: The Resurrection of the body: And the Life everlasting. *Amen.*

[All standing.]

V.—All Thy children shall be taught of Thee.

R.—*And great shall be the peace of Thy children.*

V.—Like as a father pitieth his own children.

R.—*Even so is the Lord merciful unto them that fear Him.*

V.—The LORD be with you.

R.—*And with thy spirit.*

V.—Let us pray.

[All kneeling.]

[Then after the Collect for the Day (p. 26, etc.), may follow one or more of these Prayers.]

BLESSED be Thou, O LORD, for giving us this Holy Day of Rest, for appointing one day in seven to be Thine own; to be spent in learning our Christian duty, in hearing Thy blessed Word, and in worshipping Thee in Thy holy Church. Help us, O LORD, to turn away our thoughts from pleasure, folly, and worldly cares, and teach us to join in Thy service with delight; and to be serious and attentive; and may Thy Holy Spirit be with us this day in our goings out and comings in, for JESUS CHRIST's sake. *Amen.*

O LORD Most High, who art our life, our strength and joy, our ever present helper and defender, we come to confess our sins before Thee, and to pray for what we need. Give us the mind which was in CHRIST JESUS our LORD. Make us gentle and obedient, loving, brave, and true. Keep our childhood holy, and our youth pure and good, so that the longer we live we may grow more and more into the likeness of the perfect man. Thou knowest our temptations, Heavenly FATHER: help us to watch against them, and to win the victory over them, remembering that Thou hast promised to those who are faithful unto death a crown of life. Pity our weakness, O LORD, for we are Thy children and the work of Thy hands; Thou hast called us by our names; we are Thine. Send down upon us, for our present need, the dew of Thy heavenly grace. Bless us in the work before us now. Make us quick to learn and eager to be taught; may the good seed of Thy Word, planted in our hearts to-day, bring forth abundant fruit in days to come. Thou hast made our bodies the temples of Thy presence; may our lives show forth Thy praise. LORD, hear our prayer, and let our cry come unto Thee for the sake of Thy dear Son, our SAVIOUR JESUS CHRIST. *Amen.*

KEEP us in Thy fold, O Thou Shepherd of Israel, and lead us forth continually by the green pastures and the still waters, till, supported by Thy rod and staff, we pass through the dark valley of the shadow of death, fearing no evil, for Thou art with us, and enter Thy Courts of Light and Joy, there to dwell with Thee for ever. *Amen.*

O LORD JESUS CHRIST, who didst sit lowly in the midst of the doctors, both hearing them and asking them questions; grant unto us, Thy servants, both aptness to teach, and willingness to learn Thy blessed will; who livest and reignest with the FATHER, and the HOLY GHOST, one GOD, world without end. *Amen.*

THE LORD bless us and keep us. The LORD make His face to shine upon us, and be gracious unto us. The LORD lift up His countenance upon us, and give us peace, both now and evermore. *Amen.*

Second Service.

OPENING OF THE SCHOOL.

[*All standing, the Minister or Superintendent shall say :*]
In the Name of the Father, and of the Son, and of the Holy Ghost. *Amen.*
(*Then may be sung a Canticle, Psalm or Hymn.*)
(*Then may follow a Lesson from Holy Scripture.*) ·
[*Then shall be said, all standing,*]

I BELIEVE in God the Father Almighty, Maker of heaven and earth :
And in Jesus Christ his only Son our.Lord : Who was conceived by the Holy Ghost, Born of the Virgin Mary : Suffered under Pontius Pilate, Was crucified, dead, and buried : He descended into hell ; The third day he rose again from the dead : He ascended into heaven, And sitteth on the right hand of God the Father Almighty : From thence he shall come to judge the quick and the dead.

I believe in the Holy Ghost : The Holy Catholic Church ; The Communion of Saints : The Forgiveness of sins : The Resurrection of the body : And the Life everlasting. Amen.

V.— The Lord be with you.
R. — And with thy spirit.
Let us pray.

[*All kneeling.*]

OUR FATHER, who art in heaven, Hallowed be thy Name. Thy kingdom come. Thy will be done on earth, As it is in heaven. Give us this day our daily bread. And forgive us our trespasses, As we forgive those who trespass against us. And lead us not into temptation ; But deliver us from evil : For thine is the kingdom, and the power, and the glory, for ever and ever. Amen.

[*Then after the Collect for the Day (p, 26, etc.), may follow one or more of these Prayers.*]

O LORD JESUS, our merciful REDEEMER, who didst call children to Thee, and didst take them in Thine arms and bless them ; give Thy blessing to us also, we beseech Thee, this day, and through the whole course of our lives. Grant that we may ever love Thee above all things, and with our whole hearts ; and that we may earnestly seek after that happiness for which we were created. Bless our dear parents, relations, teachers, pastors, and benefactors ; preserve them from all evil, and direct them to all good ; and grant that we may meet in Thy eternal kingdom ; and to Thee, with the Father and the Holy Spirit, shall be all praise, now and for ever. *Amen.*

O LORD GOD, we humbly beseech Thee to direct our thoughts and prayers this day : purify our hearts from every evil and false imagination, and may no vain and worldly desires have their abode in us. Keep us from all wandering looks and ways, from an undevout mind, and careless prayers. Let the Voice of Thy Love enter into our souls, that we may study Thy Word with reverence and holy fear, with fervour and delight. O GOD, Thou seest us : help us to look up unto Thee ; for the sake of Thy SON, JESUS CHRIST our LORD. *Amen.*

THE grace of our LORD JESUS CHRIST, and the love of GOD, and the fellowship of the HOLY GHOST, be with us all evermore. *Amen.*

Third Service.

OPENING OF THE SCHOOL.

[All standing, the Minister or Superintendent shall say :]

In the Name of the Father, and of the Son and of the Holy Ghost. *Amen.*

V. — Let us pray.

[All kneeling.]

OUR Father, who art in heaven, Hallowed be thy Name. Thy kingdom come. Thy will be done on earth, As it is in heaven. Give us this day our daily bread. And forgive us our trespasses, As we forgive those who trespass against us. And lead us not into temptation; But deliver us from evil: For thine is the kingdom, and the power, and the glory, for ever and ever. *Amen.*

(Then may be sung one of the Canticles or Psalms. Then may follow these Prayers.)

V. — The LORD be with you.

R. — *And with thy spirit.*

V. — Let us pray.

ALMIGHTY and everlasting God, the Giver of every good and perfect gift, send thy blessing, we beseech thee, on all who teach in this school, and so strengthen them by the grace of thy HOLY SPIRIT, that they may build up in the faith and love of thy dear Son those for whom he died and rose again : through the same thy SON JESUS CHRIST our Lord. *Amen.*

ALMIGHTY and everlasting God, heavenly FATHER, we give thee humble thanks that thou hast vouchsafed to call us to the knowledge of thy grace and faith in thee. Increase this knowledge, and confirm this faith in us evermore. Give thy HOLY SPIRIT to these children; that they, being born again, and being made heirs of everlasting salvation, through our LORD JESUS CHRIST, may continue thy servants, and attain thy promises; through the same our LORD JESUS CHRIST thy SON, who liveth and reigneth, with thee and the HOLY SPIRIT, now and for ever. *Amen.*

THE Lord bless us and keep us. The Lord make his face to shine upon us, and be gracious unto us. The LORD lift up his countenance upon us, and give us peace, both now and evermore. *Amen.*

(Then may follow a Hymn.)

Suggested Forms of Service.

OPENING.	CLOSING.
HYMN.	CATECHISING OR REVIEW OF LESSON.
SENTENCES.	OFFERING WITH OFFERTORY SENTENCE.
THE LORD'S PRAYER.	HYMN.
CANTICLE OR PSALM.	COLLECTS.
CREED.	"THE BLESSING OF GOD ALMIGHTY, ETC."
VERSICLES AND COLLECTS.	
"THE GRACE OF OUR LORD JESUS CHRIST, ETC."	

𝔄 Closing Service

FOR EVERY SUNDAY.

[*The Service shall begin with*]

A Hymn.

[*Then shall be said*]

V. — Let Thy merciful kindness, O LORD, be upon us.

R. — *As we do put our trust in Thee.*

V. — Let us pray.

[*Then, all kneeling, shall be said, unless it has been previously said in the Opening Service, the Collect for the Day. pp. 26, etc.*]

[*Then may follow any other of the Collects, and the following Prayer.*]

WE thank Thee, O LORD, for this Thy Holy Day, and for all the blessings which it brings us; and we beseech Thee of Thy great goodness, that these days which bear Thy Name may never cease to be unto us as days of heaven upon earth, and lights to guide us from earth to heaven. Give us, we pray Thee, some work to do for Thee during the week upon which we have now entered; and whatever it be, may we do it with all our might. In all our duties and employments, in the least as in the greatest, let us be mindful of Thy Presence, that it may be seen by our ways and behaviour whose we are. Lord, we are Thine: let us not grieve Thee, nor do hurt to others, by our faithlessness. Restrain all that is evil in us, and strengthen and confirm what is Thine own; for our SAVIOUR'S sake. *Amen.*

[*The following Prayer may be used if the Sunday School precedes the Church Service.*]

O LORD, we beseech Thee let Thy Presence be with us in Thy House of Prayer, that it may be unto us a sanctuary of strength and beauty. Let Thy Spirit descend upon us, that our hearts may be filled with pure and holy worship, until at last, of Thine infinite mercy, it is granted unto us to enter Thy Temple above, to live in Thy Presence, and to give Thee praise for ever. *Amen.*

MAY the Almighty and merciful LORD, the FATHER, the SON, and the HOLY GHOST, bless us, and defend us from all evil, and bring us to everlasting life. *Amen.*

Short Service for a Day School.

[There may first be read a short Lesson from Holy Scripture. Then, a Psalm or Hymn having been sung, the teacher shall say:]

Let us pray.

[All kneeling.]

OUR FATHER, who art in heaven, Hallowed be thy Name. Thy kingdom come. Thy will be done on earth, As it is in heaven. Give us this day our daily bread. And forgive us our trespasses, As we forgive those who trespass against us. And lead us not into temptation; But deliver us from evil: For thine is the kingdom, and the power, and the glory, for ever and ever. *Amen.*

[Then after the Collect for the Day or other Collects, (p. 26, etc.,) may follow one or more of these Prayers.]

BLESSED LORD, who hast given us a new commandment that we should love one another as Thou hast loved us, and hast taught us that where envy and strife are, there are confusion and every evil work, give us grace to be kindly affectioned, and to love one another with a pure heart. Put far from us all anger and evil speaking, that we may obtain the blessing of the peace-makers, and walk in love, even as Thou hast loved us; through Thy merits, O blessed SAVIOUR and REDEEMER. *Amen.*

O MERCIFUL FATHER, do Thou enable us day by day to increase in wisdom and holiness. May we never forget that Thine eye is always upon us, and that Thou art about our path, and art acquainted with all our ways. Enable us to resist the sins that we deplore, and to strive to do those things that Thou wouldest have done. O God, may Thy HOLY SPIRIT never leave our hearts, but guide us continually and lead us into all truth, for our SAVIOUR's sake. *Amen.*

O GREAT and gracious God, do Thou look down with mercy and love on this school; if Thou be with us, none can be against us. Bless us each and all in our several stations, and enable us humbly and conscientiously to fulfil those duties which Thou hast entrusted to us, not with eye-service as men-pleasers, but in single-ness of heart serving Thee. Do Thou make us to live in unity one with another, and in peace with all men. May we seek the good of one another rather than of our-selves, remembering that we are not our own, but bought with a price. O God, may thy Name be hallowed, not only with our lips, but in our lives, and Thy will be done with all our heart and with all our strength. So shall Thy blessing be with us for Christ's sake. *Amen.*

O GOD, who didst reveal Thyself to Thy Prophet Samuel while he was yet a child; grant unto us, Thy children, the knowledge of Thy will, that we may ever walk in Thy commandments, through Jesus Christ our Lord. *Amen.*

THE LORD bless us and keep us. The LORD make His face to shine upon us, and be gracious unto us. The LORD lift up His countenance upon us, and give us peace, both now and evermore. *Amen.*

A Short Choral Service.

FOR A SUNDAY OR DAY SCHOOL.

(All standing.)

SUPERINTENDENT OR TEACHER.   **SCHOOL.**

In the Name of the Father, and of the Son, and of the Holy Ghost.   A - men.

[All kneeling and repeating together.]

OUR Father, who art in heaven, Hallowed be thy Name. Thy king-dom come. Thy will be done on earth, As it is in heaven. Give us this day our daily bread. And forgive us our trespasses, As we forgive those who trespass against us. And lead us not into temptation; But deliver us from evil: For thine is the kingdom, and the power, and the glory, for ever and ever.

A - MEN.

SUPT. OR TEACHER.   **SCHOOL.**

Let us pray. O Lord. open thou our lips; And our mouth shall show forth thy praise.

SUPT. OR TEACHER.   **SCHOOL.**

O God, make speed to save us.   O Lord, make haste to help us.

ORG.

SUPT. OR TEACHER.   *[All standing.]*

Glory be to the FATHER, and to the SON, and to the HOLY GHOST;

SCHOOL.

As it was in the beginning, is now, and ever shall be, world with-out end. A-men.

ORG.

Supt. or Teacher.   **School.**

Praise ye the Lord.   The Lord's name be prais - ed.

Org.

(Then may follow a Lesson from Holy Scripture, or a Psalm.)
(Then shall be sung the Apostle's Creed, by all, standing.)

I believe in God the Father Almighty, Maker of Heaven and Earth:

And in Jesus Christ his only Son, our Lord: Who was conceived by the Holy Ghost, Born of the Virgin Mary: Suffered under Pontius Pilate, Was crucified, dead, and buried: He descended into hell; The third day he rose again from the dead: He ascended into heaven, And sitteth on the right hand of God the Father Almighty: From thence he shall come to judge the quick and the dead.

A - MEN.

I believe in the Holy Ghost: The Holy Catholic Church; The Communion of Saints: The Forgiveness of sins: The Resurrection of the body: And the Life everlasting.

Supt. or Teacher.   **School.**   **Supt. or Teacher.**

The Lord be with you.   And with thy spir - it.   Let us pray.

Org.

Supt.
or Teacher.   *(Any of the Collects, p 26, etc., may first be said.)*

O God of Abraham, God of Isaac, God of Jacob; bless these Thy children, and sow the seed of eternal life in their hearts; that whatsoever in Thy holy Word they shall profitably learn, they may in deed

A - MEN.

fulfil the same. Look, O Lord, mercifully upon them from heaven, and bless them, that they, observing Thy will, and alway being in safety under Thy protection, may abide in Thy love unto their lives' end; through Jesus Christ our Lord.

Supt.
or Teacher.   O Lord Jesus Christ, who didst sit lowly in the midst of the doctors, both hearing them and asking them questions; grant unto us, Thy servants, both aptness to teach, and willingness to learn Thy blessed will, Who livest and reignest with the Father and the Holy Ghost, one God, world without end.

A - MEN.

THE grace of our Lord Jesus Christ, and the love of God, and the fellowship of the Holy Ghost, be with us all evermore.

A - MEN.

The Collects.

THE FIRST SUNDAY IN ADVENT.

For Preparation for Judgment. ALMIGHTY GOD, give us grace that we may cast away the works of darkness, and put upon us the armour of light, now in the time of this mortal life, in which thy Son Jesus Christ came to visit us in great humility; that in the last day, when he shall come again in his glorious majesty to judge both the quick and dead, we may rise to the life immortal, through him who liveth and reigneth with thee and the Holy Ghost, now and ever. *Amen.*

¶ *This Collect is to be repeated every day, with the other Collects in Advent, unto Christmas-day.*

THE SECOND SUNDAY IN ADVENT.

For Love of God's Word. BLESSED LORD, who hast caused all Holy Scriptures to be written for our learning; Grant that we may in such wise hear them, read, mark, learn, and inwardly digest them, that by patience, and comfort of thy holy Word, we may embrace, and ever hold fast, the blessed hope of everlasting life, which thou hast given us in our Saviour Jesus Christ. *Amen.*

THE THIRD SUNDAY IN ADVENT.

For the Clergy and People. O LORD JESUS CHRIST, who at thy first coming didst send thy messenger to prepare thy way before thee; Grant that the ministers and stewards of thy mysteries may likewise so prepare and make ready thy way, by turning the hearts of the disobedient to the wisdom of the just, that at thy second coming to judge the world we may be found an acceptable people in thy sight, who livest and reignest with the Father and the Holy Spirit ever, one God, world without end. *Amen.*

THE FOURTH SUNDAY IN ADVENT.

For Grace and Guidance. O LORD, raise up, we pray thee, thy power, and come among us, and with great might succour us; that whereas, through our sins and wickedness, we are sore let and hindered in running the race that is set before us, thy bountiful grace and mercy may speedily help and deliver us; through the satisfaction of thy Son our Lord, to whom, with thee and the Holy Ghost, be honour and glory, world without end. *Amen.*

CHRISTMAS-DAY, AND THE SUNDAY AFTER CHRISTMAS-DAY.

For Spiritual Renewal. ALMIGHTY GOD, who hast given us thy only begotten Son to take our nature upon him, and as at this time to be born of a pure virgin; Grant that we being regenerate, and made thy children by adoption and grace, may daily be renewed by thy Holy Spirit: through the same our Lord Jesus Christ, who liveth and reigneth with thee and the same Spirit ever, one God, world without end. *Amen.*

CHRISTMAS-DAY.

O GOD, who makest us glad with the yearly remembrance of the birth of thine only Son Jesus Christ; Grant that as we joyfully receive him for our Redeemer, so we may with sure confidence behold him when he shall come to be our Judge, who liveth and reigneth with thee and the Holy Ghost, one God, world without end. *Amen.*

SAINT STEPHEN'S DAY.

GRANT, O Lord, that, in all our sufferings here upon earth for the **For the Imi-** testimony of thy truth, we may steadfastly look up to heaven, **tation of the** and by faith behold the glory that shall be revealed; and, being filled **Saints.** with the Holy Ghost, may learn to love and bless our persecutors by the example of thy first Martyr Saint Stephen, who prayed for his murderers to thee, O blessed Jesus, who standest at the right hand of God to succour all those who suffer for thee, our only Mediator and Advocate. *Amen.*

SAINT JOHN THE EVANGELIST'S DAY.

MERCIFUL Lord, we beseech thee to cast thy bright beams of **For the Guid-** light upon thy Church, that it being instructed by the doctrine **ance of the** of thy blessed Apostle and Evangelist Saint John, may so walk in **Church.** the light of thy truth, that it may at length attain to everlasting life; through Jesus Christ our Lord. *Amen.*

THE INNOCENTS' DAY.

O ALMIGHTY God, who out of the mouths of babes and sucklings **For Purity of** hast ordained strength, and madest infants to glorify thee by **Life.** their deaths; Mortify and kill all vices in us, and so strengthen us by thy grace, that by the innocency of our lives, and constancy of our faith even unto death, we may glorify thy holy Name; through Jesus Christ our Lord. *Amen.*

THE CIRCUMCISION OF CHRIST.

ALMIGHTY GOD, who madest thy blessed Son to be circumcised, **For Purity of** and obedient to the law for man; Grant us the true circumcision **Heart and** of the Spirit; that, our hearts, and all our members, being mortified **Life.** from all worldly and carnal lusts, we may in all things obey thy blessed will; through the same thy Son Jesus Christ our Lord. *Amen.*

THE EPIPHANY, OR THE MANIFESTATION OF CHRIST TO THE GENTILES.

O GOD, who by the leading of a star didst manifest thy only be- **For the En-** gotten Son to the Gentiles; Mercifully grant that we, who know **joyment of** thee now by faith, may after this life have the fruition of thy glo- **God in Heav-** rious Godhead; through Jesus Christ our Lord. *Amen.* **en.**

THE FIRST SUNDAY AFTER THE EPIPHANY.

O LORD, we beseech thee mercifully to receive the prayers of thy **For Grace** people who call upon thee: and grant that they may both per- **and Guid-** ceive and know what things they ought to do, and also may have grace **ance.** and power faithfully to fulfil the same; through Jesus Christ our Lord. *Amen.*

THE SECOND SUNDAY AFTER THE EPIPHANY.

ALMIGHTY and everlasting God, who dost govern all things in **For Peace.** heaven and earth; Mercifully hear the supplications of thy people, and grant us thy peace all the days of our life; through Jesus Christ our Lord. *Amen.*

For Help in Trouble or Danger.

ALMIGHTY and everlasting God, mercifully look upon our infirmities, and in all our dangers and necessities stretch forth thy right hand to help and defend us; through Jesus Christ our Lord. *Amen.*

For Protection against Dangers and Adversities.

O GOD, who knowest us to be set in the midst of so many and great dangers, that by reason of the frailty of our nature we cannot always stand upright; Grant to us such strength and protection, as may support us in all dangers, and carry us through all temptations; through Jesus Christ our Lord. *Amen.*

For Protection of the Church.

O LORD, we beseech thee to keep thy Church and household continually in thy true religion; that they who do lean only upon the hope of thy heavenly grace may evermore be defended by thy mighty power; through Jesus Christ our Lord. *Amen.*

For Purity.

O GOD, whose blessed Son was manifested that he might destroy the works of the devil, and make us the sons of God, and heirs of eternal life; Grant us, we beseech thee, that, having this hope, we may purify ourselves, even as he is pure; that, when he shall appear again with power and great glory, we may be made like unto him in his eternal and glorious kingdom; where with thee, O Father, and thee, O Holy Ghost, he liveth and reigneth ever, one God, world without end. *Amen.*

For Pardon.

O LORD, we beseech thee favourably to hear the prayers of thy people; that we, who are justly punished for our offences, may be mercifully delivered by thy goodness, for the glory of thy Name; through Jesus Christ our Saviour, who liveth and reigneth with thee and the Holy Ghost ever, one God, world without end. *Amen.*

For Defence against Adversity.

O LORD GOD, who seest that we put not our trust in anything that we do; Mercifully grant that by thy power we may be defended against all adversity; through Jesus Christ our Lord. *Amen.*

For Love.

O LORD, who hast taught us that all our doings without charity are nothing worth; Send thy Holy Ghost, and pour into our hearts that most excellent gift of charity, the very bond of peace and of all virtues, without which whosoever liveth is counted dead before thee. Grant this for thine only Son Jesus Christ's sake. *Amen.*

THE FIRST DAY OF LENT, COMMONLY CALLED ASH-WEDNESDAY.

ALMIGHTY and everlasting God, who hatest nothing that thou hast made, and dost forgive the sins of all those who are penitent; Create and make in us new and contrite hearts, that we, worthily lamenting our sins and acknowledging our wretchedness, may obtain of thee, the God of all mercy, perfect remission and forgiveness; through Jesus Christ our Lord. *Amen.*

For Contrition.

THE FIRST SUNDAY IN LENT.

O LORD, who for our sake didst fast forty days and forty nights; Give us grace to use such abstinence, that, our flesh being subdued to the Spirit, we may ever obey thy godly motions in righteousness, and true holiness, to thy honour and glory, who livest and reignest with the Father and the Holy Ghost, one God, world without end. *Amen.*

For Abstinence.

THE SECOND SUNDAY IN LENT.

ALMIGHTY GOD, who seest that we have no power of ourselves to help ourselves; Keep us both outwardly in our bodies, and inwardly in our souls; that we may be defended from all adversities which may happen to the body, and from all evil thoughts which may assault and hurt the soul; through Jesus Christ our Lord. *Amen.*

For Defence in Trouble or Danger.

THE THIRD SUNDAY IN LENT.

WE BESEECH THEE, Almighty God, look upon the hearty desires of thy humble servants, and stretch forth the right hand of thy majesty, to be our defence against all our enemies; through Jesus Christ our Lord. *Amen.*

For Deliverance from Enemies.

THE FOURTH SUNDAY IN LENT.

GRANT, we beseech thee, Almighty God, that we, who for our evil deeds do worthily deserve to be punished, by the comfort of thy grace may mercifully be relieved; through our Lord and Saviour Jesus Christ. *Amen.*

For Pardon.

THE FIFTH SUNDAY IN LENT.

WE BESEECH THEE, Almighty God, mercifully to look upon thy people; that by thy great goodness they may be governed and preserved evermore, both in body and soul; through Jesus Christ our Lord. *Amen.*

For Guidance and Protection.

THE SUNDAY NEXT BEFORE EASTER.

ALMIGHTY and everlasting God, who, of thy tender love towards mankind, hast sent thy Son, our Saviour Jesus Christ, to take upon him our flesh, and to suffer death upon the cross, that all mankind should follow the example of his great humility; Mercifully grant, that we may both follow the example of his patience, and also be made partakers of his resurrection; through the same Jesus Christ our Lord. *Amen.*

For Humility and Patience.

GOOD FRIDAY.

ALMIGHTY GOD, we beseech thee graciously to behold this thy family, for which our Lord Jesus Christ was contented to be betrayed, and given up into the hands of wicked men, and to suffer death upon the cross; who now liveth and reigneth with thee and the Holy Ghost ever, one God, world without end. *Amen.*

For Mercy through the Cross of Christ.

For the whole Church.

ALMIGHTY and everlasting God, by whose Spirit the whole body of the Church is governed and sanctified; Receive our supplications and prayers, which we offer before thee for all estates of men in thy holy Church, that every member of the same, in his vocation and ministry, may truly and godly serve thee; through our Lord and Saviour Jesus Christ. *Amen.*

For the Conversion of the Heathen.

O MERCIFUL GOD, who hast made all men, and hatest nothing that thou hast made, nor desirest the death of a sinner, but rather that he should be converted and live; Have mercy upon all Jews, Turks, infidels and heretics; and take from them all ignorance, hardness of heart, and contempt of thy Word; and so fetch them home, blessed Lord, to thy flock, that they may be saved among the remnant of the true Israelites, and be made one fold under one Shepherd, Jesus Christ our Lord, who liveth and reigneth with thee and the Holy Spirit, one God, world without end. *Amen.*

EASTER-EVEN.

For Burial and Resurrection with Christ.

GRANT, O Lord, that as we are baptized into the death of thy blessed Son, our Saviour Jesus Christ, so by continual mortifying our corrupt affections we may be buried with him; and that through the grave, and gate of death, we may pass to our joyful resurrection; for his merits, who died, and was buried, and rose again for us, thy Son Jesus Christ our Lord. *Amen.*

EASTER-DAY, AND MONDAY AND TUESDAY IN EASTER WEEK.

For Grace and Guidance.

ALMIGHTY GOD, who through thine only begotten Son Jesus Christ hast overcome death, and opened unto us the gate of everlasting life; We humbly beseech thee that, as by thy special grace preventing us thou dost put into our minds good desires, so by thy continual help we may bring the same to good effect; through Jesus Christ our Lord, who liveth and reigneth with thee and the Holy Ghost ever, one God, world without end. *Amen.*

O GOD, who for our redemption didst give thine only begotten Son to the death of the Cross, and by his glorious resurrection hast delivered us from the power of our enemy; Grant us so to die daily from sin, that we may evermore live with him in the joy of his resurrection; through the same Christ our Lord. *Amen.*

THE FIRST SUNDAY AFTER EASTER.

For Purity of Heart and Life.

ALMIGHTY FATHER, who hast given thine only Son to die for our sins, and to rise again for our justification; Grant us so to put away the leaven of malice and wickedness, that we may always serve thee in pureness of living and truth; through the merits of the same thy Son Jesus Christ our Lord. *Amen.*

THE SECOND SUNDAY AFTER EASTER.

For the Imitation of Christ.

ALMIGHTY GOD, who hast given thine only Son to be unto us both a sacrifice for sin, and also an ensample of godly life; Give us grace that we may always most thankfully receive that his inestimable benefit, and also daily endeavour ourselves to follow the blessed steps of his most holy life; through the same Jesus Christ our Lord. *Amen.*

THE THIRD SUNDAY AFTER EASTER.

ALMIGHTY GOD, who showest to them that are in error the light **For Sincerity.** of thy truth, to the intent that they may return into the way of righteousness; Grant unto all those who are admitted into the fellowship of Christ's religion, that they may avoid those things that are contrary to their profession, and follow all such things as are agreeable to the same; through our Lord Jesus Christ. *Amen.*

THE FOURTH SUNDAY AFTER EASTER.

O ALMIGHTY GOD, who alone canst order the unruly wills and **For Love of** affections of sinful men; Grant unto thy people, that they may **God and His** love the thing which thou commandest, and desire that which thou **Laws.** dost promise; that so, among the sundry and manifold changes of the world, our hearts may surely there be fixed, where true joys are to be found; through Jesus Christ our Lord. *Amen.*

THE FIFTH SUNDAY AFTER EASTER.

O LORD, from whom all good things do come; Grant to us thy **For the Di-** humble servants, that by thy holy inspiration we may think **rection of the** those things that are good, and by thy merciful guiding may perform **Holy Spirit.** the same; through our Lord Jesus Christ. *Amen.*

THE ASCENSION-DAY.

GRANT, we beseech thee, Almighty God, that like as we do believe **For Heaven-** thy only-begotten Son our Lord Jesus Christ to have ascended **ly Minded-** into the heavens; so we may also in heart and mind thither ascend, **ness.** and with him continually dwell, who liveth and reigneth with thee and the Holy Ghost, one God, world without end. *Amen.*

SUNDAY AFTER ASCENSION-DAY.

O GOD, the King of glory, who hast exalted thine only Son Jesus **For the Com-** Christ with great triumph unto thy kingdom in heaven; We be- **fort of the** seech thee, leave us not comfortless; but send to us thine Holy Ghost **Holy Ghost.** to comfort us, and exalt us unto the same place whither our Saviour Christ is gone before, who liveth and reigneth with thee and the Holy Ghost, one God, world without end. *Amen.*

WHITSUNDAY, AND MONDAY AND TUESDAY IN WHITSUN-WEEK.

O GOD, who as at this time didst teach the hearts of thy faithful **For a Right** people, by sending to them the light of thy Holy Spirit; Grant **Judgment in** us by the same Spirit to have a right judgment in all things, and **All Things.** evermore to rejoice in his holy comfort; through the merits of Christ Jesus our Saviour, who liveth and reigneth with thee, in the unity of the same Spirit, one God, world without end. *Amen.*

TRINITY-SUNDAY.

ALMIGHTY and everlasting God, who hast given unto us thy ser- **For Stead-** vants grace, by the confession of a true faith, to acknowledge **fastness in** the glory of the eternal Trinity, and in the power of the divine Maj- **the Faith.** esty to worship the Unity; We beseech thee that thou wouldest keep us steadfast in this faith, and evermore defend us from all adversities, who livest and reignest, one God, world without end. *Amen.*

THE FIRST SUNDAY AFTER TRINITY.

For Grace and Guidance.

O GOD, the strength of all those who put their trust in thee; Mercifully accept our prayers; and because, through the weakness of our mortal nature, we can do no good thing without thee, grant us the help of thy grace, that in keeping thy commandments we may please thee, both in will and deed; through Jesus Christ our Lord. *Amen.*

THE SECOND SUNDAY AFTER TRINITY.

For the Protection of God's Providence.

O LORD, who never failest to help and govern those whom thou dost bring up in thy stedfast fear and love; Keep us, we beseech thee, under the protection of thy good providence, and make us to have a perpetual fear and love of thy holy Name; through Jesus Christ our Lord. *Amen.*

THE THIRD SUNDAY AFTER TRINITY.

For Aid and Defence in danger.

O LORD, we beseech thee mercifully to hear us; and grant that we, to whom thou hast given an hearty desire to pray, may, by thy mighty aid, be defended and comforted in all dangers and adversities; through Jesus Christ our Lord. *Amen.*

THE FOURTH SUNDAY AFTER TRINITY.

For God's Guidance through things temporal.

O GOD, the protector of all that trust in thee, without whom nothing is strong, nothing is holy; Increase and multiply upon us thy mercy; that, thou being our ruler and guide, we may so pass through things temporal, that we finally lose not the things eternal. Grant this, O heavenly Father, for Jesus Christ's sake our Lord. *Amen.*

THE FIFTH SUNDAY AFTER TRINITY.

For the Peace of the Church.

GRANT, O Lord, we beseech thee, that the course of this world may be so peaceably ordered by thy governance, that thy Church may joyfully serve thee in all godly quietness; through Jesus Christ our Lord. *Amen.*

THE SIXTH SUNDAY AFTER TRINITY.

For Love of God and his Laws.

O GOD, who hast prepared for those who love thee such good things as pass man's understanding; Pour into our hearts such love toward thee, that we, loving thee above all things, may obtain thy promises, which exceed all that we can desire; through Jesus Christ our Lord. *Amen.*

THE SEVENTH SUNDAY AFTER TRINITY.

For Increase in Righteousness.

LORD of all power and might, who art the author and giver of all good things; Graft in our hearts the love of thy Name, increase in us true religion, nourish us with all goodness, and of thy great mercy keep us in the same; through Jesus Christ our Lord. *Amen.*

THE EIGHTH SUNDAY AFTER TRINITY.

For Defence against all evil.

O GOD, whose never-failing providence ordereth all things both in heaven and earth; We humbly beseech thee to put away from us all hurtful things, and to give us those things which are profitable for us; through Jesus Christ our Lord. *Amen.*

THE NINTH SUNDAY AFTER TRINITY.

GRANT to us, Lord, we beseech thee, the spirit to think and do always such things as are right; that we, who cannot do anything that is good without thee, may by thee be enabled to live according to thy will; through Jesus Christ our Lord. *Amen.*

For the Spirit to do Right.

THE TENTH SUNDAY AFTER TRINITY.

LET thy merciful ears, O Lord, be open to the prayers of thy humble servants; and, that they may obtain their petitions, make them to ask such things as shall please thee; through Jesus Christ our Lord. *Amen.*

For the acceptance of our prayers.

THE ELEVENTH SUNDAY AFTER TRINITY.

O GOD, who declarest thy almighty power chiefly in showing mercy and pity; Mercifully grant unto us such a measure of thy grace, that we, running the way of thy commandments, may obtain thy gracious promises, and be made partakers of thy heavenly treasure; through Jesus Christ our Lord. *Amen.*

For Grace to keep God's Commandments

THE TWELFTH SUNDAY AFTER TRINITY.

ALMIGHTY and everlasting God, who art always more ready to hear than we to pray, and art wont to give more than either we desire or deserve; Pour down upon us the abundance of thy mercy; forgiving us those things whereof our conscience is afraid, and giving us those good things which we are not worthy to ask, but through the merits and mediation of Jesus Christ, thy Son, our Lord. *Amen.*

For Mercy and Forgiveness.

THE THIRTEENTH SUNDAY AFTER TRINITY.

ALMIGHTY and merciful God, of whose only gift it cometh that thy faithful people do unto thee true and laudable service; Grant, we beseech thee, that we may so faithfully serve thee in this life, that we fail not finally to attain thy heavenly promises; through the merits of Jesus Christ our Lord. *Amen.*

For Fruitfulness in Good Works.

THE FOURTEENTH SUNDAY AFTER TRINITY.

ALMIGHTY and everlasting God, give unto us the increase of faith, hope, and charity; and, that we may obtain that which thou dost promise, make us to love that which thou dost command; through Jesus Christ our Lord. *Amen.*

For the Love of God's Laws.

THE FIFTEENTH SUNDAY AFTER TRINITY.

KEEP, we beseech thee, O Lord, thy Church with thy perpetual mercy; and, because the frailty of man without thee cannot but fall, keep us ever by thy help from all things hurtful, and lead us to all things profitable to our salvation; through Jesus Christ our Lord. *Amen.*

For Defence Against all Evil.

THE SIXTEENTH SUNDAY AFTER TRINITY.

O Lord, we beseech thee, let thy continual pity cleanse and defend thy Church; and, because it cannot continue in safety without thy succour, preserve it evermore by thy help and goodness; through Jesus Christ our Lord. *Amen.*

For the Purity and Defence of the Church.

**For Fruitful-
ness in good
Works.**
LORD, we pray thee that thy grace may always prevent and follow
us, and make us continually to be given to all good works;
through Jesus Christ our Lord. *Amen.*

**For Strength
to resist
Temptation.**
LORD, we beseech thee, grant thy people grace to withstand the
temptations of the world, the flesh and the devil; and with pure
hearts and minds to follow thee, the only God; through Jesus Christ
our Lord. *Amen.*

**For the Di-
rection of the
Holy Spirit.**
O GOD, forasmuch as without Thee we are not able to please
thee; Mercifully grant that thy Holy Spirit may in all things
direct and rule our hearts; through Jesus Christ our Lord. *Amen.*

**For Protec-
tion in Trou-
ble and
Danger.**
O ALMIGHTY and most merciful God, of thy bountiful goodness
keep us, we beseech thee, from all things that may hurt us; that
we, being ready both in body and soul, may cheerfully accomplish
those things which thou commandest; through Jesus Christ our
Lord. *Amen.*

**For the
Pardon of
Sin.**
GRANT, we beseech thee, merciful Lord, to thy faithful people
pardon and peace, that they may be cleansed from all their sins,
and serve thee with a quiet mind; through Jesus Christ our Lord.
Amen.   *Amen.*

**For the Peace
of the
Church.**
LORD, we beseech thee to keep thy household the Church in
continual godliness; that through thy protection it may be free
from all adversities, and devoutly given to serve thee in good works,
to the glory of thy Name; through Jesus Christ our Lord. *Amen.*

**For the Ac-
ceptance of
our Prayers.**
O GOD, our refuge and strength, who art the author of all godliness; Be ready, we beseech thee, to hear the devout prayers of
thy Church; and grant that those things which we ask faithfully we
may obtain effectually; through Jesus Christ our Lord. *Amen.*

**For Pardon
of Sin.**
O LORD, we beseech thee, absolve thy people from their offences;
that through thy bountiful goodness we may all be delivered
from the bands of those sins, which by our frailty we have committed. Grant this,
O heavenly Father, for Jesus Christ's sake, our blessed Lord and Saviour. *Amen.*

SUNDAY NEXT BEFORE ADVENT.

STIR UP, we beseech thee, O Lord, the wills of thy faithful people; **For Fruitful-** that they, plenteously bringing forth the fruit of good works, may **ness in Good** by thee be plenteously rewarded; through Jesus Christ our Lord. **Works.** *Amen.*

SAINT ANDREW'S DAY.

ALMIGHTY GOD, who didst give such grace unto thy holy Apostle **For Ready** Saint Andrew, that he readily obeyed the calling of thy Son Jesus **Obedience to** Christ, and followed him without delay; Grant unto us all, that we, **God's Will.** being called by thy holy Word, may forthwith give up ourselves obediently to fulfil thy holy commandments; through the same Jesus Christ our Lord. *Amen.*

SAINT THOMAS THE APOSTLE.

ALMIGHTY and ever living God, who, for the greater confirmation **For Stead-** of the faith, didst suffer thy holy Apostle Thomas to be doubtful **fastness in** in thy son's resurrection; Grant us so perfectly, and without all doubt, **the Faith.** to believe in thy Son Jesus Christ, that our faith in thy sight may never be reproved. Hear us, O Lord, through the same Jesus Christ, to whom, with thee and the Holy Ghost, be all honour and glory, now and for evermore. *Amen.*

THE CONVERSION OF SAINT PAUL.

O GOD, who, through the preaching of the blessed Apostle Saint **For Obedi-** Paul, hast caused the light of the Gospel to shine throughout the **ence to the** world; Grant, we beseech thee, that we, having his wonderful con- **Doctrine of** version in remembrance, may show forth our thankfulness unto thee **the Gospel.** for the same, by following the holy doctrine which he taught; through Jesus Christ our Lord. *Amen.*

THE PRESENTATION OF CHRIST IN THE TEMPLE, COMMONLY CALLED THE PURIFICATION OF SAINT MARY THE VIRGIN.

ALMIGHTY and ever-living God, we humbly beseech thy Majesty, **For Purity** that, as thy only begotten Son was this day presented in the temple **of Heart.** in substance of our flesh, so we may be presented unto thee, with pure and clean hearts, by the same thy Son Jesus Christ our Lord. *Amen.*

SAINT MATTHIAS'S DAY.

O ALMIGHTY God, who into the place of the traitor Judas didst **For the Faith-** choose thy faithful servant Matthias to be of the number of the **fulness of** twelve Apostles; Grant that thy Church, being alway preserved from **Ministers.** false Apostles, may be ordered and guided by faithful and true pastors; through Jesus Christ our Lord. *Amen.*

THE ANNUNCIATION OF THE BLESSED VIRGIN MARY.

WE beseech thee, O Lord, pour thy grace into our hearts; that as **For the Bene-** we have known the incarnation of thy Son Jesus Christ by the **fits of Christ's** message of an Angel, so by his cross and passion we may be brought **Death.** unto the glory of his resurrection; through the same Jesus Christ our Lord. *Amen.*

SAINT MARK'S DAY.

For Steadfastness in the Faith. O ALMIGHTY God, who hast instructed thy holy Church with the heavenly doctrine of thy Evangelist Saint Mark; Give us grace that, being not like children carried away with every blast of vain doctrine, we may be established in the truth of thy holy Gospel; through Jesus Christ our Lord. *Amen.*

SAINT PHILIP AND SAINT JAMES'S DAY.

For Grace and Guidance. O ALMIGHTY God, whom truly to know is everlasting life; Grant us perfectly to know thy Son Jesus Christ to be the way, the truth, and the life; that, following the steps of thy holy Apostles, Saint Philip and Saint James, we may stedfastly walk in the way that leadeth to eternal life; through the same thy Son Jesus Christ our Lord. *Amen.*

SAINT BARNABAS THE APOSTLE.

For the Manifold Gifts of the Holy Ghost. O LORD God Almighty, who didst endue thy holy Apostle Barnabas with singular gifts of the Holy Ghost; Leave us not, we beseech thee, destitute of thy manifold gifts, nor yet of grace to use them alway to thy honour and glory; through Jesus Christ our Lord. *Amen.*

SAINT JOHN BAPTIST'S DAY.

For Christian Courage. ALMIGHTY GOD, by whose providence thy servant John Baptist was wonderfully born, and sent to prepare the way of thy Son our Saviour by preaching repentance; Make us so to follow his doctrine and holy life, that we may truly repent according to his preaching; and after his example constantly speak the truth, boldly rebuke vice, and patiently suffer for the truth's sake; through Jesus Christ our Lord. *Amen.*

SAINT PETER'S DAY.

For the Clergy and People. O ALMIGHTY God, who by thy Son Jesus Christ didst give to thy Apostle Saint Peter many excellent gifts, and commandedst him earnestly to feed thy flock; Make, we beseech thee, all Bishops and Pastors diligently to preach thy holy Word, and the people obediently to follow the same, that they may receive the crown of everlasting glory; through Jesus Christ our Lord. *Amen.*

SAINT JAMES THE APOSTLE.

For Purity of Heart and Life. GRANT, O merciful God, that as thine holy Apostle Saint James, leaving his father and all that he had, without delay was obedient unto the calling of thy Son Jesus Christ, and followed him; so we, forsaking all worldly and carnal affections, may be evermore ready to follow thy holy commandments; through Jesus Christ our Lord. *Amen.*

THE TRANSFIGURATION OF CHRIST.

For the Beatific Vision. O GOD, who on the mount didst reveal to chosen witnesses thine only-begotten Son wonderfully transfigured, in raiment white and glistering; Mercifully grant that we, being delivered from the disquietude of this world, may be permitted to behold the King in his beauty, who with thee, O Father, and thee, O Holy Ghost, liveth and reigneth, one God, world without end. *Amen.*

SAINT BARTHOLOMEW THE APOSTLE.

O ALMIGHTY and everlasting God, who didst give to thine Apostle Bartholomew grace truly to believe and to preach thy Word; Grant, we beseech thee, unto thy Church, to love that Word which he believed, and both to preach and receive the same; through Jesus Christ our Lord. *Amen.*

That the Church may receive and preach the Word.

SAINT MATTHEW THE APOSTLE.

O ALMIGHTY GOD, who by thy blessed Son didst call Matthew from the receipt of custom to be an Apostle and Evangelist; Grant us grace to forsake all covetous desires, and inordinate love of riches, and to follow the same thy Son Jesus Christ, who liveth and reigneth with thee and the Holy Ghost, one God, world without end. *Amen.*

Against Covetousness.

SAINT MICHAEL AND ALL ANGELS.

O EVERLASTING God, who hast ordained and constituted the services of Angels and men in a wonderful order; Mercifully grant that, as thy holy angels always do thee service in heaven, so, by thy appointment, they may succour and defend us on earth; through Jesus Christ our Lord. *Amen.*

For the Guardianship of Angels.

SAINT LUKE THE EVANGELIST.

A LMIGHTY GOD, who calledst Luke the Physician, whose praise is in the Gospel, to be an Evangelist, and Physician of the soul; May it please thee that, by the wholesome medicines of the doctrine delivered by him, all the diseases of our souls may be healed; through the merits of thy Son Jesus Christ our Lord. *Amen.*

For the Healing of our Sins.

SAINT SIMON AND SAINT JUDE, APOSTLES.

O ALMIGHTY God, who hast built thy Church upon the foundation of the Apostles and Prophets, Jesus Christ himself being the head corner-stone; Grant us so to be joined together in unity of spirit by their doctrine, that we may be made an holy temple acceptable unto thee; through Jesus Christ our Lord. *Amen.*

For the Unity of the Church.

ALL SAINTS' DAY.

O ALMIGHTY GOD, who hast knit together thine elect in one communion and fellowship, in the mystical body of thy Son Christ our Lord; Grant us grace so to follow thy blessed Saints in all virtuous and godly living, that we may come to those unspeakable joys which thou hast prepared for those who unfeignedly love thee; through Jesus Christ our Lord. *Amen.*

For the Final Blessedness of the Saints.

FROM THE OFFICE OF HOLY COMMUNION.

A LMIGHTY GOD, unto whom all hearts are open, all desires known, and from whom no secrets are hid; Cleanse the thoughts of our hearts by the inspiration of thy Holy Spirit, that we may perfectly love thee, and worthily magnify thy holy Name; through Christ our Lord. *Amen.*

For Purity of Heart and Life.

For Guidance in Keeping God's Commandments.

O ALMIGHTY LORD, and everlasting God, vouchsafe, we beseech thee, to direct, sanctify, and govern, both our hearts and bodies, in the ways of thy laws, and in the works of thy commandments; that, through thy most mighty protection, both here and ever, we may be preserved in body and soul; through our Lord and Saviour Jesus Christ. Amen.

For God's gracious Defence.

ASSIST us mercifully, O Lord, in these our supplications and prayers, and dispose the way of thy servants towards the attainment of everlasting salvation; that, among all the changes and chances of this mortal life, they may ever be defended by thy most gracious and ready help; through Jesus Christ our Lord. Amen.

For the Grafting of the Holy Word in our Hearts.

GRANT, we beseech thee, Almighty God, that the words which we have heard this day with our outward ears, may, through thy grace, be so grafted inwardly in our hearts, that they may bring forth in us the fruit of good living, to the honour and praise of thy Name; through Jesus Christ our Lord. Amen.

For God's continual Guidance.

DIRECT US, O Lord, in all our doings, with thy most gracious favour, and further us with thy continual help; that in all our works begun, continued, and ended in thee, we may glorify thy holy Name, and finally, by thy mercy, obtain everlasting life; through Jesus Christ our Lord. Amen.

For the Acceptance of our Prayers.

ALMIGHTY GOD, the fountain of all wisdom, who knowest our necessities before we ask, and our ignorance in asking; We beseech thee to have compassion upon our infirmities; and those things, which for our unworthiness we dare not, and for our blindness we cannot ask, vouchsafe to give us, for the worthiness of thy Son Jesus Christ our Lord. Amen.

For the Acceptance of our Prayers.

ALMIGHTY GOD, who hast promised to hear the petitions of those who ask in thy Son's Name; We beseech Thee mercifully to incline thine ears to us who have now made our prayers and supplications unto thee; and grant that those things which we have faithfully asked according to thy will, may effectually be obtained, to the relief of our necessity, and to the setting forth of thy glory; through Jesus Christ our Lord. Amen.

FROM THE ORDER OF CONFIRMATION.

For the Increase of the Gifts of Grace.

ALMIGHTY and ever-living God, who hast vouchsafed to regenerate these thy servants by water and the Holy Ghost, and hast given unto them forgiveness of all their sins; Strengthen them, we beseech thee, O Lord, with the Holy Ghost, the Comforter, and daily increase in them thy manifold gifts of grace; the spirit of wisdom and understanding, the spirit of counsel and ghostly strength, the spirit of knowledge and true godliness; and fill them, O Lord, with the spirit of thy holy fear, now and for ever. Amen.

FROM THE ORDER FOR THE BURIAL OF THE DEAD.

ALMIGHTY GOD, with whom do live the spirits of those who **Thanks for** depart hence in the Lord, and with whom the souls of the faith- **the Exam-** ful, after they are delivered from the burden of the flesh, are in joy and **ples of the** felicity; We give thee hearty thanks for the good examples of all **Dead in the** those thy servants, who, having finished their course in faith, do now **Lord.** rest from their labours. And we beseech thee, that we, with all those who are departed in the true faith of thy holy Name, may have our perfect consummation and bliss, both in body and soul, in thy eternal and everlasting glory; through Jesus Christ our Lord. *Amen.*

O MERCIFUL GOD, the Father of our Lord Jesus Christ, who is **That we may** the Resurrection and the Life; in whom whosoever believeth, **obtain the** shall live, though he die; and whosoever liveth, and believeth in him, **Resurrection** shall not die eternally; who also hath taught us, by his holy Apostle **of Life.** Saint Paul, not to be sorry, as men without hope, for those who sleep in him; We humbly beseech thee, O Father, to raise us from the death of sin unto the life of righteousness; that, when we shall depart this life, we may rest in him; and that, at the general resurrection in the last day, we may be found acceptable in thy sight; and receive that blessing, which thy well-beloved Son shall then pronounce to all who love and fear thee, saying, Come, ye blessed children of my Father, receive the kingdom prepared for you from the beginning of the world. Grant this, we beseech thee, O merciful Father, through Jesus Christ, our Mediator and Redeemer. *Amen.*

MOST merciful Father, who hast been pleased to take unto thyself **For Re-union** the soul of this thy servant [*or* this child]; Grant to us who are **with the** still in our pilgrimage, and who walk as yet by faith, that having **Saints.** served thee with constancy on earth, we may be joined hereafter with thy blessed saints in glory everlasting; through Jesus Christ our Lord. *Amen.*

O LORD Jesus Christ, who by thy death didst take away the sting **That we may** of death; Grant unto us thy servants so to follow in faith where **Sleep in** thou hast led the way, that we may at length fall asleep peacefully in **Jesus.** thee, and awake up after thy likeness; through thy mercy, who livest with the Father and the Holy Ghost, one God, world without end. *Amen.*

ALMIGHTY and ever-living God, we yield unto thee most high **For Grace** praise and hearty thanks, for the wonderful grace and virtue **to follow** declared in all thy saints, who have been the choice vessels of thy **the Saints.** grace, and the lights of the world in their several generations; most humbly beseeching thee to give us grace so to follow the example of their steadfastness in thy faith, and obedience to thy holy commandments, that at the day of the general Resurrection, we, with all those who are of the mystical body of thy Son, may be set on his right hand, and hear that his most joyful voice: Come, ye blessed of my Father, inherit the kingdom prepared for you from the foundation of the world. Grant this, O Father, for Jesus Christ's sake, our only Mediator and Advocate. *Amen.*

FROM THE OFFICE OF INSTITUTION.

For the Clergy. MOST GRACIOUS God, the giver of all good and perfect gifts, who of thy wise providence hast appointed divers Orders in thy Church; Give thy grace, we beseech thee, to thy servant, to whom the charge of this congregation is now committed; and so replenish him with the truth of thy doctrine, and endue him with innocency of life, that he may faithfully serve before thee, to the glory of thy great Name, and the benefit of thy holy Church; through Jesus Christ, our only Mediator and Redeemer. *Amen.*

For the Clergy. O HOLY Jesus, who hast purchased to thyself an universal Church, and hast promised to be with the Ministers of Apostolic Succession to the end of the world; Be graciously pleased to bless the ministry and service of him who is now appointed to offer the sacrifices of prayer and praise to thee in this house, which is called by thy Name. May the words of his mouth, and the meditation of his heart, be alway acceptable in thy sight, O Lord, our strength and our Redeemer. *Amen.*

For the Congregation. O GOD, Holy Ghost, Sanctifier of the faithful, visit, we pray thee, this congregation with thy love and favour; enlighten their minds more and more with the light of the everlasting Gospel: graft in their hearts a love of the truth; increase in them true religion; nourish them with all goodness; and of thy great mercy keep them in the same, O blessed Spirit, whom, with the Father and the Son together, we worship and glorify as one God, world without end. *Amen.*

For the Unity and Peace of the Church, and its Defence against Heresy and Schism. O ALMIGHTY God, who hast built thy Church upon the foundation of the Apostles and Prophets, Jesus Christ himself being the chief corner-stone; Grant that, by the operation of the Holy Ghost, all Christians may be so joined together in unity of spirit, and in the bond of peace, that they may be an holy temple acceptable unto thee. And especially to this congregation present, give the abundance of thy grace; that with one heart they may desire the prosperity of thy holy Apostolic Church, and with one mouth may profess the faith once delivered to the Saints. Defend them from the sins of heresy and schism; let not the foot of pride come nigh to hurt them, nor the hand of the ungodly to cast them down. And grant that the course of this world may be so peaceably ordered by thy governance, that thy Church may joyfully serve thee in all godly quietness; that so they may walk in the ways of truth and peace, and at last be numbered with thy Saints in glory everlasting; through thy merits, O blessed Jesus, thou gracious Bishop and Shepherd of our souls, who art with the Father and the Holy Ghost one God, world without end. *Amen.*

Special Prayers.

FOR THE UNITY OF GOD'S PEOPLE.

O GOD, the Father of our Lord Jesus Christ, our only Saviour, the Prince of Peace; Give us grace seriously to lay to heart the great dangers we are in by our unhappy divisions. Take away all hatred and prejudice, and whatsoever else may hinder us from godly union and concord: that as there is but one Body and one Spirit, and one hope of our calling, one Lord, one Faith, one Baptism, one God and Father of us all, so we may be all of one heart and of one soul, united in one holy bond of truth and peace, of faith and charity, and may with one mind and one mouth glorify thee; through Jesus Christ our Lord. *Amen.*

FOR MISSIONS.

O GOD, who hast made of one blood all nations of men for to dwell on the face of the whole earth, and didst send thy blessed Son to preach peace to them that are far off and to them that are nigh; Grant that all men everywhere may seek after thee and find thee. Bring the nations into thy fold, and add the heathen to thine inheritance. And we pray thee shortly to accomplish the number of thine elect, and to hasten thy kingdom; through the same Jesus Christ our Lord. *Amen.*

FOR A SICK CHILD.

ALMIGHTY God, and merciful Father, to whom alone belong the issues of life and death; Look down from heaven, we humbly beseech thee, with the eyes of mercy, upon the sick *child* for whom our prayers are desired. Deliver *him*, O Lord, in thy good appointed time, from *his* bodily pain, and visit *him* with thy salvation; that if it should be thy good pleasure to prolong *his* days here on earth, *he* may live to thee, and be an instrument of thy glory, by serving thee faithfully, and doing good in *his* generation. Or else receive *him* into those heavenly habitations, where the souls of those who sleep in the Lord Jesus enjoy perpetual rest and felicity. Grant this, O Lord, for the love of thy Son, our Saviour, Jesus Christ. *Amen.*

THANKSGIVING FOR A CHILD'S RECOVERY FROM SICKNESS.

ALMIGHTY GOD and heavenly Father, we give thee humble thanks for that thou hast been graciously pleased to deliver from *his* bodily sickness the *child* in whose behalf we bless and praise thy Name, in the presence of all thy people. Grant, we beseech thee, O gracious Father, that *he*, through thy help, may both faithfully live in this world according to thy will, and also may be partaker of everlasting glory in the life to come; through Jesus Christ our Lord. *Amen.*

The Benedictions.

THE GRACE of our Lord Jesus Christ, and the love of God, and the fellowship of the Holy Ghost, be with us all evermore. *Amen.*

THE LORD bless us and keep us. The LORD make His face to shine upon us, and be gracious unto us. The LORD lift up His countenance upon us, and give us peace, both now and evermore. *Amen.*

THE PEACE of God, which passeth all understanding, keep your hearts and minds in the knowledge and love of God, and of His Son Jesus Christ our Lord: and the blessing of God Almighty, the Father, the Son, and Holy Ghost, be amongst you, and remain with you always. *Amen.*

THE GOD of peace, who brought again from the dead our Lord Jesus Christ, the great Shepherd of the sheep, through the blood of the everlasting covenant; make you perfect in every good work to do His will, working in you that which is well-pleasing in His sight; through Jesus Christ, to whom be glory for ever and ever. *Amen.*

Canticles and Psalms.

Venite, exultemus Domino.

(F = FULL. The Asterisk (*) is a direction to take breath.)

Ff O COME, let us sing | unto · the | LORD: let us heartily rejoice in the | strength of | our sal | vation.

2 Let us come before his presence with | thanks · = | giving: and show ourselves | glad in | him with | psalms.

3 For the LORD is a | great · = | God: and a great | King a | bove all | gods.

4 In his hand are all the corners | of the | earth: and the strength of the | hills is | his · = | also.

5 The sea is his | and he | made it: and his hands pre | pared · the | dry · = | land.

p 6 O come let us worship and | fall · = |
(42)

down: and kneel be | fore the | LORD our | Maker.

mf 7 For he is the | Lord our | God: and we are the people of his pasture * and the | sheep of | his · = | hand.

p 8 O worship the LORD in the | beauty · of | holiness: (cr) let the whole earth | stand in | awe of | him.

dim. 9 For he cometh, for he cometh to | judge the | earth: and with righteousness to judge the world and the | people | with his | truth.

Ff Glory be to the Father | and · to the | Son: and | to the | Holy | Ghost;

As it was in the beginning * is now, and | ever | shall be: world without | end · = | A · = | men.

Te Deum laudamus.

6 BULLINGER.

7 TURLE.

8 HODGES.

9 WESLEY.

NOTE. — *If more than one chant is used, the first change may be made at the words,* "WHEN THOU TOOKEST, etc.," *and the second change at the words* "DAY BY DAY, etc."

Ky WE práise | thee O | God : we ac- | knowledge | thee to | be the | Lord.

2 All the earth doth | worship | thee : the | Father | ever | lasting.

3 To thee all A'ngels | cry a | loud : the | Heavens, and | all the | Powers there | in;

4 To thee Chérubim and | Sera | phim : cón | tinual | ly do | cry,

p 5 Hóly | Holy | Holy : Lórd | God of | Saba | oth;

f 6 Heaven and earth are fúll of the | Majes | ty : óf | thy ' = | glo ' = | ry.

mf 7 The glorious cómpany | of ' the A | postles : (*full*) práise | = ' = | = ' = | thee.

8 The goodly féllowship | of the | Prophets: (*full*) práise | = ' = | = ' = | thee.

2d. 9 The nóble | army ' | of | Martyrs : *Part.* (*full*) práise | = ' = | = ' = | thee.

f 10 The holy Chúrch throughout | all the | world : doth ac | know ' = | ledge ' = | thee ;

mf 11 Thé | Fa ' = | ther : óf an | in | finite | Majes | ty :

12 Thíne ad | ora ' ble | true : ánd | on ' = | = ' ly | Son :

13 A'lso the | Holy | Ghost : thé | Com ' = | fort ' = | er.

f 14 Thóu art the | King of | Glory : O' | = ' = | = ' = | Christ.

15 Thou art the éver | lasting | Son : óf | = ' the | Fa ' = | ther.

pp 16 When thou tookest upon thée to de | liver | man : thou didst humble thy- | sélf to be | born ' = | of a | Virgin.

p 17 When thou hadst overcóme the | sharpness ' of | death : (*cr*) thou didst open the Kíngdom of | Heaven to | all be | lievers.

f 18 Thou sittest at the ríght | hand of | God : ín the | glory | of the | Father.

p 19 We belíeve that | thou shalt | come : tó | be ' = | our ' = | Judge.

20 We therefore práy thee | help thy | servants : whom thou hast redéemed | with thy | precious blood.

mf 21 Make them to be númbered | with thy | Saints : ín | glory | ever | lasting.

22 O Lórd | save thy | people : ánd | bless thine | herit | age.

23 Góv | = ' ern | them : ánd | lift them | up for | ever.

f 24 Dáy | by ' = | day : wé | magni | fy ' = | thee;

25 A'nd we | worship ' thy | Name : éver | world with | out ' = | end.

p 26 Vóuch | safe O | Lord : to kéep us this | day with | out ' = | sin.

27 O Lórd | have | mercy ' up | on us : háve | mercy ' up | on ' = | us.

28 O Lord | let thy | mércy | be up | on us: ás our | trust ' = | is in | thee.

f 29 O Lord in thée | have I | trusted : lét me | never | be con | founded.

Benedicite, omnia opera Domini.

10   GILBERT.

11   ANCIENT CHANT.

12   HOPKINS.

13   WEBBE.

14   HAVERGAL.

(If a second Chant is used, make a change at verse 18. and return to the first Chant at verse 26.)

Ff O ALL ye Works of the Lórd | bless · ye the | Lord: práise him, and | magnify | him for | ever.

• 2 O ye Angels of the Lórd | . . . .

mf 3 O ye Héavens | . . . .

4 O ye Waters that be above the firmament | . . . .

5 O all ye Powers of the Lórd | . . . .

6 O ye Sun and Móon | . . . .

7 O ye Stars of Héaven | . . . .

8 O ye Showers and Déw | . . . .

9 O ye Winds of Gód | . . . .

10 O ye Fire and Héat | . . . .

11 O ye Winter and Súmmer | . . . .

12 O ye Dews and Frósts | . . . .

13 O ye Frost and Cóld | . . . .

14 O ye Ice and Snów | . . . .

15 O ye Nights and Dáys | . . . .

16 O ye Light and Dárkness | . . . .

17 O ye Lightnings and Clóuds | . . . .

f 18 O let the Eárth | bless the | Lord: yea let it práise him, and | magnify | him for | ever.

mf 19 O ye Mountains and Hílls | . . . .

20 O all ye Green Things upon the eárth | . . . .

21 O ye Wélls | . . . .

22 O ye Seas and Flóods | . . . .

23 O ye Whales, and all that move in the wáters | . . . .

24 O all ye Fowls of the aír | . . . .

25 O all ye Beasts and Cáttle | . . . .

26 O ye Children of Mén | . . . .

f 27 O let I'srael | bless the | Lord: práise him, and | magnify | him for | ever.

28 O ye Priests of the Lórd | . . . .

mf 29 O ye Servants of the Lórd | . . . .

p 30 O ye Spirits and Souls of the Ríghteous | . . . .

31 O ye holy and humble Men of héart | . . . .

Ff   Glory be to the Fáther | and | to the | Son: ánd | to the | Holy | Ghost;

As it was in the beginning * is nów, and | ever | shall be: wórld without | end · = | A · = | men.

Benedictus.

15 CROFT.

16 ALDRICH.

17 CROTCH.

18 CROTCH.

19 HAYES.

20

Ff BLESSED be the Lórd | God of | Israel: for he hath vísited | and re | deemed · his | people;

2 And hath raised up a míghty sal | vation | for us: in the house | of his | servant | David;

mf 3 As he spake by the móuth of his | holy | Prophets: which have béen | since the | world be | gan;

4 That we should be sáved | from our | enemies: and fróm the | hand of | all that | hate us.

5 To perform the mercy prómised to | our fore | fathers: ánd to re | member · his | holy | covenant;

6 To perform the oath which he sware to our fórefather | Abra | ham: thát | he would | give · = | us;

p 7 That we being delivered out of the hánd | of our | enemies: might sérve | him with | out · = | fear;

8 In holiness and ríghteous | ness be | fore him: áll the | days · = | of our | life,

mf 9 And thou child, shalt be called the próphet | of the | Highest: for thou shalt go before the face of the Lórd | to pre | pare his | ways;

10 To give knowledge of salvátion | unto · his | people: fór the re | mission | of their | sins,

11 Through the tender mércy | of our | God: whereby the day-spring fróm on | high hath | visit · ed | us;

12 To give light to them that sit in darkness * and ín the | shadow · of | death: (*p*) and to guide our féet | into · the | way of | peace.

F f Glory be to the Fáther | and · to the | Son: ánd | to the | Holy | Ghost;

As it was in the beginning * is nów, and | ever | shall be: wórld without | end · = | A · = | men.

Jubilate Deo.

Ff *O* BE joyful in the Lórd | all ye | lands:
serve the LORD with gladness * and
come befóre his | presence | with a |
song.

2 Be ye sure that the LORD he is
God * it is he that hath made us ánd
not | we our | selves: we are his
people, and the | sheep of | his · = | pas-
ture.

3 O go your way into his gates with
thanksgiving * and into his | courts with |

praise: be thankful unto hím, and |
speak good | of his | Name.

mf 4 For the LORD is gracious * his mér-
cy is | ever | lasting: (cr) and his truth
endureth from géner | ation · to | gen-
er | ation.

Ff Glory be to the Fáther | and · to the |
Son: ánd | to the | Holy | Ghost:

As it was in the beginning * is nów, and
| ever | shall be: world without | end ·
= | A · = | men.

Gloria in excelsis.

29

OLD CHANT.

GLORY bé to | God on | high : and on
eárth, | peace, good | will towards |
men.

We praise thee, we bless thée, we |
worship | thee : we glorify Thee, we give
thánks to | thee for | thy great | glory.

O Lord Gód, | heavenly | King : Gód
the | Father | Al · = | mighty.

O Lord, the only begotten Són | Je-
sus | Christ : O Lord God, Lámb of |
God, Son | of the | Father,

p

That takest awáy the | sins · of the |
world : have mércy | upon | us.
Thou that takest awáy the | sins · of
the | world : have mércy | upon | us.

Thou that takest awáy the | sins · of
the | world : ré | ceive our | prayer.
Thou that sittest at the right hánd
of | God the | Father : have mércy | up-
on | us.

A - MEN

For thou ónly | art · = | holy :
Thóu | only | art the | Lord.

Thou only. O Chríst, with the | Holy |
Ghost : art most hígh in the | glory ·
of | God the | Father.

Magnificat.

30   WEBBE.

31   CRESER.

32   ROGERS.

33   NARES.

34   OUSELEY.

35

Fmf MY soul doth magni | fy the | Lord: and my spirit hath re | joiced · in | God my | Saviour.

2 For he | hath re | garded: the lowli | ness of | his hand | maiden.

3 For be | hold from | henceforth: (*f*) all gener | ations · shall | call me | bless-ed.

4 For he that is mighty hath | magni · fied | me: (*p*) and | holy | is his | Name.

p 5 And his mercy is on | them that | fear him: through | out all | gener | ations.

f 6 He hath showed strength | with his | arm: he hath scattered the proud in the imagin | ation | of their | hearts.

7 He hath put down the mighty | from their | seat: and hath ex | alted · the | humble · and | meek.

p 8 He hath filled the hungry with | good · = | things: and the rich he hath | sent · = | empty · a | way.

24 part. 9 He remembering his mercy hath holpen his | servant | Israel: as he promised to our forefathers * A'braham | and his | seed for | ever.

Ff Glory be to the Father | and · to the | Son: and | to the | Holy | Ghost;

As it was in the beginning * is now, and | ever | shall be: world without | end · = | A · = | men.

Cantate Domino.

36 RUSSELL.

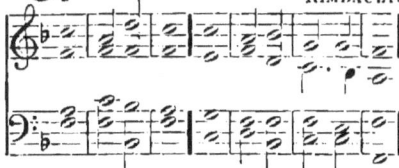

37 RIMBAULT.

38 LEMON.

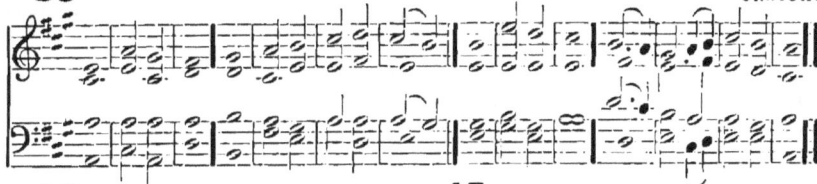

39 CROTCH.

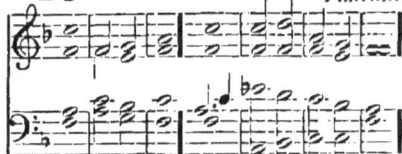

40 FELTON.

41

Fj O SING unto the LORD a | new ˙ = | song : for he hath | done˙ = | marvellous | things.

2 With his own right hand * and with his | holy | arm: hath he | gotten ˙ him | self the | victory.

mf 3 The LORD declared | his sal | vation: his righteousness hath he openly showed in the | sight ˙ = | of the | heathen.

4 He hath remembered his mercy and truth toward the | house of | Israel: and all the ends of the world have seen the sal | vation | of our | God.

f 5 Show yourselves joyful unto the LORD | all ye | lands: sing, re | joice and | give ˙ = | thanks.

6 Praise the LORD up | on the | harp: sing to the harp with a | psalm of | thanks ˙ = | giving.

7 With trumpets | also ˙ and | shawms: O show yourselves joyful be | fore the | LORD | the King.

8 Let the sea make a noise * and all that | therein | is: the round world, and | they that | dwell there | in.

9 Let the floods clap their hands * and let the hills be joyful together be | fore the | LORD: for he | cometh ˙ to | judge the | earth.

mf 10 With righteousness shall he | judge the | world: and the | people | with ˙ = | equity.

Ff Glory be the Father | and ˙ to the | Son: and | to the | Holy | Ghost;

As it was in the beginning * is now, and | ever | shall | be: world without | end ˙ = | A ˙ = | men.

Bonum est.

42   ANON.

43   FARRANT.

44   STEPHENS.

45   GOLDWIN.

46   HENLEY.

47   DUPUIS.

48   TRAVERS.

49

F/ IT is a good thing to give thánks | un-
to · the | LORD: and to sing praises
únto thy | Name · = | O Most | Highest;

2 To tell of thy loving-kindness éarly |
in the | morning: and of thy trúth | in
the | night · = | season;

3 Upon an instrument of ten strings *
ánd up | on the | lute: upon a loud ín-
strument | and up | on the | harp.

4 For thou, LORD, hast made me
glád | through thy | works: and I will
rejoice in giving praise for the óper |
ations | of thy | hands.

F/ Glory be to the Fáther | and · to the |
Son: ánd | to the | Holy | Ghost; .

As it was in the beginning * is nów,
and | ever | shall be: wórld without |
end · = | A · = | men.

Nunc Dimittis.

50 BARRY.

51 BLOW.

Ped.

52 ANON.

53 MEDLEY.

54 MONK.

55 BULLINGER.

56 LANGDON.

57 ANON.

58

F*mf* LORD, now lettest thou thy sér- | vant de | part in | peace: &c | cording | to thy | word.

2 For mine | eyes have | seen: thỹ | = · sal | va · = | tion,

3 Which thou | hast pre | pared: before the | face of | all · = | peo- ple;

4 To be a líght to | lighten · the | Gentiles: and to be the glóry | of thy | people | Israel.

F*f* Glory be to the Fáther | and · to the | Son: and | to the | Holy | Ghost;

As it was in the beginning * is nów, and | ever | shall be: wórld without | end · = | A · = | men.

Deus misereatur.

59   ALDRICH.   **60**   BARNBY.

61   BOYCE.

62   HIGGINS.

63   MONK.   **64**

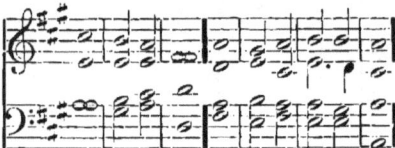

F mf GOD be merciful únto | us and | bless us: and show us the light of his countenance * ánd be | merci · ful | unto | us;

2 That thy wáy may be | known up · on | earth: thy sáving | health a | mong all | nations.

f 3 Let the people práise | thee O | God: yéa let | all the | people | praise thee.

mf 4 O let the nations rejóice | and be | glad: for thou shalt judge the folk right-eously * and góvern the | nations · up | on · = | earth.

f 5 Let the people práise | thee O | God: yéa let | all the | people | praise thee.

mf 6 Then shall the eárth bring | forth her | increase: and God, even our own Gód, shall | give · = | us his | blessing.

F f 7 Gód shall | bless · = | us: and all the énds of the | world shall | fear · = | him.

Glory be to the Fáther | and · to the | Son: ánd | to the | Holy | Ghost;

As it was in the beginning * is nów and | ever | shall be: wórld without | end · = | A · = | men.

Benedic, anima mea.

65 BATTISHILL.

66 ANON.

67 NORRIS.

68 WOODWARD.

69 BELLAMY.

70

F f PRAISE the Lo'rd | O my | soul:
and all that is within me | praise
his | holy | Name.

2 Praise the Lo'rd | O my | soul: ánd
for | get not | all his | benefits:

mf 3 Who forgíveth | all thy | sin: and
healeth | all · = | thine in | firmities;

4 Who saveth thy life | from de |
struction: and crowneth thée with |
mercy · and | loving | kindness.

f 5 O praise the Lord ye angels of his *
ye that ex | cel in | strength: ye that
fulfil his commandment * and hearken

unto the | voice · = | of his | word.

6 O praise the Lo'rd, all | ye his |
hosts: ye sérvants of | his that | do his |
pleasure.

2d part. 7 O speak good of the Lord, all ye
works of his * in all pláces of | his do |
minion: praise thóu the | Lord · = | O
my | soul.

F f Glory be to the Fáther | and · to the |
Son: ánd | to the | Holy | Ghost;

As it was in the beginning * is nów,
and | ever | shall be: wórld without |
end · = | A · = | men.

Easter Day.

Instead of the VENITE EXULTEMUS DOMINO.

71   SAVAGE.   **72**   FISHER.

73   MORNINGTON.

74   CROTCH.

75   EDWARDS.   **76**

Ff CHRIST our Passover is sacri | ficed · for | us : therefore | let us | keep the | feast.

2 Not with old leaven * neither with the leaven of | malice · and | wicked- ness: but with the unleavened bread of sin | ceri | ty and | truth. 1 *Cor.* v. 7.

Ff CHRIST being raised from the dead | dieth no | more: death hath no more do | minion | over | him.

p 4 For in that he died * he died unto | sin · = | once: (*f*) but in that he liveth he | liveth | unto | God.

5 Likewise reckon ye also yourselves to be dead indeed | unto | sin: but alive unto God through | Jesus | Christ our | Lord. *Rom.* vi. 9.

Ff CHRIST is risen | from · the | dead: them that | slept.

p 7 For since by | man came | death : (*cr*) by man came also the resur | rec- tion | of the | dead.

p 8 For as in A'dam | all · = | die: (*cr*) Even so in Christ shall | all be | made a | live. 1 *Cor.* xv. 20.

Ff Glory be to the Father | and · to the | Son: and | to the | Holy | Ghost;

As it was in the beginning * is now, and | ever | shall be: world without | end · = | A · = | men.

Thanksgiving=Day.

Instead of the VENITE EXULTEMUS DOMINO.

77   SMITH.   **78**   BARCROFT.

79   DUPUIS.

80   CROTCH.

81   **82**

F f   O PRAISE the LORD * for it is a good thing to sing praises | unto · our | God: yea, a joyful and pleasant thing it is | to be | thank · = | ful.

2 The LORD doth build up Je | rusa | lem: and gather together | the out | casts of | Israel.

p 3 He healeth those that are | broken · in | heart: and giveth | medicine · to | heal their | sickness.

4 O sing unto the LORD with | thanks · = | giving: sing praises upon the | harp · = | unto · our | God:

mf 5 Who covereth the heaven with clouds * and prepareth rain | for the | earth: and maketh the grass to grow upon the mountains * and herb | for the | use of | men;

6 Who giveth fodder | unto · the | cattle: and feedeth the young | ravens · that | call up | on him.

f 7 Praise the LORD, O · Je | rusa | lem: praise | = · thy | God O | Sion.

8 For he hath made fast the bars | of thy | gates: and hath | blessed · thy | children · with | in thee.

2d part. 9 He maketh peace | in thy | borders: and filleth thee | with the | flour of | wheat.

F f Glory be to the Father | and · to the | Son: and | to the | Holy | Ghost;

As it was in the beginning * is now, and | ever | shall be: world without | end · = | A · = | men.

Psalms.

(While any one of these Psalms may be appropriately used at almost any Service, some of them are the "Proper Psalms" for the Holy Days of the Church, as is indicated in the following Table:)

Day.	Psalm.	Day.	Psalm.
1st Sunday in Advent	{ 8 96 97 }	Ascension	{ 8 15 24 }
Christmas	{ 19 85 }	Whitsunday	{ 47 48 145 }
Circumcision	{ 40 65 103 }	Trinity Sunday	{ 93 97 150 }
Epiphany	{ 46 47 48 }	Transfiguration	{ 84 93 }
Purification	84		{ 34 91 }
Ash-Wednesday	{ 32 130 }	St. Michael and All Angels	{ 91 103 148 }
Annunciation	138		
Good Friday	40		{ 1 15 }
Easter-Even	30	All Saints' Day	{ 112 121 }
Easter-Day	{ 111 118 }		

Psalm 1.

Beatus vir, qui non abiit.

83. FARRANT.

F mf **B**LESSED is the man that hath not walked in the counsel of the ungodly * nor stóod in the | way of | sinners: and hath not sát in the | seat · = | of the | scornful.

2 But his delight is in the láw |of the | Lord: and in his law will he exercíse him | self · = | day and | night.

3 And he shall be like a tree plánted bý the | water | side: that will bring fórth his | fruit in | due · = | season.
(56)

4 His léaf also | shall not | wither: and look, whatsoéver he | doeth | it shall | prosper.

mp 5 As for the ungodly, it is nót | so with | them: but they are like the chaff* which the wind scattereth awáy from the | face · = | of the | earth.

6 Therefore the ungodly shall not be able to stánd | in the | judgment: neither the sinners in the cóngre | gation | of the | righteous.

7 But the Lord knoweth the wáy | of the | righteous: (*dim.*) and the wáy of 'he un | godly | shall · = | perish.

At the end of every Psalm may be repeated the GLORIA PATRI, as follows: —

f Glory be to the Fáther | and · to the | Son: ánd | to the | Holy | Ghost;

As it was in the beginning, is nów, and | ever | shall be: wórld without | end · = | A · = | men.

PSALM 8. *Domine, Dominus noster.*

84 ANON.

Ff O LORD our Governor * how excel- | lent is thy | Name in | all the | world: thou that hast set thy | glory · a | bove the | heavens!

2 Out of the mouth of very babes and sucklings hast thou ordained strength * because | of thine | enemies: that thou mightest still the | enemy | and · the a | venger.

3 For I will consider thy heavens *

even the works | of thy | fingers: the moon and the stars | which thou | hast or | dained.

p 4 What is man, that thou art | mind- ful · of | him: and the son of man | that thou | visitest | him?

5 Thou madest him lower | than the | angels: (*cr*) to crown | him with | glory · and | worship.

f 6 Thou makest him to have dominion of the works | of thy | hands: and thou hast put all things in sub | jection | un- der · his | feet;

7 All | sheep and | oxen: yea and the | beasts · = | of the | field;

8 The fowls of the air, and the fishes | of the | sea: and whatsoever walketh through the | paths · = | of the | seas.

F 9 O · | Lord our | Governor: how ex- cellent is thy | Name in | all the | world!

PSALM 15. *Domine, quis habitabit?*

85 JONES.

F L ORD, who shall dwell in thy | tab- | *mf* er | nacle: or who shall rest up | on thy | holy | hill?

2 Even he that leadeth an | uncorrupt | life: and doeth the thing which is right * and speaketh the | truth · = | from his | heart.

3 He that hath used no deceit in his tongue * nor done evil | to his | neigh- bour: and | hath not | slandered · his | neighbour.

4 He that setteth not by himself * but is lowly in his | own · = | eyes: and maketh much of | them that | fear the | Lord.

5 He that sweareth unto his neigh- bour * and disap | pointeth | him | not: though it | were to | his own | hin- drance.

6 He that hath not given his money up | on · = | usury: nor taken reward a | gainst the | inno | cent.

7 Whoso | doeth · these | things: shall | nev · = | er · = | fall.

PSALM 19. *Cœli enarrant.*

86 NARES.

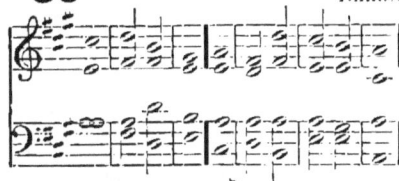

Ff THE heavens declare the | glory · of | God: and the firmament | showeth · his | handy | work.

2 One day | telleth · an | other: and one night | certi | fieth · an | other.

3 There is neither | speech nor | lan- guage: but their | voices · are | heard a- mong them.

4 Their sound is gone out into | all · = | lands: and their words into the | ends · = | of the | world.

5 In them hath he set a tabernacle | for the | sun: which cometh forth as a bridegroom out of his chamber * and re- joiceth as a | giant · to | run his | course.

6 It goeth forth from the uttermost part of the heaven * and runneth about unto the end of | it a | gain: and there is nothing hid | from the | heat there | of.

86

NARES.

7 The law of the Lord is an undefiled láw con | verting · the | soul: the testimony of the Lord is sure * and gíveth | wisdom | unto · the | simple.

8 The statutes of the Lord are ríght and re | joice the | heart: the commandment of the Lord is pure * and gíveth | light un | to the | eyes.

dim. 9 The fear of the Lord is cléan and en | dureth · for | ever: the judgments of the Lord are trúe and | righteous | alto | gether.

mp 10 More to be desired are they than gold * yéa than | much fine | gold: sweeter also than hóney | and the | honey | comb.

11 Moreover by thém is thy | servant | taught: and in kéeping of them | there is | great re | ward.

p 12 Who can tell how óft | he of | fendeth: O cleanse thou mé | from my | secret | faults.

13 Keep thy servant also from presumptuous sins * lest they get the domínion | over | me: so shall I be undefiled, and ínnocent | from the | great of | fence.

cr 14 Let the words of my mouth * and the meditátion | of my | heart: be álway ac | ceptable | in thy | sight,

f 15 O' | = · = | Lord: mý | strength and | my re | deemer.

87

PSALM 23.   *Dominus regit me.*

BARNBY.

F | THE Lórd | is my | shepherd: thére-
mf   fore | can I | lack · = | nothing.

2 He shall féed me in a | green · = | pasture: and lead me fórth be | side the | waters · of | comfort.

3 Hé shall con | vert my | soul: and bring me forth in the paths of ríghteousness | for his | Name's · = | sake.

4 Yea, though I walk through the valley of the shadow of death * I' will I fear no | evil: for thou art with me * thy ród and thy | staff · = | comfort | me.

5 Thou shalt prepare a table before me against thém that | trouble | me: thou hast anointed my head with óil and my | cup · = | shall be | full.

6 But thy loving-kindness and mercy shall follow me all the dáys | of my | life: and I will dwell in the hóuse | of the | Lord for | ever.

88

PSALM 24.   *Domini est terra.*

DUPUIS.

F*f* | THE earth is the Lord's * and áll
  that | therein | is: the compass of the wórld, and | they that | dwell there | in.

2 For he hath fóunded it up | on the | seas: and prepared | it up | on the | floods.

p 3 Who shall ascend into the híll | of the | Lord: or who shall rise úp | in his | holy | place?

4 Even he that hath clean hánds and a | pure · = | heart: and that hath not lift up his | mind unto vanity * nor swórn | to de | ceive his | neighbour.

5 He shall receive the bléssing | from the | Lord: and righteóusness fróm the | God of | his sal | vation.

6 This is the generátion of | them that | seek him: even of thém that | seek thy | face O | Jacob.

F*f* 7 Lift up your heads O ye gates * and be ye lift up ye éver | lasting | doors: and the Kíng of | glory | shall come | in.

p 8 Whó is this | King of | glory: (*f*) it is the Lord strong and mighty * éven the | Lord · = | mighty · in | battle.

F*f* 9 Lift up your heads O ye gates * and be ye lift up ye éver | lasting | doors: and the Kíng of | glory | shall come | in.

p 10 Whó is this | King of | glory: (*f*) even the Lord of hósts | he · is the | King of | glory.

PSALM 27. *Dominus illuminatio.*

89 HAYES.

mf F THE Lord is my light and my salva- tion * whóm then I shall I I fear: the Lord is the strength of my life * of whóm then I shall I I be a I fraid?

2 When the wicked * even mine ene- mies and my foes * came upon me to eat I up my I flesh: théy I stumbled I and · = I fell.

3 Though an host of men were laid a- gainst me * yet shall not my héart I be a I fraid: and though there rose up war against me * yét will I I put my I trust in I him.

mf 4 One thing have I desired of the Lórd which I I will re I quire: even that I may dwell in the house of the Lord all the days of my life * to behold the fair beau- ty of the Lórd I and to I visit · his I tem- ple.

5 For in the time of trouble he shall hide mé in his I taber I nacle: yea in the secret place of his dwelling shall he hide me * and set me úp up I on a I rock of I stone.

6 And now shall he lĭft I up mine I head: above mine énemies I round a I bout · = I me.

f 7 Therefore will I offer in his dwelling an oblátion with I great · = I gladness: I will sing and spéak I praises I unto · the I Lord.

mp 8 Hearken unto my voice O Lord * when I crý I unto I thee: have mércy up I on me · and I hear · = I me.

9 My heart hath talked of thee * Séek I ye my I face: Thý I face Lord I will I I seek.

10 O hide not thóu thy I face from I me: nor cast thy sérvant a I way · = I in dis I pleasure.

11 Thóu hast I been my I succour: leave me not, neither forsáke me O I God of I my sal I vation.

12 When my fáther and my I mother · for I sake me : the Lórd I taketh I me · = I up.

13 Teach me thý I way O I Lord: and lead me in the right wáy be I cause of I mine · = I enemies.

14 Deliver me not over into the wĭll of mine I adver I saries: for there are false witnesses risen up against me, ánd I such as I speak · = I wrong.

mf 15 I should útterly I have · = I fainted: but that I believe verily to see the good- ness of the Lórd in the I land · = I of the I living.

16 O tarry thóu the I Lord's · = I lei- sure: (*cr*) be strong and he shall com- fort thine heart * and put thóu thy I trust · = I in the I Lord.

PSALM 30. *Exaltabo te, Domino.*

90 BATTISHILL.

p F I WILL magnify thee O Lord * for thóu hast I set me I up: and not made my fóes to I triumph I over I me.

2 O Lord my God, I crĭed I unto I thee: ánd I thou hast I healed I me.

3 Thou Lord hast brought my sóul I out of I hell: thou hast kept my life from thém that go I down · = I to the I pit.

4 Sing praises unto the Lórd, O ye I saints of I his: and give thanks unto him * fór a re I membrance I of his I holiness.

5 For his wrath endureth but the twinkling of an eye * and ĭn his I pleas- ure · is I life: heaviness may endure for a night * but jóy I cometh I in the I morn- ing.

6 And in my prosperity I said * I shall néver I be re I moved: thou Lord of thy góodness hast I made my I hill so I strong.

p 7 Thou didst tŭrn thy I face from I me: ánd I I · = I was · = I troubled.

8 Then cried I únto I thee O I Lord: and gát me I to my I Lord right I humbly.

9 What profit ĭs there I in my I blood: when I go I down · = I to the I pit?

10 Shall the dust give thánks I unto I thee: ŏr shall I it de I clare thy I truth?

11 Hear O Lord, and háve I mercy · up I on me: Lórd be I thou · = I my · = I helper.

cr 12 Thou hast turned my héaviness I into I joy: thou hast put off my sáck- cloth and I girded I me with I gladness. .

f 13 Therefore shall every good man sing of thy práise with I out · = I ceas- ing: O my God, I will give thánks I un- to I thee for I ever.

PSALM 32. *Beati quorum.*

91   HEYWOOD.

F **BLESSED** is he whose unrighteous-
mp ness | is for | given: ånd whose |
sin · = | is · = | covered.

2 Blessed is the man unto whom the
Lord im | puteth · no | sin: and in whose |
spirit · there | is no | guile.

3 For whilst I | held my | tongue: my
bones consumed away | through my |
daily · com | plaining.

4 For thy hand is heavy upon me | day
and | night: and my moisture is | like
the | drought in | summer.

5 I will acknowledge my sin | unto |
thee: and mine unrighteouness | have
I | not · = | hid.

6 I said, I will confess my sins | unto ·
the | Lord: and so thou forgåvest the |
wickedness | of my | sin.

7 For this shall every one that is godly make his prayer unto thee * in a time
when thou | mayest · be | found: (cr)
but in the great water-floods | they shall |
not come | nigh him.

8 Thou art a place to hide me in * thou
shalt preserve | me from | trouble: thou
shalt compass me about with | songs ·
= | of de | liverance.

mf 9 I will inform thee, and teach thee in
the way wherein | thou shalt | go: and
I' will | guide thee | with mine | eye.

10 Be ye not like to horse and mule *
which have no | under | standing: whose
mouths must be held with bit and bri-
dle | lest they | fall up | on thee.

11 Great plagues remain | for the · un |
godly: but whoso putteth his trust in
the Lord * mercy embraceth | him on |
every | side.

f 12 Be glad O ye righteous * and re-
joice | in the | Lord: and be joyful all
ye | that are | true of | heart.

PSALM 34. *Benedicam Dominum.*

92   MONK.

F **I WILL** alway give thånks | unto ·
f the | Lord: his praise shall | ever ·
be | in my | mouth.

2 My soul shall make her boast | in
the | Lord: the humble shall hear there |
of · = | and be | glad.

3 O praise the | Lord with | me: and
let us magni | fy his | Name to | gether.

mf 4 I sought the Lord | and he | heard
me: yea, he delivered me | out of | all
my | fear.

5 They had an eye unto him | and
were | lightened: ånd their | faces ·
were | not a | shamed.

6 Lo the poor crieth, and the Lord |
heareth | him: yea, and saveth him |
out of | all his | troubles.

7 The angel of the Lord tarrieth round
about | them that | fear him: ånd | = ·
de | livereth | them.

p 8 O taste and see how gracious the |
Lord · = | is: (cr) blessed is the | man
that | trusteth · in | him.

9 O fear the Lord ye that | are his |
saints: for they that | fear · = | him
lack | nothing.

mf 10 The lions do láck and | suffer |
hunger: but they who seek the Lord
shall want no manner of | thing · = |
that is | good.

11 Come ye children, and hearken |
unto | me: I will teach you the | fear ·
= | of the | Lord.

12 What man is he that | lusteth · to |
live: ånd would | fain · = | see good |
days?

13 Keep thy | tongue from | evil: and
thy lips | that they | speak no | guile.

14 Eschew evil | and do | good: seek |
peace · = | and en | sue it.

15 The eyes of the Lord are | over ·
the | righteous: and his ears are | open |
unto · their | prayers.

16 The countenance of the Lord is
against them that | do · = | evil: to root
out the remembrance | of them | from
the | earth.

17 The righteous cry, and the Lord |
heareth | them: and delivereth them |
out of | all their | troubles.

18 The Lord is nigh unto them that are of a | contrite | heart: and will save such as | be · of an | humble | spir-it.

p 19 Great are the troubles | of the | righteous: (*cr*) but the Lórd de | livereth · him | out of | all.

20 He kéepeth | all his | bones: só

that not | one of | them is | broken.

21 But misfortune shall sláy | the un | godly: and they that háte the | right-eous | shall be | desolate.

22 The Lord delivereth the sóuls | of his | servants: and all they that put their trúst in | him shall | not be | desti-tute.

PSALM 40. *Expectans expectavi.*

93 LAMB.

F I WAITED pátiently | for the | Lord:
mf and he inclíned unto | me and | heard my | calling.

2 He brought me also out of the hor-rible pit * óut of the | mire and | clay: and set my feet upon the róck and | or-dered | my · = | goings.

3 And he hath put a new sóng | in my | mouth: even a thánks | giving | un-to · our | God.

4 Mány shall | see it · and | fear: and shall pút their | trust · = | in the | Lord.

5 Blessed is the man that hath set his hópe | in the | Lord: and turned not unto the proud * and to súch as | go a | bout with | lies.

6 O Lord my God, great are the won-drous works which thou hast done * like as he also thy thóughts which | are to | us-ward: and yet there is no man that órdereth | them · = | unto | thee.

7 If I should decláre them and | speak of | them: they should be more then I· am | able | to ex | press.

8 Sacrifice and meat-óffering thou | wouldest | not: but mine | ears · = | hast thou | opened.

9 Burnt-offerings and sacrifice for sin hast thóu | not re | quired: thén | said I | Lo I | come;

10 In the volume of the book it is written of me * that I should fulfil thy wíll | O my | God: I am content to do it * yea thy láw | is with | in my | heart.

11 I have declared thy righteousness in the gréat | congre | gation: lo, I will not refrain my líps O | Lord and | that thou | knowest.

12 I have not hid thy ríghteousness with | in my | heart: my talk hath been of thy trúth | and of | thy sal | vation.

13 I have not kept back thy lóving | mercy · and | truth: fróm the | great · = | congre | gation.

mf 14 Withdraw not thou thy mércy from | me O | Lord: let thy loving-kindness and thy trúth | alway · pre | serve · = | me.

15 For innumerable troubles are come about me * my sins have taken such hold upon me * that I am not áble | to look | up: yea, they are more in number than the hairs of my head * ánd my | heart hath | failed | me.

mp 16 O Lord, let it be thy pléasure to de | liver | me: máke | haste O | Lord to | help me.

mf 17 Let them be ashamed and confound-ed together * that seek after my sóul | to de | stroy it: let them be driven back-ward and pút to re | buke that | wish me | evil.

18 Let them be desolate ánd re | warded · with | shame: that say unto me, Fie up | on thee | fie up | on thee!

f 19 Let all those that seek thee be jóy-ful and | glad in | thee: and let such as love thy salvation say álway, The | Lord be | prais · = | ed.

p 20 As for mé I am | poor and | needy: (*cr*) but the | Lord · = | careth | for me.

21 Thou art my hélper | and re | deem-er: make nó long | tarrying | O my | God,

PSALM 42.   *Quemadmodum.*

94   Hɪɴᴇ.

F **L**IKE as the hart desíroth the |
mf water | brooks: so longeth my
sóul | after | thee O | God.

2 **My** soul is athirst for God * yea e-
ven fór the | living | God: when shall I
come to appéar be | fore the | presence ·
of | God?

3 My tears have been my méat | day
and | night: while they daily sáy unto
me | Where is | now thy | God?

4 Now when I think thereupon * I
pour out my héart | by my | self: for I
went with the multitude * and brought
them fórth | into · the | house of |
God;

5 In the voice of práise and | thanks ·
= | giving: among súch | as keep | holy |
day.

p 6 Why art thou so full of héaviness |
O my | soul: and why art thou só dis |
quiet | ed with | in me.

mf 7 Pút thy | trust in | God: for I will
yet give him thánks for the | help · = |
of his | countenance.

8 My God, my sóul is | vexed · with |
in me: therefore will I remember thee
concerning the land of Jordan * ánd
the | little | hill of | Hermon.

9 One deep calleth another * because
of the nóise of thy | water | pipes: all
thy waves and stórms | are gone | over |
me.

10 The Lord hath granted his loving-
kíndness | in the | day - time: and in the
night-season did I sing of him * and
made my prayer únto the | God · = | of
my | life.

11 I will say unto the God of my
strength * why hast thóu for | gotten |
me: why go I thus heavily * while
the | ene · my op | presseth | me?

p 12 My bones are smitten asúnder as |
with a | sword: while mine enemies that
tróuble me | cast me | in the | teeth;

13 Namely, while they say dáily | un-
to | me: Where | = · is | now thy |
God?

p 14 Why art ᴍᴏᴏ so véxed | O my |
soul: and why art thou só dis | quiet |
ed with | in me?

cr f 15 O pút thy | trust in | God: for I
will yet thank him * which is the hélp
of my | counte · nance | and my | God.

PSALM 46.   *Deus noster refugium.*

95   Lᴇᴇ.

F **G**O'D is our | hope and | strength:
f a véry | present | help in | trouble.

2 Therefore will we not fear, thóugh
the | earth be | moved: and though the
hills be carried ínto the | midst · = | of
the | sea.

3 Though the waters theréof | rage
and | swell: and though the mountains
sháke at the | tempest | of the | same.

4 The rivers of the flood thereof shall
make glád the | city · of | God: the holy
place of the tábernacle | of the | Most ·
= | Highest.

5 God is in the midst of her * there-
fore shall she nót | be re | moved: Gód
shall | help her · and | that right | ear-
ly.

6 The heathen make much adó and
the | kingdoms · are | moved: but God
hath showed his vóice and the | earth
shall | melt a | way.

F 7 The Lórd of | hosts is | with us:
mf 8 O come hither, and behold the
wórks | of the | Lord: what destruction
hé hath | brought up | on the | earth.

9 He maketh wars to céase in | all
· the | world: he breaketh the bow, and
knappeth the spear in sunder * and
búrneth the | chariots | in the | fire.

p cr 10 Be still then, and knów that | I
am | God: I will be exalted among the
heathen * and I will bé ex | alted | in
the | earth.

F *f* 11 The Lórd of | hosts is | with us:
the Gód of | Jacob | is our | refuge.

PSALM 47. *Omnes gentes, plaudite.*

96   RUSSELL.

Ff O CLAP your hands together | all
ye | people: O sing unto God |
with the | voice of | melody.

mf 2 For the Lord is high and | to be |
feared: he is the great King up | on ˙ = |
all the | earth.

3 He shall subdue the people | under |
us: and the | nations | under ˙ our | feet.

4 He shall choose out an | heritage |
for us: even the worship of | Jacob |
whom he | loved.

f 5 God is gone up with a | merry | noise:
and the Lord with the | sound ˙ = | of
the | trump.

6 O sing praises, sing praises | unto ˙
our | God: O sing praises sing | praises |
unto ˙ our | King.

7 For God is the King of | all the |
earth: sing ye | praises ˙ with | under |
standing.

8 God reigneth | over ˙ the | heathen:
God sitteth up | on his | holy | seat.

9 The princes of the people are joined
unto the people of the God of | Abra |
ham: for God which is very high
exalted * doth defend the earth as it |
were ˙ = |with a | shield.

PSALM 48. *Magnus Dominus.*

97   HOPKINS.

Ff GREAT is the Lord, and highly | to
be | praised: in the city of our
God, even up | on his | holy | hill.

mf 2 The hill of Sion is a fair place * and
the joy of the | whole ˙ = | earth: upon
the north side lieth the city of the great
King * God is well known in her palaces |
as a | sure ˙ = | refuge.

3 For lo the kings | of the | earth: are
gathered and | gone ˙ = | by to | gether.

4 They marvelled to | see such |
things: they were astonished and |
sudden | ly cast | down.

p 5 Fear came there upon | them and |

sorrow: as upon a | woman | in her |
travail.

6 Thou shalt break the ships | of the |
sea: through | = ˙ the | east ˙ = | wind.

7 Like as we have heard * so have we
seen in the city of the Lord of hosts *
in the city | of our | God: God up | hold-
eth ˙ the | same for | ever.

mf 8 We wait for thy loving | kindness ˙
O | God: in the | midst of | thy ˙ = |
temple.

9 O God according to thy Name * so
is thy praise unto the | world's ˙ = | end:
thy right hand is | full of | righteous |
ness.

f 10 Let the mount Sion rejoice * and the
daughter of | Judah ˙ be | glad: be |
cause of | thy ˙ = | judgments.

11 Walk about Sion, and go | round a |
bout her: and | tell the | towers there | of.

12 Mark well her bulwarks, set | up
her | houses: that ye may tell | them
that I come ˙ = | after.

f 13 For this God is our God for | ever ˙
and | ever: he shall be our | guide ˙ = |
unto | death.

98 BLOW.

F HAVE mercy upon me O God *
p after I thy great I goodness: according to the multitude of thy mercies
do a I way · = I mine of I fences.

pp 2 Wash me throughly I from my I
wickedness: and I cleanse me I from
my I sin.

3 For I ac I knowledge · my I faults:
and my I sin is I ever · be I fore me.

4 Against thee only have I sinned and
done this evil I in thy I sight: that thou
mightest be justified in thy saying and I
clear when I thou art I judged.

5 Behold I was I shapen · in I wickedness: and in sin hath my I mother · con I
ceived I me.

p 6 But lo thou requirest truth in the I
inward I parts: and shalt make me to
understand I wisdom I secret I ly.

7 Thou shalt purge me with hyssop,
and I I shall be I clean: thou shalt wash
me, and I I shall be I whiter · than I snow.

8 Thou shalt make me hear of I joy

and I gladness: that the bones which
thou hast I broken I may re I joice.

9 Turn thy face I from my I sins: and
put out I all · = I my mis I deeds.

10 Make me a clean I heart O I God:
and re I new a · right I spirit · with I in me.

11 Cast me not away I from thy I presence: and take not thy I holy I Spirit I
from me.

cr 12 O give me the comfort of thy I help
a I gain: and stablish me I with thy I
free · = I Spirit.

13 Then shall I teach thy ways I unto ·
the I wicked: and sinners shall be con I
verted I unto I thee.

p 14 Deliver me from blood guiltiness O
God * thou that art the God I of my I
health: (cr) and my tongue shall sing I
of thy I righteous I ness.

mf 15 Thou shalt open my I lips O I Lord:
and my I mouth shall I show thy I praise.

16 For thou desirest no sacrifice * else
would I I give it I thee: but thou delightest I not in I burnt · = I off'rings.

p 17 The sacrifice of God is a I troubled I
spirit: a broken and a contrite heart O
God I shalt thou I not de I spise.

18 O be favourable and gracious I unto I
Sion: (cr) build thou the walls I of Je I
rusa I lem.

mf 19 Then shalt thou be pleased with the
sacrifice of righteousness * with the
burnt offerings I and ob I lations: then
shall they offer young I bullocks · up I
on thine I altar.

99 CROTCH.

F O GOD, thou I art my I God: early I
mf will I I seek · = I thee.

2 My soul thirsteth for thee * my flesh
also longeth I after I thee: in a barren
and dry land I where no I water I is.

3 Thus have I looked for I thee in I
holiness: that I might be I hold thy I
power · and I glory.

4 For thy loving-kindness is better
than the I life it I self: my I lips shall I
praise · = I thee.

5 As long as I live will I I magnify

thee I in this I manner: and lift up my I
hands in I thy · = I name.

6 My soul shall be satisfied * even as
it were with I marrow · and I fatness:
when my mouth praiseth I thee with I
joyful I lips.

7 Have I not remembered thee I in my I
bed: and thought upon I thee when I I
was I waking?

8 Because thou hast I been my I helper:
therefore under the shadow of thy I
wings will I I re I joice.

9 My soul hangeth I upon I thee: thy
right hand I hath up I holden I me.

10 These also that seek the hurt I of
my I soul: they shall I go · = I under ·
the I earth.

11 Let them fall upon the edge I of the I
sword: that they may I be a I portion ·
for I foxes.

12 But the King shall rejoice in God *
all they also that swear by him shall I be
com I mended: for the mouth of them
that speak I lies · = I shall be I stopped.

PSALM 65. *Te decet hymnus.*

100 TURNER.

f F THOU O God art | praised · in | Si-
on: and unto thee shall the vow be
performed | in Je | rusa | lem.
dim 2 Thou that | hearest · the | prayer:
unto | thee shall | all flesh | come.
p 3 My misdeeds pre | vail a | gainst
me: O be thou | merciful | unto · our |
sins.
f 4 Blessed is the man whom thou
choosest and receivest | unto | thee: he
shall dwell in thy court * and shall be
satisfied with the pleasures of thy
house * even | of thy | holy | temple.
mf 5 Thou shalt show us wonderful
things in thy righteousness * O God
of | our sal | vation: thou that art the
hope of all the ends of the earth * and
of them that remain | in the | broad · = |
sea.

6 Who in his strength setteth | fast
the | mountains: and is | girded · a |
bout with | power.
dim. 7 Who stillest the raging | of the | sea:
and the noise of his waves and the |
madness | of the | people.
p 8 They also that dwell in the uttermost
parts of the earth * shall be afraid | at
thy | tokens: thou that makest the out-
goings of the morning and | evening ·
to | praise · = | thee.
f 9 Thou visitest the earth and | bless-
est | it: thou | makest · it | very | plen-
teous.
10 The river of God is | full of | wa-
ter: thou preparest their corn * for so
thou pro | videst | for the | earth.
11 Thou waterest her furrows * thou
sendest rain into the little | valleys ·
there | of: thou makest it soft with the
drops of rain and | blessest · the | in-
crease | of it.
12 Thou crownest the year | with thy |
goodness: and thy | clouds · = | drop ·
= | fatness.
13 They shall drop upon the dwell-
ings | of the | wilderness: and the lit-
tle hills shall re | joice on | every | side.
14 The folds shall be | full of | sheep:
the valleys also shall stand so thick
with corn that | they shall | laugh and |
sing.

PSALM 84. *Quam dilecta!*

101 MACFARREN.

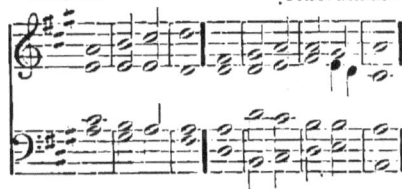

mf F O HOW amiable | are thy | dwell-
ings: thou | Lord · = | of · = |
hosts!
2 My soul hath a desire and longing
to enter into the courts | of the | Lord:
my heart and my flesh rejoice | in the |
living | God.
3 Yea, the sparrow hath found her an
house * and the swallow a nest where

she may | lay her | young: even thy al-
tars O Lord of hosts, my | King · = |
and my | God.
4 Blessed are they that dwell | in
thy | house: they will be | alway | prais-
ing | thee.
5 Blessed is the man whose strength |
is in | thee: in whose | heart · = | are
thy | ways.
6 Who going through the vale of mis-
ery use it | for a | well: and the | pools
are | filled · with | water.
7 They will go from | strength to |
strength: and unto the God of gods ap-
peareth every | one of | them in | Sion.
p 8 O Lord God of hosts | hear my |
prayer: hearken | O · = | God of | Ja-
cob.
9 Behold O God | our de | fender: and
look upon the | face of | thine a | noint-
ed.

101 MACFARREN.

cr 10 For one day | in thy | courts: is | better | than a | thousand.

11 I had rather be a door-keeper in the house | of my | God: than to dwell in the tents | of un | godli | ness.

f 12 For the Lord God is a light | and de | fence: the Lord will give grace and worship * and no good thing shall be withheld from them that | live a | god- ly | life.

13 O Lord | God of | hosts: blessed is the man that | putteth · his | trust in | thee.

PSALM 85. *Benedixisti, Domine.*

102 NARES.

F | LORD, thou art become gracious |
mp unto · thy | land: thou hast turned away the cap | tivi | ty of | Ja- cob.

2 Thou hast forgiven the offence | of thy | people: and | covered | all their | sins.

3 Thou hast taken away all | thy dis | pleasure: and turned thyself from thy | wrathful | indig | nation.

p 4 Turn us then O | God our | Saviour: and let thine | anger | cease from | us.

5 Wilt thou be displeased at | us for | ever: and wilt thou stretch out thy wrath from one gener | ation | to an | other.

cr 6 Wilt thou not turn again and | quicken | us: that thy people | may re | joice in | thee?

7 Show us thy | mercy · O | Lord: and | grant us | thy sal | vation.

mf 8 I will hearken what the Lord God will say con | cerning | me: for he shall speak peace unto his people and to his saints * that they | turn · = | not a | gain.

9 For his salvation is nigh | them that | fear him: that glory may | dwell · = | in our | land.

10 Mercy and truth are | met to | geth- er: righteousness and | peace have | kissed · each | other.

11 Truth shall flourish | out · of the | earth: and righteousness hath | looked | down from | heaven.

12 Yea, the Lord shall show | loving | kindness: and our | land shall | give her | increase.

13 Righteousness shall | go be | fore him: and he shall direct his | going | in the | way.

PSALM 91. *Qui habitat.*

103 CROTCH.

F | WHOSO dwelleth under the de-
mf fence of the | Most · = | High: shall abide under the | shadow · of | the Al | mighty.

2 I will say unto the Lord * Thou art my hope and | my strong | hold: my God, in | him · = | will I | trust.

3 For he shall deliver thee from the snare | of the | hunter: and | from the | noisome | pestilence.

4 He shall defend thee under his wings * and thou shalt be safe | under · his | feathers: his faithfulness and truth shall be thy | shield and | buckler.

5 Thou shalt not be afraid for any | terror · by | night: nor for the | arrow · that | flieth · by | day:

6 For the pestilence that | walketh · in | darkness: nor for the sickness that de | stroyeth | in the | noonday.

7 A thousand shall fall beside thee * and ten thousand at | thy right | hand: but it shall | not come | nigh · = | thee.

8 Yea with thine éyes shalt | thou be |
hold: and sée the re | ward of | the un |
godly.
f 9 For thou Lórd | art my | hope: thou
hast set thine hóuse of de | fence · = |
very | high.
10 There shall no evil háppen | unto |
thee: neither shall ány | plague come |
nigh thy | dwelling.
11 For he shall give his angels
chárge | over | thee: to kéep | thee in |
all thy | ways.
12 They shall béar thee | in their |
hands: that thou hurt nót thy | foot a |
gainst a | stone.

f 13 Thou shalt go upón the | lion ·
and | adder: the young lion and the
dragon shált thou | tread un | der thy |
feet.
14 Because he hath set his love upon
me, therefore will I' de | liver | him: I
will set him up becáuse | he hath |
known my | Name.
15 He sha'l call upon mé and | I will |
hear him: yea I am with him in trou-
ble * I will deliver hím and | bring · = |
him to | honour.
16 With long lífe will I | satisfy | him:
ánd | show him | my sal | vation.

PSALM 93. *Dominus regnavit.*

104
BACON.

F THE Lord is King * and hath put on
f glóri | ous ap | parel: the Lord hath
put on his appárel and | girded · him |
self with | strength.

2 He hath máde the round | world so |
sure: thát | it can | not be | moved.
3 Ever since the world began hath thy
séat | been pre | pared: thóu | art from |
ever | lasting.
4 The floods are risen O Lord * the
floods have líft | up their | voice : thé |
floods lift | up their | waves.
5 The waves of the sea are míghty
and | rage · = | horribly: but yet the Lórd
who | dwelleth · on | high is | mightier.
6 Thy testimonies O Lórd are | very |
sure: hóliness be | cometh · thine |
house for | ever.

PSALM 96. *Cantate Domino.*

105
BELLAMY.

F O SING unto the Lórd a | new · = |
f song: sing unto the Lórd | all the |
whole · = | earth.
2 Sing unto the Lórd and | praise his |
Name: be telling of hís sal | vation ·
from | day to | day.
3 Declare his hónour | unto · the |
heathen: and his wónders | unto | all ·
= | people.
4 For the Lord is great, and cannot
wórthi | ly be | praised: he is móre to
be | feared | than all | gods.
mf 5 As for all the gods of the héathen,
they | are but | idols: but it ís the |
Lord that | ma·le the | heavens.

6 Glory and wórship | are be | fore
him: pówer and | honour are | in his |
sanctuary.
f 7 Ascribe unto the Lord, O ye kín-
dreds | of the | people: ascribe únto
the | Lord · = | worship · and | power.
8 Ascribe unto the Lord the honour
dúe | unto · his | Name: bring présents
and | come · = | into · his | courts.
mf 9 O worship the Lord in the | beauty ·
of | holiness: (*or*) let the whole éarth |
stand in | awe of | him.
f 10 Tell it out among the héathen that
the | Lord is | King· and that it is he
who hath made the round world so fast
that it cannot be moved * and how that
he shall júdge the | people | righteous |
ly.
11 Let the heavens rejoice, and lét the |
earth be | glad: let the sea make a nóise
and | all that | therein | is.
12 Let the field be jóyful and | all that ·
is | in it: then shall all the trees of the
wóod re'l joice be | fore the | Lord.
dim 13 For he cometh, for he cómeth to |
judge the | earth: and with righteous-
ness to judge the wórld and the | people |
with his | truth.

PSALM 97. *Dominus regnavit.*

106   MACFARREN.

F ' THE Lord is King * the earth may
f be | glad there | of: yea, the mul-
titude of the isles | may be | glad there |
of.

2 Clouds and darkness are | round a | bout him: righteousness and judgment are the habi | tation | of his | seat.

f 3 There shall go a | fire be | fore him: and burn up his | ene · mies on | every | side.

4 His lightnings gave shine | unto · the | world: the earth | saw it · and | was a | fraid.

5 The hills melted like wax at the pres-ence | of the | Lord: at the presence of

the Lord | of the | whole · = | earth.

6 The heavens have declared his | righteous | ness: and all the | people · have | seen his | glory.

mf 7 Confounded be all they that worship carved images * and that delight in | vain · = | gods: worship | him · = | all ye | gods.

8 Sion heard of it | and re | joiced: and the daughters of Judah were glad* because of thy | judgments | O · = | Lord.

f 9 For thou Lord, art higher than all that are | in the | earth: thou art exalted | far a | bove all | gods.

dim 10 O ye that love the Lord * see that ye hate the thing | which is | evil: the Lord preserveth the souls of his saints * he shall deliver them from the | hand of | the un | godly.

cr 11 There is sprung up a light | for the | righteous: and joyful gladness for | such as | are true | hearted.

f 12 Rejoice in the | Lord ye | righteous: and give thanks for a re | membrance | of his | holiness.

PSALM 101. *Misericordiam et judicium.*

107   BUNNETT.

F MY song shall be of | mercy · and |
f judgment: unto thee O | Lord · = | will I | sing.

mf 2 O let me have | under | standing: in the | way of | godli | ness!

3 When wilt thou come | unto | me: I will walk in my house | with a | perfect | heart.

4 I will take no wicked thing in hand * I hate the sins | of un | faithfulness:

there shall no such | cleave · = | unto | me.

5 A froward heart shall de | part from | me: I will not | know a | wicked | person.

6 Whoso privily slander | eth his | neighbour: him | = · will | I de | stroy.

7 Whoso hath also a proud look | and high | stomach: I' | will not | suffer | him.

8 Mine eyes look upon such as are faithful | in the | land: that | they may | dwell with | me.

9 Whoso leadeth a | godly | life: he | = · shall | be my | servant.

10 There shall no deceitful person dwell | in my | house: he that telleth lies shall not | tarry | in my | sight.

11 I shall soon destroy all the ungodly that are | in the | land: that I may root out all wicked doers from the | city | of the | Lord.

PSALM 103. *Benedic, anima mea.*

108 ALDRICH.

F **PRAISE** the Lórd | O my | soul:
f and all that is withín me | praise
his | holy | Name.

2 Praise the Lórd | O my | soul: ánd
for | get not | all his | benefits.

3 Who forgíveth | all thy | sin: and
héaleth | all · = | thine in | firmities;

4 Who saveth thy lífe | from de | struc-
tion: and crowneth thée with | mercy
and | loving | kindness;

5 Who satisfieth thy móuth with |
good · = | things: making thee yóung
and | lusty | as an | eagle.

mf 6 The Lord executeth ríghteous | ness
and | judgment: for all thém that | are
op | pressed · with | wrong.

7 He showed his wáys | unto | Moses:
his wórks | unto · the | children · of | Israel.

mf 8 The Lord is fúll of com | passion ·
and | mercy: long-súffering | and of |
great · = | goodness.

9 He wíll not | alway · be | chiding:
neither kéepeth | he his | anger · for | ever.

10 He hath not déalt with us | after ·
our | sins: nor rewarded us accórding |
to our | wicked | nesses.

11 For look how high the heaven is in
compárison | of the | earth: so great is
his mercy also tóward | them that |
fear · = | him.

12 Look how wide also the éast is | from
the | west: so fár hath he | set our | sins
from | us.

13 Yea, like as a father pítieth his |
own · = | children: even so is the Lord
mérciful | unto | them that | fear him.

p 14 For he knoweth wheróf | we are |
made: he remémbereth | that we | are
but | dust.

15 The days of mán are | but as | grass:
for he flourisheth ás a | flower | of the |
field.

16 For as soon as the wind goeth óver
it | it is | gone: and the place theréof
shall | know it | no · = | more.

cr 17 But the merciful goodness of the
Lord * endúreth for ever and éver upon |
them that | fear him: and his ríghteous-
ness up | on · = | children's | children;

18 Even upon súch as | keep his | cove-
nant: and think upon his com | mand · = |
ments to | do them.

f 19 The Lord hath prepáred his | seat
in | heaven: and his kíngdom | ruleth |
over | all.

ff 20 O praise the Lord ye angels of his *
ye that ex | cel in | strength: ye that
fulfil his commandment * and hearken
únto the | voice · = | of his | words.

21 O praise the Lórd all | ye his | hosts:
ye sérvants of | his that | do his | pleasure.

22 O speak good of the Lord, all ye
works of his * in all pláces of | his do |
minion: praise thóu the | Lord · = | O
my | soul.

PSALM 111. *Confitebor tibi.*

109 SEWELL.

F **I WILL** give thanks unto the Lórd
f with my | whole · = | heart: secretly
among the fáithful and | in the | congre |
gation.

2 The wórks of the | Lord are | great:

sought out of all thém | that have |
pleasure · there | in.

mf 3 His work is worthy to be práised
and | had in | honour: and his ríghteous |
ness en | dureth · for | ever.

4 The merciful and gracious Lord
hath so dóne his | marvellous | works:
that they óught to be | had · = | in re |
membrance.

5 He hath given méat unto | them
that | fear him: he shall éver be | mind-
ful | of his | covenant.

6 He hath showed his people the
pówer | of his | works: that he may
give thém the | heritage | of the | hea-
then.

109

SEWELL.

7 The works of his hands are vérity I
and   ' = I judgment: áll I his com I
mandmants ' are I true.

8 They stand fást for I ever ' and I
ever: and are dóne in I truth and I equi I
ty.

f 9 He sent redémption I unto ' his I
people: he hath commanded his covenant for ever * hóly and I reverend I is
his I Name.

mf 10 The fear of the Lórd is the be I
ginning ' of I wisdom: a good understanding have all they that do there-
after * the práise of I it en I dureth '
for I ever.

PSALM 112.   *Beatus vir.*

110

JACKSON.

F   B LESSED is the mán that I feareth '
mf   the I Lord: he hath gréat de I
light in I his com I mandments.

2 His seed shall be míghty up I on ' = I
earth: the generátion of the I faithful I
shall be I blessed.

3 Riches and plenteousness shall bé I
in his I house: and his ríghteous I ness
en I dureth ' for I ever.

4 Unto the godly there ariseth up

light I in the I darkness: hé is I merciful I
loving ' and I righteous.

5 A good man is mérci I ful and I lend-
eth: and will gúide his I words ' = I
with dis I cretion.

6 For hé shall I never ' be I moved:
and the righteous shall be hád in I ever I
lasting ' re I membrance.

7 He will not be afraid of ány I evil I
tidings: for his heart standeth fást and
be I lieveth I in the I Lord.

8 His heart is estáblished and I will
not I shrink: until he sée his de I sire
up I on his I enemies.

9 He hath dispersed abroad, and gíven I
to the I poor: and his righteousness re-
maineth for ever * his hórn shall I be ex I
alted ' with I honour.

10 The ungodly shall sée it, and I it
shall I grieve him: he shall gnash with
his teeth and consume away * the de-
síre of the un I godly I shall ' = I perish.

PSALM 118.   *Confitemini Domino.*

111

HAYES.

F   O GIVE thanks unto the Lórd, for I
f   he is I gracious: becáuse his I
mercy ' en I dureth ' for I ever.

2 Let Israel now conféss that I he is I
gracious: and thát his I mercy ' en I
dureth ' for I ever.

3 Let the house of Aáron I now con I
fess: thát his I mercy ' en I dureth ' for I
ever.

4 Yea, let them now that féar the I
Lord con I fess: thát his I mercy ' en I
dureth ' for I ever.

mf 5 I called upón the I Lord in I trouble:
and the Lórd I heard ' = I me at I large.

6 The Lórd is I on my I side: I will
not fear what mán I doeth I unto I me.

7 The Lord taketh my párt with I
them that I help me: therefore shall I
sée my de I sire up I on mine I enemies.

8 It is better to trúst I in the I Lord:
than to pút any I confi I dence in I man.

9 It is better to trúst | in the | Lord: than to pút any | confi | dence in | princes.

10 All nations cómpassed me | round a | bout: but in the Náme of the | Lord will | I de | stroy them.

dim 11 They kept me in on every side * they kept me in I sáy on | every | side: (*cr*) but in the Náme of the | Lord will | I de | stroy them.

12 They came about me like bees * and are extinct even as the fíre a | mong the | thorns: for in the Náme of the | Lord I | will de | stroy them.

p 13 Thou hast thrust sore at mé, that | I might | fall: (*cr*) bút the | Lord · = | was my | help.

mf 14 The Lord is my stréngth | and my | song: and ís he | come · = | my sal | vation.

15 The voice of joy and health is in the dwéllings | of the | righteous: the right hand of the Lórd bringeth | míghty | things to | pass.

16 The right hand of the Lórd | hath · the pre | eminence: the right hand of the Lórd bringeth | mighty | things to | pass.

17 I sháll not | die but | live: and de- cláre the | works · = | of the | Lord.

18 The Lord hath chastened ánd cor | rected | me: but he hath not gíven me | over | unto | death.

19 Open me the gátes of | righteous | ness: that I may go into them * ánd give | thanks · = | unto · the | Lord.

20 This is the gáte | of the | Lord: the ríghteous shall | enter | into | it.

21 I will thánk thee for | thou hast | heard me: and árt he | come · = | my sal | vation.

22 The same stóne which the | build- ers · re | fused: is becóme the | head- stone | in the | corner.

23 Thís is the | Lord's · = | doing: ánd it is | marvellous | in our | eyes.

24 This is the dáy which the | Lord hath | made: we will rejóice | and be | glad in | it.

25 Hélp me | now O | Lord: O Lórd | send us | now pros | perity.

26 Blessed be he that cometh in the Náme | of the | Lord: we have wished you good luck * ye that áre of the | house · = | of the | Lord.

27 God is the Lórd who hath | showed · us | light: bind the sacrifice with cords * yea, even únto the | horns · = | of the | altar.

f 28 Thou art my Gód, and | I will | thank thee: thou art my | God and | I will | praise thee.

29 O give thanks unto the Lórd, for | he is | gracious: ánd his | mercy · en- dureth · for | ever.

PSALM 121. *Levavi oculos.*

112   MEDLEY.

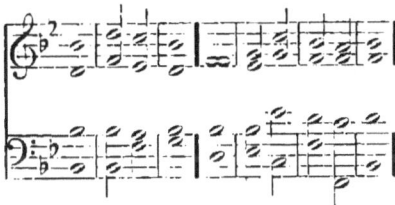

F I WILL lift up mine éyes | unto |
mf the | hills: fróm | whence · = |
cometh · my | help.

2 My help cometh éven | from the | Lord: whó hath | made · = | heaven and | earth.

3 He will not suffer thy fóot | to be | moved: and hé that | keepeth · thee | will not | sleep.

4 Behold, hé that | keepeth | Israel: shall | neither | slumber · nor | sleep.

5 The Lord himsélf | is thy | keeper: the Lord is thy defénce up | on thy | right · = | hand;

6 So that the sun shall not búrn | thee by | day: néither the | moon · = | by · = | night.

7 The Lord shall presérve thee | from all | evil: yea it is even hé | that shall | keep thy | soul.

8 The Lord shall preserve thy going out * ánd thy | coming | in: from thís time | forth for | ever | more.

PSALM 122 *Lætatus sum.*

113
CHILDE.

F I WAS glad when they said | unto |
f me: We will go into the | house ·
= | of the | Lord.

2 Our feet shall stand | in thy | gates:
O· | = · Je | rusa | lem.

3 Jerusalem is built | as a | city: that
is at | unity | in it | self.

4 For thither the tribes go up * even
the tribes | of the | Lord: to testify un-
to Israel * to give thanks unto the |
Name · = | of the | Lord.

5 For there is the | seat of | judgment:
even the seat | of the | house of | David.

p 6 O pray for the peace | of Je | rusa-
lem: they shall | prosper | that love |
thee.

7 Peace be with | in thy | walls: (*cr*)
and plenteous | ness with | in thy | pala-
ces.

8 For my brethren and com | panions' |
sakes: I· will | wish · = | thee pros | perity.

9 Yea because of the house of the |
Lord our | God: I· will | seek to | do
thee | good.

PSALM 125. *Qui confidant.*

114
RUSSELL.

F THEY that put their trust in the
mf Lord shall be even as the |
mount · = | Sion: which may not be
removed, but | standeth | fast for | ever.

2 The hills stand about Je ' rusa |
lem: even so standeth the Lord round
about his people * from this time | forth
for | ever | more.

3 For the rod of the ungodly cometh
not into the lot | of the | righteous: lest
the righteous put their | hand · = | unto |
wickedness.

p 4 Do | well O | Lord: unto those that
are | good and | true of | heart.

5 As for such as turn back unto their
own | wicked | ness: the Lord shall lead
them forth with the evil doers * but
peace shall | be up | on · = | Israel.

PSALM 130. *De profundis.*

115
GILBERT.

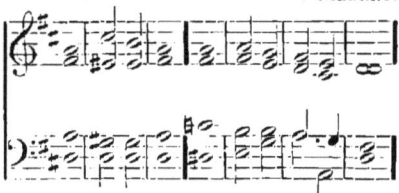

F OUT of the deep have I called unto |
p thee O | Lord: Lord | hear · = |
my · = | voice.

2 O let thine ears con | sider | well:
the | voice of | my com | plaint.

3 If thou Lord, wilt be extreme to
mark what is | done a | miss: O Lord |
who · = | may a | bide it?

4 For there is | mercy · with | thee:
therefore | shalt · = | thou be | feared.

5 I look for the Lord; my soul doth |
wait for | him: in his | word · = | is my |
trust.

6 My soul fleeth | unto · the | Lord:
before the morning watch I say, be | fore
the | morning | watch.

cr 7 O Israel trust in the Lord * for with
the Lord | there is | mercy: and with |
him is | plenteous · re | demption.

8 And he shall re | deem · = | Israel:
from | all · = | his · = | sins.

PSALM 138. *Confitebor tibi.*

116

PURCELL.

F *I* WILL give thanks unto thee O
f Lord, with my | whole · = | heart:
even before the gods will I sing |
praise · = | unto | thee.

2 I will worship toward thy holy temple, and praise thy Name * because of
thy loving | kindness · and | truth: for
thou hast magnified thy Name, and thy |
word a | bove all | things.

3 When I called upon thee, thou |
heardest | me: and enduedst my | soul
with | much · = | strength.

4 All the kings of the earth shall
praise | thee O | Lord: for they have
heard the | words · = | of thy | mouth.

5 Yea, they shall sing in the ways |
of the | Lord: that great is the | glory |
of the | Lord.

p 6 For though the Lord be high * yet
hath he respect | unto · the | lowly: as
for the proud, he beholdeth | them a |
far · = | off.

7 Though I walk in the midst of
trouble * yet shalt | thou re | fresh me:
thou shalt stretch forth thy hand upon
the furiousness of mine enemies * and |
thy right | hand shall | save me.

cr 8 The Lord shall make good his loving-
kindness | toward | me: yea, thy mercy
O Lord endureth for ever * despise
not then the | works of | thine own |
hands.

PSALM 139. *Domine, probasti.*

117

LANGDON.

F *O* LORD, thou hast searched me |
mf out and | known me: thou know-
est my down-sitting and mine up-rising *
thou understandest my | thoughts · = |
long be | fore.

2 Thou art about my path, and a |
bout my | bed: and | spiest · out | all
my | ways.

3 For lo, there is not a word | in my |
tongue: but thou O Lord | knowest · it |
alto | gether.

4 Thou hast fashioned me behind |
and be | fore: and | laid thine | hand up |
on me.

mp 5 Such knowledge is too wonderful
and | excellent | for me: I cannot at |
tain · = | unto | it.

6 Whither shall I go then | from thy |
Spirit: or whither shall I | go then |
from thy | presence?

7 If I climb up into heaven | thou art |
there: if I go down to hell | thou art |
there · = | also.

8 If I take the wings | of the | morn-
ing: and remain in the uttermost |
parts · = | of the | sea;

9 Even there also shall | thy hand |
lead me: and | thy right | hand shall |
hold me.

10 If I say, Peradventure the dark-
ness shall | cover | me: then shall my |
night be | turned · to | day.

11 Yea, the darkness is no darkness
with thee * but the night is as clear | as
the | day: the darkness and light to |
thee are | both a | like.

12 For my | reins are | thine: thou
hast covered me | in my | mother's |
womb.

13 I will give thanks unto thee * for
I am fearfully and wonder | fully |
made: marvellous are thy works * and
that my | soul · = | knoweth · right |
well.

mp 14 My bones are not | hid from | thee:
though I be made secretly * and fashion-
ed be | neath · = | in the | earth.

15 Thine eyes did see my substance,
yet I being · im | perfect: and in thy
book were | all my | members | written;

16 Which day by | day were | fashion-
ed: when as yet | there was | none of |
them!

117

LANGDON.

mf 17 How dear are thy counsels únto |
me O | God: O how gréat | is the | sum
of | them.

18 If I tell them, they are more in
númber | than the | sand: when I wake
úp | I am | present · with | thee.

mp 19 Wilt thou not sláy the | wicked ·
O | God: Depart from mé ye | blood · = |
thirsty | men.

20 For they speak unríghteously a |
gainst · = | thee: and thine énemies |
take thy | Name in | vain.

21 Do not I hate them O Lórd, that |
hate · = | thee: and am not I grieved
with thóse that | rise · = | up a | gainst
thee?

22 Yea I háte | them right | sore:
éven as | though they | were mine | ene-
mies.

p 23 Try me O God, and seek the
gróund | of my | heart: próve me | and
ex | amine · my | thoughts.

24 Look well if there be any wáy of |
wickedness | in me: and léad me in the |
way · = | ever | lasting.

PSALM 145. *Exaltabo te, Deus.*

118

WOODWARD.

F I WILL magnify thée O | God my |
f King: and I will práise thy | Name
for | ever · and | ever.

2 Every day will I give thánks | unto |
thee: and práise thy | Name for | ever ·
and | ever.

3 Great is the Lord, and marvellous
wórthy | to be | praised: there ís no |
end · = | of his | greatness.

4 One generation shall praise thy
wórks | unto · an | other: ánd de |
clare · = | thy · = | power.

f 5 As for me, I will be tálking | of thy |
worship: thy glóry thy | praise and |
wondrous | works;

6 So that men shall speak of the
míght of thy | marvellous | acts: and
I will álso | tell · = | of thy | greatness.

7 The memorial of thine abundant
kíndness | shall be | showed: and men
shall síng | of thy | righteous | ness.
p 8 The Lórd is | gracious · and | merci-
ful: long-súffering | and of | great · = |
goodness.

9 The Lord is lóving unto | every |

man: and his mércy is | over | all his |
works.
f 10 All thy works práise | thee O |
Lord: and thy sáints give | thanks · = |
unto | thee.

11 They show the glóry | of thy |
kingdom: ánd | talk · = | of thy | power;

12 That thy power, thy glory, and
míghtiness | of thy | kingdom: míght
be | known · = | unto | men.

13 Thy kingdom is an éver | lasting |
kingdom: and thy domínion en | dureth·
through | out all | ages.
mp 14 The Lord uphóldeth all | such as |
fall: and lifteth úp all | those · = | that
are | down.

15 The eyes of all wáit upon | thee O |
Lord: and thou givest thém their | meat
in | due · = | season.

16 Thóu | openest · thine | hand: and
fillest áll things | living · with | plen-
teous | ness.
mf 17 The Lord is ríghteous in | all his |
ways: ánd | holy · in | all his | works.

18 The Lord is nigh unto all thém
that | call up | on him: yea all such as
cáll up | on him | faithful | ly.

19 He will fulfil the desíre of | them
that | fear him: he also will hear their
crý | and will | help · = | them.

20 The Lord presérveth all | them that |
love him: but scattereth abróad | all ·
the un | god · = | ly.
f 21 My mouth shall speak the práise |
of the | Lord: and let all flesh give
thanks unto his hóly | Name for | ever ·
and | ever.

PSALM 147. *Laudate Dominum.*

119 BROWNSMITH.

F O PRAISE the Lord * for it is a
f good thing to sing praises | unto ·
our | God: yea, a joyful and pleasant
thing it | is to | be · = | thankful.
  2 The Lord doth build | up Je | rusa-
lem: and gather together | the out | casts
of | Israel.
p 3 He healeth those that are | broken ·
in | heart: and giveth | medicine · to |
heal their | sickness.
  4 He telleth the number | of the |
stars: and calleth them | all · = | by
their | names.
f 5 Great is our Lord * and great | is
his | power: yea | and his | wisdom · is |
infinite.
  6 The Lord setteth | up the | meek:
and bringeth the ungodly | down · = |
to the | ground.
  7 O sing unto the Lord with | thanks·
= | giving: sing praises upon the | harp·
= | unto · our | God;
mf 8 Who covereth the heaven with
clouds * and prepareth rain | for the |
earth: and maketh the grass to grow up-

on the mountains * and herb | for the |
use of | men;
  9 Who giveth fodder | unto · the | cat-
tle: and feedeth the young | ravens ·
that | call up | on him.
  10 He hath no pleasure in the strength|
of an | horse: neither delighteth | he in |
any · man's | legs.
  11 But the Lord's delight is in | them
that | fear him: and put their | trust ·
= | in his | mercy.
f 12 Praise the Lord O' Je | rusa | lem:
praise | = · thy | God O | Sion.
  13 For he hath made fast the bars | of
thy | gates: and hath | blessed · thy |
children · with | in thee.
p 14 He maketh peace | in thy | borders:
(cr) and filleth thee | with the | flour of |
wheat.
mf 15 He sendeth forth his command-
ment up | on · = | earth: and his word |
runneth | very | swiftly.
  16 He giveth | snow like | wool: and
scattereth the | hoar · = | frost like |
ashes.
  17 He casteth forth his | ice like |
morsels: who is able | to a | bide his |
frost.
  18 He sendeth out his word, and |
melteth | them: he bloweth with his
wind | and the | waters | flow.
  19 He showeth his word | unto | Jacob:
his statutes and ordinances | unto | Is-
ra | el.
  20 He hath not dealt so with | any |
nation: neither have the heathen | know-
ledge | of his | laws.

PSALM 148. *Laudate Dominum.*

120 OUSELEY.

F O PRAISE the | Lord of | heaven:
f praise | = · him | in the | height.
  2 Praise him all ye | angels · of | his:
praise | = · him | all his | host.
  3 Praise him | sun and | moon: praise
him | all ye | stars and | light.
  4 Praise him | all ye | heavens: and ye
waters that | are a | bove the | heavens.
  5 Let them praise the Name | of the |
Lord: for he spake the word and they
were made * he commanded | and they |

  6 He hath made them fast for | ever ·
and | ever: he hath given them a law |
which shall | not be | broken.
mf 7 Praise the Lord up | on · = | earth:
ye | dragons | and all | deeps;
  8 Fire and hail | snow and | vapours:
wind and | storm ful | filling · his | word;
  9 Mountains | and all | hills: fruitful |
trees and | all · == | cedars;
  10 Beasts | and all | cattle: worms |
= · and | feathered | fowls.
  11 Kings of the earth | and all | peo-
ple: princes and all | judges | of the |
world;
f 12 Young men and maidens, old men
and children * praise the Name | of the |
Lord: for his Name only is excellent *
and his praise a | bove · = | heaven and
earth.
  13 He shall exalt the horn of his peo-
ple * all his | saints shall | praise him:
even the children of Israel * even the |
people · that | serveth | him.

PSALM 150.   *Laudate Dominum.*

121

HUMPHREYS.

F O PRAISE God | in his | holiness:
f   praise him in the | firmament |
of his | power.

2 Praise him in his | noble | acts:
praise him according | to his | excellent |
greatness.

3 Praise him in the sound | of the |
trumpet: praise him up | on the | lute
and | harp.

4 Praise him in the | cymbals · and |
dances: praise him up | on the | strings
and | pipe.

5 Praise him upon the well | tuned |
cymbals: praise him up | on the | loud ·
=· | cymbals.

6 Let every thing | that hath | breath:
praise | = · = | = · the | Lord.

Hymns and Carols.

[The bracketted Numbers refer to Hymns in the "Church Hymnal."]

Morning.

122 [2]

Joyful.

MORNING HYMN.
L. M.

A - wake, my soul, and with the sun Thy dai - ly course of du - ty run: Shake off dull sloth, and ear - ly rise To pay thy morn - ing sac - ri - fice. A - MEN.

2 Let all thy converse be sincere.
Thy conscience as the noon-day clear;
Think how the all-seeing God, thy ways
And all thy secret thoughts surveys.

3 Wake, and lift up thyself, my heart,
And with the angels bear thy part;
Who all night long unwearied sing,
"Glory to Thee, eternal King."

4 Lord, I my vows to Thee renew;
Scatter my sins as morning dew;
Guard my first springs of thought and will,
And with Thyself my spirit fill.

5 Direct, control, suggest this day
All I design, or do, or say,
That all my powers, with all their **might**,
In Thy sole glory may unite.

6 Praise God, from whom all blessings flow,
Praise Him, all creatures here below;
Praise Him above, ye heavenly host:
Praise Father, Son, and Holy Ghost.

123[1]

Moderate.

MELCOMBE.
L. M.

New ev-ery morning is the love Our wak-ing and up-ris-ing prove;

Thro' sleep and darkness safely brought, Restored to life, and pow'r, and thought. AMEN.

2 New mercies, each returning day,
Hover around us while we pray;
New perils past, new sins forgiven,
New thoughts of God, new hopes of heaven.

3 If on our daily course our mind
Be set to hallow all we find,
New treasures still of countless price,
God will provide for sacrifice.

4 The trivial round, the common task,
Will furnish all we ought to ask:
Room to deny ourselves: a road
To bring us daily nearer God.

5 Only, O Lord, in Thy dear love
Fit us for perfect rest above;
And help us this, and every day,
To live more nearly as we pray.

124

Cheerful.

SMALLWOOD.
7s.

Now the drear-y night is done, Comes a - gain the glo-rious sun;

Crimson clouds and sil-ver white Wait up - on his breaking light. A - MEN.

2 Child of Mary, Thou dost know
What of danger, joy, or woe
Shall to-day my portion be,—
Let me meet it all in Thee.

Thou wast meek and undefiled—
Make me holy too, and mild;
Thou didst foil the tempter's power;
Help me in temptation's hour.

4 Thou didst love Thy mother here—
Make me gentle, kind, and dear;
Thou wast subject to her word—
Teach me to obey, O Lord.

5 Fretful feelings, passion, pride
Never did with Thee abide:
Make me watch myself to-day,
That they lead me not astray.

125

THE MORNING BRIGHT.
P. M.

Cheerful.

The morning bright, With ro - sy light, Hath waked me from my sleep;

Fa - ther, I own Thy love a-lone Thy lit - tle one doth keep. A - MEN.

2 All through the day,
I humbly pray.
Be Thou my Guard and Guide;
My sins forgive,
And let me live,
Blest Jesus, near Thy side.

3 Oh make Thy rest
Within my breast,
Great Spirit of all grace;
Make me like Thee,
Then shall I be
Prepared to see Thy face.

126

FERRIER.
7s.

Moderate.

Je - sus, ho - ly, un - de - filed, Lis - ten to a lit - tle child;

Thou hast sent the glo-rious light, Chasing far the si - lent night. A - MEN.

2 Thou hast sent the sun to shine
O'er this glorious world of Thine;
Warmth to give, and pleasant glow,
On each tender flower below.

3 Now the little birds arise.
Chirping gaily in the skies;
Thee their tiny voices praise
In the early songs they raise.

4 Thou by whom the birds are fed,
Give to me my daily bread;
And Thy Holy Spirit give.
Without whom I cannot live.

5 Make me, Lord. obedient. mild,
As becomes a little child;
All day long. in every way,
Teach me what to do and say.

6 Make me, Lord, in work and play,
Thine more truly every day;
And when Thou at last shall come,
Take me to Thy heavenly home.

127

DAWN.
C. M.

Moderate.

The breaking morn comes back to bless The earth from pole to pole;

So come, sweet Sun of Righteous-ness, And shine in-to my soul. A - MEN.

2 A silver mist along the lawn,
  From every dewy sod,
Goes up to heaven; and so at dawn
I lift my thoughts to God.

3 I think how Thou didst wake, O Lord,
  Before the break of day,
And seek the lonely mountain sward;
  So teach my lips to pray.

4 I think how Thou didst sleep and rise,
  So many nights and days,
A Child obedient, holy, wise,
  And perfect in Thy ways.

5 The dawn of day, the dawn of life,
  Were blest alike to Thee;
Thou know'st the danger and the strife;
  Lord bless them both to me.

128

S. HELEN.
L. M.

Quietly.

O God, who, when the night was deep, Hast kept me safe and lent me sleep,

Now with Thy sun Thou bid'st me rise, And look around with older eyes. A - MEN.

2 Each happy morning Thou dost give,
  I have one morning less to live;
O help me so this day to spend,
  To make me fitter for the end.

3 O bid all wicked thoughts to fly;
  The fretful word, the idle eye;
Help me to think in all I do,
  "God sees me:—would He have it so?"

4 Make my first wish and thought to be
  For others sooner than for me;
And let me pardon them, as I
  Hope for God's pardon when I die.

5 Be with me when I work and play;
  Be with me now and every day:
Be near me, when I pray Thee hear;
  And when I pray not,—Lord! be near.

129

AWAKE, AND AWAY.
6s. 5s. *with Chorus.*

Joyous.

The morning light fling-eth Its wak - en - ing ray; And as the day

bringeth The work of the day, The hap - py heart singeth, A-wake, and a - way!

Chorus after each verse.

A - wake,.... and a - way! A - wake,.... and a - way!

A - wake, a-wake, and a - way, a-way! Awake, awake, and a-way, a-way!

The hap-py heart sing - eth, A-wake, and a - way! A - MEN.

2 No life can be dreary,
  When work is delight;
Though evening be weary,
  Rest cometh at night,
And all will be cheery,
  If faithful and right.
CHORUS.—Awake, and away, &c.

3 When duty is pleasure,
  And labour is joy,
How sweet is the leisure
  Of ended employ!
Then only can pleasure
  Be free from alloy.
CHORUS.—Awake, and away, &c.

130 [12]   𝔈𝔟𝔢𝔫𝔦𝔫𝔤.

EVENTIDE.
10s.

Quietly.   (If preferred, the tune "Ellers" (No. 201) can be used for this hymn.)

A - bide with me: fast falls the e - ven - tide; The dark-ness

deep - ens; Lord, with me a - bide; When oth - er help - ers

fail, and comforts flee, Help of the helpless, O a - bide with me. A-MEN.

2 Swift to its close, ebbs out life's little day;
Earth's joys grow dim, its glories pass away;
Change and decay in all around I see;
O Thou, who changest not, abide with me.

3 I need Thy presence every passing hour;
What but Thy grace can foil the tempter's power?
Who like Thyself my guide and stay can be?
Through cloud and sunshine, Lord, abide with me.

4 I fear no foe, with Thee at hand to bless:
Ills have no weight, and tears no bitterness.
Where is death's sting? where, grave, thy victory?
I triumph still, if Thou abide with me.

5 Hold Thou Thy Cross before my closing eyes;
Shine through the gloom, and point me to the skies;
Heaven's morning breaks, and earth's vain shadows flee;
In life, in death, O Lord, abide with me.

(SECOND TUNE.)   TROYTE No. 1.

A-MEN.

131 [11]

HURSLEY.
L. M.

Moderate.

Sun of my soul. Thou Sav - iour dear, It is not night if Thou be near;

O may no earth-born cloud a - rise To hide Thee from Thy servant's eyes. A-MEN.

2 When the soft dews of kindly sleep
My weary eyelids gently steep.
Be my last thought, how sweet to rest
For ever on my Saviour's breast.

3 Abide with me from morn till eve,
For without Thee I cannot live;
Abide with me when night is nigh,
For without Thee I dare not die.

4 If some poor wandering child of Thine
Have spurn'd to-day the voice divine,

Now, Lord, the gracious work begin;
Let him no more lie down in sin.

5 Watch by the sick; enrich the poor
With blessings from Thy boundless store;
Be every mourner's sleep to-night.
Like infant slumbers, pure and light.

6 Come near and bless us when we wake,
Ere through the world our way we take,
Till in the ocean of Thy love
We lose ourselves in heaven above.

132

DAY IS PAST.
P. M.

Moderate.

Day is past and gone; Dark - ness has - tens on;

Blessed Lord, in mer-cy keep An - gel-guards a - round Thy sheep. A - MEN.

2 Work again is past;
Rest has come at last;
Blessèd Lord, forgive, I pray,
All I have done wrong to-day.

3 Soon in silence deep
God will give me sleep:
Blessèd Lord, be Thou my light,
In the watches of the night.

4 When the night is o'er,
And I wake once more,
Blessèd Lord, who lovest me,
Make Thy child to follow Thee.

133 [22]

STELLA.
Six 8s.

Moderate.

Sweet Sav-iour, bless us ere we go; Thy word in - to our minds in - stil:

And make our lukewarm hearts to glow With low-ly love and fervent will.

Through life's long day and death's dark night, O gen-tle Je-sus, be our light. A - MEN.

2 The day has gone, its hours have run,
  And Thou hast taken count of all,
The scanty triumphs grace hath won,
  The broken vow, the frequent fall.
Through life's long day and death's dark
    night,
O gentle Jesus, be our light.

3 Grant us, dear Lord, from evil ways
  True absolution and release;
And bless us, more than in past days,
  With purity and inward peace.
Through life's long day and death's dark
    night,
O gentle Jesus, be our light.

4 Labour is sweet, for Thou hast toil'd;
  And care is light, for Thou hast cared;
Ah! never! let our works be soil'd
  With strife, or by deceit ensnared.
Through life's long day and death's dark
    night,
O gentle Jesus, be our light.

5 For all we love, the poor, the sad,
  The sinful, unto Thee we call;
O let Thy mercy make us glad;
  Thou art our Jesus, and our all.
Through life's long day and death's dark
    night,
O gentle Jesus, be our light,

6 Sweet Saviour, bless us; night is come;
  Through night and darkness near us be,
Good angels watch about our home,
  And we are one day nearer Thee.
Through life's long day and death's dark night,
O gentle Jesus, be our light.

134 [18]

TALLIS'S CANON.
L. M.

Moderate.

All praise to Thee, my God, this night, For all the blessings of the light:

Keep me, O keep me, King of kings, Un-der Thine own Al - might-y wings. A-MEN.

2 Forgive me, Lord, for Thy dear Son.
The ills that I this day have done;
That with the world, myself, and Thee,
I, ere I sleep, at peace may be.

3 Teach me to live, that I may dread
The grave as little as my bed;
Teach me to die, that so I may
Rise glorious at the awful day,

4 O may my soul on Thee repose,
And with sweet sleep mine eyelids close;

Sleep, that may me more vigerous make
To serve my God, when I awake.

5 When in the night I sleepless lie,
My soul with heavenly thoughts supply;
Let no ill dreams disturb my rest,
No powers of darkness me molest

6 Praise God, from whom all blessings flow;
Praise Him, all creatures here below;
Praise Him above, ye heavenly host;
Praise Father, Son, and Holy Ghost.

135

GERMAN EVENING HYMN.
7s.

Quietly.

Now the light has gone a - way, Sa-viour, lis - ten while I pray,

Ask-ing Thee to watch and keep, And to send me quiet sleep. A - MEN.

2 Jesus, Saviour, wash away,
All that has been wrong to-day;
Help me every day to be
Good and gentle, more like Thee.

3 Let my near and dear ones be,
Always near and dear to Thee;
O bring me and all I love
To Thy happy Home above.

4 Now my evening praise I give;
Thou didst die that I might live,
All my blessings come from Thee,
O how good Thou art to me!

5 Thou my best and kindest Friend,
Thou wilt love me to the end!
Let me love Thee more and more,
Always better than before.

136 [19]

SOUTHGATE'S.
8s. 4s.

Moderate.

God, that madest earth and heaven, Dark-ness and light; Who the day for

toil hast giv-en, For rest the night: May Thine an-gel guards de-fend us,

Slumber sweet Thy mer-cy send us, Ho-ly dreams and hopes at-tend us,

This live-long night. A-MEN.

Guard us waking, guard us sleeping.
And, when we die,
May we in Thy mighty keeping,
All peaceful lie:
When the last dread trump shall wake us,
Do not Thou, our Lord, forsake us,
But to reign in glory take us
With Thee on high.

137 [16]

S. ANATOLIUS.
P. M.

Quietly.

The day is past and o-ver; All thanks, O Lord, to Thee!

EVENING.

I pray Thee that of - fence - less The hours of dark may be.

O Je-sus, keep me in Thy sight, And save me thro' the com - ing night. A-MEN.

2 The joys of day are over;
I lift my heart to Thee,
And call on Thee that sinless
The hours of gloom may be.
O Jesus, make their darkness light,
And save me through the coming night.

3 The toils of day are over;
I raise the hymn to Thee,
And ask that free from peril
The hours of fear may be:
O Jesus, keep me in Thy sight,
And guard me through the coming night.

4 Lighten mine eyes, O Saviour,
Or sleep in death shall I,
And he, my wakeful tempter,
Triumphantly shall cry.
"Against him I have now prevailed:
Rejoice! the child of God has failed!"

5 Be Thou my soul's Preserver,
O God! for Thou dost know,
How many are the perils
Through which I have to go.
O loving Jesus, hear my call,
And guard and save me from them all!

138

S. SYLVESTER.
8s. 7s.

Quietly.

Hear Thy children, gentle Je - sus, While we breathe our evening prayer;

Save us from all harm and dan - ger, Take us 'neath Thy sheltering care. A - MEN.

2 Save us from the wiles of Satan,
'Mid the lone and silent night
Sweetly may bright guardian angels
Keep us 'neath their watchful sight.

3 Gentle Jesus, look in pity
From Thy great white throne above:

All the night Thy care is watchful;
Never closed Thine eyes of love.

4 Shades of evening fast are falling,
Day is fading into gloom:
When the shades of death fall round us
Lead Thy ransomed children home.

139 [17]

RUSSIAN HYMN.
8s. 7s. with Refrain.

Cheerful. 1st and 3d verses.

1 { Sa - viour, breathe an eve - ning blessing, Ere re-pose our spir - its seal:
Sin and want we come con-fess - ing, Thou canst save, and Thou canst heal.

3 { Though de-struc-tion walk a-round us, Though the ar-row past us fly,
An - gel-guards from Thee surround us, We are safe if Thou art nigh.

2d and 4th verses.

2 { Though the night be dark and drear - y, Darkness can - not hide from Thee;
Thou art He, who, ne - ver wea - ry, Watch-est where Thy peo - ple be.

4 { Should swift death this night o'ertake us, And our couch be - come our tomb,
May the morn in heaven a - wake us, Clad in light and death - less bloom.

After each verse.

Hal - le - lu - jah, Hal - le - lu - jah, Hal - le - lu - jah. A - MEN.

140

S. FULDA.
7s. 6s. D.

Moderate.

When eve - ning shad-ows ga - ther, And twi - light gent - ly fades:

When all is still and si - lent In mid-night's dark - er shades;

Then, O my God, be near me, Do Thou pro-tect my bed;

From e - vil and from dan - ger Let An-gels guard my head. A-MEN.

2 We know not, when we slumber,
　That we shall e'er awake,
　To see another day begin,
　Another dawning break:
　But Thou art ever watching,
　Thou wilt our vigils keep,
　And, trusting in Thy mercy,
　We sink in peaceful sleep.

3 But, ere our eyelids closing,
　We humbly seek Thy face,
　And pray for Thy forgiveness,
　And Thy sustaining grace:
　For we are weak and erring,
　And need Thy mighty power;
　O Jesus, ever guard us
　In dark temptation's hour.

4 We pray for those who languish
　In sickness and distress,
　That Thou wilt soothe their anguish,
　And their afflictions bless:
　We pray for those in peril
　Upon the mighty sea;
　We pray for friends and loved ones;—
　Do Thou their Guardian be.

5 And now to Thee we render
　Our thanks for mercies past,
　With grateful hearts imploring
　Thy favour to the last.
　And at the great awakening
　May we be found above.—
　With saints and angels praising
　Thy providence and love.

141

Moderate.

Sa-viour, a - bide with us! The day is now far gone: We would ob-tain a

blessing thus By coming to Thy throne. A-MEN.

2 We have not reached that land,
　That happy land, as yet,
　Where holy Angels round Thee
　stand,
　Whose sun can never set.

3 Our sun is sinking now;
　Our day is almost o'er;
　O Sun of Righteousness, do
　Thou
　Shine on us evermore.

142 [535]

EUDOXIA.
3s. 5s.

Quietly.

Now the day is o - ver, Night is draw - ing nigh,

Sha - dows of the eve - ning Steal a - cross the sky. A - MEN.

2 Now the darkness gathers,
   Stars begin to peep,
   Birds, and beasts, and flowers
   Soon will be asleep.

3 Jesus, give the weary
   Calm and sweet repose,
   With Thy tenderest blessing
   May our eyelids close.

4 Through the long night watches
   May Thine Angels spread

Their white wings above me,
   Watching round my bed.

5 When the morning wakens,
   Then may I arise
   Pure and fresh and sinless
   In Thy holy eyes.

6 Glory to the Father,
   Glory to the Son,
   And to Thee, blest Spirit,
   Whilst all ages run.

143 [534]

TENDER SHEPHERD.
8s. 7s.

Moderate.

Je - sus, ten - der Shepherd, hear me; Bless Thy lit - tle lamb to - night;

Thro' the darkness be Thou near me: Keep me safe till morn - ing light. A - MEN.

2 All this day Thy hand has led me,
   And I thank Thee for Thy care;
   Thou hast warmed me, clothed and fed me,
   Listen to my evening prayer.

3 Let my sins be all forgiven;
   Bless the friends I love so well;
   Take us all at last to heaven,
   Happy there with Thee to dwell.

144

The ra - diant sun, de - clin - ing, Will soon have passed a - way,

And sil - ver stars out - shin - ing, Make but a tran - sient stay;

O Light, all light ex - cell - ing, When sun or stars de - cline,

Shine forth, our gloom dis - pell - ing With light and joy di - vine. A - MEN.

2 Like sunbeams, quickly flying
  Before the dusky night,
  Or stars' fair lustre, dying
  With morning's clearer light:
  So swift beyond our measure
  Life's little day speeds on;
  A moment's fleeting pleasure,
  And light and life are gone.

3 Thou, who in human fashion
  Didst render up Thy breath,
  And by Thy bitter passion
  Destroy the sting of death:
  When life's brief day is over,
  Its toil, and care, and sin,
  Open Thine arms of mercy,
  And take the weary in.

4 O Saviour, be Thou near us
  Till all our toil is o'er,
  Till heavenly light shall cheer us
  And night return no more:
  So, to the life immortal,
  With joy we'll haste away,
  And pass through death's dark portal
  To never-ending day.

145

MOZART.

Ere the wan-ing light de - cay, God of all, to Thee we pray;

Let Thine an - gel-guards de-scend, Us to succour and de-fend. A-MEN.

2 Guard from dreams that may affright,
Guard from terrors of the night;
Guard from foes, without, within,
Outward danger, inward sin.

3 Mindful of our only stay,
Duly thus to Thee we pray;
Duly thus to Thee we raise
Solemn hymns of grateful praise.

4 Hear our prayer, Almighty King!
Hear our praises while we sing!
Hymning with the heavenly host,
Father, Son, and Holy Ghost.

146 [9]

VESPERI LUX.

Ho - ly Fa-ther, cheer our way With Thy love's per-pet - ual ray;

rall.

Grant us ev - 'ry clo - sing day . . . Light at eve - ning - time. A-MEN.

2 Holy Saviour, calm our fears
When earth's brightness disappears;
Grant us in our later years
Light at evening-time.

3 Holy Spirit, be Thou nigh,
When in mortal pains we lie;
Grant us, as we come to die,
Light at evening-time.

4 Holy, blessèd Trinity,
Darkness is not dark to Thee:
Those Thou keepest always see
Light at evening-time.

147 *Moderate.*

The hours of day are o - ver, The eve - ning calls us home;

cres. *f*

Once more to Thee, O Fa - ther, With thankful hearts we come. A - MEN.

2 For all Thy countless blessings
  We praise Thy holy Name,
And own Thy love unchanging
  Through days and years the same.

3 For all the dear affection
  Of parents, brothers, friends,
To Him our thanks we render
  Who these and all things sends.

4 But these, O Lord, can show us
  Thy goodness but in part;
Thy love would lead us onward
  To know Thee as Thou art;

5 The Teacher ever present,
  The Friend for ever nigh,
The Home prepared by Jesus
  For us above the sky.

6 Lord, gather all Thy children
  To meet Thee there at last,
When earthly tasks are ended,
  And earthly days are past.

7 With all our dear ones round us
  In that eternal Home,
Where death no more shall part us,
  And night shall never come.

148 [28] ＃the 𝕷ord's 𝕯ay.

SWABIA.
S. M.

Joyful.

This is the day of light; Let there be light to - day;

O Day Spring, rise up - on our night, And chase its gloom a - way. A - MEN.

2 This is the day of rest:
  Our failing strength renew;
On weary brain and troubled breast
  Shed Thou Thy freshening dew.

3 This is the day of peace:
  Thy peace our spirits fill;
Bid Thou the blasts of discord cease,
  The waves of strife be still.

4 This is the day of prayer:
  Let earth to heaven draw near;
Lift up our hearts to seek Thee there;
  Come down to meet us here.

5 This is the first of days:
  Send forth Thy quickening breath,
And wake dead souls to love and praise,
  O Vanquisher of death!

149

CLEETHORPES.
7s. 6s. D. with chorus.

Joyful.

Again the morn of glad-ness, The morn of light is here; And earth itself looks fair - er,

And heav'n it-self more near : The bells, like an-gel voi - ces, Speak peace to ev-ery breast,

FULL.

And all the land lies qui - et To keep the day of rest. Glo-ry be to Je - sus,

sf

Let all the children say ; He rose a-gain, He rose again, On this glad day ! A - MEN.

2 Again, O loving Saviour,
  The children of Thy grace
Prepare themselves to seek Thee
  Within Thy chosen place.
Our song shall rise to greet Thee,
  If Thou our hearts wilt raise;
If Thou our lips wilt open
  Our mouth shall shew Thy praise.
    Glory be to Jesus, &c.

3 The shining choir of angels
  That rest not day or night,
The crowned and palm-decked martyrs,
  The saints arrayed in white,
The happy lambs of Jesus
  In pastures fair above,—
These all adore and praise Him
  Whom we too praise and love.
    Glory be to Jesus, &c.

4 The Church on earth rejoices
  To join with these to-day;
In every tongue and nation
  She calls her sons to pray:
Across the Northern snow-fields,
  Beneath the Indian palms.
She makes the same "pure offering,"
  And sings the same sweet psalms.
    Glory be to Jesus, &c.

5 Toll out, sweet bells, His praises!
  Sing, children, sing His Name!
Still louder and still farther
  His mighty deeds proclaim!
Till all whom He redeemèd
  Shall own Him Lord and King,
Till every knee shall worship,
  And every tongue shall sing!
    Glory be to Jesus, &c.

150 [24]

ROTTERDAM.
7s. 6s. D.

Moderate.

O Day of rest and glad-ness, O day of joy and light,
O balm of care and sad-ness, Most beau-ti-ful, most bright;
On thee, the high and low-ly, Through a-ges join'd in tune,
Sing, Ho-ly, ho-ly, ho-ly, To the great God Tri-une. A-MEN.

2 On thee, at the Creation.
 The light first had its birth;
On thee for our salvation
 Christ rose from depths of earth;
On thee our Lord victorious
 The Spirit sent from heaven;
And thus on thee most glorious
 A triple light was given.

3 Thou art a port protected
 From storms that round us rise;
A garden intersected
 With streams of Paradise;
Thou art a cooling fountain
 In life's dry, dreary sand;
From thee, like Pisgah's mountain,
 We view our promised land.

4 To-day on weary nations
 The heavenly manna falls;
To holy convocations
 The silver trumpet calls;
Where gospel-light is glowing
 With pure and radiant beams;
And living water flowing
 With soul-refreshing streams.

5 New graces ever gaining
 From this our day of rest,
We reach the rest remaining
 To spirits of the blest;
To Holy Ghost be praises,
 To Father, and to Son;
The Church her voice upraises
 To Thee, blest Three in One.

151

BARRY.
6s. 5s. D.

Moderate.

Hap-py, hap-py Sun-day! Day of rest and peace, Which from earthly la-bours

cres.

Bringeth us re-lease; Day which tells of Je-sus Ris-ing from the

dead, *Org.* Day on which His members With His grace are fed! A-MEN.

Org.

In the absence of tenors and basses, the two upper parts may be sung as a choral duet by trebles.

2 Jewish bondage ended,
  Jewish rites surpassed, .
On this day we worship
  Christ, the First and Last;
Here in Christian freedom,
  Gladly we may sing
Hymns of praise and honour
  To our loving King.

3 Every week, in Jesus,
  Thus do we begin,
Who redeemed and called us,
  Saving us from sin;
And our week-day labours
  Are for ever blest,
By the gracious worship
  Of the Sunday Rest.

152

GRANGE.
8s. 7s. 7s.

Joyous.

Al-le-lu-ia! Fair-est morn-ing! Fair-er than our words can say!

Down we lay the hea-vy bur-den Of life's toil and care to - day;

While this morn of joy and love Brings fresh vig - our from a - bove. A-MEN.

2 Sun-day, full of holy glory!
  Sweetest rest-day of the soul!
Light upon a world of darkness
  From thy blessèd moments roll!
Holy, happy, heavenly day,
Thou canst charm our grief away.

3 In the gladness of His worship
  We will seek our joy to-day;
It is there we learn the fulness
  Of the grace for which we pray,
When the word of life is given,
Like the Saviour's voice from heaven.

4 Let the day with Thee be ended,
  As with Thee it has begun;
And Thy blessing, Lord, be granted,
  Till earth's days and weeks are done;
That at last Thy servants may
Keep eternal Sabbath-day.

153 [536]

ABELARD.
S. M.

Moderate.

We come, Lord, to Thy feet, On this Thy ho - ly day;

O come to us, while here we meet, To learn and praise and pray. A-MEN.

2 Our many sins forgive;
  The Holy Spirit send;
And teach us to begin to live
  The life that knows no end.

3 Lord, fill our hearts with love;
  Our teachers' labors own:
That we and they may meet above,
  To sing before Thy throne.

154

Moderate.

O sweet Sab - bath bells! A mes - sage of mu - si - cal chim - ing Ye bring us from God,..... and we know.... what you say;.... Now ri - sing, now fall - ing, So tune - ful - ly call - ing His chil - dren to seek Him, and praise Him to - day. A - MEN.

2 The day we love best!
.The brightest and best of the seven,
The pearl of the week, and the light of our way;
We hold it a treasure, And count it a pleasure,
To welcome its dawning, and praise Him to-day.

3 O sweet Sabbath rest!
The gift of our Father in heaven;
A herald sent down from the home far away,
With peace for the weary, And joy for the dreary,
Then, oh! let us thank Him, and praise Him to-day.

(At the close of service in the afternoon or evening.)

155 [32]

ELLERS.
10s.

Moderate.

Sa - viour, a - gain to Thy dear Name we raise

With one ac - cord our part - ing hymn of praise;

We stand to bless Thee ere our wor - ship cease,

Then, low - ly kneel - ing, wait Thy word of peace. A-MEN.

2 Grant us Thy peace upon our homeward way;
With Thee began, with Thee shall end the day;
Guard Thou the lips from sin, the hearts from shame,
That in this house have called upon Thy Name.

3 Grant us Thy peace, Lord, through the coming night,
Turn Thou for us its darkness into light;
From harm and danger keep Thy children free,
For dark and light are both alike to Thee.

4 Grant us Thy peace throughout our earthly life,
Our balm in sorrow, and our stay in strife;
Then, when Thy voice shall bid our conflict cease,
Call us, O Lord, to Thine eternal peace.

The Seasons.

SPRING.

156

Lux Eoi.
8s. 7s, D.

Joyous.

All is bright and cheerful round us, All above is soft and blue; Spring at last hath
come and found us, Spring and all its pleasures too; Ev-ery flower is full of gladness;
Dew is bright and birds are gay; Earth, with all its sin and sad-ness,
Seems a hap-py place to-day. A-MEN.

2 If the flowers, that fade so quickly,
  If a day, that ends in night,
  If the sky, that clouds so thickly
    Often cover from our sight,—
  If they all have so much beauty.
  What must be God's Land of Rest,
  Where His sons, that do their duty,
    After many toils are blest?

3 *There* are leaves that never wither,
  There are flowers that ne'er decay;
  Nothing evil goeth thither,
    Nothing good is kept away.

They that came from tribulation.
  Washed their robes and made them white,
Out of every tongue and nation,
  They have rest, and peace, and light.

SUMMER.

157

Ruth.
6s. 5s. D.

Joyous.

Summer suns are glowing O-ver land and sea, Hap-py light is flow-ing

Boun-ti - ful and free. Everything re-joi - ces In the mellow rays, All earth's thousand

voi-ces Swell the psalm of praise. A-MEN.

2 God's free mercy streameth
Over all the world,
And His banner gleameth
Everywhere unfurled.
Broad and deep and glorious
As the heaven above,
Shines in might victorious
His eternal Love.

3 Lord, upon our blindness,
Thy pure radiance pour;
For Thy loving kindness
Make us love Thee more.
And when clouds are drifting
Dark across our sky,
Then, the veil uplifting,
Father, be Thou nigh.

4 We will never doubt Thee,
Though Thou veil Thy light;
Life is dark, without Thee;
Death with Thee is bright.
Light of Light! shine o'er us
On our pilgrim way,
Go Thou still before us
To the endless day.

AUTUMN.

158

AUTUMNIA.
7s. 6s.

Quietly.

The year is swift-ly wan-ing, The sum-mer days are past;

And life, brief life, is speed-ing: The end is near-ing fast. A-MEN.

2 The ever-changing seasons
In silence come and go;
But Thou, Eternal Father,
No time or change canst know.

3 Oh! pour Thy grace upon us
That we may worthier be,
Each year that passes o'er us,
To dwell in Heaven with Thee.

4 Behold, the bending orchards
With bounteous fruit are crowned·

Lord, in our hearts more richly
Let heavenly fruits abound.

5 Oh! by each mercy sent us,
And by each grief and pain,
By blessings like the sunshine,
And sorrows like the rain,

6 Our barren hearts make fruitful
With every goodly grace,
That we Thy Name may hallow,
And see at last Thy Face.

WINTER.

159

BEDWYN.
7s.

Moderate.

Win - ter reign-eth o'er the land, Freez-ing with its i - cy breath;

Dead and bare the tall trees stand; All is chill and drear as death.

5th and 6th verses.

5. But the sleep - ing earth shall wake, And the flow'rs shall burst in bloom,

And all Na-ture ris - ing break Glo-rious from its win - try tomb. A-MEN.

2 Yet it seemeth but a day
  Since the summer flowers were here,
Since they stacked the balmy hay,
  Since they reaped the golden ear.

3 Sunny days are past and gone:
  So the years go, speeding fast,
Onward ever, each new one
  Swifter speeding than the last.

4 Life is waning; life is brief:
  Death, like winter, standeth nigh:
Each one, like the falling leaf,
  Soon shall fade, and fall, and die.

5 But the sleeping earth shall wake,
  And the flowers shall burst in bloom,
And all Nature rising break
  Glorious from its wintry tomb.

6 So, Lord, after slumber blest
  Comes a bright awakening,
And our flesh in hope shall rest
  Of a never-fading Spring.

The Christian Year.

Advent.

160 *

Briskly.

IMMANUEL.
7s. 6s. 8.

Be - hold! be-hold He com - eth, Who doth sal-va-tion bring; Lift

up your heads re-joic - ing, And wel-come Zi-on's King; With hymns of joy we

praise the Lord, Ho - san - na to th' In - car - nate Word! A-MEN.

2 Hosanna to the Saviour,
Who came on Christmas morn,
And, of a lowly Virgin,
Was in a stable born:
Immanuel! Blessèd Jesus! come!
Within Thy children make Thy home.

3 Yea, come in love and meekness
Our Saviour now to be;
Come to be formèd in us,
And make us like to Thee,
Before the Day of Wrath draw near,
When, as our Judge, Thou shalt appear.

4 Soon shalt Thou sit in glory
Upon "the great White Throne,"
And punish all the wicked,
And recompense Thine own:
When every word and deed and thought
To righteous judgment shall be brought.

5 *Here*, good and bad are mingled;
But on that Judgment Day
The Angels shall divide them,
And take the bad away:
Grant, Lord, that we be faithful found
When the last trumpet-call shall sound!

* May be sung also as a two-part Chorus by Trebles, either with or without Accompaniment.

161

Goss.
S. M.

Joyful.

Lift up the Ad - vent strain! Be - hold the Lord is nigh!

Greet His approach, ye saints, a - gain, With hymns of ho - ly joy. A-MEN.

2 The everlasting Son,
Incarnate deigns to be;
Our God the form of slave puts on,
A race of slaves to free.

3 Daughter of Sion, rise
To meet Thy lowly King,
Nor let the faithless heart despise
The peace He comes to bring.

4 As Judge in clouds of light
He shall come down again,

And all His scattered saints unite
With Him in Heaven to reign.

5 Before that dreadful day
May all our sins be gone,
The old man all be put away,
The new man all put on.

6 Jesus, all praise to Thee,
Our joy and endless rest;
We pray Thee here our Guide to be
Our crown amid the blest.

162 *

JENNER.
6s.

Moderate.

Dear chil - dren, ev - er - more In God your Lord re - joice;

And ren-der prais-es meet, With heart, and soul, and voice. A-MEN.

2 In all things sober be,
For Jesus is at hand;
So live that when He comes
Accepted ye may stand.

3 Cast ye aside all care,
And with glad heart alway,
Make known your every want;
God loves to hear you pray.

4 With every meek request
Let praises glad ascend,

For praise like incense sweet
Should with petition blend.

5 A glad and thankful heart
Wins blessings from the skies,
And is a sacrifice
Most precious in God's eyes.

6 Then in the Lord alway,
O children dear, rejoice;
And glorify His Name,
With heart, and soul, and voice.

* May be used at other seasons.

Hark! the voice e-ter-nal, Robed in maj-es-ty, Call-ing in-to be-ing Earth and sea and sky, Hark! in countless num-bers, All the an-gel-throng. Hail cre-a-tion's morning With one burst of song. High in re-gal glo-ry, 'Mid e-ter-nal light, Reign, O King im-mor-tal, Ho-ly, in-fi-nite. A-MEN.

2 Long the nations waited,
  Through the troubled night,
Looking, longing, yearning
  For the promised light.
Prophets saw the morning
  Breaking far away,
Minstrels sang the splendour
  Of that opening day.
    Whilst in regal glory,
      'Mid eternal light,
    Reigned the King immortal,
      Holy, infinite.

3 Brightly dawned the Advent
  Of the new-born King,
Joyously the watchers
  Heard the angels sing.
Sadly closed the evening
  Of His hallowed life,
As the noon-tide darkness
  Veiled the last dread strife.
    Lo! again in glory,
      'Mid eternal light,
    Reigns the King immortal,
      Holy, infinite.

4 Lo! again He cometh,
  Robed in clouds of light,
As the Judge eternal,
  Armed with power and might.
Nations to His footstool,
  Gathered then shall be;
Earth shall yield her treasures,
  And her dead, the sea.
    Till the trumpet soundeth,
      'Mid eternal light
    Reign, Thou King Immortal,
      Holy, infinite,

5 Jesus! Lord and Master,
  Prophet, Priest and King,
To Thy feet triumphant
  Hallowed praise we bring.
Thine the pain and weeping,
  Thine the victory;
Power, and praise, and honour,
  Be, O Lord, to Thee.
    High in regal glory,
      'Mid eternal light,
    Reign, O King immortal,
      Holy, infinite.

164 [48]

STUTGARD.
8s, 7s.

Joyful.

Come, Thou long-ex-pect-ed Je-sus, Born to set Thy peo-ple free;

From our fears and sins re-lease us; Let us find our rest in Thee. A-MEN.

2 Israel's strength and consolation,
   Hope of all the earth Thou art;
Dear desire of every nation,
   Joy of every longing heart.

3 Born Thy people to deliver,
   Born a child, and yet a King,
Born to reign in us for ever,
   Now Thy gracious kingdom bring.

4 By Thine own eternal Spirit,
   Rule in all our hearts alone:
By Thine all-sufficient merit,
   Raise us to Thy glorious throne.

165 [47]

SALFORD.
C. M.

Joyful.

Hark! the glad sound, the Saviour comes, The Sav-iour prom-ised long!

Let ev-'ry heart pre-pare a throne, And ev-'ry voice a song. A-MEN.

2 He comes, the prisoners to release,
   In Satan's bondage held;
The gates of brass before Him burst,
   The iron fetters yield.

3 He comes, from thickest films of vice
   To clear the mental ray,
And on the eyes oppressed with night
   To pour celestial day.

4 He comes, the broken heart to bind,
   The bleeding soul to cure,
And with the treasures of His grace,
   To enrich the humble poor.

5 Our glad Hosannas, Prince of Peace,
   Thy welcome shall proclaim;
And heaven's eternal arches ring
   With Thy beloved Name.

Also the following:

303. Holy Bible, Book divine.

311. Rock of ages, cleft for me.

Christmas.
The Story of the Nativity.

I.—THE HOLY CHILD.

166

Quietly.

Cradled in a man-ger, In a stable bare, Lies a lit-tle infant, Pure and fair.

O-ver him his mother Bends with loving eye, While an old man watches, Standing by.

3 Far from home, and friendless,
Who so poor as they!
From the crowded inn door
Turned away.
4 Wearied with the journey,
And the hard world's scorn,
Here the mother welcomes
Her first born.

5 Oxen share his shelter,
Cold the night wind blows,
Straw his bed, and rough his
Swaddling clothes.
6 Weak as other infants,
Child of want and care,
Claims he aught but pity,
Lying there?

II.—THE MIGHTY GOD.

Softly.

Why does that pale mother Gaze and tremble so, Showing deeper joy than Mo-thers know?

2 Why, before her baby
Does that mother kneel?
Whence the holy light her
Eyes reveal?

Moderate.

Cra-dled in that man-ger Lies the E - ter - nal Son, Who is with the Fa-ther, E - ver One.

On that mother's bosom Sleeps in slumber still He who ru-leth all things By His will.

3 Mary's child the prophets
Called Immanuel,—
God, with us His creatures
Come to dwell.
4 And the name of Jesus
God by Gabriel gave;
For, from sin His people
He shall save.

5 Faith can see the Angels
Watch around Him now,
And, before the infant,
Humbly bow.
6 Faith can hear them singing
Sweetest songs of praise,
Faith can catch the meaning
Of their lays.

III.—THE SAVIOUR OF THE WORLD.

Moderate.

Ho-ly Babe, we worship At Thy manger throne, And our Lord and Master Thee we own.

2 Oh! what love has led Thee
To be born for us,
All Thy power and glory
Hidden thus!

3 Shall Thy love yet bring Thee
Into deeper woe
Than our coarser natures
Ever know?

4 Shalt Thou long and labour
Wandering souls to gain,
Calling sinners to Thee,
And in vain?

5 Shall those hands so tender,
Feel the piercing nails,
While Thy life in torment
Sinks and fails?

6 Shall Thy form hang naked
On the shameful tree—
Friends all fled, and foes all
Mocking Thee?

7 Yes, for this Thou camest
From Thy throne on high,
For us men to suffer,
And to die.

8 On Thy path no sorrow
Shall unlooked for fall,
Thou, from the beginning
Knowest all.

9 Yet, Thy joys are deeper
Than Thy sorrows are,
And Thy zeal to save us
Stronger far.

10 Thou wouldst have us joyful,
Even as Thou art,
Though we keep Thy sorrow
In our heart.

11 We may hail Thy coming,
Saviour, Healer, Friend,
And, with Thee, look forward
To the end.

12 When in our frail nature
Thou hast toiled and died,
Thou shalt rise to heaven,
Glorified.

13 Souls shall fill the mansions
In the home above,
Trophies of Thy sorrow
And Thy love.

IV.—THE PRINCE OF PEACE.

Joyous.

Now the new Cre-a-tion Is in Thee be-gun, All that A-dam lost us More than won.

Thou art the In-car-nate, God with man made one, Giving man once more the Place of Son. A-MEN.

3 Thou art born to free us
From the power of earth,
Binding us to Thee in
The New Birth.

4 Thou art born to save us
From the power of sin,
From the evil round us
And within.

5 Thou art born to change us
By Thy grace Divine,
And to make our natures
Like to Thine.

6 Thou hast left Thy glory,
Far beyond the skies,
That with Thee to heaven
We may rise.

7 One with Thee, O Saviour,
May our lives be blest,
One with Thee O bring us
To Thy rest.

8 While by faith we see Thee,
May our hearts adore,
Till our eyes behold Thee
Evermore.

167 [49]

ADESTE FIDELES.
P. M.

Cheerful.

1. O come, all ye faith-ful, Joy-ful and tri-um-phant, O
2. God of God Light of Light
3. Sing, choirs of An-gels, Sing in ex-ul-ta-tion,
4. Yea, Lord, we greet Thee, Born this hap-py morn-ing,

come ye, O come ye to Beth - le-hem;
Lo! He ab - hors not the Vir - gin's womb;
Sing, all ye ci - ti - zens of heav'n a - bove:
Je - sus, to Thee be glo - ry giv'n;

Come, and be - hold Him Born, the King of An - gels;
Ve - ry God, Be - got - ten, not cre - a - ted;
Glo - ry to God In the high - est;
Word of the Fa - ther, Now in flesh ap - pear-ing;

After each verse.

O come, let us a - dore Him, O come, let us a - dore Him, O

come, let us a - dore Him, Christ, the Lord. A - MEN

168 [51]

MENDELSSOHN.
7s. D.

Joyful.

Hark! the her-ald an-gels sing Glo-ry to the newborn King; Peace on earth, and mer-cy mild, God and sin-ners rec-on-cil'd! Joy-ful all ye na-tions, rise, Join the triumph of the skies; With th' an-gel-ic host proclaim Christ is born in Beth-lehem. Hark! the herald an-gels sing Glo-ry to the new-born King. A-MEN.

Organ Pedal.

2 Christ, by highest heaven adored,
Christ, the Everlasting Lord,
Late in time behold Him come,
Offspring of the Virgin's womb.
Veiled in flesh the Godhead see;
Hail the Incarnate Deity,
Pleased as Man with men to dwell,
Jesus, our Emmanuel.
    Hark! the herald-angels sing
    Glory to the new-born King.

3 Risen with healing in His wings,
Light and life to all He brings.
Hail, the Sun of Righteousness;
Hail, the heaven-born Prince of Peace!
Holy Father, Holy Son,
Holy Spirit, Three in One!
Glory, as of old, to Thee,
Now and evermore shall be!
    Hark! the herald-angels sing
    Glory to the new-born King.

169 [56]

YORKSHIRE
Six 10s.

Joyful.

Christians, a-wake, sa-lute the hap-py morn, Whereon the Saviour of man-kind was born;

Rise to a-dore the mys-te-ry of love, Which hosts of angels chanted from a bove;

With them the joy-ful tidings first be-gun Of God In-car-nate and the Vir-gin's Son. A-MEN.

2 Then to the watchful shepherds it was told,
Who heard the angelic herald's voice: "Behold
I bring good tidings of a Saviour's birth
To you and all the nations upon earth:
This day hath God fulfill'd His promised word,
This day is born a Saviour, Christ the Lord."

3 He spake; and straightway the celestial choir
In hymns of joy, unknown before, conspire:
The praises of redeeming love they sang,
And heaven's whole arch with alleluias rang:
God's highest glory was their anthem still,
Peace upon earth, and unto men good-will.

4 To Bethlehem straight the happy shepherds ran
To see the wonder God had wrought for man:
And found with Joseph and the blessed maid,
Her Son, the Saviour, in a manger laid;
Amazed, the wondrous story they proclaim,
The earliest heralds of the Saviour's Name.

5 Let us, like these good shepherds, then employ
Our grateful voices to proclaim the joy;
Trace we the Babe, who hath retrieved our loss,
From His poor manger to His bitter Cross;
Treading His steps, assisted by His grace,
Till man's first heavenly state again takes place.

6 Then may we hope, the angelic thrones among,
To sing, redeemed, a glad triumphal song;
He, that was born upon this joyful day
Around us all His glory shall display;
Saved by His love, incessant we shall sing,
Eternal praise to heaven's Almighty King.

170 [59]

Joyful.

CAROL.
C. M. D.

It came up-on the midnight clear, That glo-rious song of old,

From an-gels bend-ing near the earth, To touch their harps of gold:

"Peace on the earth, good-will to men From heaven's all gra-cious King;"

The world in sol-emn stillness lay To hear the an-gels sing.   A - MEN.

2 Still through the cloven skies they come,
  With peaceful wings unfurl'd;
And still their heavenly music floats
  O'er all the weary world:
Above its sad and lowly plains
  They bend on hovering wing,
And ever o'er its Babel sounds
  The blessèd angels sing.

3 O ye beneath life's crushing load,
  Whose forms are bending low,
Who toil along the climbing way,
  With painful steps and slow!
Look now, for glad and golden hours
  Come swiftly on the wing;
O rest beside the weary road,
  And hear the angels sing.

4 For lo, the days are hastening on,
  By prophets seen of old,
When with the ever-circling years
  Shall come the time foretold,
When the new heaven and earth shall own
  The Prince of Peace their King.
And the whole world send back the song
  Which now the angels sing.

171 *Cheerful.*

HEAVENLY SONG.
P. M.

Hark, the Heaven's sweet melo-dy Echoes now on earth, And the bands of those on high

Sing the Virgin-Birth; What mean ye, O ye pas-sers-by, Share ye not their mirth? A-MEN.

2 Shepherds watch their flocks by night;
  Angel notes they hear;
  Songs of glory in the height,
  Peace and love brought near;
  To us they sing, through Love's dear might,
  Praise to CHRIST they bear.

3 Of His Birth the bright stars tell,
  Pouring floods of light;
  Shepherds seek out Bethlehem's cell,
  All those stars in sight;
  They find the King of Heaven where dwell
  Ox and ass of right.

4 There, within the manger laid,
  They their LORD descry:
  We that Child of Mother-maid
  Sing with praises high;
  With homage, LORD, thus duly paid
  We to Thee draw nigh.

172 [61]

Cheerful.

HOLY VOICES.
8s, 7s.

Hark! what mean those ho-ly voi-ces, Sweetly sounding thro' the skies?

Lo, th' angel-ic host re-joic-es, Heavenly Al-le-lu-ias rise. A-MEN.

2 Listen to the wondrous story,
  Which they chant in hymns of joy—
  "Glory in the highest, glory!
  Glory be to God most high!

3 "Peace on earth, good-will from heaven,
  Reaching far as man is found;
  Souls redeemed and sins forgiven,
  Loud our golden harps shall sound.

4 "Christ is born; the great Anointed!
  Heaven and earth His praises sing!
  O receive whom God appointed
  For your Prophet, Priest, and King!

5 "Hasten, mortals, to adore Him;
  Learn His Name to magnify,
  Till in heaven ye sing before Him,
  Glory be to God most high!"

Christmas.

173 [54]

SPES CELESTIS.
C. M. D.

While shepherds watch'd their flocks by night, All seat - ed on the ground, The an - gel of the
Lord came down, And glo - ry shone a - round. "Fear not," said he, for migh - ty dread
Had seiz'd their troubled mind, "Glad tidings of great joy I bring To you and all man kind. A - MEN.

2 "To you, in David's town this day
    Is born of David's line.
The Saviour, who is Christ the Lord,
    And this shall be the sign.
"The heavenly Babe you there shall find,
    To human view display'd,
All meanly wrapt in swathling bands,
    And in a manger laid."

3 Thus spake the seraph: and forthwith
    Appeared a shining throng
Of angels, praising God, who thus
    Addressed their joyful song:
"All glory be to God on high,
    And to the earth be peace;
Good-will henceforth from heaven to men
    Begin, and never cease."

174

MONKTON COMBE.
88, 78.

Chris - tian chil - dren, wake and list - en, Songs are break - ing o'er the earth;
While the stars in hea - ven glist - en, Hear the news of Je - sus' birth. A - MEN.

2 Long ago, to lonely meadows,
    Angels brought the message down';
Still each year, thro' midnight shadows,
    It is heard in every town.

3 What is this that they are telling,
    Singing in the quiet street,
While their voices high are swelling,
    What sweet words do they repeat?

4 Words to bring us greater gladness,
    Though our hearts from care are free,

Words to chase away our sadness,
    Cheerless though our heart may be.

5 Christ has left His throne of glory,
    And a lowly cradle found:
Well might angels tell the story,
    Well may we their words resound.

6 Christian children, wake and listen,
    Songs are ringing through the earth,
While the stars in heaven glisten.
    Hail with joy your Saviour's birth!

175

JUBILEE.

Hark! what mean those thrilling voi - ces, Strange-ly sound-ing in the skies;

There th'an-gel - ic host re-joic-es, There those Al - le - lu - ias rise;

Lo! they sing a won-drous sto - ry, Tell - ing of the Sa-viour nigh!

Glo - ry in the high-est, Glo - ry, Glo - ry be to God on high! A - MEN.

2 Peace on earth, good will from heaven
  Reaching far as man is found:
Man redeemed and sin forgiven;
  Hear the golden harps resound.
Christ is born, the great Anointed,
  Heaven and earth glad welcome sing,
Hail! Lord Christ, the God appointed,
  As our Prophet, Priest, and King.

3 Let us sing the wondrous story
  Of our great Redeemer's birth,
That the brightness of His glory
  Spread and cover all the earth;
Born to reign, let all adore Him,
  All creation praise its Lord,
May we ever sing before Him,
  Glory be to God on high!

176 [60] CHRISTMAS. REGENT SQUARE. 8s. 7s. 4.

Joyful.

An - gels from the realms of glo - ry, Wing your flight o'er all the earth;

Ye who sang cre - a - tion's sto - ry, Now pro - claim Mes - si - ah's birth!

Come and wor - ship, come and wor - ship, Wor - ship Christ the new - born King. A-MEN.

2 Shepherds in the field abiding,
Watching o'er your flocks by night;
God with man is now residing,
Yonder shines the infant-light:
Come and worship,
Worship Christ, the new-born King.

3 Sages, leave your contemplations;
Brighter visions beam afar:
Seek the great Desire of nations,

Ye have seen His natal star:
Come and worship,
Worship Christ, the new-born King.

4 Saints before the altar bending,
Watching long in hope and fear,
Suddenly the Lord, descending,
In His temple shall appear:
Come and worship,
Worship Christ, the new-born King.

177 *Joyful.* COLOGNE. L. M.

Give heed, my heart, lift up thine eyes; Who is it in yon mang - er lies?

Who is this Child, so young and fair? The bless-ed Christ-child li - eth there. A - MEN.

2 Ah, dearest Jesus, holy Child,
Make Thee a bed, soft, undefiled,
Within my heart, that it may be
A quiet chamber kept for Thee.

3 My heart for very joy doth leap,
My lips no more can silence keep;

I too must sing with joyful tongue,
That sweetest ancient cradle-song:

4 Glory to God in highest heaven,
Who unto man His Son hath given;
While angels sing with pious mirth,
A glad new year to all the earth.

178

Rex Infans.
8s. 7s. *with Refrain.*

Cheerful.

Once in Beth-le-hem of Ju-dah, Far a-way a-cross the sea, There was laid a

dim. *cres.*

lit-tle Ba-by On a Vir-gin Mother's knee. O Saviour, gentle Saviour! Hear Thy lit-tle

dim.

chil-dren sing, The God of our sal-va-tion, The Child that is our King. A-MEN.

2 It was not a stately palace
  Where that little Baby lay,
  With His servants to attend Him,
  And with guards to keep the way.
      O Saviour, gentle Saviour, &c.

3 But the oxen stood around Him
  In a stable, low and dim:
  In the world He had created
  There was not a room for Him!
      O Saviour, gentle Saviour, &c.

4 For He left His Father's glory,
  And the golden halls above,
  And He took our human nature
  In the greatness of His love.
      O Saviour, gentle Saviour, &c.

5 Of His infinite compassion
  He can feel our want and woe;
  For He suffered, He was tempted,
  When He lived our life below.
      O Saviour, gentle Saviour, &c.

6 Still His childhood's bright example
  Gives a light to our poor homes;
  From the blood of His atoning
  Still our hope of pardon comes.
      O Saviour, gentle Saviour, &c

7 Still He stands and pleads in heaven
  For us, weak and sin defiled,—
  God, who is a man for ever,
  Jesus, who was once a Child!
      O Saviour, gentle Saviour, &c

The joy - ful morn is break - ing, The bright-est morn of earth,

Through all cre - a - tion wak - ing The joy of Je - sus' birth.

His star a - bove is glist - ening, Where Je - sus cra- dled lies,

And all the earth is list- ening The car - ol of the skies. A - MEN.

2 High strains of praise are swelling
   From angel hosts on high,
And one soft voice is telling
   Glad tidings from the sky;
Tidings of free salvation,
   Of peace on earth below;
Through every land and nation
   The blessed word shall go!

3 His children's songs shall name Him
   In many a tongue to-day;
His Church shall yet proclaim Him
   To people far away;
Till idols fall before Him,
   Till strife and wrong shall cease
Till all the earth adore Him,
   The eternal Prince of Peace!

180

St. Winifred.
8s, 7s. D.

Cra-dled in a man-ger, mean-ly Laid the Son of God His head;

Sleep-ing His first earth-ly slum-ber, Where the ox-en had been fed.

Hap-py were those Shepherds list'ning To the ho-ly an-gels' word!

Hap-py they with-in that sta-ble, Worshipping their in-fant Lord! A-MEN.

2 Happy all who hear the message
Of His coming from above!
Happier still who hail His coming,
And with praises greet His love!
Blessèd Saviour, Christ most holy!
In a manger Thou didst rest:
Canst Thou stoop again, yet lower
And abide within my breast?

3 Evil things are there before Thee:
In the heart, where they have fed,
Wilt Thou pitifully enter,
Son of man, and lay Thy head?
Enter then, O Christ most holy;
Make a Christmas in my heart;
Make a heaven of my manger:
It is heaven where Thou art.

4 And to those who never listened
To the message of Thy birth,
Who have winter, but no Christmas
Bringing them Thy 'peace on earth,'
Send to these the joyful tidings;
By all people, in each home,
Be there heard the Christmas anthem,
'Praise to God, the Christ has come!'

181 [57]

BLESSED MORN.
7s.

Sing, O sing, this bless-ed morn, Un-to us a Child is born,

Un-to us a Son is given, God Him-self comes down from heaven.

CHORUS.

Sing, O sing, this bless-ed morn. Je-sus Christ to-day is born. A-MEN.

2 God of God, and Light of Light,
Comes with mercies infinite,
Joining in a wondrous plan
Heaven to earth, and God to man. Cho.

3 God with us, Emmanuel,
Deigns for ever now to dwell;
He on Adam's fallen race
Sheds the fulness of His grace. Cho.

4 God comes down that man may rise,
Lifted by Him to the skies;
Christ is Son of Man that we
Sons of God in Him may be. Cho.

5 O renew us, Lord, we pray,
With Thy Spirit day by day,
That we ever one may be
With the Father, and with Thee. Cho.

182

MAYLAND.
7s, 8s, 7s.

'Neath the stars that shone so bright, Shepherds watch'd their flocks by night; Suddenly, in

glo-rious guise, Came an an-gel from the skies, Stood beside them, did not chide them,

Told the tid - ings glad and free, "Christ Incar-nate deigns to be." A - MEN.

2 Born this day of David's line,
   Now behold the Babe Divine;
   Rude the raiment that enfolds Him,
   Rough the manger-bed that holds Him;
   Lord all holy, laid so lowly,
   Who from highest realm of heaven
   Stoops that man may be forgiven.

3 May we all with heart and voice,
   Still in Bethlehem rejoice,
   Thither by the bright star led
   To the House of Living Bread;
   Chant the story of His glory,
   Till His Majesty we see
   At His last Epiphany.

183

MANN.
8s, 7s.

1. Hail, sweet Ba - by, pure and ho - ly! Hail, fair Son of Ma - ry blest!
2. Filled with awe and ten - der rap ture, Tears of joy Thy moth-er weeps;

Roy - al In - fant, in a man - ger Thou art gen - tly laid to rest.
Through the night thy fos - ter - fa - ther By Thee faith-ful vig - il keeps.

3 Hovering o'er the hallowed stable
   Choirs of angels carols sing,
   Glory, glory in the highest,
   Hail to Thee, O Christ our King!

4 Shepherds, leave your flocks, and hasten
   To adore, on bended knee:
   Wrapped in swaddling clothes your Sav-
   Israel's Shepherd, ye shall see. [iour,

5 Children, year by year with gladness
   Keep Christ's birthday feast anew;
   Sing His praise with loving voices
   Who was born a babe for you.

6 Hail, sweet Baby, Child of Mary,
   Hail, King David's royal Son,
   Singing carols round Thy cradle,
   We adore Thee, Holy One.

After last verse.

ff

Al - le - lu - ia! Al - le - lu - ia! Al - le - lu - ia! A - MEN.

184 [58]

Moderate.

S. LOUIS.
P. M.

O lit-tle town of Beth-le-hem! How still we see thee lie, A-

bove thy deep and dreamless sleep, The si-lent stars go by; Yet in thy dark streets

shin-eth The ev-er-last-ing Light; The hopes and fears of all the years, Are

met in thee to-night. A-MEN.

2 For Christ is born of Mary,
And gathered all above,
While mortals sleep the angels keep
Their watch of wondering love.
O morning stars together
Proclaim the holy birth!
And praises sing to God the King,
And peace to men on earth.

3 How silently, how silently,
The wondrous gift is given;
So God imparts to human hearts
The blessings of His heaven.
No ear may hear His coming,
But in this world of sin,
Where meek souls will receive Him still,
The dear Christ enters in.

4 O holy Child of Bethlehem!
Descend to us, we pray,
Cast out our sin and enter in,
Be born in us to-day.
We hear the Christmas angels,
The great glad tidings tell,
O, come to us, abide with us,
Our Lord Emmanuel!

185

CHRISTMAS MORN.
7s.

Cheerfully.

Sing with joy, 'tis Christmas Morn, Un-to us a Child is born;

Christ hath come on earth to dwell, God with us, Im - man - u - el! A-MEN.

2 Shepherds. watching thro' the night,
Wondering at the dazzling light,
Hear the glorious Angel tell
Of the Hope of Israel.

3 Thousand thousand angels raise
Songs of glad triumphant praise;
Singing, through the starry sky,
"Glory be to God on High!"

4 Joyously the shepherds ran,
Knelt to Jesus—God and Man;
"Come," they bid us haste with them,
"See the Babe of Bethlehem"!

5 Jesus! whom we now adore,
May we love Thee more and more;
As by faith we, wondering, see
This Thy great humility!

186

Moderate.
(May be sung unaccompanied.)

CHRISTCHILD.
6s. 8s.

Be - hold a lit - tle Child Laid in a man-ger bed, The wintry blasts blow

wild.... A-round His in - fant head; But who is this so low-ly laid?

'Tis He by whom the worlds were made. A-MEN.

2 Alas! in what poor state
The Son of God is seen;
Why doth the Lord so great
Choose out a home so mean?
That we may learn from pride to flee,
And follow His humility.

3 Where Joseph plies his trade,
Lo! Jesus labours too;
The hands that all things made
An earthly craft pursue,
That weary men on Him may rest,
And faithful toil in Him be blest.

4 Among the doctors see
The Boy so full of grace:
Say, wherefore taketh He

The scholar's lowly place?
That Christian boys with reverence meet
May sit and learn at Jesus' feet.

5 Christ! once Thyself a boy,
Our boyhood guard and guide;
Be Thou its light and joy,
And still with us abide;
That Thy dear love, so great, so free,
May draw us evermore to Thee.

Also the following:

187 *[149]

Circumcision.

Moderate.

S. BEES.
7s.

Je - sus! Name of won-drous love! Name all oth - er names a - bove!

Un - to which must ev - er-y knee Bow in deep hu - mil - i - ty. A-MEN.

2 Jesus! Name decreed of old:
To the maiden mother told,
Kneeling in her lowly cell,
By the angel Gabriel.

3 Jesus! Name of priceless worth
To the fallen sons of earth,
For the promise that it gave—
"Jesus shall His people save."

4 Jesus! Name of mercy mild,
Given to the holy Child,
When the cup of human woe
First He tasted here below.

5 Jesus! only Name that's given
Under all the mighty heaven,
Whereby man, to sin enslaved,
Bursts his fetters, and is saved.

6 Jesus! Name of wondrous love!
Human name of God above;
Pleading only this we flee,
Helpless, O our God, to Thee.

188 *

Moderate.

SPRINGHILL.
8s. 7s.

Chris-tian child-ren must be ho - ly, Serv-ing God from day to day;

Ne - ver is the time too ear - ly For a Christian to o - bey. A-MEN.

2 Jesus taught us in His childhood;
Only eight short days He saw
Ere He suffered circumcision
And obeyed His Father's law.

3 He who is our great Example,
Let no moment run to loss:
Not one precious hour He wasted
From the cradle to the Cross.

4 Soon He sorrowed, soon He suffered;
We must meek and gentle be,
Little pain and childish trial
Ever bearing patiently.

5 Soon He showed a Son's obedience;
We must early learn to do
Not our own will, but our Father's,
And be found obedient too.

Also the following:

320. All hail the power of Jesus' Name. 312. How sweet the Name of Jesus sounds.
330. There is no name so sweet on earth.

* May be used at other seasons.

The New Year.

ST. COLUMB.
11s.

From glo-ry un-to glo-ry! Be this our joy-ous song, As on the King's own

high-way, we brave-ly march a-long! From glo-ry un-to glo-ry! O

word of stirring cheer, As dawns the solemn brightness of another glad New Year. A-MEN.

2 From glory unto glory! What great things He hath done,
What wonders He hath shown us, what triumphs He hath won!
From glory unto glory! What mighty blessings crown
The lives for which our Lord hath laid His own so freely down!

3 The fulness of His blessing encompasseth our way;
The fulness of His promises crowns every bright'ning day;
The fulness of His glory is beaming from above,
While more and more we learn to know the fulness of His love.

4 And closer yet and closer the golden bonds shall be,
Uniting all who love our LORD in pure sincerity;
And wider yet and wider shall the circling glory glow,
As more and more are taught of God that mighty Love to know.

5 Thus onward, ever onward, from strength to strength we go,
While grace for grace abundantly shall from His fulness flow,
To glory's full fruition, from glory's foretaste here,
Until His very presence crown our happiest New Year.

190

Standing at the por - tal of the op-'ning year, Words of comfort meet us,

hush - ing ev -'ry fear; Spo-ken thro' the si - lence by our Fa-ther's Voice,

Ten-der, strong, and faith - ful, mak-ing us re - joice. On-ward then, and fear not,

child-ren of the day! For His word shall ne-ver, ne-ver pass a - way! A-MEN.

2 I, the Lord, am with thee, be thou not afraid,
I will help and strengthen, be thou not dismayed!
Yea, I will uphold thee with My own Right Hand,
Thou art called and chosen in My sight to stand.
Onward then, etc.

3 For the year before us, O what rich supplies!
For the poor and needy living streams shall rise;
For the sad and sinful shall His grace abound;
For the faint and feeble perfect strength be found.
Onward then, etc.

4 He will never fail us, He will not forsake;
His eternal covenant He will never break.
Resting on His promise, what have we to fear?
God is all sufficient for the coming year.
Onward then, etc.

191 [204]

CHOPE.
7s.

Moderate.

For Thy mer-cy and Thy grace, Faith-ful through an - o-ther year,

Hear our song of thank-ful-ness; Fa-ther, and Re - deem-er, hear. A-MEN.

2 In our weakness and distress,
Rock of Strength, be Thou our Stay,
In the pathless wilderness
Be our true and living Way.

3 Who of us death's awful road,
In the coming year shall tread;
With Thy rod and staff, O God,
Comfort Thou his dying head.

4 Make us faithful, keep us pure,
Keep us evermore Thine own;
Help, O help us to endure;
Fit us for the promised crown.

5 So within Thy palace gate
We shall praise, on golden strings,
Thee, the only Potentate,
Lord of lords, and King of kings.

192

Epiphany.

S. OSWALD.
8s. 7s.

Moderate.

Beth-le - hem! of no - blest cit - ies, None can once with thee com - pare;

Thou a - lone the LORD from Heaven Didst for us In - car-nate bear. A-MEN.

2 Fairer than the sun at morning;
Was the star that told His birth;
To the lands their God announcing,
Hid beneath a form of earth.

3 By its radiant beauty guided,
See, the Eastern kings appear!
See them bend, their gifts to offer,
Gifts of incense, gold, and myrrh.

4 Offerings of mystic meaning!
Incense doth the God disclose;
Gold a Royal Child proclaimeth,
Myrrh the future tomb foreshows.

5 Holy Jesus! in Thy brightness
To the Gentile world displayed,
With the Father and the Spirit,
Endless praise to Thee be paid.

193. [62]

LISSANT.
7s, 6s. D.

From the East-ern moun-tains, Press-ing on they come, Wise men in their
wis - dom, To His hum-ble Home; Stirred by deep de - vo - tion, Hast-ing from a -
far . . Ev - er journeying on - ward, Guid - ed by a Star. A - MEN.

2 There their Lord and Saviour
  Meek and lowly lay,
  Wondrous light that led them
  Onward on their way:
  Ever now to lighten
  Nations from afar,
  As they journey Homeward,
  By that guiding Star.

3 Thou who in a Manger,
  Once hast lowly lain,
  Who dost now in glory
  O'er all kingdoms reign,
  Gather in the heathen
  Who in lands afar,
  Ne'er have seen the brightness
  Of Thy guiding Star.

4 Onward through the darkness
  Of the lonely night,
  Shining still before them,
  With Thy kindly Light,
  Guide them, Jew and Gentile,
  Homeward from afar,
  Young and old together
  By Thy guiding Star.

5 Until every nation,
  Whether bond or free,
  'Neath Thy star-lit Banner,
  Jesu, follows Thee,
  O'er the distant mountains,
  To that Heavenly Home,
  Where nor sin nor sorrow
  Evermore shall come.

194

THREE KINGS.
8. 6. 8. 6. 8. 8.

Smoothly.

There came three Kings, ere break of day, All on E - piph - a - nie; Their gifts they bare both rich and rare, All, all, Lord Christ for Thee : Gold, frank-incense and

myrrh are there, Where is the King? O where? O where? O where is the King? O where? A-MEN.

2 The Star shone brightly overhead,
  The air was calm and still,
O'er Bethlehem's fields its rays were shed,
  The dew lay on the hill ;
We see no throne, no palace fair—
Where is the King? O where? O where?

3 An old man knelt at a manger low,
  A Babe lay in the stall ;
The starlight played on the Infant brow,
  Deep silence lay o'er all ;
A Maiden bent o'er the Babe in prayer—
There is the King! O there! O there!

195

S. MARK.
8, 6, 8, 6, 8, 8.

O'er Bethlehem's hill, in time of old, Came wise men from afar, Bringing their cost-ly

gifts of gold, For they had seen the star, In princely pomp, with presents meet,

They came to worship at His feet. A - MEN.

2 The silvery light through all the night
  Led on their eager way,
Until upon His lowly home
  Was shed its gentle ray ;
And there they found the infant King,
And on the ground fell worshipping.

3 So, gracious Spirit, by Thy light
  Shine Thou upon our way,
To guide our feet to Christ our Lord,
  Who would our homage pay ;
For He who is the children's King
Will not disdain what children bring.

4 For gifts : we give ourselves to Thee,
  Our hearts shall be Thy throne ;
For gold : we give Thee all our love.
  O, make it all Thine own !
As incense sweet Thy praise we sing.
And bless Thy name, our Saviour-King.

196*[323]

Joyful.

ZOAN.
7s. 6s. D.

Hail to the Lord's A - noint - ed, Great Da-vid's greater Son! Hail, in the time ap - point - ed, His reign on earth be - gun! He comes to break op-pres - sion, To set the cap-tive free; To take a-way trans - gres-sion, And rule in e - qui - ty. A-MEN.

2 He comes with succour speedy,
To those who suffer wrong,
To help the poor and needy,
And bid the weak be strong;
To give them songs for sighing,
Their darkness turn to light,
Whose souls, condemn'd and dying,
Were precious in His sight.

3 He shall descend like showers
Upon the fruitful earth;
And love and joy, like flowers,
Spring in His path to birth:
Before Him, on the mountains,
Shall peace, the herald, go;
And righteousness, in fountains,
From hill to valley flow.

4 To Him shall prayer unceasing,
And daily vows ascend:
His kingdom still increasing,
A kingdom without end:
The tide of time shall never,
His covenant remove,
His Name shall stand forever;
That Name to us is Love.

* *May be used at other seasons.*

197 [66]

Joyful.

WEBER.
11s. 10s.

Bright-est and best of the sons of the morn - ing, Dawn on our darkness, and lend us Thine aid: Star of the East, the ho - ri - zon a -

dorn-ing, Guide where our in - fant Re - deem - er is laid. A - MEN.

2 Cold on His cradle the dew-drops are shining,
Low lies His head with the beasts of the stall;
Angels adore Him in slumber reclining,
Maker and Monarch and Saviour of all.

Say, shall we yield Him in costly devotion,
Odours of Edom, and offerings divine,
Gems of the mountain, and pearls of the ocean,
Myrrh from the forest, and gold from the mine?

4 Vainly we offer each ample oblation,
Vainly with gifts would His favour secure;
Richer by far is the heart's adoration,
Dearer to God are the prayers of the poor.

5 Brightest and best of the sons of the morning,
Dawn on our darkness, and lend us Thine aid
Star of the East, the horizon adorning,
Guide where our infant Redeemer is laid.

198 [65]

DIX.
Six 7s.

Moderate.

{ As with gladness men of old Did the guid-ing star be - hold; }
{ As with joy they hail'd its light, Leading on-ward, beaming bright; }

So, most gracious Lord, may we Ev - er-more be led to Thee. A-MEN.

2 As with joyful steps they sped
To that lowly manger-bed,
There to bend the knee before
Him whom Heaven and earth adore;
So may we with willing feet
Ever seek the mercy-seat.

3 As they offer'd gifts most rare
At that manger rude and bare;
So may we with holy joy,
Pure and free from sin's alloy,
All our costliest treasures bring,
Christ, to Thee, our heavenly King.

4 Holy Jesus, every day
Keep us in the narrow way;
And, when earthly things are past,
Bring our ransom'd souls at last
Where they need no star to guide,
Where no clouds Thy glory hide.

5 In the heavenly country bright
Need they no created light;
Thou its Light, its Joy, its Crown,
Thou its Sun, which goes not down;
There for ever may we sing
Alleluias to our King.

Also the following.
265. Jesus shall reign where'er the sun.

Lent.
The Story of the Cross.

199 [106]   I.—THE QUESTION.

Quietly. Voices in unison.

In His own raiment clad—With His Blood dyed; Women walk sorrow-ing By His side.

2 Heavy that Cross to Him—
    Weary the weight—
One who will help Him waits
    At the gate.

3 See! they are travelling
    On the same road—
Simon is sharing with
    Him the load.

4 Oh, whither wandering,
    Bear they that tree?
He who first carries it—
    Who is He?

Quietly.   II.—THE ANSWER.

Fol-low to Cal-va-ry—Tread where He trod—He who for e-ver was Son of God.

2 You who would love Him, stand,
    Gaze at His face;
Tarry awhile on your
    Earthly race.

3 As the swift moments fly
    Through the Blest Week,
Read the great story the
    Cross will teach.

4 Is there no beauty to
    You who pass by
In that lone figure which
    Marks the sky?

Quietly.   III.—THE STORY.

On the Cross lift - ed Thy Face I scan— Bearing that Cross for me, Son of Man.

2 Thorns form Thy diadem,
    Rough wood Thy throne—
For us Thy Blood is shed—
    Us alone.

3 No pillow under Thee
    To rest Thy Head—
Only the splintered Cross
    Is Thy bed.

4 Nails pierce Thy Hands and Feet,
    Thy Side the Spear;
No voice is nigh, to say
    Help is near.

5 Shadows of midnight fall,
    Though it is day—
Thy friends and kinsfolk stand
    Far away.

6 Loud is Thy bitter cry:
　Sunk on Thy breast
　Hangeth Thy bleeding Head
　　Without rest.

7 Loud scoffs the dying thief,
　Who mocks at Thee—
　Can it, my Saviour, be
　　All for me?

8 Gazing afar from Thee,
　Silent and lone,
　Stand those few weepers Thou
　　Call'st Thine own.

9 I see Thy title, Lord,
　Inscribed above—
　"JESUS of Nazareth,"
　　King of Love!

10 What, O my Saviour,
　Here didst Thou see,
　Which made Thee suffer and
　　Die for me?

IV—THE APPEAL FROM THE CROSS.

Moderate.　　Part IV should, if possible, be sung by a Tenor or Bass voice.

Child of my grief and pain, Watch'd by my love, I came to call thee to Realms a love.

2 I saw thee wandering
　Far off from me:
　In love I seek for thee—
　　Do not flee.

3 For thee My blood I shed—
　For thee alone;
　I came to purchase thee—
　　For Mine own.

4 Weep not for My grief,
　Child of my love—
　Strive to be with Me in
　　Heaven above.

V.—THE CRY TO JESUS.

Cheerful.

Oh, I will follow Thee, Star of my soul, Thro' the deep shades of life To the goal.

Yes, let Thy Cross be borne Each day by me, Mind not how heavy if But with Thee. A-MEN.

3 Lord, if Thou only wilt
　Make me Thine own,
　Give no companion, save
　　Thee alone.

4 Grant through each day of life
　To stand by Thee;
　With Thee, when morning breaks,
　　Ever to be.

200 *[89]

Quietly.

Sa - viour, when in dust to Thee, Low we bow th' a - dor-ing knee;

When, re - pent-ant, to the skies Scarce we lift our streaming eyes;

O, by all Thy pains and woe, Suf-fered once for man be - low,

Bending from Thy throne on high, Hear our sol-emn lit - a - ny. A-MEN.

2 By Thy birth and early years,
By Thy human griefs and fears,
By Thy fasting and distress
In the lonely wilderness,
By Thy victory in the hour
Of the subtle tempter's power;
Jesus, look with pitying eye,
Hear our solemn litany.

3 By Thy conflict with despair,
By Thine agony of prayer,
By the purple robe of scorn,
By Thy wounds, Thy crown of thorn,
By Thy cross, Thy pangs, and cries,
By Thy perfect sacrifice;
Jesus, look with pitying eye;
Hear our solemn litany.

4 By Thy deep expiring groan,
By the seal'd sepulchral stone,
By Thy triumph o'er the grave,
By Thy power from death to save;
Mighty God, ascended Lord,
To Thy throne in heaven restored,
Prince and Saviour, hear our cry,
Hear our solemn litany.

* May be used at other seasons

201*

HEAVENLY GUIDE.
6s, 5s.
TWELVE LINES.

VOICES IN UNISON.

When my feet have wandered From the narrow way, Out in-to the des-ert,

Gone like sheep a-stray, Soil'd and sore with trav-el, Thro' the ways of men, . . .

rit. Ped. *Tempo.*

All too weak to bear me Back to Thee a-gain; Hear me then, my Fa-ther,

rit. molto. *rall e dim.*

From Thy mercy-seat; Save me by the Pas-sion Of the Bleeding Feet. A-MEN.

2 When my hands, unholy
  Through some sinful deed
Wrought in me, have freshly
  Made my Saviour's bleed;
And I cannot lift up
  Mine to Thee in prayer,
Tied, and bound, and holden
  Back by my despair;
Then, my Father, loose them,
  Break for me their bands,
Save me by the Passion
  Of the Bleeding Hands.

3 When my thoughts, unruly,
  Dare to doubt of Thee,
And Thy ways to question,
  Deem is to be free,
Till through clouds and darkness
  Wholly gone astray,

They find no returning
  To the narrow way;
Then, my God, mine only
  Trust and truth art Thou,
Save me by the Passion
  Of the Bleeding Brow.

4 When my heart, forgetful
  Of the Love, that yet,
Though by man forgotten,
  Never can forget,
All its best affections
  Spent on things below,
In its sad despondings
  Knows not where to go:
Then, my God, mine only .
  Hope and Help Thou art,
Save me by the Passion
  Of the Bleeding Heart.

* *May be used at other seasons.*

202* [339]

GRACE CHURCH.
L. M.

Moderate.

O Thou to whose all-search-ing sight The darkness shin-eth as the light,

Search, prove my heart, it looks to Thee, O burst its bonds, and set it free. A-MEN.

2 Wash out its stains, remove its dross,
Bind my affections to the Cross;
Hallow each thought; let all within
Be clean, as Thou, my Lord, art clear.

3 If in this darksome wild I stray,
Be Thou my light, be Thou my way;
No foes, no violence I fear,
No harm, while Thou, my God, art near.

4 When rising floods my soul o'erflow,
When sinks my heart in waves of woe,
Jesus, Thy timely aid impart,
And raise my head, and cheer my heart.

5 Saviour, where'er Thy steps I see,
Dauntless, untired, I follow Thee:
O let Thy hand support me still,
And lead me to Thy holy hill.

203* [88]

S. PHILIP.
Three 7s.

Quietly.

Lord, in this Thy mer-cy's day, Ere the time shall

pass a-way, On our knees we fall and pray. A-MEN.

2 Holy Jesus, grant us tears,
Fill us with heart-searching fears,
Ere the hour of doom appears.

3 Lord, on us Thy Spirit pour,
Kneeling lowly at Thy door,
Ere it close for evermore.

4 By Thy night of agony,
By Thy supplicating cry,
By Thy willingness to die,

5 By Thy tears of bitter woe
For Jerusalem below,
Let us not Thy love forego.

6 Judge and Saviour of our race,
When we see Thee face to face,
Grant us 'neath Thy wings a place.

7 On Thy love we rest alone,
And that love will then be known
By the pardon'd round Thy throne.

* May be used at other seasons.

204* [606]

S. CRISPIN.

Moderate.   8s. 6s.

Just as I am,—with-out one plea, But that Thy Blood was shed for me,

And that Thou bidd'st me come to Thee, O Lamb of God, I come, I come. A-MEN.

2 Just as I am,—though toss'd about,
  With many a conflict, many a doubt,
  Fightings and fears, within, without,
    O Lamb of God, I come.

3 Just as I am,—poor, wretched, blind—
  Sight, riches, healing of the mind,
  Yea, all I need, in Thee to find,
    O Lamb of God, I come.

4 Just as I am,—Thou wilt receive,
  Wilt welcome, pardon, cleanse, relieve;
  Because Thy promise I believe,
    O Lamb of God, I come.

5 Just as I am,—Thy love unknown
  Has broken every barrier down;
  Now to be Thine, yea, Thine alone,
    O Lamb of God, I come.

* *May be used at other seasons.*

205

SION.
8s. 7s.

Joyous.

Si - on, Si - on, haste to meet Him, Lo, He comes, your Lord and King;

Wave the bright palm-branch before Him, And with joy Ho - san - nas sing. A-MEN.

2 See the eager crowd around Him
  Strew with garments fair His way,
  Honour to the Son of David,
  With glad voices hear them say.

3 Even little tender children,
  Haste their loving Lord to meet;
  Sing Hosannas with sweet voices,
  Strew palm-branches at His feet.

206 [90]

S. THEODULPH.

7s. 6s. with Refrain.

Joyous.

{ All glo - ry, laud, and hon - our, To Thee, Re - deem - er, King! }
{ To whom the lips of chil - dren, Made sweet Ho - san - nas ring. }

The 2d and following verses.

Thou art the King of Is - rael, Thou Da - vid's roy - al Son,

Who in the Lord's Name com - est, The King and Bless-ed One.

After each verse.

{ All glo - ry, laud, and hon - our, To Thee, Re - deem-er, King! }
{ To whom the lips of chil - dren, Made sweet Ho - san - nas ring. } A - MEN.

3 The company of angels
　Are praising Thee on high;
And mortal men and all things
　Created, make reply.
　　　　All glory, &c.

4 The people of the Hebrews
　With palms before Thee went:
Our praise and prayer and anthems
　Before Thee we present.
　　　　All glory, &c.

5 To Thee before Thy passion
　They sang their hymns of praise:
To Thee, now high exalted
　Our melody we raise.
　　　　All glory, &c.

6 Thou didst accept their praises;
　Accept the prayers we bring,
Who in all good delightest,
　Thou good and gracious King.
　　　　All glory, &c.

207*

HOLY CITY.
8s, 7s. D.

"Is not this our King and Prophet?" Ring ho-san - na, wave the palm,

Let the chil-dren from the tem-ple Ech-o back the peo-ple's psalm;

"Bless-ed is the Son of Da - vid,"Bless-ed is the Christ of God,

Wel-come to the hill of Si - on, Deck the path-way, strew the sod! A-MEN.

2 "Meek and lowly One," He cometh,
　And the anthem greets His ears;
Lo, the city lies before Him,
　But He sees it through His tears;
Looking from the Mount of Olives,
　Towers and marble temples rise;
Is thy peace, O well-loved Salem
　"Hid for ever from thine eyes?"

3 Sees He now, in solemn vision,
　Calvary "without the gate?"
Israel fallen "house and city
　Left unto her desolate?"
Yes, O Saviour all enduring!
　Thou wast watching every heart—[Thee,
Which would love Thee, which forsake
　Which would do the traitor's part.

4 Pity, Lord, man's hollow praises,
　Then and now, which greet Thee thus;
"By Thy Cross, and by Thy Passion,"
　O have mercy yet on us!
Now Thou reignest with the Father,
　And the Spirit evermore;
Lord, look down upon Thy servants,
　Who repent and would adore.

* *May be used at other seasons.*

208*

BRADFORD.
7s. 6s. D.

Bold.

Ho - san - na! loud ho - san - na! The lit - tle child - ren sang; Through
pillar'd court and tem - ple The love - ly an - them rang; To Je - sus, who had
bless'd them, Close folded to His breast, The children sang their prais - es,
The sim - plest and the best. A - MEN.

2 From Olivet they followed.
  'Midst an exultant crowd,
Waving the victor palm branch,
  And shouting clear and loud;
Bright angels joined the chorus,
  Beyond the cloudless sky—
"Hosanna in the highest!
  Glory to God on high!"

3 Fair leaves of silvery olive
  They strewed upon the ground,
Whilst Salem's circling mountains
  Echoed the joyful sound;
The Lord of men and angels
  Rode on in lowly state,
Nor scorned that little children
  Should on His bidding wait.

4 "Hosanna in the highest!"
  That ancient song we sing,
For Christ is our Redeemer,
  The Lord of Heaven our King.
Oh! may we ever praise Him,
  With heart, and life, and voice,
And in His blissful presence
  Eternally rejoice!

* *May be used at other seasons.*

209

ROYAL SAVIOUR.
6s. 5s. D.

Moderately slow.

Je - sus! Roy - al Je - sus! Son of God most high, Saviour meek and low - ly,

LENT.

Riding forth to die! On a colt Thou sit-test, While the peo-ple sing, "Glo-ry in the

High-est, Bless-ed be the King!" AMEN.

2 Tell we forth Thy praises,
   Palms in triumph wave;
   Blessing, with hosannas,
   Whom we hail to save.
   We with hearts and voices
   Honour Thee with them
   Who Thy footsteps welcomed
   To Jerusalem.

3 Soon will these, O Jesus!
   Raise the Cross on high,
   And the crowd, so faithless,
   Shout "Him crucify."
   Dearest Lord, increase us
   With Thy perfect love,
   That through all temptations,
   We may faithful prove.

4 Grant us Thee to follow,
   And Thy Cross to bear,
   So Thy Resurrection
   We at last may share;
   So that we may praise Thee
   On Thy Heavenly Throne,
   Who art, with the Father,
   And the Spirit, One!

210*

Earnestly.

SALEM.
8s. 7s. 4.

Once was heard the song of chil-dren By the Sa-viour when on earth; Joy-ful

in the sa-cred tem-ple Shouts of youthful praise had birth; And Ho-san-nas, And Ho-

sannas Loud to David's Son broke forth. AMEN.

2 Palms of victory strewn around Him,
   Garments spread beneath His feet,
   Prophet of the Lord they crowned Him,
   In fair Salem's crowded street,
   While Hosannas
   From the lips of children greet.

3 God o'er all in heaven reigning,
   We this day Thy glory sing;
   Not with palms Thy pathway strewing,
   We would loftier tribute bring,—
   Glad Hosannas
   To our Prophet, Priest, and King.

4 O, though humble is our offering,
   Deign accept our grateful lays;
   Those from children once proceeding
   Thou didst deem "perfected praise."
   Now Hosannas,
   Saviour, Lord, to Thee we raise.

* *May be used at other seasons.*

211 *[544]

Moderate.

HORSLEY.
C. M.

There is a green hill far a - way, With - out a cit - y wall,

Where the dear Lord was cru - ci - fied Who died to save us all. A-MEN.

2 We may not know, we cannot tell,
What pains He had to bear,
But we believe it was for us
He hung and suffered there.

3 He died that we might be forgiven,
He died to make us good,
That we might go at last to heaven,
Saved by His precious blood.

4 There was no other good enough
To pay the price of sin,
He only could unlock the gate
Of heaven, and let us in.

5 Oh, dearly, dearly has He loved,
And we must love Him too,
And trust in His redeeming blood,
And try His work to do.

212 *[101]

Moderate.

ROCKINGHAM.
L. M.

When I sur - vey the wondrous Cross On which the Prince of Glo - ry died,

My rich-est gain I count but loss, And pour contempt on all my pride. A-MEN.

2 Forbid it, Lord, that I should boast,
Save in the Cross of Christ, my God;
All the vain things that charm me most,
I sacrifice them to Thy Blood.

3 See, from His head, His hands, His feet,
Sorrow and love flow mingled down!
Did e'er such love and sorrow meet?
Or thorns compose a Saviour's crown?

4 Were the whole realm of nature mine,
That were a tribute far too small;
Love so amazing, so divine,
Demands my soul, my life, my all.

* *May be used at other seasons.*

213 *[104]

BATTY.
8s. 7s.

Quietly.

Sweet the mo-ments, rich in blessing, Which be-fore the Cross I spend,

Life, and health, and peace possess-ing From the sin-ner's dy-ing Friend. A-MEN.

2 Here I'll rest forever viewing
Mercy poured in streams of blood:
Precious drops, my soul bedewing,
Plead, and claim my peace with God.

3 Truly blessèd is the station,
Low before His Cross to lie;
Whilst I see divine compassion
Beaming in His languid eye.

4 Lord, in ceaseless contemplation
Fix my thankful heart on Thee,
Till I taste Thy full salvation,
And Thine unveil'd glory see.

214 *

THURGAU.
8s. 7s.

Quietly.

Hear Thy chil-dren, gen-tle Je-sus, Hear Thy chil-dren cry to Thee;

Self and sin no more shall please us; Hear our sol-emn Lit-a-ny. A-MEN.

2 Thou didst suffer, gentle Jesus,
Bitter shame and agony;
From sin's bondage to release us,
Thou didst hang upon the tree.

3 But our sins it was that stung Thee,
Not the scourge, and nails and spear;
'Twas our sins alone that hung Thee
On the cross, O Saviour dear!

4 Thou wert pierced, O holy Jesus,
Pierced that sinners might not die;
Oh, let sin no longer please us,
Make us Thine eternally.

5 Gentle Jesus, Thou hast won us
By Thy Passion and Thy love;
Gentle Jesus, deign to own us
In the land of rest above.

Also the following.

310. Jesus, Lover of my soul.
349. My God, my Father, while I stray.
433. Lord, Thy children guide and keep.
489—492. Litany Hymns.

* *May be used at other seasons.*

Easter Even.

215 [107]

Quietly.

REDHEAD, 76.
Six 7s.

Rest - ing from His work to - day, In the tomb the Sa - viour lay;

Still He slept, from Head to Feet, Shrouded in the wind - ing - sheet,

Ly - ing in the rock a - lone, Hid - den by the seal - ed stone. A - MEN.

2 Late at even there was seen
Watching long the Magdalene;
Early, ere the break of day,
Sorrowful she took her way
To the holy garden glade,
Where her buried Lord was laid.

3 So with Thee, till life shall end,
I would solemn vigil spend:
Let me hew Thee, Lord, a shrine
In this rocky heart of mine,
Where in pure embalmèd cell
None but Thou may ever dwell.

4 Myrrh and spices will I bring,
True affection's offering;
Close the door from sight and sound
Of the busy world around;
And in patient watch remain
Till my Lord appear again.

Easter.

The Story of the Resurrection.

I.—THE QUESTION.

216 *Not fast.*

Ear-ly with blush of dawn, Speeding a - way, Shrouded in mourning robes, Say, who are they?

2 See, in their hands they bear
Spices most sweet,
Whom are they hastening
Early to greet?

3 Whose is that garden-fold
Eager they seek,
Why that stone rolled away
Baffling the weak?

4 Why are they pausing now
Close by the Cave?
Whom are they seeking for
In the dark grave?

II.—THE ANSWER.

Not fast.

These are the Ma-ries three, Je-sus they seek, Who to the Cross was nailed, Gentle and meek.

2 This is the garden-fold
Wherein they laid,
Loving, His lifeless form,
Bold, yet afraid.

3 Trembling, they now behold
Where He had lain,
Clothèd in shining robes,
Bright angels twain.

4 Hark! they are speaking now—
"Fear not," they say;
"Whom you are seeking here
Is risen to-day!"

III.—THE STORY.

A little faster.

Long ere the morning dawn, O'er the seal'd stone; O'er where the keepers watch'd, Swift, He hath gone.

2 Lo! as with haste they came,
Bringing their tale,
Greeting, His voice was heard—
"Children, all hail!"

* When fell the eventide
Through the closed door
To His disciples came
Jesus once more.

4 See, at His feet they kneel,
Blessings to win,
"Peace," He is whispering,
"Pardon from sin,"

5 "Peace," once again He breathes,
"Bear it abroad,
Peace to the contrite soul
Thirsting for God!"

6 Thomas the eighth day come,
Chiding, He bade
Touch the deep scars and wounds
The nails had made.

7 In the fair morning hour,
Nigh to the sea
Asked He of Jonas' son—
"Lovest thou Me?"

8 "Feed this dear flock of Mine,
Bought with My Blood,
Preach ye, baptize, and win
Souls to their God.

9 To your and My Father-God
Now I ascend,
Yet in My Church abide
On to the end!"

10 Then on Ascension Day,
By His own might,
Jesus to Heaven went
Up in their sight.

IV.—OUR CRY TO JESUS.

Not fast.

Mas-ter, we cry to Thee, Leave not a-lone; Keep e-ver close to Thee, Je-su! Thine own. A - MEN.

2 Send us Thy Holy Ghost,
Comfort and Guide,
Joyful and true to make
This Easter-tide.

3 Make us to share with Thee,
Thy risen life,
So to be conquerors
All through the strife.

4 Gather our hearts to Thee,
Burning with love,
Till Thy blest Face we see
Cloudless above!

217 [112]

WORGAN.
7s. with *Alleluia.*

Joyful.

Je - sus Christ is risen to - day, Al - le - lu - ia!

Our tri - um - phant ho - ly day; Al - le - lu - ia!

Who did once up - on the Cross Al - le - lu - ia!

Suf - fer to re - deem our loss. Al - le - lu - ia! A - MEN.

2 Hymns of praise then let us sing, Alleluia!
Unto Christ, our heavenly King, Alleluia!
Who endured the Cross and grave, Alleluia!
Sinners to redeem and save. Alleluia!

3 But the pains which He endured, Alleluia!
Our salvation have procured; Alleluia!
Now above the sky He's King, Alleluia!
Where the angels ever sing, Alleluia!

218 [111]

Joyful.

WHITNEY.
7s.

Christ, the Lord, is risen to-day, Sons of men and an-gels say:

Raise your joys and tri-umphs high, Sing, ye heav'ns; and earth, re-ply A-MEN.

2 Love's redeeming work is done,
Fought the fight, the victory won:
Jesus' agony is o'er,
Darkness veils the earth no more.

3 Vain the stone, the watch, the seal;
Christ hath burst the gates of hell;
Death in vain forbids Him rise,
Christ hath open'd Paradise.

4 Soar we now where Christ hath led,
Following our exalted Head;
Made like Him, like Him we rise;
Ours the cross, the grave, the skies.

219 [116]

Joyful.

ARIMATHEA.
P. M.

An - gels, roll the rock a - way! Death, yield up the might - y Prey!

See, the Sa - viour quits the tomb, Glow - ing with im - mor - tal bloom.

ff *p* *f*
Al - le - lu - ia, Al - le - lu - ia, Christ the Lord is risen to - day. A - MEN.

2 Shout, ye seraphs; angels, raise
Your eternal song of praise:
Let the earth's remotest bound
Echo to the blissful sound.
Alleluia! alleluia!
Christ the Lord is risen to day.

3 Holy Father, Holy Son,
Holy Spirit, Three in One,
Glory as of old to Thee,
Now and evermore shall be.
Alleluia! alleluia!
Christ the Lord is risen to-day.

220 [122]

S. ALBINUS.
7s. 8s.

Bold.

Je - sus lives! no long-er now Can thy ter-rors, Death ap - pal us; Je-sus

lives! by this we know Thou, O Grave, canst not enthral us. Al - le - lu - ia! A - MEN.

2 Jesus lives! henceforth is death
But the gate of life immortal;
This shall calm our trembling breath,
When we pass its gloomy portal.
Alleluia!

3 Jesus lives! for us He died;
Then, alone to Jesus living,
Pure in heart may we abide,
Glory to our Saviour giving.
Alleluia!

4 Jesus lives! our hearts know well
Nought from us His love shall sever;
Life, nor death, nor powers of hell
Tear us from His keeping ever.
Alleluia!

5 Jesus lives! to Him the Throne
Over all the world is given;
May we go where He is gone,
Rest and reign with Him in Heaven.
Alleluia!

221*

EASTER DAWN.
P. M.

Moderate.

Eas - ter Day hath dawn'd a - gain, Past the night of grief and pain,

cres. *pp* *rit.*

Vain the guard, the tomb in vain, To hold our bu-ried Je - sus! A - MEN.

* May be sung as an accompanied melody, or as a two-part chorus with or without accompaniment.

2 Faithful hearts their watch have kept,
Loving eyes have mourned and wept,
Where, it seemed, He lately slept,
So still and silent, Jesus!

3 Now, all tears have passed away
With the early morning ray;
From the grave, where once He lay,
There hath arisen Jesus!

4 On this blessèd Even-tide,
Two there were He walked beside,
And they prayed—"With us abide!"
Although they knew not Jesus!

5 Jesus, Lord! I pray to Thee,
Though Thy Face not yet I see,
Evermore abide with me—
My Lord—my God—my Jesus!

222

VIA DOLOROSA.
8s, 7s. D.

By the thorn-y way of sor-row, Counting earth-ly gain but loss;

Wins the Church her glad to-mor-row, In re-demp-tion by the Cross.

Lent-en clouds a-way have drift-ed, Comes at length her great re-ward,

And her eyes are now up-lift-ed, To the glo-ry of her Lord. A-MEN.

2 Alleluia! King Eternal!
  Lord of life! the strife is o'er;
Thou hast quelled the powers infernal;
  Throwing wide the heaven's door;
Alleluia! He has risen!
  And His own, in Him shall rise;
Broken are the bars of prison;
  Won the rest of Paradise.

3 Forth His Church shall go to meet Him
  In the breaking of the dawn!
At her altars kneel to greet Him!
  On this glorious Easter morn:
Whom His chalice veils enfolding
  Very Bread! and very Wine!
We adore by faith beholding;
  In His Eucharist divine.

4 In His manhood, Christ victorious
    Won for man o'er death the strife;
  In His Godhead ever glorious:
    Grants the gift of endless life;
  Hail! all Hail! the King immortal!
    Who shall with His Church abide
  Till we pass through death's dark portal
    To the eternal Eastertide.

223 [121]

VICTORY.
P. M.

The strife is o'er, the bat - tle done; The vic - to - ry of life is won;

The song of tri - umph has be - gun. Al - le - lu - ia! A - MEN.

2 The powers of Death have done their worst,
But Christ their legions hath dispersed:
Let shout of holy joy outburst,
Alleluia!

3 The three sad days are quickly sped;
He rises glorious from the dead:
All glory to our risen Head!
Alleluia!

4 He closed the yawning gates of hell,
The bars from heaven's high portals fell;
Let hymns of praise His triumphs tell!
Alleluia!

5 Lord! by the stripes which wounded Thee,
From Death's dread sting Thy servants free,
That we may live and sing to Thee,
Alleluia!

After last verse.

Al - le - lu - ia! Al - le - lu - ia! Al - le - lu - ia! A - MEN.

Org.

224 [115]

CRAMER.
7s. 6s. D.

Moderate.

The day of Re-sur-rec-tion! Earth, tell it out a broad; The Pass-o-ver of glad-ness, The Pass-o-ver of God. From death to life e-ter-nal, From this world to the sky, Our Christ hath brought us o-ver, With hymns of vic-to-ry. A-MEN.

2 Our hearts be pure from evil,
    That we may see aright
The Lord in rays eternal
    Of resurrection-light;
And, listening to His accents,
    May hear so calm and plain
His own "All hail!" and hearing,
    May raise the victor-strain.

3 Now let the heavens be joyful!
    Let earth her song begin!
Let the round world keep triumph,
    And all that is therein
Invisible and visible
    Their notes let all things blend,
For Christ the Lord hath risen,
    Our Joy that hath no end.

225

ALNWICK.
7s. 5s.

Moderate.

Rise, the ris-en Sa-viour saith! Rise to high-er things; Draw a-new thy quick-en'd breath, Use Thy new made wings! A-MEN.

2 Broken down thy prison walls;
    Sit no more forlorn;
Every chain and hindrance falls
    On glad Easter Morn.

3 Therefore sing thy glad new song,
    Live as children free;
Raise with voices loud and strong
    Shouts of Jubilee!

226 [110]

S. KEVIN.
7s. 6. D.

Joyful.

Come ye faith-ful, raise the strain Of tri - um - phant glad - ness;

God hath brought His Is - ra - el In - to joy from sad - ness;

Loosed from Pha-raoh's bit - ter yoke Ja - cob's sons and daugh-ters;

Led them with un - moistened foot Through the Red Sea wa - ters. A - MEN.

2 'Tis the Spring of souls to-day:
Christ hath burst His prison;
And from three days' sleep in death
As a sun hath risen;
All the winter of our sins,
Long and dark, is flying
From His light, to whom we give
Laud and praise undying.

3 Now the Queen of Seasons, bright
With the day of splendour,
With the royal Feast of feasts,
Comes its joy to render;
Comes to glad Jerusalem,
Who with true affection,
Welcomes in unwearied strains
Jesus' Resurrection.

4 Alleluia now we cry
To our King Immortal,
Who triumphant burst the bars
Of the tomb's dark portal;
Alleluia, with the Son
God the Father praising;
Alleluia yet again
To the Spirit raising.

Also the following.

Ascension.

227 [545]

S. THERESA.
6s. 8s. D.

Joyful.

Gold-en harps are sounding, An-gel voi-ces ring, Pear-ly gates are o-pened,
O-pened for the King. Christ the King of glo-ry, Je-sus, King of Love,
Is gone up in triumph, To His Home a-bove. All His work is end-ed,

Unison.

Joy-ful-ly we sing, Je-sus hath as-cend-ed! Glo-ry to our King. A-MEN.

2 He who came to save us,
  He who bled and died,
Now is crowned with glory
  At His Father's side;
Never more to suffer;
  Never more to die;
Jesus, King of glory,
  Is gone up on high.
    All His work is ended, &c.

3 Praying for His children
  In that blessed place,
Calling them to glory,
  Sending them His grace;
His bright home preparing,
  Little ones for you;
Jesus ever liveth
  Ever loveth too.
    All His work is ended, &c.

230 [128] ASCENSION. ASCENSION.
7s. with Alleluia.

Joyful.

Hail the day that sees Him rise, Al - le - lu - ia! To His throne a -
bove the skies; Al - le - lu - ia! Christ the Lamb for sin - ners given, Al - le -
lu - ia! En - ters now the high-est heav'n. Al - le - lu - ia! A-MEN.

2 There for Him high triumph waits, Alleluia!
Lift your heads, eternal gates; Alleluia!
He hath conquered death and sin, Alleluia!
Take the King of glory in. Alleluia!

3 Lo, the heaven its LORD receives, Alleluia!
Yet He loves the earth He leaves; Alleluia!

Though returning to His throne, Alleluia!
Still He calls mankind His own. Alleluia!

4 LORD, though parted from our sight, Alleluia!
Far above the starry height, Alleluia!
Grant our hearts may thither rise, Alleluia!
Seeking Thee above the skies. Alleluia!

231 *Cheerfully.* OLIVET.
7s. 6s. 7.

For - ty days on earth He spent Since glad Easter day, Then from His A - pos-tles' sight
Je - sus pass'd away; Ev - er-more th' In-carnate Son Sits on God the Father's Throne. A-MEN.

2 "Lift your heads, Eternal gates,"
  So the Angels sing;
"Everlasting doors, make way
  For the Glorious King!"
Satan's power is overthrown,
Christ the Victor reigns alone!

3 With the Angels we, O Lord,
  Songs of triumph raise;
With the twelve, at Bethany,
  Up to Heaven we gaze;
Soon Thou wilt return—may we
Watch with joy to welcome Thee!

Also the following:

320. All hail the power of Jesus' Name. **328.** Glory to the Blessed Jesus.

232* [375]

Moderate.

S. CUTHBERT.
P. M.

Our blest Redeem-er, ere He breathed His ten-der, last fare-well,

A Guide, a Com-fort-er, bequeathed With us to dwell. A-MEN.

2 He came in semblance of a Dove
With sheltering wings outspread,
The holy balm of peace and love
On earth to shed.

3 He came sweet influence to impart,
A gracious, willing guest,
While He can find one humble heart
Wherein to rest.

4 And His that gentle voice we hear,
Soft as the breath of even,
That checks each thought,that calms each
And speaks of heaven. [fear,

5 And every virtue we possess,
And every victory won,
And every thought of holiness
Are His alone.

6 Spirit of purity and grace,
Our weakness, pitying, see:
O make our hearts Thy dwelling-place,
And meet for Thee.

7 O praise the Father; praise the Son;
Blest Spirit, praise to Thee;
All praise to God, the Three in One,
The One in Three.

233* [379]

Moderate.

FEDERAL STREET.
L. M.

Come gracious Spir-it, heavenly Dove, With light and comfort from a-bove;

Be Thou our Guardian,Thou our Guide, O'er every thought and step pre-side. A-MEN.

2 The light of truth to us display,
And make us know and choose Thy way;
Plant holy fear in every heart,
That we from Thee may ne'er depart.

3 Lead us to Christ, the living way,
Nor let us from His precepts stray;

Lead us to holiness, the road
That we must take to dwell with God.

4 Lead us to heaven, that we may share
Fulness of joy for ever there:
Lead us to God, our final rest,
To be with Him for ever blest.

* *May be used at other seasons.*

234*[76]

Moderate.

CAPETOWN.
7s. 5.

Gra - cious Spir-it, Ho - ly Ghost, Taught by Thee we cov - et most,

Of Thy gifts at Pen - te - cost, Ho - ly, heaven - ly Love. A-MEN.

2 Love is kind, and suffers long,
Love is meek, and thinks no wrong,
Love than death itself more strong;
Therefore, give us Love.

3 Prophecy will fade away,
Melting in the light of day;
Love will ever with us stay;
Therefore, give us Love.

4 Faith will vanish into sight;
Hope be emptied in delight;
Love in heaven will shine more bright;
Therefore, give us Love.

5 Faith and Hope and Love we see
Joining hand in hand agree;
But the greatest of the three,
And the best, is Love.

6 From the overshadowing
Of Thy gold and silver wing,
Shed on us who to Thee sing,
Holy, heavenly Love.

235*

Moderate.

HOLY COMFORTER.
7s.

Ho - ly Spir-it, Bless - ed Dove, Sent by Je - sus from a - bove,

Sent to be our Friend most dear, And a Comfort - er to cheer. A-MEN.

2 Gentle Guide and Helper sweet,
Lead our weary wayworn feet
Safely through this world of care,
Till they reach Thy dwelling fair.

Tender Friend, Companion blest,
Deign to be our constant Guest,
All that grieves Thee put away,
And with us for ever stay.

4 Form in us each good desire,
Quicken them with holy fire,
Till the life on love's strong wing
Upward soar, and soaring sing.

5 Holy Spirit, Blessèd Dove,
Comforter, Whose Name is Love,
Helper, Friend, Companion, Guide,
Evermore with us abide.

* *May be used at other seasons.*

236*

Moderate.

PENTECOST.
SIX 7s.

Gracious Spir-it, dwell with me,—I myself would gracious be; And, with words that help and heal,

Would Thy life in mine re-veal; And, with actions bold and meek, Would for Christ, my Saviour, speak. A-MEN.

2 Truthful Spirit, dwell with me,—
I myself would truthful be;
And with wisdom kind and clear,
Let Thy life in mine appear;
And, with actions brotherly,
Speak my Lord's sincerity.

3 Tender Spirit, dwell with me,—
I myself would tender be;
Shut my heart up like a flower
At temptation's darksome hour;
Open it, when shines the sun,
And his love by fragrance own.

4 Holy Spirit, dwell with me,—
I myself would holy be;
Separate from sin, I would
Choose and cherish all things good;
And whatever I can be
Give to Him who gave me Thee.

237

Cheerful.

WOLHAYES.
7s.

Thou, who cam-est from a-bove, Bring-ing light and breathing love,

Teaching us Thy per-fect way, Giv-ing gifts to men to-day. A-MEN.

2 Thou, who once did change our state,
Making us regenerate,
Help us evermore to be
Faithful subjects unto Thee.

3 Often have we grieved Thee sore;
May we never grieve Thee more;
Thou the feeble canst protect,
Thou the wandering direct.

4 We are dark: be Thou our Light;
We are blind; be Thou our Sight;
Be our Comfort in distress:
Guide us through the wilderness.

5 Praise the blessed Three in One,
Praise the Father and the Son;
To the Holy Ghost arise
Praise from all below the skies!

* *May be used at other seasons.*

Trinity Sunday.

Earnestly.

NICAEA.
P. M.

Ho - ly, ho - ly, ho - ly! Lord God Al - migh - ty!

(1)

Ear - ly in the morn - ing our song shall rise to Thee:

(1)

Ho - ly, ho - ly, ho - ly! mer - ci - ful and migh - ty!

God in Three Per - sons, bless - ed Trin - i - ty! A-MEN.

2 Holy, holy, holy! all the saints adore Thee,
   Casting down their golden crowns around the glassy sea,
   Cherubim and seraphim falling down before Thee,
   Which wert, and art, and evermore shalt be.

3 Holy, holy, holy! though the darkness hide Thee,
   Though the eye of sinful man Thy glory may not see,
   Only Thou art holy; there is none beside Thee
   Perfect in power, in love, and purity.

4 Holy, holy, holy! Lord God Almighty!
   All Thy works shall praise Thy Name, in earth, and sky, and sea:
   Holy, holy, holy! merciful and mighty!
   God in Three Persons, Blessèd Trinity.

(1) The small notes are intended for the second and third verses.

* *May also be sung at other seasons.*

239* [389]
Joyous.

CAPETOWN.
7s. 5.

Three in One, and One in Three, Ru-ler of the earth and sea,

rall.

Hear us, while we lift to Thee Ho-ly chant and psalm. A-MEN.

2 Light of lights! with morning, shine:
Lift on us Thy light divine;
And let charity benign
Breathe on us her balm.

3 Light of lights! when falls the even,
Let it close on sins forgiven;
Fold us in the peace of heaven,
Shed a holy calm.

4 Three in One and One in Three,
Dimly here we worship Thee:
With the saints hereafter we
Hope to bear the palm.

240* [547]
Joyous.

NUREMBERG.
7s.

Glo-ry to the Fa-ther give, God in whom we move and live:

Children's prayers He deigns to hear, Children's songs de-light His ear. A-MEN.

2 Glory to the Son we bring.
Christ our Prophet, Priest and King:
Children, raise your sweetest strain
To the Lamb, for He was slain.

3 Glory to the Holy Ghost.
He reclaims the sinner lost;
Children's minds may He inspire,
Touch their tongues with holy fire.

4 Glory in the highest be
To the Blessèd Trinity
For the Gospel from above.
For the word that " God is love."

* *May also be used at other seasons.*

241*

Moderate.

S. BARTHOLOMEW.
C. M. D.

How bright these glorious spir-its shine! Whence all their white ar - ray?

How came they to the bliss-ful seats Of ev-er-last-ing day?

Lo, these are they, from sufferings great, Who came to realms of light;

And in the blood of Christ have wash'd Those robes which shine so bright. A-MEN.

2 Now with triumphal palms they stand
Before the throne on high,
And serve the God they love amidst
The glories of the sky.
His presence fills each heart with joy,
Tunes every mouth to sing;
By day, by night, the sacred courts
With glad hosannas ring.

3 The Lamb, which reigns upon the throne,
Shall o'er them still preside;
Feed them with nourishment divine.
And all their footsteps guide.
'Mong pastures green He'll lead His flock,
Where living streams appear;
And God the Lord from every eye
Shall wipe off every tear.

* *May also be used at other seasons.*

242* [179]

Joyous.

MOULTRIE.
8s. 7s. D.

Hark! the sound of ho-ly voi-ces, Chanting o'er the crystal sea,

Al - le-lu - ia, Al - le-lu - ia, Al - le-lu - ia, Lord, to Thee;

Mul - ti-tude, which none can num-ber, Like the stars in glo-ry stands,

Clothed in white ap - par - el, hold-ing Palms of vic-tory in their hands. A-MEN.

2 Patriarch, and Holy Prophet,
  Who prepared the way of Christ,
King, Apostle, Saint, Confessor,
  Martyr and Evangelist,
Saintly Maiden, Godly Matron,
  Widows who have watched to prayer,
Joined in holy concert, singing
  To the Lord of all, are there.

3 They have come from tribulation,
  And have wash'd their robes in blood,
Wash'd them in the blood of Jesus;
  Tried they were, and firm they stood;
Mock'd, imprison'd, stoned, tormented,
  Sawn assunder, slain with sword,
They have conquer'd death and Satan
  By the might of Christ the Lord.

4 Marching with Thy Cross their banner,
  They have triumph'd, following
Thee, the Captain of salvation,
  Thee, their Saviour and their King;
Gladly, Lord, with Thee they suffer'd;
  Gladly, Lord, with Thee they died;
And by death to life immortal
  They were born and glorified.

5 Now they reign in heavenly glory,
  Now they walk in golden light,
Now they drink, as from a river,
  Holy bliss and infinite:
Love and peace they taste for ever,
  And all truth and knowledge see
In the beatific vision
  Of the Blessèd Trinity.

* *May also be used at other seasons.*

243

MYNTHURST.
8. 7. 8. 7. 7. 7.

Who can paint that love-ly ci-ty, Ci-ty of true peace di-vine, . .

Whose pure gates for ev-er o-pen, Each in pear-ly lus-tre shine;

Whose a-bodes of glo-ry clear Nought de-fi-ling cometh near. A-MEN.

2 There no sun his circuit wheeleth;
  There no moon or stars appear;
Thither night and darkness come not;
  Death hath no dominion there:
But the Lamb's pure beaming ray
Scatters round eternal day.

3 There the Saints of God resplendent
  As the sun in all its might,
Ever more rejoice together,
  Crowned with diadems of light,
And from peril safe at last
Reckon up their triumphs past.

4 Happy he, who with them seated
  Doth in all their glory share;
O that I, my days completed,
  Might be but admitted there!
There with them the praise to sing
Of my gracious God and King.

244*

ANNANDALE.
7s, 6s. D.

We know the guar - dian An - gels' Blest work and sweet em - ploy

Is aye to keep from e - vil, And fill with ho - ly joy;

The Saints all gone be - fore us Must love and watch us still,

And do for each re - deemed one Ac - cord - ing to God's will. A-MEN.

2 But chief, they lead us onward,
And heavenward point the way
To every earth-born wand'rer,
Lest he should go astray;
They hold on high Christ's banner,
With Holy Cross and shield,
And bid us all, full bravely,
Take now the battle-field.

3 And then, above us shining,
They show the golden Crown,
The palm branch and the lily,
The streets with roses strown,
The harping of the victors
Upon the sea of glass;
The gates for those all open
Who into glory pass.

4 Then to the throne of Jesus,
They lead our trembling feet,
Until, with Him safe sheltered,
We rest in pastures sweet;
The pastures green of Eden
Above the starry skies,
The waters of the sheep-fold
All still in Paradise.

5 O Shepherd dear, we thank Thee
For all Thy Saints so blest,
Who lead us ever onward
To our dear Home of rest;
O never, never leave us,
But keep us in the way,
Until at last we see Thee,
In everlasting Day.

* May be used at other seasons.

245 [507]

ALL SAINTS.
C. M. D.

The Son of God goes forth to war, A king-ly crown to gain:

His blood-red ban-ner streams a-far; Who fol-lows in His train?

Who best can drink his cup of woe, Tri-umph-ant o-ver pain;

Who pa-tient bears his cross be-low, He fol-lows in His train. A-MEN.

2 The martyr first, whose eagle eye
   Could pierce beyond the grave,
Who saw his Master in the sky,
   And call'd on Him to save:
Like Him, with pardon on his tongue,
   In midst of mortal pain,
He pray'd for them that did the wrong:
   Who follows in his train?

A glorious band, the chosen few,
   On whom the Spirit came:
Twelve valiant saints, their hope they know,
   And mock'd the cross and flame,
They met the tyrant's brandish'd steel,
   The lion's gory mane;
They bow'd their necks the death to feel:
   Who follows in their train?

4 A noble army, men and boys,
   The matron and the maid,
Around the Saviour's throne rejoice,
   In robes of light array'd:
They climbed the steep ascent of Heaven
   Through peril, toil, and pain:
O God, to us may grace be given
   To follow in their train. AMEN.

* *May be used at other seasons.*

245 (SECOND TUNE.)

LAMBETH.
C. M.

With spirit.

The Son of God goes forth to war; A king-ly crown to gain;

His blood red ban-ner streams a-far; Who fol-lows in His train? A-MEN.

2 Who best can drink his cup of woe,
Triumphant over pain;
Who patient bears his cross below
He follows in His train.

3 The martyr first, whose eagle eye
Could pierce beyond the grave;
Who saw his Master in the sky,
And call'd on Him to save:

4 Like Him, with pardon on his tongue,
In midst of mortal pain,
He prayed for them that did the wrong:
Who follows in His train.

5 A glorious band, the chosen few,
On whom the Spirit came:

Twelve valiant saints, their hopes they
And mock'd the cross and flame, [knew.

6 They met the tyrant's brandish'd steel,
The lion's gory mane;
They bow'd their necks the death to feel:
Who follows in their train?

7 A noble army, men and boys,
The matron and the maid;
Around the Saviour's throne rejoice,
In robes of light array'd:

8 They climb'd the steep ascent to heaven
Through peril, toil and pain:
O God, to us may grace be given
To follow in their train.

246*

NEW CALABAS.
7 s.

Lord, to Thee glad songs of praise, For Thine In-no-cents we raise,

First-lings of Thy Mar-tyr band, Slain by Her-od's cru-el hand. A-MEN.

2 First to follow Thee, the Lamb,
Triumphing with crown and palm,
Death shall never touch them more,
Pain and grief for them are o'er.

3 Infant martyrs round Thy throne,
Thou dost keep them for Thine own;

Thy blest steps they follow still,
Praise Thy Name, and work Thy will.

4 With their anthems, Lord, we sing
"Glory to the new-born King,
Glory to the Father, Son,
Holy Spirit, Three in One."

*May be used at other seasons.

The Church.

247 [490]

AUSTRIA.
8s. 7s. D.

Earnestly.

Glo-rious things of thee are spo-ken, Zi-on, cit-y of our God;

He, whose word can-not be bro-ken, Form'd thee for His own a-bode;

On the Rock of A-ges found-ed, What can shake thy sure re-pose?

With sal-va-tion's walls surrounded, Thou may'st smile at all thy foes. A-MEN.

2 See, the streams of living waters,
  Springing from eternal love,
Well supply thy sons and daughters,
  And all fear of want remove;
Who can faint, while such a river
  Ever flows their thirst t' assuage?
Grace, which like the Lord, the **Giver,**
  Never fails from age to age.

3 Round each habitation hovering,
  See the cloud and fire appear,
For a glory and a covering,
  Showing that the Lord is near.
Blest inhabitants of Zion,
  Wash'd in the Redeemer's blood!
Jesus, whom our souls rely on,
  Makes them kings and priests to **God.**

248 [491]

AURELIA.
7s. 6s. D.

Moderate.

The Church's one foun - da - tion   Is   Je-sus Christ her   Lord;

She   is   His   new   cre - a - tion   By   wa - ter and the   word:

From heaven He   came and sought her   To   be   His ho - ly   bride;

With His own blood He bought her,   And   for her life He   died. A-MEN.

2 Elect from every nation,
   Yet one o'er all the earth,
Her charter of salvation
   One Lord, one faith, one birth;
One Holy Name she blesses,
   Partakes one holy food,
And to one hope she presses,
   With every grace endued.

3 Though with a scornful wonder
   Men see her sore opprest,
By schisms rent asunder,
   By heresies distrest;
Yet saints their watch are keeping,
   Their cry goes up, "How long?"
And soon the night of weeping
   Shall be the morn of song.

4 'Mid toil and tribulation,
   And tumult of her war,
She waits the consummation
   Of peace for evermore;
Till with the vision glorious
   Her longing eyes are blest,
And the great Church victorious
   Shall be the Church at rest.

5 Yet she on earth hath union
   With God the Three in One,
And mystic sweet communion
   With those whose rest is won:
O happy ones and holy!
   Lord, give us grace that we
Like them, the meek and lowly,
   On high may dwell with Thee.

249 [489]

MAIDSTONE.
7s. D.

Joyous.

Pleas-ant are Thy courts a-bove, In the land of light and love;

Pleas-ant are Thy courts be-low, In this land of sin and woe.

O, my spir-it longs and faints For the con-verse of Thy saints,

For the brightness of Thy face, King of Glo-ry, God of grace! A-MEN.

2 Happy birds that sing and fly
Round Thy altars, O Most High!
Happier souls, that find a rest,
In a Heavenly Father's breast!
Like the wandering dove, that found
No repose on earth around,
They can to their ark repair,
And enjoy it ever there.

3 Happy souls! their praises flow,
Ever in this vale of woe;
Waters in the desert rise.
Manna feeds them from the skies;
On they go from strength to strength,
Till they reach Thy throne at length;
At Thy feet adoring fall,
Who hast led them safe through all.

4 Lord, be mine this prize to win;
Guide me through a world of sin,
Keep me by Thy saving grace,
Give me at Thy side a place:
Sun and shield alike Thou art,
Guide and guard my erring heart;
Grace and glory flow from Thee,
Shower, O shower them, Lord, on me.

250 [485]

Earnestly.

S. THOMAS.
S. M.

I love Thy king-dom, Lord. The house of Thine a - bode,

The Church our blest Re - deem-er saved With His own precious blood. A-MEN.

2 I love Thy Church, O God;
   Her walls before Thee stand,
Dear as the apple of Thine eye,
   And graven on Thy hand.

3 For her my tears shall fall;
   For her my prayers ascend;
To her my cares and toils be given
   Till toils and cares shall end.

4 Beyond my highest joy
   I prize her heavenly ways,

Her sweet communion, solemn vows,
   Her hymns of love and praise.

5 Jesus, Thou Friend divine,
   Our Saviour and our King,
Thy hand from every snare and foe
   Shall great deliverance bring.

6 Sure as Thy truth shall last,
   To Sion shall be given
The brightest glories earth can yield,
   And brighter bliss of heaven.

251 [207]

Baptism.

Moderate.

BROCKLESBURY.
8s. 7s.

Saviour, who Thy flock art feeding, With the shepherd's kind-est care,

All the fee-ble gent-ly lead-ing, While the lambs Thy bo-som share; A-MEN.

2 Now these little ones receiving.
   Fold them in Thy gracious arm ;
There, we know, Thy word believing,
   Only there secure from harm.

3 Never from Thy pasture roving,
   Let them be the lion's prey ;

Let Thy tenderness, so loving,
   Keep them all life's dangerous way ;

4 Then, within Thy fold eternal,
   Let them find a resting-place ;
Feed in pastures ever vernal,
   Drink the rivers of Thy grace

252* [207]

CONSECRATION.
7s, 6s. D.

O Fa - ther, bless the chil - dren Brought hi - ther to Thy gate.

Lift up their fal - len na - ture, Re - store their lost es - tate;

Re - new Thy im - age in them, And own them by this sign,

Thy ver - y sons and daughters, New born of birth di - vine. A - MEN.

2 O Jesus, Lord, receive them;
Thy loving arms of old
Were opened wide to welcome
The children to Thy fold;
Let these, baptized, and dying,
Then rising from the dead,
Henceforth be living members
Of Thee, their living Head.

3 O Holy Spirit, keep them;
Dwell with them to the last,
Till all the fight is ended,
And all the storms are past.
Renew the gift baptismal,
From strength to strength, till each,
The troublous waves o'ercoming,
The land of life shall reach.

4 O Father, Son, and Spirit,
O Wisdom, Love, and Power,
We wait the promised blessing
In this accepted hour!
We name upon the children
The Threefold Name divine;
Receive them, cleanse them, own them,
And keep them ever Thine.

* May be used on other occasions.

253

WOODBURN.
8s, 7s.

O God, our strength, our hope, our rock, Whose prom - ise fail - eth nev - er,

In - to Thy cho - sen blood-bought flock, Re-ceive this child for ev - er. A - MEN.

2 Now sealed with Thy thrice holy Name
In these baptismal waters,
For *him* a place we humbly claim
Among Thy sons and daughters.

3 We mark the cross upon *his* brow,
The symbol of Thy Passion;
O Christ, vouchsafe *his* earliest vow
May be *his* life's confession.

4 This banner over *him* unfurled,
May *he* fight on, subduing
The flesh, the devil, and the world;
His strength in Thee renewing.

5 May nothing, Lord, in life or death
From Thee Thy servant sever:
Thy soldier true to plighted faith,
Henceforward, and for ever.

254 [210]

WHITEHEAD.
S. M.

With spirit.

Stand, sol - dier of the Cross, Thy high al - le - giance claim,

And vow to hold the world but loss For Thy Re - deem-er's Name. A - MEN.

2 Arise, and be baptized,
And wash thy sins away;
Thy league with God be solemnized,
Thy faith avouched to-day.

3 Thine is our country now,
Our Lord and Master thine,
Receive imprinted on thy brow
His Passion's awful sign.

4 No more thine own, but Christ's;
With all the saints of old,
Apostles, seers, evangelists,
And martyr throngs enrolled.

5 Oh, bright the conqueror's crown,
The song of triumph sweet,
When faith casts every trophy down
At our great Captain's feet.

255 [209]

Moderate.

S. STEPHEN.
C. M.

In to-ken that thou shalt not fear Christ cru-ci-fied to own,

We print the cross up-on thee here, And stamp thee His a-lone. A-MEN.

2 In token that thou shalt not blush
To glory in His Name,
We blazon here upon thy front
His glory and His shame.

3 In token that thou too shalt tread
The path He travell'd by,
Endure the cross, despise the shame,
And sit thee down on high;

4 Thus outwardly and visibly
We seal thee for His own;
And may the brow that wears His cross
Hereafter share His crown.

256* *Moderate.* **Confirmation.**

HOLY CROSS.
L. M.

Thy cross, O Lord, the ho-ly sign That we, here-af-ter, should be Thine,

Was traced up-on our in-fant brow, And shall we fear to own it now? A-MEN.

2 O God, forbid; before the vain,
The proud, the scoffing, the profane,
We will, through grace, our Lord confess,
His faint but faithful witnesses.

3 His strength in weakness He displays,
From youthful lips He perfects praise,
And we, His faithful soldiers, stand
Strong in the might of His right hand.

4 Smile on us, Lord, and we will fear
Nor scorn, nor shame, whilst Thou art near;
Reproach is glory, suffering rest,
If borne for Thee, if by Thee blest.

5 Great Judge of all, in that dread day,
When heaven and earth shall flee away,
Before the universe confess
Thy faint but faithful witnesses.

* May be used on other occasions.

257 * [509]

Bold.

SILVER STREET.
S. M.

Sol - diers of Christ, a - rise, And put your ar - mour on;

Strong in the strength which God sup - plies, Thro' His e - ter - nal Son. A-MEN.

2 Strong in the Lord of hosts,
And in His mighty power;
Who in the strength of Jesus trusts,
Is more than conqueror.

3 Stand then in His great might,
With all His strength endued;
And take, to arm you for the fight,
The panoply of God;

4 That having all things done,
And all your conflicts past,
Ye may behold your victory won,
And stand complete at last.

258 * [216]

Moderate.

EVERMORE.
7s.

Thine for - ev - er:— God of love, Hear us from Thy throne a - bove;

Thine for ev - er may we be, Here and in e - ter - ni - ty. A - MEN.

2 Thine for ever:—Lord of life.
Shield us through our earthly strife:
Thou the Life, the Truth, the Way,
Guide us to the realms of day.

3 Thine for ever—O how bless'd
They who find in Thee their rest!
Saviour, Guardian, heavenly Friend,
O defend us to the end.

4 Thine for ever:—Saviour, keep
These Thy frail and trembling sheep;
Safe alone beneath Thy care,
Let us all Thy goodness share.

5 Thine for ever:—Thou our Guide,
All our wants by Thee supplied,
All our sins by Thee forgiven,
Lead us, Lord, from earth to heaven.

* *May be used on other occasions.*

259 [215]

BAYNES.
8s, 7s. Six lines.

Ho - ly Spi - rit, Lord of Glo - ry, Look on us Thy flock to - day,

Meek - ly kneel-ing at Thy foot-stool For Thy sevenfold gifts we pray;

Guide us all our earth-ly jour-ney In the true and nar - row way. A-MEN.

2 Foes on every hand are round us,
   And our hearts are weak and frail;
   Gird us with Thy heavenly armour:
   Never let us yield or quail;
   Give us victory in the struggle,
   When the hosts of sin assail.

3 Blessèd Jesus, draw Thou near us,
   As before Thy Cross we bow;
   Help us to be true and faithful,
   Seal our sacramental vow;
   We Thy soldiers are, and servants;
   Hear our solemn promise now.

4 Lead us by Thy guiding presence
   Through the waste with danger rife;
   Feed us with the heavenly manna,
   That we faint not in the strife;
   Slake our weary spirits' thirsting
   From the living well of Life.

5 Looking ever unto Jesus,
   Leaning on His staff and rod;
   May we follow in His Footsteps,
   Tread the path that Jesus trod,
   Till we dwell with Him for ever,
   In the Paradise of God!

260 [213]

NELSON.
7s. Six lines.

Ho - ly Spi - rit, Lord of Love, Thou Who cam- est from a - bove,

CONFIRMATION.

Gifts of bless - ings to be - stow On Thy wait-ing Church be - low;

Once a - gain in love draw near, To Thy chil-dren gath-ered here. AMEN.

2 From their bright baptismal day,
Through their childhood's onward way,
Thou hast been their constant guide,
Watching ever by their side:
May they now till life shall end,
Choose and know Thee as their friend.

3 Give them light Thy truth to see,
Give them life to live for Thee,
Daily power to conquer sin,
Patient faith the crown to win;
Shield them from temptation's breath,
Keep them faithful unto death.

4 When the holy vow is made,
When the hands are on them laid,
Come, in this most solemn hour,
With Thy sevenfold gifts of power,
Come, Thou blessèd Spirit, come,
Make each heart Thy happy home.

261*

UNITY.
7s. 6s.

Spir - it blest, who art a - dored With the Fa - ther and the Word,

One e - ter-nal God and Lord; Hear us, Ho - ly Spir - it. A - MEN.

2 Source of strength and knowledge clear,
Wisdom, godliness sincere,
Understanding, counsel, fear:
    Hear us, Holy Spirit.

3 Thou who camest like a dove
From the opened skies above,
With the Father's power and love:
    Hear us, Holy Spirit.

4 Thou whom Jesus, from His throne,
Gave to cheer and help His own,
That they might not be alone:
    Hear us, Holy Spirit.

5 Thou who yet the Church dost fill,
Making Jesus present still,
Showing us God's perfect will:
    Hear us, Holy Spirit.

6 Come to help the hearts that yearn
More of truth divine to learn,
And with deeper love to burn:
    Hear us, Holy Spirit.

7 Now Thy sevenfold gifts bestow;
Gifts of grace, our God to know,
Gifts of strength to quell our foe:
    Hear us, Holy Spirit.

* May be used on other occasions.

262[358]
Moderate.

DEERHURST.
8s. 7s. D.

Je - sus, I my cross have tak - en, All to leave and fol - low Thee;

Des - ti - tute, de - spised, for - sak - en, Thou from hence my all shalt be:

Per - ish ev - ery fond am - bi - tion, All I've sought, or hoped, or known;

Yet how rich is my con - di - tion! God and heaven are all my own. A-MEN.

2 Man may trouble and distress me,
  'Twill but drive me to Thy breast;
Life with trials hard may press me,
  Heaven will bring me sweeter rest.
O 'tis not in grief to harm me,
  While Thy love is left to me;
O 'twere not in joy to charm me,
  Were that joy unmix'd with Thee.

3 Take, my soul, thy full salvation;
  Rise o'er sin, and fear, and care;
Joy to find in every station
  Something still to do or bear:
Think what Spirit dwells within Thee,
  What a Father's smile is thine:
What a Saviour died to win thee;
  Child of heaven, shouldst thou repine?

4 Haste then on from grace to glory,
  Arm'd by faith, and wing'd by prayer;
Heaven's eternal day's before thee,
  God's own hand shall guide thee there.
Soon shall close thy earthly mission,
  Swift shall pass thy pilgrim days;
Hope soon change to glad fruition,
  Faith to sight, and prayer to praise.

* May be used on other occasions.

Burial.

263 [248] (ON THE DEATH OF A CHILD.) MEINHOLD, P. M.

Quietly.

Ten-der Shepherd, Thou hast still'd Now Thy lit-tle lamb's brief weep-ing;

Ah, how peace-ful, pale, and mild, In its nar-row bed 'tis sleep-ing,

And no sigh of an-guish sore Heaves that lit-tle bos-om more. A-MEN.

2 In this world of care and pain,
　Lord, Thou wouldst no longer leave it;
To the sunny, heavenly plain
　Thou dost now with joy receive it;
　　Clothed in robes of spotless white,
　　Now it dwells with Thee in light.

3 Ah, Lord Jesus, grant that we
　Where it lives may soon be living,
And the lovely pastures see
　That its heavenly food are giving;
　　Then the gain of death we prove,
　　Tho' Thou take what most we love.

Also the following:

387. Hark! hark, my soul.
379. Jerusalem the golden.
220. Jesus lives, thy terrors now.
310. Jesus, Lover of my soul.
349. My God, my Father, while I stray.

388. O Paradise, O Paradise.
369. The King of love my Shepherd is.
381. There is a blessed Home.
385. We are but strangers here.
386. We speak of the realms of the blest.

264 [254]   **Missions.**

Joyful.   MISSIONARY HYMN.
7s. 6s. D.

From Greenland's i - cy mountains, From In - dia's co - ral strand,

Where A - fric's sun - ny foun-tains Roll down their gold - en sand;

From many an an-cient riv - er, From many a pal-my plain,

They call us to de - liv - er Their land from er - ror's chain. A-MEN.

2 What though the spicy breezes
　　Blow soft o'er Ceylon's isle;
　Though every prospect pleases,
　　And only man is vile:
　In vain with lavish kindness
　　The gifts of God are strewn;
　The heathen in his blindness
　　Bows down to wood and stone.

3 Shall we, whose souls are lighted
　　With wisdom from on high;
　Shall we to men benighted
　　The lamp of life deny?
　Salvation, O salvation,
　　The joyful sound proclaim,
　Till each remotest nation
　　Has learnt Messiah's **Name.**

4 Waft, waft, ye winds, His story,
　　And you, ye waters, roll,
　Till, like a sea of glory,
　　It spreads from pole to pole.
　Till o'er our ransom'd nature
　　The Lamb for sinners slain,
　Redeemer, King, Creator,
　　In bliss returns to reign.

265 *[261]

Moderate.

WARRINGTON.
L. M.

Je-sus shall reign where'er the sun Does His suc-cess-ive journeys run;

His kingdom stretch from shore to shore, Till moons shall wax and wane no more. A-MEN.

2 To Him shall endless prayer be made.
And praises throng to crown His head;
His Name like sweet perfume shall rise
With every morning sacrifice.

3 People and realms of every tongue
Dwell on His love with sweetest song;
And infant voices shall proclaim
Their early blessings on His Name.

4 Blessings abound where'er He reigns;
The prisoner leaps to burst his chains,
The weary find eternal rest,
And all the sons of want are blest.

5 Let every creature rise and bring
Peculiar honours to our King:
Angels descend with songs again,
And earth repeat the loud Amen.

266 *[253]

Bold.

CALKIN.
L. M.

Fling out the ban-ner! let it float Sky - ward and sea-ward, high and wide,

The sun shall light its shining folds, The Cross, on which the Saviour died. A-MEN.

2 Fling out the banner! Angels bend
In anxious silence o'er the sign ;
And vainly seek to comprehend
The wonder of the love divine.

3 Fling out the banner! Heathen lands
Shall see from far the glorious sight,
And nations, gathering at the call,
Their spirits kindle in its light.

4 Fling out the banner ! Sin-sick souls,
That sink and perish in the strife,
Shall touch in faith its radiant hems,
And spring immortal into life.

5 Fling out the banner ! Let it float
Skyward and seaward high and wide ;
Our glory only in the Cross,
Our only hope the Crucified.

* *May be used on other occasions.*

267*

SHILOH.
7s. 6s. D.

Moderate.

With hearts in love a - bound-ing, Pre - pare we now to sing

A lof - ty theme, re - sound-ing Thy praise, Al - migh - ty King;

Whose love, rich gifts be - stow - ing, Re-deemed the hu - man race;

Whose lips, with zeal o'er - flow-ing, Breathe words of truth and grace. A-MEN.

2 So reign, O God, of Heaven,
    Eternally the same;
And endless praise be given
    To Thy Almighty Name.
Clothed in Thy dazzling brightness
    Thy Church on earth behold,
In robe of purest whiteness,
    In raiment wrought in gold.

3 And let each Gentile nation
    Come gladly in her train,
To share Thy great salvation,
    And join her grateful strain:
Then ne'er shall note of sadness
    Awake the trembling string:
One song of joy and gladness
    The ransomed world shall sing.

268* [143]

BARTON.
8s. 7s.

Moderate.

Je - sus calls us; o'er the tu - mult Of our life's wild rest-less sea,

* *May be used on other occasions.*

Day by day His sweet voice soundeth. Soft-ly. clear-ly. "Fol - low Me." A-MEN.

2 Jesus calls us. from the evil
  In a world we cannot flee.
  From each idol that would keep us.
  Softly. clearly—"Follow Me."

3 Still in joy. and still in sadness,
  We discern His own decree:
  Still He calls. in cares and pleasures.
  Softly, clearly—"Follow Me."

4 As Saint Andrew heard thee. Saviour,
  By the Lake of Galilee.
  May we hear. and help each other
  Day by day to follow Thee.

5 Thou dost call us! May we ever
  To Thy call attentive be:
  Give our hearts to Thine obedience,
  Rise. leave all, and follow Thee.

269*

Earnestly.

POSTWICK.
P. M.

Come, la - bour on! Who dares stand i - dle on the har-vest plain, While all a-round him waves the gol-den grain? And to each ser-vant does the Mas-ter say. "Go. work to - day." A-MEN.

2 Come. labour on!
Claim the high calling angels cannot share,
To young and old the gospel glorious bear;
Redeem the time, its hours too swiftly fly,
  The night draws nigh.

3 Come. labour on!
Away with gloomy doubt and faithless fear!
No arm so weak but may do service here:
By feeblest agents can our God fulfil
  His righteous will.

4 Come. labour on!
The toil is pleasant. the reward is sure.
Blessèd are those who to the end endure:
How full their joy. how deep their rest shall be,
  O Lord, with Thee!

* *May be used on other occasions.*

270 *Bold.*

HAVERGAL.
P. M.

1. Tell it out a-mong the heath-en that the Lord is King! Tell it out! Tell it out!......

Tell it out! Tell it out! that the Lord is King! Tell it out!...............

out! Tell it out a-mong the na-tions; bid them shout and sing. Tell it

Tell it out! Tell it out! Tell it out! bid them shout and sing. Tell it

FINE. *After 3rd verse.*

out! Tell it out! A-MEN. Tell it out with a-do-ra-tion that He shall increase,

Tell it out!

out! Tell it out! Tell it out................ that He shall increase.

That the mighty King of glo-ry is the King of Peace; Tell it out with ju-bi-lation, though the

D.S.

waves may roar, That He sitteth on the wa-ter-floods, our King for ev-ermore; Tell it

2 Tell it out among the heathen that the Saviour
    Tell it out! Tell it o t! [reigns.
Tell it out among the nations bid them burst their
    Tell it out! Tell it out! [chains.
Tell it out among the weeping ones that Jesus lives;
Tell it out among the weary ones what rest He
    [gives;
Tell it out among the sinners that He came to save,
Tell it out among the dying that He triumphed
    [o'er the grave.

3 Tell it out among the heathen, Jesus reigns above!
    Tell it out! Tell it out!
Tell it out among the nations that His reign is
    Tell it out! Tell it out! [love!
Tell it out among the highways and the lanes at
    [home;
Let it ring across the mountains and the ocean
    [foam;
Like the sound of many waters let the glad shout be,
Till it echo and re-echo from the islands of the sea.

* *May be used on other occasions.*

271* [252]

WEBB.
7s, 6s. D.

The morn-ing light is breaking, The dark-ness dis-ap-pears; The sons of earth are

wak-ing To penitential tears; Each breeze that sweeps the ocean Brings tidings from a-

far, Of na-tions in com-mo-tion, Prepared for Sion's war. A- MEN.

2 See heathen nations bending
Before the God we love,
And thousand hearts ascending,
In gratitude above;
While sinners now confessing,
The Gospel call obey,
And seek the Saviour's blessing,
A nation in a day.

3 Blest river of salvation!
Pursue thy onward way;
Flow thou to every nation,
Nor in thy richness stay:
Stay not till all the lowly
Triumphant reach their home;
Stay not till all the holy
Proclaim "The Lord is come!"

272* [256]

HEBER.
8s, 7s. 4s.

Souls in hea-then dark-ness ly- ing, Where no light has bro-ken through,

Souls that Je- sus bought by dy-ing, Whom His soul in tra- vail knew:

* May be used on other occasions.

Thousand voi-ces Call us, o'er the wa - ters blue. A - MEN.

2 Christians, hearken! None has taught them
Of His love so deep and dear:
Of the precious price that bought them;
Of the nail, the thorn, the spear;
Ye who know Him,
Guide them from their darkness drear.

3 Haste, oh haste, and spread the tidings
Wide to earth's remotest strand;
Let no brother's bitter chidings

Rise against us, when we stand
In the Judgment,
From some far, forgotten land.

4 Lo! the hills for harvest whiten,
All along each distant shore;
Seaward far the islands brighten;
Light of nations! lead us o'er:
When we seek them,
Let Thy Spirit go before.

273*

ONSLOW
6s, 5s. D.

Hark, the swell-ing bree - zes, Ris - ing from a - far, Bring the sound of

con - flict From the ho - ly war. God is with our arm - ies; He the word has

given; He is watch-ing o'er you, Mes-sen-gers of Heaven. A - MEN.

2 Go, thou mighty Gospel,
Conquering on thy way;
Night upon the mountains
Changes into day.
Idols bow before Thee,
Heathen temples fall;
Soon the world shall own Thee,
Victor over all.

3 O Thou blessed Saviour,
Reigning now on high,
May Thy faithful soldiers
Find Thee ever nigh.
Bid their glorious mission
Spread from sea to sea,
Till the whole creation
Worship only Thee.

* *May be used on other occasions.*

274 [478] Offerings.

Moderate.

HOLY OFFERINGS.
P. M.

Ho-ly off'-rings rich and rare, Of-fer-ings of praise and prayer,
Pur-er life and pur-pose high, Clasp-ed hands, up-lift-ed eye,
Low-ly acts of a-do-ra-tion, To the God of our sal-va-tion—
On His al-tar laid we leave them; Christ, present them! God re-ceive them! A-MEN.

2 Vows and longings, hopes and fears,
  Broken-hearted sighs and tears,
  Dreams of what we yet might be,
  Could we cling more close to Thee,
  Which, despite of faults and failings,
  Help Thy grace in its prevailings—
  On Thine altar laid we leave them;
  Christ, present them! God receive them!

3 Homage of each humble heart,
  Ere we from Thy house depart;
  Worship fervent, deep and high,
  Adoration, ecstacy;
  All that childlike love can render
  Of devotion true and tender—
  On Thine altar laid we leave them,
  Christ, present them! God receive them!

4 To the Father, and the Son,
  And the Spirit, Three in One,
  Though our mortal weakness raise
  Off'rings of imperfect praise,
  Yet with hearts bowed down most lowly,
  Crying, Holy! Holy! Holy!
  On Thine altar laid we leave them;
  Christ, present them! God receive them!

275 [477]

GRATITUDE.
8s. 4.

Moderate.

O Lord of heaven, and earth, and sea, To Thee all praise and glo - ry be;

How shall we show our love to Thee, Giv-er of all. A - MEN.

2 The golden sunshine, vernal air,
  Sweet flowers and fruits Thy love declare;
  When harvests ripen, Thou art there,
    Giver of all.
3 For peaceful homes and healthful days,
  For all the blessings earth displays,
  We owe Thee thankfulness and praise,
    Giver of all.
4 For souls redeemed, for sins forgiven,
  For means of grace and hopes of heaven,

What can to Thee, O Lord, be given,
    Who givest all?
5 We lose what on ourselves we spend,
  We have as treasure without end,
  Whatever, Lord, to Thee we lend,
    Who givest all.
6 Whatever, Lord, we lend to Thee,
  Repaid a thousandfold will be;
  Then gladly will we give to Thee,
    Giver of all.

276 [268]

TELLEFSEN.
S. M.

Moderate.

We give Thee but Thine own, What-e'er the gift may be;

All that we have is Thine a - lone, A trust, O Lord, from Thee. A-MEN.

2 May we Thy bounties thus
  As stewards true receive,
  And gladly, as Thou blessest us,
  To Thee our first fruits give.
3 O! hearts are bruised and dead,
  And homes are bare and cold,
  And lambs for whom the Shepherd bled
  Are straying from the fold.
4 To comfort and to bless,
  To find a balm for woe,

To tend the lone and fatherless
  Is angel's work below.
5 The captive to release,
  To God the lost to bring,
  To teach the way of life and peace,
  It is a Christ-like thing.
6 And we believe Thy word,
  Though dim our faith may be;
  Whate'er for Thine we do, O Lord,
  We do it unto Thee.

Thanksgiving and Harvest Home.

277 [193]

S. George's Windsor.
7s. D.

Joyful.

Come, ye thankful peo-ple, come, Raise the song of Har-vest-home;

All is safe-ly gath-ered in, Ere the win-ter storms be-gin;

God, our Mak-er, doth pro-vide For our wants to be sup-plied;

Come to God's own tem-ple, come, Raise the song of Har-vest home. A-men.

2 All the world is God's own field,
 Fruit unto His praise to yield;
 Wheat and tares together sown,
 Unto joy or sorrow grown:
 First the blade, and then the ear,
 Then the full corn shall appear:
 Lord of harvest, grant that we
 Wholsome grain and pure may be.

3 For the Lord our God shall come,
 And shall take His harvest home:
 From His field shall in that day
 All offences purge away;
 Give His angels charge at last
 In the fire the tares to cast,
 But the fruitful ears to store
 In His garner evermore.

4 Even so, Lord, quickly come
 To Thy final Harvest-home:
 Gather Thou Thy people in,
 Free from sorrow, free from sin;
 There for ever purified,
 In Thy presence to abide:
 Come with all Thine angels, come,
 Raise the glorious Harvest-home.

278 [191]

GOLDEN SHEAVES.
8s. 7s. D.

To Thee, O Lord, our hearts we raise In hymns of a - do - ra - tion,

To Thee bring sac - ri - fice of praise With shouts of ex - ul - ta - tion;

Bright robes of gold the fields a - dorn, The hills with joy are ring - ing,

The val-leys stand so thick with corn, That e - ven they are sing - ing. A-MEN.

2 And now on this our festal day,
  Thy bounteous hand confessing,
Upon Thine altar, Lord, we lay
  The first-fruits of Thy blessing.
By Thee the souls of men are fed
  With gifts of grace supernal,
Thou who dost give us daily bread,
  Give us the Bread eternal.

3 We bear the burden of the day,
  And often toil seems dreary;
But labour ends with sunset ray,
  And rest is for the weary.
May we, the angel-reaping o'er,
  Stand at the last accepted,
Christ's golden sheaves for evermore
  To garners bright elected.

4 Oh, blessèd is that land of God,
  Where saints abide for ever;
Where golden fields spread fair and broad,
  Where flows the crystal river:
The strains of all its holy throng
  With ours to-day are blending;
Thrice blessèd is that harvest-song
  Which never hath an ending.

With spirit.

Come, chil-dren, lift your voi-ces, And sing with us to-day, As to the Lord of Har-vest, Our grate-ful vows we pay. We thank Thee, Lord, for send-ing The gen-tle show'rs of rain; For summer suns which ri-pen'd The fields of gol-den grain; Come, chil-dren, lift your voi-ces, And sing with us to-day, As to the Lord of Har-vest, Our grate-ful vows we pay. A-MEN.

p
cres - cen - do. *Full.* *f*

2 Come join our glad procession,
  As onward still we move,
Rejoicing in the tokens
  Of God our Father's love.
All good is His creation,
  All beautiful and fair,
Birds, insects, beasts, and fishes,
  Our harvest gladness share.
    Come, children, &c.

3 May we by holy living
  Thy praises echo forth,
And tell Thy boundless mercies
  To all the listening earth;
May we grow up as branches,
  In Christ, the one True Vine,
Bear fruit to Life Eternal,
  And be for ever Thine.
    Come, children, &c.

280 *Joyful.* MONKLAND.
7s.

Praise, O praise our God and King! Hymns of a - dor - a - tion sing;

For His mer - cies still en-dure, Ev - er faith-ful, ev - er sure. A-MEN.

2 Praise Him that He made the sun
  Day by day his course to run;
    For His mercies still endure,
    Ever faithful, ever sure:

3 And the silver moon by night,
  Shining with her gentle light;
    For His mercies still endure,
    Ever faithful, ever sure.

4 Praise Him that He gave the rain
  To mature the swelling grain;
    For His mercies still endure,
    Ever faithful, ever sure.

5 And hath bid the fruitful field
  Crops of precious increase yield;

    For His mercies still endure,
    Ever faithful, ever sure.

6 Praise Him for our harvest-store,
  He hath fill'd the garner-floor;
    For His mercies still endure,
    Ever faithful, ever sure:

7 And for richer Food than this,
  Pledge of everlasting bliss;
    For His mercies still endure,
    Ever faithful, ever sure.

8 Glory to our bounteous King!
  Glory let creation sing!
    Glory to the Father, Son,
    And blest Spirit, Three in One.

281 FARMER.
Cheerful. 7s. 6s. D.

The corn is ripe for reap-ing, Fields glow with ruddy grain, And we must now be

keeping Our harvest feast again; With voice of joy and singing, Our praise to God shall rise, Who, whilst the seed was springing, Rain'd blessings from the skies. A-MEN.

2 Thine, Father, is the river
That maketh rich the earth;
Through Thee, O gracious Giver,
The buried seed hath birth:
Thou on the furrows raining,
Didst make them soft with show'rs;
The thirsty crops maintaining
Through silent summer hours.

3 The year, by Thee anointed,
Is now with goodness crowned,
Robed in the robes appointed,
With gladness girded round.

We thank Thee for the blessing
Which meets us on our way,
And come, Thy love confessing,
With happy hearts to-day.

4 But whilst our *lips* are praising,
Our *lives* to Thee belong;
With them we would be raising
A nobler, sweeter song;
One that may sound for ever,
Whilst earth's great Harvest speeds,
A song of high endeavour
Rung out in earnest deeds.

National Festivals.

282 [196]

Moderate.

AMERICA.
6s, 4s.

Our fa-thers' God! to Thee, Au-thor of lib-er-ty, To Thee we

sing; Long may our land be bright With free-dom's ho-ly light;

Pro-tect us by Thy might, Great God, our King. A - MEN.

2 Bless Thou our native land!
Firm may she ever stand,
Through storm and night;
When the wild tempests rave,
Ruler of wind and wave,
Do Thou our country save
By Thy great might.

3 For her our prayer shall rise
To God, above the skies;
On Him we wait;
Thou who art ever nigh,
Guarding with watchful eye,
To Thee aloud we cry,
God save the State!

283

EMMANUEL.
C. M.

Joyous.

Ho - san - na, be the chil-dren's song To Christ, the chil - dren's King;

His praise to whom their souls be-long, Let all the chil-dren sing. A - MEN.

2 Hosanna, sound from hill to hill,
And spread from plain to plain:
While, louder, sweeter, clearer still,
Woods echo to the strain.

3 Hosanna, on the wings of light
O'er earth and ocean fly;
Till morn to eve, and noon to night,
And heaven to earth reply.

4 Hosanna, then, our song shall be,
Hosanna to our King;
This is the children's jubilee,
Let all the children sing.

284

S. BEES.
7s.

Joyous.

Lord, this day Thy chil-dren meet, In Thy courts with wil - ling feet;

Un - to Thee this day they raise, Grate-ful hearts in hymns of praise. A-MEN.

2 Not alone the day of rest
With Thy worship shall be blest;
In our pleasure and our glee
Lord, we would remember Thee.

3 Help us unto Thee to pray,
Hallowing our happy day;
From Thy presence thus to win
Hearts all pure and free from sin.

4 All our pleasures here below,
Saviour, from Thy mercy flow;
Little children Thou dost love;
Draw our hearts to Thee above.

5 Make, O Lord, our childhood shine
With all lowly grace, like Thine;
Then, through all eternity,
We shall live in heaven with Thee.

285

Come, Christian youths and maid - ens, Come, bro- thers, old and young,

Up - lift your hearts and voi - ces, Be praise on ev - ery tongue.

In God's own House we ga - ther, Our year - ly feast to hold;

Come, join our joy - ful an- them, Ye brothers, young and old. A - MEN.

2 Come, sing with us the praises
Of God's preserving care,
Who safe from harm has kept us
Throughout another year;
And crowned our lives with mercies
Unnumbered as the sand,
Which day by day have reached us
From His all-gracious Hand.

3 Come, sing with us the praises
Of God's Redeeming Love,
That song which never ceases
Around the Throne above;
The voice of many Angels,
"Worthy the Lamb of God;
For He was slain to save us
By His most precious Blood."

4 Come, praise Him for glad tidings
Heard in this hallowed place—
Glad tidings of salvation,
By free and sovereign grace;
For gifts of Holy Scripture,
Known from our childhood's days;
For call from Heaven to serve Him
In wisdom's happy ways.

5 Come, praise Him for the promise
Of strength in weakness given;
For means of grace provided;
For blessèd hope of Heaven.
Oh, Christian youths and maidens!
Oh, brothers, old and young!
Uplift your hearts and voices,
And let His praise be sung.

286.

HAWKSLEY.
7s. 6s. Twelve lines.

Cheerfully. TREBLES AND ALTOS.

mf
It is a day of glad-ness, When all our friendly band, Christ's
members, thus to - ge - ther, In Him u - ni - ted stand; To - ge - ther lift our
voi - ces To praise Him for His love, And pray that we may wor - thy Of
all His mer - cies prove.

CHORUS.

Haste for-ward, then, dear chil-dren, Reach to the glo-rious
prize, The mark of our high call - ing. The Crown a-bove the skies. A - MEN.

2 In lowliness and meekness
   May we from day to day
Still in our Master's Footsteps
   Press on our heavenward way ;
O make us, blessed Master,
   Pure, even as Thou art pure,
And grant as faithful servants
   We to the end endure !—CHO.

3 Bright Angels hover round us,
   And saints before the Throne
Make ceaseless intercession
   That sin may be o'erthrown ;

They, like to us once tempted,
   The tempter overcame,
In strength of the Almighty,
   In power of Jesus' Name.—CHO.

4 Oh, joy within the vineyard
   To labour for the Lord,
Joy on this happy feast-day
   To praise with one accord ;
Joy of all joys the greatest
   To hear Him say, "Well done !
Rest, good and faithful servant,
   Thy heavenly Crown is won !"—CHO.

287[*]

Joyous.

SCHUMANN.
C. M. with Chorus.

Let ev' ry heart rejoice and sing, Let cho-ral anthems rise; Let old and young to-

CHORUS.

ge-ther bring To God their sa - cri-fice. For He is good; the Lord is good,

And kind are all His ways; With songs and honours sounding loud, The Lord Jehovah praise.

While the rocks and the rills, while the vales and the hills, A glo-rious an-them raise;

Let all pro-long their grateful song, And the God of our fathers praise. A-MEN.

2 He bids the sun to rise and set;
In heaven His power is known;
And earth subdued to Him shall yet
Bow low before His throne.
CHO.— For He is good, &c.

Also the following:

329. Above the clear blue sky
498. Brightly gleams our banner.
326. Hosanna we sing, like the children.

327. Come, praise your Lord and Saviour.
324. Come sing with holy gladness.
409. We plough the fields and scatter.

[*] *May be used on other occasions.*

General Hymns.

288 [284]

ZOAN.
7s. 6s. D.

Moderate.

O word of God in - car - nate, O wis - dom from on high,

O truth unchang'd, un - chang - ing, O Light of our dark sky!

We praise Thee for the ra - diance That from the hal - low'd page,

A lan - tern to our foot - steps, Shines on from age to age. A-MEN.

2 The Church from her dear Master
 Received the gift divine,
And still that light she lifteth
 O'er all the earth to shine.
It is the golden casket
 Where gems of truth are stored,
It is the heaven-drawn picture
 Of Christ the living Word.

3 It floateth like a banner
 Before God's host unfurl'd,
It shineth like a beacon
 Above the darkling world;
It is the chart and compass
 That o'er life's surging sea,
Mid mists, and rocks, and quicksands
 Still guide, O Christ, to Thee.

4 O make Thy Church, dear Saviour
 A lamp of burnish'd gold,
To bear before the nations
 Thy true light as of old;
O teach Thy wandering pilgrims
 By this their path to trace,
Till, clouds and darkness ended,
 They see Thee face to face.

289

WARFARE.
6s. 6s.

Faith - ful Shep-herd, feed me In the pas - tures green ;

Faith - ful Shep-herd, lead me Where Thy steps are seen. A - MEN.

2 Hold me fast, and guide me
In the narrow way :
So with Thee beside me,
I shall never stray.

3 Daily bring me nearer
To the heavenly shore ;
May my faith grow clearer,
May I love Thee more.

4 Hallow every pleasure,
Every gift and pain ;
Be Thyself my Treasure,
Though none else I gain

5 Give me joy or sadness,
This be all my care,
That eternal gladness
I with Thee may share.

6 Day by day prepare me
As Thou seest best,
Then let angels bear me
To Thy promised rest.

290

S. CYRIL.
C. M.

Be - fore the Throne of God a - bove The glo - rious an - gels stand ;

Their on - ly wish, their on - ly joy, To do their Lord's command. A - MEN.

2 Some ever bow before His face,
And praise Him all day long.
And sing in never-ending strains
Their blessed joyous song.

3 These holy Angels never choose,
And never wish nor ask
For other work than what God gives
To be their daily task.

4 And we must like the Angels be—
Not choosing good or ill,
But humbly striving day by day
To do God's holy will.

291

Mont Dol.
12s. 9s.

We are sol - diers of Christ, Who is migh - ty to save, And His
ban - ner the Cross is un - furled; We are pledg'd to be faith - ful and
stead - fast and brave Against Sa - tan, the flesh, and the world. A - MEN.

2 We are brothers and comrades, we stand side by side,
And our faith and our hope are the same;
And we think of the Cross on which Jesus has died.
When we bear the reproach of His Name.

3 We will watch ready armed if the tempter draw near,
If he come with a frown or a smile;
We will heed not his threats, nor his flatteries hear,
Nor be taken by storm nor by wile.

4 For the world's love we live not, its hate we defy,
And we will not be led by the throng;
We'll be true to ourselves, to our Father on high,
And the bright world to which we belong.

5 Now let each cheer his comrade, let hearts beat as one,
While we follow where Christ leads the way;
'Twere dishonour to yield, or the battle to shun,
We will fight, and will watch, and will pray.

6 Though the warfare be weary, the trial be sore,
In the might of our God we will stand;
Oh, what joy to be crowned and be pure evermore,
In the peace of our own Fatherland!

292

COLLEGE HOUSE.
7s, 5s.

Hear Thy chil - dren's hymn of praise, Lord of earth and sea,

Which our joy - ful voi - ces raise, Fa - ther un - to Thee. A - MEN.

2 Gentle Jesus, Thou didst love
  Little children here ;
  Bid Thine angels guard us well
  From all harm and fear.

3 Blessed Spirit, be Thou near
  When temptations rise ;
  Keep Thy faithful ones from sin,
  Fix their wandering eyes.

4 When the battle's fought and won,
  Weary warfare o'er,
  Angels bright will bear us home
  Safe to heaven's shore.

5 Alleluia ! let us sing
  To the Father, Son,
  With the Holy Spirit blest,
  Ever Three in One.

293

LOWESTOFT.
7s.

Let us sing! The An - gels sing, High a - bove the cloud-less sky,

Where they see their Heav'nly King, In His ho - ly ma - jes - ty. A - MEN.

2 Let us sing ! the children sang,
  When to Sion Jesus rode ;
  And the stately temple rang
  With hosannas to their God.

3 Let us sing ! rejoice, rejoice !
  Jesus listens while we sing,
  Jesus loves an infant's voice,
  And the praises children bring.

4 Let us sing our hymns below !
  Sing at morn, at noon, at even,
  'Till, through Jesus Christ, we go,
  Sweeter songs to sing in heaven.

294 [583]

BELGARD.
7s. 6s.

Work, for the night is com - ing; Work, thro' the morn- ing hours;

Work, while the dew is spark - ling; Work 'mid the spring-ing flowers.

Work, when the day grows bright - er, Work in the glow-ing sun;

Work, for the night is com - ing When man's work is done. A - MEN.

2 Work, for the night is coming,
  Work through the sunny noon ;
Fill brightest hours with labour,
  Rest will come sure and soon :
Give every flying minute
  Something to keep in store :
Work, for the night is coming
  When man works no more.

3 Work, for the night is coming,
  Under the sunset skies ;
While their bright tints are glowing
  Work, for the daylight flies :
Work till the last beam fadeth,
  Fadeth to shine no more ;
Work, while the night is darkening
  When man's work is o'er.

295 [549]

BENEDICT.
7s.

King of Glo-ry! Sa-viour dear! Grant us grace to per-se-vere;

Lead-er of the hosts of God, May we tread where Thou hast trod! A-MEN.

2 Once for Thee, the Crucified,
Many a faithful martyr died,
How can we, Thy children show
All our love for all Thy woe?

3 They for Thee bore axe and wheel,
Fire, and beasts, and piercing steel:
Like them, may we suffer shame,
Pain or loss for Thy dear Name.

4 Bearing calmly for our Lord
Thoughtless jest or spiteful word;
Curbing angry speech and tear,
Strong in Thee to persevere.

5 Persevere, Thy yoke is light;
Persevere, Thy crown is bright;
Persevere, and we shall sing
In the palace of our King!

296

OUR FATHER'S VOICE.
8s, 7s.

Come! our Fa-ther's voice is call-ing, One by one His chil-dren dear;

He will raise the weak, the fall-ing, He the faint-ing heart will cheer. A-MEN.

2 Come! our Shepherd waits to lead us,
He who once for sinners died,
Where the Bread of Heaven will feed us,
Where the living streams abide.

3 Come! the Spirit now will seal us,
Heirs of God for evermore;
Strong to help, and kind to heal us,
When our souls are weak and sor

4 Come! our King Himself will arm us,
For the fight we must endure;
'Neath His shield, when foes alarm us,
He will keep our life secure.

5 Come! the Cross, our banner glorious,
Onward guides the host of God;
We may march, in hope victorious,
By the path our Saviour trod.

297

THEODOSIA.
C. M.

Fa - ther of love, our Guide and Friend, Oh, lead us gent - ly on,

Un - til life's tri - al - time shall end, And heavenly peace be won. A - men.

2 We know not what the path may be,
  As yet by us untrod;
  But we can trust our all to Thee,
  Our Father and our God.

3 If called, like Abraham's child, to climb
  The hill of sacrifice;
  Some angel may be there in time,
  Deliverance shall arise.

4 Or if some darker lot be good,
  Oh, teach us to endure

The sorrow, pain, and solitude,
  That make the spirit pure.

5 Christ by no flowery pathway came,
  And we His followers here,
  Must do Thy will, and praise Thy Name,
  In hope, and love, and fear.

6 And till in Heaven we sinless bow,
  And faultless anthems raise,
  O Father, Son, and Spirit, now
  Accept our feeble praise.

298

WIMBLETON.
7s. 6s.

Look - ing up - ward ev - ery day, Sun - shine on our fac - es;

Press-ing on-ward ev - ery day Towards the heavenly pla - ces. A - MEN.

2 Growing every day in awe,
  For Thy Name is holy;
  Learning every day to love
  With a love more lowly.

3 Walking every day more close
  To our Elder Brother;
  Growing every day more true
  Unto one another.

4 Leaving every day behind
  Something which might hinder;
  Running swifter every day,
  Growing purer, kinder.

5 Lord, so pray we every day
  Hear us in Thy pity,
  That we enter in at last,
  To the Holy City.

299

EUNICE.
10s.

God will take care of you. All thro' the day Je - sus is near you to

keep you from ill; Wak-ing or rest-ing, at work or at play, Je - sus is

with you, and watching you still. AMEN.

2 He will take care of you. All through
the night
Jesus, the Shepherd, His faithful one
keeps;
Darkness to Him is the same as the light,
He never slumbers and He never sleeps.

3 He will take care of you. All through
the year,
Crowning each day with His kindness
and love,
Sending you blessings, and shielding from
fear,
Leading you on to the bright home above.

4 He will take care of you. Yes; to the end
Nothing can alter His love for His own;
Children, be glad that you have such a Friend;
He will not leave you one moment alone.

300

PERSEVERANTIA.
7s. 6s. D.

My Lord, in glo - ry reign-ing, Up - on the glass-y sea,

By an - gel hosts sur -round - ed, Is think-ing still on me.

My heart for joy is dan - cing, My lamp is burn-ing clear;

The Bride-groom bids me en - ter, If I but per - se - vere. A - MEN.

2 My Lord a land is ruling,
  The land of pure delight,
Whence hate and might are banished,
  And all is love and light.
What though my lot be lowly,
  What though my way be drear;
'T is mine, 'tis mine, that kingdom,
  If I but persevere.

3 My Lord a home is building,
  A mansion passing fair,
Of pearl and gold all burnished,
  Of jewels, costly, rare;

A home where nothing lacketh,
  Away with doubt, and fear!
'T is mine, 't is mine, that mansion,
  If I but persevere.

4 My Lord a song is teaching
  The Angels' choirs on high:
They strike their harps and cymbals,
  And sound the psaltery.
A song to greet the wanderer,
  To Heaven's gate drawing near;
'T is mine, 'tis mine, the welcome,
  If I but persevere.

301

GOLDEN DAYS.
8s, 7s.

Hope on, hope on, the gold-en days Are not as yet a-dawn-ing,

The mists of night Pre-cede the light And ush - er in the morn - ing. A-MEN.

2 Hope on, hope on, though black the clouds,
Dark shadows intertwining,
  Yet calm and still,
  O'er heath and hill,
The sun shall soon be shining.

3 Hope on, hope on, through frost and snow,
Through trouble, toil and sorrow;

Though wind and rain,
  And tears and pain,
The sun shall pierce to-morrow.

4 Hope on, hope on, though friends be few,
And dark the way before thee,
  A God of love
  From Heaven above
Shall shed His radiance o'er thee.

302 [283]

CHESTERFIELD.
C. M.

Joyful.

Fa - ther of mer - cies! in Thy word What end - less glo - ry shines! For

e - ver be Thy Name a - dored For these ce - les - tial lines. A - MEN.

2 Here the Redeemer's welcome voice,
Spreads heavenly peace around;
And life and everlasting joys
Attend the blissful sound.

3 O may these heavenly pages be
My ever dear delight;

And still new beauties may I see,
And still increasing light.

4 Divine Instructor, gracious Lord,
Be Thou for ever near;
Teach me to love Thy sacred word,
And view my Saviour there.

303

BATTISHILL.
7s.

Cheerful.

Ho - ly Bi - ble! book di - vine, Price-less treas-ure, thou art mine;

Mine to tell me whence I came, Mine to teach me what I am. A - MEN.

2 Mine, to chide me when I rove;
Mine, to show a Saviour's love;
Mine art thou to guide my feet,
Mine, to judge, condemn, acquit.

3 Mine, to comfort in distress,
If the Holy Spirit bless;
Mine, to show by living faith
Man can triumph over death.

4 Mine to tell of joys to come,
Light and life beyond the tomb;
Holy Bible, book divine,
Priceless treasure, thou art mine.

304

GEOFFREY.
P. M.

cres.

p

Light in the East-ern sky, Je-sus re-turn-ing; Light in the

West-ern sky, Je-sus is near; Soon shall the na-tions, His

dim.

Ad-vent dis-cern-ing, Hail Him with glad-ness or see Him with fear:

CHORUS.

p

Lord, by Thy hands that were nail-pierc'd and torn, Lord! by the crown that they

ril.

wove of the thorn, Lord! by Thy Pas-sion in Geth-sem-a-ne, Christ of all ten - der - ness! Plead Thou for me. A - - - MEN.

2 Bright be our lamps, as we watch for the dawning;
Girded our loins, that our strength may not fail;
So as He shines through the mists of the morning
We may be ready to cry Him, "All Hail."
Lord! by Thy hands, etc.

3 Not as at Nazareth, lowly they found Him;
He as the Judge cometh back from the sky;
Borne on the whirlwind of Angels around Him;
Veiling their face from His glory so nigh.
Lord! by Thy hands, etc.

4 Judge of the earth, Who in mercy unfailing,
Offered Thyself as atonement for sin,
In that great day, by Thy love all prevailing,
Grant us the rest of Thy Heaven to win.
Lord! by Thy hands, etc.

305

WOODWARD.
8s, 7s.

Fa - ther, help - less, how shall I Learn to live, and how to die?

Who, O Lord, my guide can be? Who shall lead Thy child to Thee? AMEN.

2 Blessèd Father, Gracious One,
Thou hast sent Thy Holy Son;
He will give the light I need,
He my trembling steps will lead.

3 Through this world, uncertain, dim,
Let me ever lean on Him;
From His precepts wisdom draw,
Make His life my solemn law.

4 Thus in deed, and thought, and word,
Led by Jesus Christ, the Lord,
In my meekness, thus shall I
Learn to live and learn to die.

306

GENTLE SAVIOUR.
7s, 6s. D.

O kind and gen-tle Sav-iour, Who art the chil-dren's Friend,

We pray Thee now re-ceive us, Thy bless-ing on us send.

Our joys and all our sor-rows, Thou will-est we should bring,

And lay them all be-fore Thee, Our good and gracious King. A-MEN.

2 To Thee of old their children
   The people came and brought;
From Thee Thy grace and favour
   For little ones they sought;
And Thou didst not forbid them,
   For Thou art good and kind;
In Thee a loving Saviour
   May we, Thy children, find.

3 Let not our ways and doings
   Dishonour Thy dear Name,
Nor words, nor deeds of evil
   Our Christian calling shame.
Grant us Thy grace, that boldly
   We may our Lord confess;
While for all gifts Thou givest
   Thy Holy Name we bless.

307

Moderate.

ADORATION.
6s. 5s. D.

Hail the Cross of Je-sus; Lift it up on high: Hail the migh-ty Sig - nal,

Pointing to the sky! Hail the Guide of pil-grims,Through the des-ert drear!

Hail the Sign of Je - sus, Chas-ing far our fear! A - MEN.

2 God forbid we glory,
   Save in that blest Sign—
Sign of Him who saved us
   Through His love divine.
Hail the Cross of Jesus,
   Lifted up on high!
Hail the mighty Signal,
   Pointing to the sky!

3 Stands the Cross of Jesus
   Foremost in the fight,
Drawing ever all men
   By Its wondrous might.
Hail the Cross of Jesus,
   Lifted up on high!
Hail the mighty Standard,
   Pointing to the sky!

4 See! It moveth onward:
   Gladly follow we:
Wheresoe'er It goeth
   Should Christ's soldiers be.
Hail the Cross of Jesus,
   Lifted up on high!
Hail the mighty Standard,
   Pointing to the sky!

5 Lo! It reacheth Jordan,
   Cleaves the surging wave,
Lighteth up the portals
   Of the opening grave.
Hail the Cross of Jesus,
   Lift It up on high!
Hail the guide of pilgrims,
   Pointing to the sky!

6 Then, O then, what glory
   Shines upon our eyes,
From the sunny pastures
   Spread in Paradise!
Lo! the Cross of Jesus,
   Pointing to the sky,
Hath His children guided
   Home to victory.

308 [442]

Moderate.

TRUST.
8s. 7s.

Sa - viour, source of ev - ery bless-ing, Tune my heart to grateful lays;

Streams of mer - cy nev - er ceas-ing, Call for ceaseless songs of praise. A-MEN.

2 Teach me some melodious measure,
    Sung by raptured saints above;
Fill my soul with sacred pleasure,
    While I sing redeeming love.

3 Thou did'st seek me when a stranger,
    Wandering from the fold of God;

    Thou to save my soul from danger,
    Didst redeem me with Thy blood.

4 By Thy hand restored, defended,
    Safe through life thus far I've come;
· Safe, O Lord, when life is ended,
    Bring me to my heavenly home.

309

Quietly.

S. RAPHAEL.
7s. 5.

Je - sus, when He left the sky, And for sin - ners came to die,

In His mer - cy passed not by Lit - tle ones like me. A-MEN.

2 Mothers then the Saviour sought
In the places where He taught,
And to Him their children brought—
    Little ones like me.

3 Did the Saviour say them nay?
No, He kindly bade them stay;
Suffered none to turn away
    Little ones like me.

4 'Twas for them His life He gave,
To redeem them from the grave;
Jesus able is to save
    Little ones like me.

5 Children, then, should love Him too,
Strive His holy will to do,
Pray to Him, and praise Him too—
    Little ones like me.

310 [335]   HOLLINGSIDE.

Moderate.   7s. D.

Je - sus, Lov - er of my soul, Let me to Thy bo - som fly,

While the near - er wa - ters roll, While the tem - pest still is high;

Hide me, O my Sa - viour, hide, Till the storm of life be past;

Safe in - to the ha - ven guide, O re - ceive my soul at last. A-MEN.

2 Other refuge have I none,
   Hangs my helpless soul on Thee;
 Leave, ah! leave me not alone,
   Still support and comfort me:
 All my trust on Thee is stay'd;
   All my help from Thee I bring;
 Cover my defenceless head
   With the shadow of Thy wing.

3 Plenteous grace with Thee is found,
   Grace to cover all my sin;
 Let the healing streams abound,
   Make and keep me pure within:
 Thou of life the fountain art,
   Freely let m take of Thee:
 Spring Thou up within my heart,
   Rise to all eternity.

311 [336]

Quietly.

REDHEAD, No. 76.
Six 7s.

Rock of A - ges, cleft for me, Let me hide my - self in Thee: Let the wa - ter

and the blood, From Thy riv - en side which flow'd, Be of sin the dou - ble cure,

Cleanse me from its guilt and power. A - MEN.

2 Not the labours of my hands
  Can fulfil Thy law's demands;
  Could my zeal no respite know,
  Could my tears for ever flow,
  All for sin could not atone,
  Thou must save, and Thou alone.

3 Nothing in my hand I bring:
  Simply to Thy Cross I cling;
  Naked, come to Thee for dress;
  Helpless, look to Thee for grace:
  Foul, I to the fountain fly;
  Wash me, Saviour, or I die.

4 While I draw this fleeting breath,
  When my eyelids close in death,
  When I soar through tracts unknown,
  See Thee on Thy judgment throne,
  Rock of Ages, cleft for me,
  Let me hide myself in Thee.

312 [433]

Moderate.

S. PETER.
C. M.

How sweet the Name of Je - sus sounds In a be - liev - er's ear!

It soothes his sor-rows, heals his wounds, And drives a - way his fear. A-MEN.

2 It makes the wounded spirit whole,
  And calms the troubled breast;
  'Tis manna to the hungry soul,
  And to the weary rest.

3 Dear Name, the rock on which I build
  My shield and hiding-place,
  My never-failing treasury, filled
  With boundless stores of grace.

4 Jesus! my Shepherd, Husband, Friend,
  My Prophet, Priest and King,

My Lord, my life, my way, my end,—
  Accept the praise I bring.

5 Weak is the effort of my heart,
  And cold my warmest thought:
  But when I see Thee as Thou art,
  I'll praise Thee as I ought.

6 Till then I would Thy love proclaim
  With every fleeting breath;
  And may the music of Thy Name
  Refresh my soul in death.

313

GARDINER.
7s. 6s. D.

Moderate.

Go when the morn-ing shi-neth, Go when the moon is bright;

Go when the day de - cli - neth, Go in the hush of night;

Go with pure heart and feel - ing, Cast earth-ly thoughts a - way,

And in thy cham - ber kneel-ing, Do thou in se-cret pray. A-MEN.

2 Remember all who love thee;
   All who are loved by thee;
Pray, too, for those who hate thee,
   If any such there be.
Then for thyself in meekness,
   A blessing humbly claim;
And link with each petition
   Thy great Redeemer's Name.

3 But if 'tis e'er denied thee
   In solitude to pray,
Should holy thoughts come o'er thee,
   When friends are round the way—
E'en then, in silence breathing,
   The spirit, rais'd above,
Will reach the throne of glory,
   Of mercy, truth, and love.

4 When'er thou pin'st in sickness
   Before His foot-stool fall;
Remember in thy gladness,
   His love who gave thee all.
Oh! not a joy or blessing
   With this we can compare,
The power which He has given,
   To approach His throne in prayer.

314

Moderate.

EMMAUS.
C. M.

There is an Eye that ne - ver sleeps Be - neath the wing of night;

There is an Ear that ne - ver shuts When sink the beams of light. A - MEN.

2 There is an Arm that never tires
  When human strength gives way;
There is a Love that never fails
  When earthly loves decay.

3 That Eye is fixed on Seraph throngs;
  That Arm upholds the sky;
That Ear is filled with Angel songs;
  That Love is throned on high.

4 But there's a power which man can wield,
  When mortal aid is vain,
That Eye, that Arm, that Love to reach,
  That listening Ear to gain.

5 That power is Prayer, which soars on high
  Through Jesus to the throne,
And moves the Hand which moves the world
  To bring salvation down.

315

Moderate.

PRAYER.
8s. 6s. 8s.

Lord of my life whose ten - der care Hath led me on till now,

Here low - ly, at the hour of prayer, Be - fore Thy throne I bow;

I bless Thy gracious hand, and pray For - giveness for an - oth - er day. A - MEN.

2 Oh, may I daily, hourly strive
   In heavenly grace to grow;
   To Thee and to Thy glory live,
   Dead to all else below;
   Tread in the path my Saviour trod,
   Though thorny, yet the path of God.

3 With prayer, my humble praise I bring,
   For mercies day by day:
   Lord, teach my heart, Thy love to sing,
   Lord, teach me how to pray.
   All that I am and have, to Thee
   I offer through eternity.

316

SURSUM CORDA.
7s. 5s. 7s.

Moderate.

Fold thy hands in prayer, my child, Gent - ly bow thine head;

To our glo - rious God in heaven Chil-dren's prayers are said;

And the An-gels pure and fair Bow be - fore His pres - ence there. A - MEN.

The last two lines to be sung more slowly.

2 Close thine eyes in prayer, my child,
   Close thy roving eyes:
   Wandering looks would fill thine heart
   With all vanities.
   Kneeling to the King of kings,
   Would thou gaze on earthly things?

3 Guard thine heart in prayer, my child,
   Closely guard thine heart,
   Lest with holy, earnest thoughts
   Bad ones have their part:
   When we to our Father pray
   Let us mean the things we say.

317

McKAY.
7s. 6s. D.

Thou bid'st us seek Thee ear-ly, And we shall sure-ly find;

We come, O bless-ed Je - - sus, Our Sav-iour true and kind!

We come in time of glad - ness, We come in hours of grief,

With childhood's joys so tran - sient, With child-hood's sor-row brief. A - MEN.

2 We have not seen the glory
   Which Bethlehem's shepherds saw,
   Nor heard the midnight anthem
   They heard with wondering awe ;
   In rapturous haste they sought Thee,
   The Christ so lowly born ;
   We, too, would seek Thee early
   In life's rejoicing morn.

3 Lord, give us now Thy Spirit ;
   Grant us Thy constant grace,
   Till, having sought Thee early,
   At length we see Thy face ;
   See Thee in cloudless glory,
   The Lamb who once was slain ;
   And join the host of ransomed
   Who follow in Thy train.

318 [476]

Joyful.

VIENNA.
7s.

Songs of praise the An - gels sang, Heav'n with Al - le - lu - ias rang,

When Je - ho - vah's work be - gun, When He spake and it was done. A-MEN.

2 Songs of praise awoke the morn,
When the Prince of Peace was born;
Songs of praise arose, when He
Captive led captivity.

3 Heaven and earth must pass away;
Songs of praise shall crown that day:
God will make new heavens and earth;
Songs of praise shall hail their birth.

4 And shall man alone be dumb
Till that glorious kingdom come?

No; the Church delights to raise
Psalms, and hymns, and songs of praise.

5 Saints below, with heart and voice,
Still in songs of praise rejoice;
Learning here, by faith and love,
Songs of praise to sing above.

6 Borne upon their latest breath,
Songs of praise shall conquer death;
Then, amidst eternal joy,
Songs of praise their powers employ.

319

S. WINIFRED.
8s. 7s.

Moderate.

Hum- ble prais - es, ho - ly Je - sus, In - fant voi - ces raise to Thee:

In Thy mer - cy O re-ceive us! Suf - fer us Thy lambs to be. A-MEN.

2 Blessed Jesus! Thou hast bidden
Babes like us to come to Thee,
Though by Thy disciples chidden,
Thou didst tell them not to flee.

3 Saviour, condescend to feed us;
Richly let Thy mercy flow:
Send Thy Spirit, blessed Jesus!
Light and Life on us bestow.

320 [450]

MILES LANE.
C. M.

Bold.

All hail the power of Je - sus' Name, Let an - gels pros-trate

fall; Bring forth the roy - al di - a - dem, And crown Him,

Last verse. ff

crown Him, crown Him, crown Him Lord of all. A-MEN.

2 Crown Him, ye martyrs of our God,
Who from His altar call;
Extol the Stem of Jesse's rod,
And crown Him Lord of all.

3 Hail Him, the Heir of David's line,
Whom David, Lord did call;
The God Incarnate! Man divine,
And crown Him Lord of all!

4 Ye seed of Israel's chosen race,
Ye ransomed of the fall,

Hail Him who saves you by His grace,
And crown Him Lord of all.

5 Sinners, whose love can ne'er forget
The wormwood and the gall,
Go, spread your trophies at His feet,
And crown Him Lord of all.

6 Let every kindred, every tribe,
On this terrestrial ball,
To Him all Majesty ascribe,
And crown Him Lord of all.

321 [458]

DULCE CARMEN.
8s. 7s. Six lines.

Bold.

Praise, my soul, the King of heav-en, To His feet thy trib-ute bring;

Ransomed, healed, re-stored, for-giv-en, Ev-er-more His prais-es sing;

Al-le-lu-ia! Al-le-lu-ia! Praise the ev-er-last-ing King. A-men.

2 Praise Him for His grace and favour
To our fathers in distress;
Praise Him still the same as ever,
Slow to chide, and swift to bless;
Alleluia! Alleluia!
Glorious in His faithfulness.

3 Father-like, He tends and spares us,
Well our feeble frame He knows;
In His hands He gently bears us,
Rescues us from all our foes;
Alleluia! Alleluia!
Widely yet His mercy flows.

4 Angels in the height adore Him!
Ye behold Him face to face;
Saints triumphant bow before Him!
Gathered in from every race:
Alleluia! Alleluia!
Praise with us the God of grace.

322 [559]

Joyous.

CHESALON.
C. M.

Ho-san-na! raise the peal-ing hymn To Da-vid's Son, and Lord,

With cher-u-bim and ser-a-phim Ex-alt th'In-car-nate Word. A-men.

2 Hosanna! Lord, our feeble tongue
No lofty strains can raise,
But Thou wilt not despise the young
Who feebly sing Thy praise.

3 Hosanna! Master, may we bring
Our offerings to Thy throne:
Not gold, nor myrrh, nor mortal thing,
But hearts to be Thine own.

4 Hosanna! once Thy gracious ear
Approved a youthful throng:
Be gracious now, and deign to hear
Our humble, grateful song.

5 O Saviour, if redeemed by Thee,
Thy Temple we behold,
Thy praises through eternity
We'll sing to harps of gold.

323 [461]

Joyful.

TROYTE, No. 2.

Al - le - lu - ia! Alle - lu - ia! A-MEN.

THE strain upraise of joy and *praise,* Alle | luia!
To the glory of their King
Shall the *ransom'd* | people sing, ‖ *Alle-* | luia! ‖ *Alle-* | luia!
And the *choirs* that | dwell on high,
Shall re-*echo* | through the sky, ‖ *Alle-* | luia! ‖ *Alle-* | luia!

They in the *rest* of | Paradise who dwell,
The blessèd ones with *joy* the | chorus swell, ‖ *Alle-* | luia! ‖ *Alle-* | luia!
The planets beaming *on* their | heavenly way,
The shining constella*tions,* | join and say, ‖ *Alle-* | luia! ‖ *Alle-* | luia!

Ye clouds that onward sweep,
   Ye *winds* on | pinions light,
Ye thunders, echoing loud and deep,
   Ye light*nings,* | wildly bright,
In *sweet* con- | sent unite ‖ *your* Alle- | luia!

Ye floods and ocean billows,
   Ye *storms* and | winter snow,
Ye days of cloudless beauty,
   Hoar *frost* and | summer glow:
Ye groves that wave in spring,
And *glorious* | forests, sing, ‖ *Alle-* | luia!

First let the birds, with *painted* | plumage gay,
Exalt their great Crea*tor's* | praise, and say, ‖ *Alle-* | luia! ‖ *Alle-* | luia!
Then let the beasts of *earth,* with | varying strain,
Join in creation's *hymn* and | cry again, ‖ *Alle-* | luia! ‖ *Alle-* | luia!

Here let the mountains thunder *forth* so- | norous, ‖ *Alle-* | luia!
There let the valleys sing in *gentler* | chorus, ‖ *Alle-* | luia!
Thou jubilant ab*yss* of | ocean, cry, ‖ *Alle-* | luia!
Ye tracts of earth and *conti-* | nents, reply ‖ *Alle-* | luia!

To God, who *all* cre- | ation made,
The frequent *hymn* be | duly paid: ‖ *Alle-* | luia! ‖ *Alle-* | luia!
This is the strain, the eternal strain, the *Lord* Al- | mighty loves: ‖ *Alle-* | luia!
This is the song, the heavenly song, that *Christ,* the | King, approves: ‖ *Alle-* | luia!
Wherefore we sing, both heart and *voice* a- | waking, ‖ *Alle-* | luia!
And children's voices echo, an*swer* | making, ‖ *Alle-* | luia!

Now from all *men* | be outpoured
Allelu*ia* | to the Lord;—
With Allelu*ia* | evermore
The Son and Spi*rit* | we adore.
Praise be *done* to the | Three in One,
   Alle- | luia! ‖ *Alle-* | luia! ‖ *Alle-* | luia!

324

ELLACOMBE.
7s. 6s. D.

Joyous.

Come sing with ho - ly glad - ness, High al - le - lu - ias sing,

Up - lift your loud ho - san - nas, To Je - sus, Lord and King;

Sing, boys, in joy - ful cho - rus Your hymn of praise to - day,

And sing, ye gen - tle maid - ens, Your sweet re - sponsive lay. A-MEN.

2 'Tis good for boys and maidens
   Sweet hymns to Christ to sing,
   'Tis meet that children's voices
   Should praise the children's King;
   For Jesus is salvation,
   And glory, grace, and rest;
   To babe and boy and maiden
   The one Redeemer blest.

3 O boys be strong in Jesus,
   To toil for Him is gain,
   And Jesus wrought with Joseph,
   With chisel, saw, and plane;
   O maidens live for Jesus,
   Who was a maiden's Son;
   Be patient, pure and gentle,
   And perfect grace begun.

4 Soon in the golden City
   The boys and girls shall play,
   And through the dazzling mansions
   Rejoice in endless day;
   O Christ, prepare Thy children
   With that triumphant throng
   To pass the burnished portals,
   And sing th' eternal song.

325

TRISAGION.

Moderate.

6s. 5s. D. with Refrain.

Round the throne of glo - ry, Cir-cling che - ru - bim Raise their hal-low'd voi - ces,

In the sa - cred hymn. True their notes are blend - ed, Loud the strains they raise,

Through the courts e - ter - nal, Rolls the song of praise; Ho - ly, Ho - ly, Ho - ly,

Bless-ed Tri - ni - ty, Heav'n and earth are fill - ed With Thy Ma - jes - ty! A-MEN.

2 Earth hath many voices
　Blended with the sea,
Pealing forth the anthem
　Of their praise to Thee;
Night and day it rises,
　Mingling with the song
Which these sacred singers
　Endlessly prolong.
　　Holy, Holy, Holy, &c.

3 Where the city steeple
　And the village spire
Point each faithful toiler
　To His soul's desire,
There in faith we gather,
　There our homage pay,
Prayer and praise we offer
　On each hallowed day.
　　Holy, Holy, Holy, &c.

4 One our heavenly Father,
　Round whose throne we meet,
One our great Redeemer,
　One our Paraclete;
Bound in living union,
　By one holy tie,
In Thy sacred presence,
　Triune God, we cry:
　　Holy, Holy, Holy, &c.

5 Raise the hymn of triumph!
　Heaven and earth and sea,
Roll your thousand voices
　Forth in harmony!
Voices young and aged,
　Voices grand in song,
Blend them, singers holy,
　Loud the strain prolong.
　　Holy, Holy, Holy, &c.

326 [560]

HOSANNA WE SING.
P. M.

Joyous. In Unison or in Harmony.

1. Ho-san-na we sing, like the chil-dren dear, In the old-en days when the
2. Ho-san-na we sing, for He bends His ear, And re-joices the hymns of His

Lord lived here; He bless'd little children and smil'd on them, While they chanted His praise in Je-
own to hear; We know that His heart will ne-ver wax cold To the lambs that He feeds in His

ru-sa-lem. Al-le-lu-ia we sing, like the chil-dren bright With their
earth-ly fold. Al-le-lu-ia we sing in the Church we love, Al-le-

harps of gold and their rai-ment white, As they fol-low their Shepherd with
lu-ia re-sounds in the Church a-bove; To Thy lit-tle ones, Lord, may such

lov-ing eyes, Thro' the beau-ti-ful val-leys of Par-a-dise.
grace be given, That we lose not our part in the song of heaven. A-MEN.

327 [533]

Joyous.

ALL—*Verses 1 and 4.*

LOCHBIE.
7s. 6s. D.

1. Come praise your Lord and Saviour, In strains of ho - ly mirth: Give thanks to Him, O children,
4. O Lord, with voi - ces blend-ed We sing our songs of praise: Be Thou the Light and Pattern

1. Who lived a Child on earth. He loved the lit-tle child - ren, And called them to His side,
4. Of all our childhood's days; And lead us e-ver on-ward, That, while we stay be - low,

1. His lov - ing Arms em - braced them, And for their sake He died.
4. We may, like Thee, O Je - sus, In grace and wis-dom grow. A-MEN.

Verse 2 for BOYS *only.* *Verse 3 for* GIRLS *only.*

2. O Je - sus, we would praise Thee With songs of ho - ly joy,
3. O Je - sus, we too praise Thee, The low - ly Mai - den's Son:

2. For Thou on earth didst so - journ, A pure and spot-less Boy.
3. In Thee all gen - tlest gra - ces Are gath - ered in - to one.

2. Make us like Thee, o - be - dient, Like Thee, from sin - stains free,
3. Oh, give that best a - dorn - ment, That Chris - tian maid can wear,

2 Like Thee, in God's own tem - ple, In low - ly home like Thee.
3 The meek and qui - et spir - it, Which shone in Thee so fair.

328 [537]

Moderate.

BERNARD.
P. M.

Glo - ry to the Bless - ed Je - sus! Who for us was born,

In the sta - ble, cold and poor, On glad Christ - mas morn. A - MEN.

2 Glory to the Blessèd Jesus!
  Who was crucified
  On Good Friday for our sins;
  Loving us He died.

3 Glory to the Blessèd Jesus!
  Who for sinners lay
  In the tomb, and rose upon
  Happy Easter Day.

4 Glory to the Blessèd Jesus!
  He who is our Way

Went up in a cloud to heaven
  On Ascension Day.

5 Glory to the Blessèd Jesus!
  Who at Whitsuntide
  Sent His Holy Spirit down
  With us to abide.

6 Glory to the Blessèd Jesus!
  We will praise His love,
  All our days on earth below,
  And for aye above.

329 [570]

Joyous.

A-bove the clear blue sky, In heaven's bright a-bode, The An-gel host on

high Sing praises to their God. Al - le - lu - ia!

They love to sing to God their King Al - le - lu - ia! A - MEN.

2 But God from infant tongues
  On earth receiveth praise;
We then our cheerful songs
  In sweet accord will raise:
    Alleluia!
  We too will sing
  To God our King
    Alleluia!

3 O Blessed Lord, Thy Truth
  To us Thy babes impart,
And teach us in our youth
  To know Thee as Thou art.
    Alleluia!
  Then shall we sing
  To God our King
    Alleluia!

4 O may Thy holy Word
  Spread all the world around;
And all with one accord
  Uplift the joyful sound,
    Alleluia!
  All then shall sing
  To God their King
    Alleluia!

330

Riseholme.
8s. 7s. D.

Moderate.

There is no name so sweet on earth, No name so dear in hea - ven,

As that be - fore His won-drous birth To Christ the Sa-viour giv - en.

f and a little faster.

We love to sing un - to our King, And hail Him bles - sed Je - sus!

For there's no word ear ev - er heard, So dear, so sweet as Je - sus. A-men.

2 'Twas Gabriel first that did proclaim
To His most blessèd Mother
That Name which now and evermore
We praise above all other.
We love to sing unto our King,
And hail Him blessèd Jesus!
For there's no word ear ever heard,
So dear, so sweet as Jesus!

3 And when He hung upon the Cross,
They wrote this Name above Him,
That all might see the reason we
For evermore must love Him.
We love to sing unto our King,
And hail Him blessèd Jesus!
For there's no word ear ever heard,
So dear, so sweet as Jesus!

4 So now upon His Father's throne,
Almighty to release us
From sin and pains, He ever reigns
The Prince and Saviour Jesus!
We love to sing unto our King,
And hail Him blessèd Jesus!
For there's no word ear ever heard,
So dear, so sweet as Jesus.

331

Joyous.

INNOCENTS.
7s.

God e - ter - nal, migh-ty King, Un - to Thee our praise we bring;

All the earth doth wor - ship Thee, We a - mid the throng would be. A-MEN.

2 Holy, Holy, Holy! cry
Angels round Thy Throne on high;
Lord of all the heavenly powers,
Be the same loud anthem ours.

3 Glorified Apostles raise
Night and day continual praise;
Hast Thou not a mission too
For Thy children here to do?

4 With the Prophets' goodly line
We in mystic bond combine;
For Thou hast to babes revealed
Things that to the wise were sealed.

5 Martyrs, in a noble host,
Of the cross are heard to boast;
O that we our cross may bear,
And a crown of glory wear.

6 All Thy Church in heaven and earth,
Jesus, hail Thy spotless birth;
Own the God who all has made,
And the Spirit's soothing aid.

332 [550]

S. SAVIOUR
6s. 5s.

Moderate.

Je - sus, high in glo - ry, Lend a listen - ing ear,

When we bow be - fore Thee, Chil-dren's prais - es hear. A-MEN.

2 Though Thou art so holy,
Heaven's Almighty King,
Thou wilt stoop to listen,
When Thy praise we sing.

3 We are little children,
Weak and apt to stray;
Saviour, guide and keep us
In the heavenly way.

4 Save us, Lord, from sinning,
Watch us day by day;
Help us now to love Thee;
Take our sins away:

5 Then, when Jesus calls us
To our heavenly Home,
We would gladly answer,
"Saviour, Lord, we come."

333

HENRY.
8s. 7s. D.

Joyous.

Al - le - lu - ia! thanks and glo - ry, High a - dor - ing praise we bring,

Hearts and voi-ces both up - lift - ed To our crown'd and con-quering King!

Chil-dren in the tem-ple prais'd Thee, Thou the children's praise didst own;

Now let children's praise accepted Reach Thee on Thy ra-diant throne. A-MEN.

2 Alleluia! King, Redeemer,
  Saviour of our Eden lost!
Though but children, sinful children,
  We are Thine by priceless cost;
Though but children, weak and wayward,
  Yet through Thy redeeming love
Washed, forgiven, sealed for glory,
  We shall reign with Thee above.

3 Alleluia! Oh! the mercy!
  Oh! the goodness, love, and grace!
Mercy rich, and free, and glorious,
  Passing bound of time and space!
Let Thy children sing Hosanna,
  Sing and say, in faith divine,
"Such a Saviour, such salvation,
  Such eternal joys are mine!"

4 Alleluia! O most holy,
  O most patient, O most true,
Ever faithful, all-forgiving,
  Still bestowing mercies new!
Day by day has mercy kept us,
  Soul and body kept from ill;
Night by night, in peace descending,
  Cometh mercy, mercy still.

5 Then to Him, the Fount of mercy,
  Jesus Christ, the children's King,
Blessing, honour, thanks, and glory,
  Let His children ever bring.
Let their mighty Alleluia
  Fill the earth from shore to shore,
Till with that new song it mingles,
  Sung in heaven for evermore!

334

TINTERN ABBEY.
7s. 6s. D.

Moderate.

God, who hath made the dai - sies And ev' - ry love - ly thing;

He will ac - cept our prai - ses, And heark-en while we sing.

He says, though we are sim - ple, Though ig - no-rant we be,

"Suf - fer the lit - tle chil-dren, And let them come to Me." A-MEN.

2 Though we are young and simple,
  In praise we may be bold;
The children in the temple
  He heard in days of old.
And if our hearts are humble,
  He says to you and me,
"Suffer the little children,
  And let them come to Me."

3 He sees the bird that wingeth
  Its way o'er earth and sky;
He hears the lark that singeth
  Up in the heaven so high;
He sees the heart's low breathings,
  And says (well pleased to see),
"Suffer the little children,
  And let them come to Me."

4 Therefore we will come near Him,
  And joyfully we'll sing;
No cause to shrink or fear Him,
  We'll make our voices ring:
For in our temple speaking,
  He says to you and me,
"Suffer the little children,
  And let them come to Me."

335

Moderate.

Upward where the stars are burn-ing, Si - lent, si - lent in their turning,

Round the nev - er changing pole; Up-ward where the sky is bright-est,

Upward where the blue is light-est,— Lift I now my long-ing soul. A - MEN.

2 Far beyond that arch of gladness,
  Far beyond these clouds of sadness.
    Are the many mansions fair:
  Far from pain and sin and folly,
  In that palace of the holy—
    I would find my mansion there.

3 Where the Lamb on high is seated,
  By ten thousand voices greeted:
    Lord of lords, and King of kings!
  Son of man, they crown, they crown Him
  Son of God, they own, they own Him,
    With His Name the palace rings.

4 Blessing, honour, without measure,
  Heavenly riches, earthly treasure,
    Lay we at His blessèd feet:
  Poor the praise that now we render,
  Loud shall be our voices yonder,
    When before His throne we meet.

336

PENTECOST.
Six 7s.

Cheerful.

For the beau-ty of the earth, For the glo-ry of the skies,

For the love which from our birth O - ver and a - round us lies;

Christ, our Lord, to Thee we raise This our hymn of grate-ful praise. A - MEN.

2 For the wonder of each hour
  Of the day and of the night;
  Hill and vale, and tree and flower,
  Sun and moon, and stars of light;
  Christ, our Lord, to Thee we raise
  This our hymn of grateful praise.

3 For the joy of human love,
  Brother, sister, parent, child;
  Friends on earth, and friends above,
  Pleasures pure and undefiled;
  Christ, our Lord, to Thee we raise
  This our hymn of grateful praise.

4 For Thy Church that evermore
  Lifts her holy hands above,
  Offering up on every shore
  Her pure sacrifice of love;
  Christ, our Lord, to Thee we raise
  This our hymn of grateful praise.

337

HOSANNA.
7s. 6s. D.

Joyous.

Ho - san-na! loud ho - san - na! From Heav'nly choirs peal, And from the earth's glad bo - som The echoes upward steal, From sacred fanes upspringing, From aisles mid leafy

grove, From in-fant voi-ces tell - ing The mys-te-ry of love. A-MEN.

2 Hosanna! loud Hosannas
  To Mary's Holy Child.
Emmanuel! to dwell with us
  The sinless, undefiled.
Come, kneel in adoration
  While angels hymn His praise,
The Lord of our salvation!
  To Him an anthem raise.

3 Hosanna! loud Hosannas
  Unto the Prince of Peace,
The Wonderful, the Counsellor,
  Who maketh strife to cease.
Now may our joy triumphant
  Unite with songs on high;
And earth in strains exultant
  Her noblest praise employ.

338

Joyful.

CARTER.
8s. 7s.

Day by day we mag-ni-fy Thee, When our hymns in school we raise;

Dai-ly work be-gun and end-ed, With the dai-ly voice of praise. A-MEN.

2 Day by day we magnify Thee—
  When as each new day is born,
On our knees at home we bless Thee
  For the mercies of the morn.

3 Day by day we magnify Thee—
  In our hymns before we sleep;
Angels hear them, watching by us,
  Christ's dear lambs all night to keep.

4 Day by day we magnify Thee
  Not in words of praise alone;
Truthful lips and meek obedience
  Show Thy glory in Thine own.

5 Day by day we magnify Thee—
  When, for Jesus' sake, we try
Every wrong to bear with patience,
  Every sin to mortify.

6 Day by day we magnify Thee—
  Till our days on earth shall cease,
Till we rest from these our labours,
  Waiting for Thy Day in peace!

7 Then, on that eternal morning,
  With Thy great redeemèd host,
May we fully magnify Thee—
  Father, Son and Holy Ghost!

339 [444]

Joyous.

O Saviour, pre-cious Sa-viour, Whom yet un-seen we love,

O Name of might and fa-vour, All o-ther names a-bove;

We wor-ship Thee, we bless Thee, To Thee a-lone we sing;

We praise Thee and con-fess Thee, Our ho-ly Lord and King. A-MEN.

2 O Bringer of salvation,
  Who wondrously hast wrought,
Thyself the revelation
  Of love beyond our thought;
We worship Thee, we bless Thee,
  To Thee alone we sing;
We praise Thee and confess Thee,
  Our gracious Lord and King.

3 In Thee all fulness dwelleth,
  All grace and power divine;
The glory that excelleth,
  O Son of God, is Thine;
We worship Thee, we bless Thee,
  To Thee alone we sing;
We praise Thee and confess Thee,
  Our glorious Lord and King.

4 Oh, grant the consummation
  Of this our song above,
In endless adoration
  And everlasting love;
Then shall we praise and bless Thee,
  Where perfect praises ring,
And evermore confess Thee,
  Our Saviour and our King.

340 [554]

Joyous.

ALLHALLOWS.
C. M. D.

Come, Christian chil-dren, come and raise Your voice with one ac - cord;

Come, sing in joy - ful songs of praise The glo - ries of your Lord.

Sing of the won-ders of His Love, And loud-est prai - ses give,

To Him who left His throne above, And died that you might live. A - MEN.

2 Sing of the wonders of His Truth,
  And read in every page
The promise made to earliest youth
  Fulfilled to latest age.
Sing of the wonders of His Power,
  Who with His own right arm
Upholds and keeps you hour by hour,
  And shields from every harm.

3 Sing of the wonders of His Grace,
  Who made and keeps you His,
And guides you to the appointed place
  At His right hand in bliss.
Sing of the wonders of His Name,
  And Jesus Christ adore;
Him for your Lord and God proclaim,
  And praise Him evermore.

Dear Sa-viour, we ga-ther, our trib-ute to bring, The off'-rings of

love, like the blos-soms of Spring; Our gra - cious Re - deem - er! we

grate - ful - ly raise Our hearts and our voi - ces to

hymn Thy great praise. Hal-le - lu - jah! Hal-le - lu - jah! Ho-san-na to the

Slower

Lord! Hal-le - lu - jah! Hal-le - lu-jah! Ho-san - na to the Lord. A - MEN.

2 When stooping to earth from the brightness of heaven,
Thy blood for our ransom so freely was given,
Thou deignedst to listen while children adored,
With joyful hosannas the Bless'd of the Lord.
             Hallelujah, &c.

3 Those arms which embraced little children of old,
Still love to encircle the lambs of the fold;
That grace which inviteth the wandering home,
Hath never forbidden the youngest to come.
             Hallelujah, &c.

4 Hosanna! Hosanna! Great Teacher, we raise
Our hearts and our voices in hymning Thy praise
For precept and promise so graciously given,
For blessings of earth, and the glories of heaven.
             Hallelujah, &c.

342 [558]

Joyful.

Mehul.
7s. 6s. D., with Refrain.

When, His salvation bringing, To Zi-on Jesus came,
The chil-dren all stood sing-ing Ho-san-na to His Name.
Nor did their zeal of-fend Him, But, as He rode a-long.
He let them still at-tend Him, And smiled to hear their song:
Ho-san-na, Ho-san-na, to Jesus they sang. A-MEN.

2 And since the Lord retaineth
  His love for children still:
Though now as King He reigneth
  On Zion's heavenly hill;
We'll flock around His banner,
  Who sits upon the throne,
And cry aloud, Hosanna
  To David's royal Son:
    Hosanna to Jesus we'll sing.

3 For should we fail proclaiming
  Our great Redeemer's praise,
The stones, our silence shaming,
  Would their Hosannas raise.
But shall we only render
  The tribute of our words?
No, while our hearts are tender,
  They too shall be the Lord's.
    Hosanna to Jesus, our King.

343 [344]

Earnestly.

S. EDMUND.
6s. 4s.

Near - er, my God, to Thee, Near - er to Thee,

E'en though it be a cross That rais - eth me;

Still all my song shall be, Near - er, my God, to Thee,

Near - er, my God, to Thee, Near - er to Thee. A - MEN.

2 Though like a wanderer,
  Weary and lone,
Darkness comes over me,
  My rest a stone;
Yet in my dreams I'd be
Nearer, my God, to Thee,
  Nearer to Thee.

3 There let my way appear
  Steps unto heaven;
All that Thou sendest me
  In mercy given;
Angels to beckon me
Nearer, my God, to Thee,
  Nearer to Thee.

4 Then, with my waking thoughts
  Bright with Thy praise,
Out of my stony griefs
  Altars I'll raise;
So by my woes to be
Nearer, my God, to Thee,
  Nearer to Thee.

5 Or, if on joyful wing,
  Cleaving the sky,
Sun, moon, and stars forgot,
  Upward I fly,
Still all my song shall be
Nearer, my God, to Thee,
  Nearer to Thee.

344

HOLLANDISH AIR.
C. M. D.

Moderate.

As help-less as a child who clings, Fast to his fa-ther's arm.

And casts his weak-ness on the strength That keeps him safe from harm;

So I, my Fa-ther, cling to Thee, And ev-ery pass-ing hour

Would link my earth-ly fee-ble-ness To Thine Al-migh-ty power. A-MEN.

2 As trustful as a child who looks
Up in his mother's face,
And all his little griefs and fears
Forgets in her embrace;
So I to Thee, my Saviour, look,
And in Thy face Divine,
Can read the love that will sustain
As weak a faith as mine.

3 As loving as a child who sits
Close by his parent's knee,
And knows no want while it can have
That sweet society;
So, sitting at Thy feet, my heart
Would all its love outpour,
And pray that Thou wouldst teach me, Lord,
To love Thee more and more.

345

THE DIVINE FRIEND.
8s. 7s. D.

Moderate.

There's no oth-er friend like Je-sus, None so faith-ful, none so true; Though the
waves break wildly o'er us, He will guide us safe-ly through; Storms and tempests
shrink be-fore Him, He can calm them at His will: Je - sus, calm our stormy
passions With Thy wondrous "Peace, be still." A-MEN.

2 There's no other friend like Jesus,
  He who died our souls to save;
  He who dwelt on earth in meekness;
  Healed, and pitied, and forgave.
  Still He pities, still He loves us,
  In His holy, happy home,
  And with voice of gracious mercy,
  Bids the wandering sinner, come.

3 There's no other friend like Jesus,
  Holy angels, chant the song;
  Sing His love and wondrous mercy;
  Children, join the heavenly throng.

Raise the joyful, happy chorus,
  Thank Him for His loving grace,
  Let it be your happy portion
  To proclaim the Saviour's praise.

346 [552]

BUCKLAND.
7s.

Joyful.

Lov - ing Shep-herd of Thy sheep, Keep Thy lamb, in safe - ty keep;

Noth-ing can Thy power withstand, None can pluck me from Thy hand. A-MEN.

2 Loving Saviour, Thou did'st give
Thine own life that we might live,
And the Hands outstretched to bless
Bear the cruel nails' impress.

3 I would praise Thee every day,
Gladly all Thy will obey,
Like Thy blessèd ones above,
Happy in Thy precious love.

4 Loving Shepherd, ever near,
Teach Thy lamb Thy voice to hear,
Suffer not my steps to stray,
From the straight and narrow way

5 Where Thou leadest I would go,
Walking in Thy steps below,
Till before my Father's Throne
I shall know as I am known.

347

PRINCETHORPE.
6s. 5s. D.

Moderate.

Je-sus is our Shepherd, Well we know His voice; How the gentlest whis-per,

Makes our hearts re-joice! E-ven when He chid-eth, Ten-der is His

tone; None but He shall guide us; We are His a-lone. A-MEN.

2 Jesus is our Shepherd;
Guided by His Arm,
Though the wolves may raven,
None can do us harm:
When we tread death's valley,
Dark with fearful gloom,
We will fear no evil,
Victors o'er the tomb.

3 Jesus is our Shepherd;
With His goodness now
And His tender mercy,
He doth us endow!
Let us sing His praises
With a gladsome heart,
Till in heaven we meet Him,
Never more to part.

348

HANFORD.
8s. 4.

Moderate.

Through good re-port and e - vil, Lord, Still gui-ded by Thy faithful Word,

Our staff, our buck-ler, and our sword— We fol - low Thee. A - MEN.

2 In silence of the lonely night,
In the full glow of day's clear light,
Through life's strange wanderings, dark or
      We follow Thee.   [bright,

3 Strengthened by Thee we forward go,
'Mid smile or scoff of friend or foe,
Through pain or ease, through joy or woe,
      We follow Thee.

4 With enemies on every side,
We lean on Thee, the Crucified,
Forsaking all on earth beside,
      We follow Thee.

5 O Master, point Thou out the way,
Nor suffer Thou our steps to stray;
Then in the path that leads to Day,
      We follow Thee.

6 Thou hast passed on before our face;
Thy footsteps on the way we trace;
Oh, keep us, aid us by Thy grace:
      We follow Thee.

7 Whom have we in the heaven above,
Whom on this earth, save Thee, to love?
Still in Thy light we onward move;
      We follow Thee.

349 [667]

TROYTE, No. 1.

Calmly.

A - MEN.

1 My God, my Father, while I stray
Far from my home, on life's rough way,
O teach me from my heart to say,
      " Thy will be done."

2 Though dark my path, and sad my lot,
Let me be still and murmur not,
And breathe the prayer divinely taught,
      " Thy will be done."

3 What though in lonely grief I sigh
For friends beloved no longer nigh,
Submissive still would I reply,
      " Thy will be done."

4 If Thou should'st call me to resign
What most I prize—it ne'er was mine;
I only yield Thee what is Thine—
      " Thy will be done."

5 Renew my will from day to day,
Blend it with Thine, and take away
All that now makes it hard to say,
      " Thy will be done."

6 Let but my fainting heart be blest
With Thy sweet Spirit for its Guest,
My God, to Thee I leave the rest;
      " Thy will be done."

350

All that's good, and great, and true, All that is and is to be,

Be it old or be it new, Comes, O Fa-ther, all from Thee. A - MEN.

2 Mercies dawn with every day,
　Newer, brighter, than before,
And the sun's declining ray
　Layeth others up in store.

3 Not a bird that doth not sing
　Sweetest praises to Thy Name;
Not an insect on the wing
　But Thy wonders doth proclaim.

4 Far and near, o'er land and sea,
　Mountain top and wooded dell,
All in singing, sing of Thee,
　Songs of love ineffable.

5 Fill us then with love divine;
　Grant that we, though toiling here,
May, in spirit being Thine,
　See and hear Thee everywhere.

6 May we all, with songs of praise,
　Whilst on earth, Thy Name adore;
Till with Angel choirs we raise
　Songs of praise for evermore.

SECOND TUNE.

S. GURON.

All that's good, and great, and true, All that is and is to be,

Be it old or be it new, Comes, O Fa - ther, all from Thee. A - MEN.

351

Moderate.

PASTOR BONUS.
6s. 5s. D.

Christ, who once a - mongst us As a child did dwell, Is the children's

Sa - viour, And He loves us well; If we keep our prom-ise Made Him at the

Font, He will be our Shep-herd, And we shall not want. A-MEN.

2 Then it was they laid us
    In those tender Arms,
Where the lambs are carried
    Safe from all alarms;
If we trust His promise,
    He will let us rest
In His Arms forever,
    Leaning on His Breast.

3 Though we may not see Him
    For a little while,
We shall know He holds us,
    Often feel His smile;
Death will be to slumber
    In that sweet embrace,
And we shall awaken
    To behold His Face.

4 He will be our Shepherd
    After as before,
By still heavenly waters
    Lead us evermore;
Make us lie in pastures
    Beautiful and green,
Where none thirst or hunger,
    And no tears are seen.

5 Jesus, our good Shepherd,
    Laying down Thy life,
Lest Thy sheep should perish
    In the cruel strife,
Help us to remember
    All Thy love and care,
Trust in Thee, and love Thee,
    Always, everywhere.

352

Tenderly.

PALMER.
5s. 4s. D.

1. Rest of the wea - ry, Joy of the sad; Hope of the
2. Pil - low, where, ly - ing, Love rests its head; Peace of the

drea - ry, Light of the glad; Home of the stran - ger, Strength to the
dy - ing, Life of the dead; Path of the low - ly, Prize at the

p dim.

end; Re-fuge from dan - ger, Sa - viour and Friend.
end; Breath of the ho - ly, Sa - viour and Friend. A - MEN.

3 When my feet stumble, I'll to Thee cry;
Crown of the humble, cross of the high:
When my steps wander, over me bend,
Truer and fonder, Saviour and Friend.

4 Ever confessing Thee, I will raise
Unto Thee blessing, glory, and praise:—
All my endeavour, world without end,
Thine to be ever, Saviour and Friend.

353

S. OSWALD.
8s. 7s.

Moderate.

Ho - ly Fa - ther, Thou hast taught me I should live to Thee a - lone;

Year by year Thy hand hath brought me On through dangers oft un-known. A-MEN.

2 When I wandered, Thou hast found me;
When I doubted, sent me light;
Still Thine Arm has been around me,
All my paths were in Thy sight.

3 In the world will foes assail me,
Craftier, stronger far than I.
And the strife may never fail me,
Well I know, before I die.

4 Therefore, Lord, I come believing
Thou canst give the power I need;
Through the prayer of faith, receiving
Strength—the Spirit's strength indeed.

5 I would trust in Thy protection,
Wholly rest upon Thine Arm,
Follow wholly Thy direction,
Thou mine only Guard from harm.

6 Keep me from mine own undoing;
Let me turn to Thee when tried,
Still my footsteps, Father, viewing,
Keep me ever at Thy side.

354 [511]

PILGRIM BAND.
7s. 6s. D.

Joyful.

O hap-py band of pil-grims, If on-ward ye will tread,

With Je-sus as your fel-low, To Je-sus as your Head;

O hap-py if ye la-bour As Je-sus did for men;

O hap-py if ye hun-ger As Je-sus hungered then. A-MEN.

2 The Cross that Jesus carried
  Was carried as your due;
The Crown that Jesus weareth
  He weareth it for you.
The trials that beset you,
  The sorrows ye endure,
The manifold temptations,
  That death alone can cure;

3 What are they but His jewels
  Of right celestial worth?
What are they but the ladder
  Set up to heaven on earth?
O happy band of pilgrims,
  Look upward to the skies,
Where such a light affliction
  Shall win so great a prize.

355 [452]

Joyous.

PLEYEL'S HYMN.
7s.

Chil-dren of the heavenly King, As ye jour-ney sweet-ly sing:

Sing your Saviour's wor-thy praise, Glorious in His works and ways. A-MEN.

2 We are travelling home to God,
  In the way the fathers trod:
  They are happy now, and we
  Soon their happiness shall see.

3 Banish'd once, by sin betray'd,
  Christ our Advocate was made;

Pardon'd now, no more we roam,
Christ conducts us to our home.

4 Lord, obediently we go,
  Gladly leaving all below;
  Only Thou our Leader be,
  And we still will follow Thee.

356

Joyful.

HULLAH.
6s. 5s. D.

We are lit-tle pilgrims, We are strangers here, We are hast'ning onward

Harmony.   *rall.*   *a tempo.*

To our Home most dear; All that stays our progress We will cast aside, Sinful lusts and

rall.

passions, E-vil tho'ts and pride. A-MEN.

2 Ofttimes we are weary,
  Oftentimes in pain;
  But the hope of Heaven
  Cheers our souls again.
  Grief will there be rapture,
  Toil will there be rest;
  Each day brings us nearer
  To our Home most blest.

357 [432]

WESTON.
8s. 7s. D.

Moderate.

Ory. Ped.

Love di-vine, all love ex-cel-ling, Joy of heaven, to earth come down!

Fix in us Thy hum-ble dwell-ing, All Thy faith-ful mer-cies crown.

Je-sus, Thou art all com-pas-sion, Pure un-bound-ed love Thou art;

Vis-it us with Thy sal-va-tion, En-ter ev-ery trembling heart. A-MEN.

2 Breathe, O breathe Thy loving Spirit
 Into every troubled breast;
Let us all in Thee inherit,
 Let us find Thy promised rest;
Take away the love of sinning,
 Alpha and Omega be,—
End of faith, as its beginning,
 Set our hearts at liberty.

3 Come, Almighty to deliver,
 Let us all Thy grace receive;
Suddenly return, and never,
 Never more Thy temples leave.
Thee we would be always blessing;
 Serve Thee as Thy hosts above;
Pray, and praise Thee without ceasing,
 Glory in Thy perfect love.

4 Finish then Thy new creation,
 Pure and spotless let us be:
Let us see Thy great salvation,
 Perfectly restored in Thee.
Changed from glory into glory,
 Till in heaven we take our place:
Till we cast our crowns before Thee,
 Lost in wonder, love, and praise.

358

Joyously.

ANGEL VOICES.
7s. 6s. D.

I love to hear the sto-ry Which an-gel voi-ces tell,

How once the King of glo-ry Came down on earth to dwell. A-MEN. *Fine.*

I am both weak and sin-ful, But this I sure-ly know,

The Lord came down to save me, Be-cause He loved me so. *rit. dim.* *D.S.*

2 I'm glad my Blessed Saviour
   Was once a child like me,
To show how pure and holy
   His little ones might be;
And if I try to follow
   His footsteps here below,
He never will forget me,
   Because He loves me so.
      I love to hear the story
         Which Angel voices tell,
      How once the King of glory
         Came down on earth to dwell.

3 To sing His love and mercy
   My sweetest songs I'll raise;
And though I cannot see Him,
   I know He hears my praise;
For He has kindly promised
   That even I may go
To sing among His Angels,
   Because He loves me so.
      I love to hear the story
         Which Angel voices tell,
      How once the King of glory
         Came down on earth to dwell.

359

Amor.
7s. 6s. D.

Moderate.

How dear - ly God must love us, And this poor world of ours,

To spread blue skies a - bove us, And deck the earth with flowers!

There's not a weed so low - ly, Nor bird that cleaves the air,

But tells, in ac-cents ho - ly, His kind-ness and His care. A-MEN.

2 He bids the sun to warm us,
    And light the path we tread;
At night, lest aught should harm us,
He guards our welcome bed:
He gives our needful clothing,
    And sends our daily food;
His love denies us nothing
His wisdom deemeth good.

3 The Bible, too, He sends us,
    That tells how Jesus came,
Whose word can save and cleanse us
From guilt and sin and shame.
O may God's mercies move us
    To serve Him with our powers,
For O how He must love us,
    And this poor world of ours!

360

S. Salvador.
7s.

Smoothly.

All things beau - ti - ful and fair, Earth and sky and balm - y air;

Sun-ny field and sha-dy grove, Gent-ly whis-per, "God is love!" A-MEN.

2 Every tree and flower we pass,
Every tuft of waving grass,
Every leaf and opening bud,
Seem to tell us "God is good"
3 Little streams that glide along,
Verdant, mossy banks among,

Shadowing forth the clouds above,
Softly murmur, "God is love."

4 He who dwelleth high in heaven,
Unto us has all things given;
Let us, as through life we move,
Ever feel that "God is love".

361

SHERBROOKE.
8s. 7s. 7.

Moderate.

One there is a-bove all o-thers, Well deserves the name of Friend;

His is love be-yond a bro-ther's, Cost-ly, free, and knows no end;

They who once His kindness prove, Find it ev-er-last-ing love. A-MEN.

ORG.

2 Which of all our friends, to save us,
Could, or would, have shed His blood?
Christ the Saviour died to have us
Reconciled in Him to God:
This was boundless love indeed!
Jesus is a Friend in need.

3 When He lived on earth abased.
Friend of sinners was His name;
Now above all glory raised,
He rejoices in the same.
Still He calls them brethren, friends;
And to all their wants attends.

4 Oh, for grace our hearts to soften!
Teach us, Lord, at length to love;
We, alas! forget too often
What a Friend we have above;
But, when home our souls are brought,
We will love Thee as we ought.

362 *Moderate.*

CARITAS.
8s. 4s.

One there is a-bove all o-thers, O how He loves! His is love be-

yond a bro-ther's, O how He loves! Earthly friends may fail or leave us,

One day soothe, the next day grieve us, But this Friend will ne'er de-ceive us,

O how He loves! A-MEN.

2 'Tis eternal life to know Him,
    O how He loves!
Think, O think how much we owe Him,
    O how He loves!
With His precious blood He bought us,
In the wilderness He sought us,
To His fold He safely brought us,
    O how He loves!

3 We have found a friend in Jesus,
    O how He loves!
'Tis His great delight to bless us,
    O how He loves!
How our hearts delight to hear Him—
Bid us dwell in safety near Him:
Why should we distrust or fear Him?
    O how He loves!

4 Through His Name we are forgiven,
    O how He loves!
Backward shall our foes be driven,
    O how He loves!
Best of blessings He'll provide us,
Nought but good shall e'er betide us,
Safe to glory He will guide us,
    O how He loves!

363 *Moderate.*

PERRY.
8s. 7s.

God is love; His mer-cy bright-ens All the path in which we rove;

Bliss He wakes, and woe He lightens; God is wis-dom, God is love. A-MEN.

2 Chance and change are busy ever,
  Man decays and ages move;
  But His mercy waneth never;
  God is wisdom, God is love.

3 E'en the hour that darkest seemeth
  Will His changeless goodness prove;
  From the mist His brightness streameth,
  God is wisdom, God is love.

4 He with earthly care entwineth
  Hope and comfort from above;
  Everywhere His glory shineth;
  God is wisdom, God is love.

364

Moderate.

HEAVENLY SHEPHERD.
8s. 7s. Six lines.

Heavenly Shep-herd, guide and feed us Thro' our pil - grim-age be - low;

And by liv - ing wa-ters lead us Where Thy flock rejoic - ing go;

Heavenly Shepherd, Heavenly Shepherd, Thou hast loved us, Thine we are. A - MEN.

2 Lord, Thy guardian presence ever,
  Meekly bending, we implore;
  We have found Thee, and would never,
  Never wander from Thee more.
  Heavenly Shepherd, Heavenly Shepherd,
  Thou hast loved us, Thine we are.

365

POSEN.
7s.

Joyful.

Fa-ther, lead me, day by day, E - ver in Thine own sweet way;

Teach me to be pure and true, Show me what I ought to do. A-MEN.

2 When in danger, make me brave;
  Make me know that Thou canst save:
  Keep me safe by Thy dear side;
  Let me in Thy love abide.

3 When I'm tempted to do wrong,
  Make me steadfast, wise, and strong;
  And when all alone I stand,
  Shield me with Thy mighty hand.

4 When my heart is full of glee,
  Help me to remember Thee,—

Happy most of all to know
That my Father loves me so.

5 When my work seems hard and dry,
  May I press on cheerily;
  Help me patiently to bear
  Pain and hardship, toil and care.

6 May I do the good I know,
  Be Thy loving child below,
  Then at last go home to Thee,
  Evermore Thy child to be.

366 [563]

PERCIVALS.
7s.

Joyful.

Sa-viour, teach me, day by day, Love's sweet les - son to o - bey;

Sweet-er les-son can-not be— Lov-ing Him who first loved me. A-MEN.

2 With a childlike heart of love,
  At Thy bidding may I move;
  Prompt to serve and follow Thee,
  Loving Him who first loved me.

3 Teach me all Thy steps to trace,
  Strong to follow in Thy grace,
  Learning how to love from Thee,
  Loving Him who first loved me.

4 Love in loving finds employ,
  In obedience all her joy;
  Ever new that joy will be
  Loving Him who first loved me.

5 Thus may I rejoice to show
  That I feel the love I owe;
  Singing, till Thy face I see,
  Of His love who first loved me.

367

Moderate.

CLAUGHTON.
8s. 7s.

Je - sus loves me, Je - sus loves me; He is al-ways, al-ways near:

If I try to please Him tru-ly, There is nought that I can fear. A-MEN.

2 Jesus loves me,—well I know it,
  For to save my soul He died:
  He for me bore pain and, sorrow,
  Nailed hands and piercèd side.

3 Jesus loves me,—night and morning
  Jesus hears the prayers I pray;
  And He never, never leaves me,
  When I work or when I play.

4 Jesus loves me,—and He watches
  Over me with loving eye,
  And He sends His Holy Angels,
  Safe to keep me, till I die.

5 Jesus loves me,—O Lord Jesus,
  Now I pray Thee by Thy love,
  Keep me ever pure and holy,
  Till I come to Thee above!

368

Moderate.

HART.
7s.

Christ is mer - ci - ful and mild; He was once a lit - tle child;

He whom heavenly hosts a-dore, Lived on earth a - mong the poor. A-MEN.

2 Thus He laid His glory by,
  When for us He stooped to die;
  How I wonder, when I see
  His unbounded love to me.

3 He the sick to health restored,
  To the poor He preached the word;
  Even children had a share
  Of His love and tender care.

4 Every bird can build its nest;
  Foxes have their place of rest;
  He, by whom the world was made,
  Had not where to lay His head.

5 He who is the Lord most high,
  Then was poorer far than I,
  That I might hereafter be
  Rich to all eternity.

369 [412]

DOMINUS REGIT ME.
8s. 7s.

Joyful.

The King of love my Shepherd is, Whose good-ness fail-eth nev - er;

I noth-ing lack if I am His, And He is mine for ev - er. A-MEN.

2 Where streams of living water flow
My ransom'd soul He leadeth,
And, where the verdant pastures grow,
With food celestial feedeth.

3 Perverse and foolish, oft I stray'd,
But yet in love He sought me,
And on His shoulder gently laid,
And home, rejoicing brought me.

4 In death's dark vale I fear no ill
With Thee, dear Lord, beside me;
Thy rod and staff my comfort still,
Thy Cross before to guide me.

5 Thou spreadst a table in my sight,
Thy unction grace bestoweth,
And O the transport of delight
With which my cup o'erfloweth.

6 And so, through all the length of days,
Thy goodness faileth never;
Good Shepherd, may I sing Thy praise
Within Thy house forever!

370 *Moderate.*

BROCKLESBURY.
8s. 7s.

Yes! for me, for me He car-eth, With a bro-ther's ten - der care,

Yes! with me, with me He shar-eth Ev - ery bur-den, ev - ery care. A-MEN.

2 Yes! o'er me, o'er me He watcheth,
Ceaseless watcheth night and day;
Yes! e'en me, e'en me He snatcheth
From the perils of the way.

3 Yes! for me He standeth pleading
At the mercy-seat above;
Ever for me interceding,
Constant in untiring love.

4 Yes! in me, in me He dwelleth,
I in Him, and He in me;
And my empty soul He filleth,
Here, and through eternity.

5 Thus I wait for His returning,
Singing all the way to heaven;
Such the joyful song of morning,
Such the joyful song of even.

371 [521]

S. ASAPH.
8s. 7s. D.

Boldly.

Through the night of doubt and sor - row, Onward goes the pil-grim band,

Sing - ing songs of ex - pec - ta - tion, Marching to the Promised Land.

Clear be - fore us through the darkness Gleams and burns the guid - ing Light;

Broth - er clasps the hand of brother, Stepping fearless through the night. A-MEN.

2 One the Light of God's own Presence,
O'er His ransom'd people shed,
Chasing far the gloom and terror,
Brightening all the path we tread;
One the object of our journey,
One the faith which never tires,
One the earnest looking forward,
One the hope our God inspires.

3 One the strain the lips of thousands
Lift as from the heart of one;
One the conflict, one the peril,
One the march in God begun;
One the gladness of rejoicing
On the far eternal shore,
Where the one Almighty Father
Reigns in love for evermore.

4 Onward, therefore, pilgrim brothers,
Onward, with the Cross our aid!
Bear its shame, and fight its battle,
Till we rest beneath its shade!
Soon shall come the great awaking;
Soon the rending of the tomb;
Then, the scattering of all shadows,
And the end of toil and gloom!

372 [506]

UNIVERSITY COLLEGE.
7s.

Boldly.

Oft in dan-ger, oft in woe, On-ward, Chris-tians, on-ward go:

Fight the fight, main-tain the strife, Strengthen'd with the bread of life. A - MEN.

2 Onward, Christians, onward go,
  Join the war and face the foe:
  Will ye flee in danger's hour?
  Know ye not your Captain's power?

3 Let your drooping hearts be glad;
  March in heavenly armor clad:
  Fight, nor think the battle long,
  Victory soon shall tune your song.

4 Let not sorrow dim your eye,
  Soon shall every tear be dry;
  Let not fears your course impede,
  Great your strength, if great your need.

5 Onward then in battle move,
  More than conquerors ye shall prove:
  Though opposed by many a foe,
  Christian soldiers, onward go.

373 [510]

VICTORY.
7s. 6s. D.

Boldly.

{ Go for-ward, Chris-tian sol-dier! Be-neath His ban-ner true;
{ The Lord Him-self thy Lead-er, Shall all thy foes sub-due:

His love fore-tells thy tri - als; He knows thine hour-ly need;

He can with bread of hea - ven Thy faint-ing spir - it feed. A - MEN.

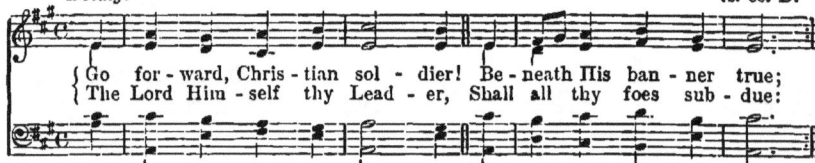

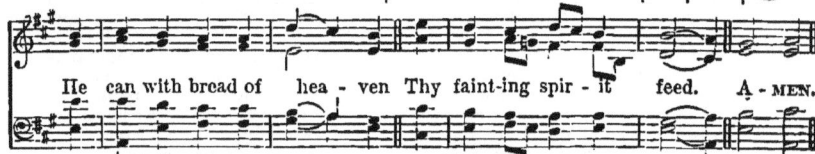

2 Go forward, Christian soldier!
  Fear not the secret foe;
  Far more o'er thee are watching
  Than human eyes can know;
  Trust only Christ, thy Captain;
  Cease not to watch and pray;
  Heed not the treacherous voices
  That lure thy soul astray.

3 Go forward, Christian soldier!
  Nor dream of peaceful rest,
  'Till Satan's host is vanquished,
  And heaven is all possessed;

'Till Christ Himself shall call thee
  To lay thine armor by,
  And wear in endless glory
  The crown of victory.

4 Go forward, Christian soldier!
  Fear not the gathering night,
  The Lord has been thy Shelter,
  The Lord will be thy Light.
  When morn His face revealeth,
  Thy dangers all are past;
  Oh, pray that faith and virtue
  May keep thee to the last!

374 [503]

CHRISTMAS.
C. M.

Earnestly.

A-wake, my soul, stretch every nerve, And press with vigour on; A heavenly

race demands thy zeal, And an immor-tal crown, And an immortal crown. A-MEN.

2 A cloud of witnesses around
  Hold thee in full survey;
Forget the steps already trod,
  And onward urge thy way.

3 'Tis God's all animating voice
  That calls thee from on high,

'Tis His own hand presents the prize
  To thine uplifted eye.

4 Then wake, my soul, stretch every nerve,
  And press with vigour on;
A heavenly race demands thy zeal,
  And an immortal crown.

375 [577]

MABEL.
8s. 7s. 4.

Moderate.

In the vine-yard of our Fa-ther, Dai-ly work we find to do; Scattered

gleanings we may gather, Though we are but young and few; Lit-tle clusters, Lit-tle

clusters Help to fill the garners too. A-MEN.

2 Toiling early in the morning,
  Catching moments through the day,
Nothing small or lowly scorning
  While we work, and watch, and pray;
    Gathering gladly
  Free-will offerings by the way.

3 Not for selfish praise or glory,
  Not for objects nothing worth,
But to send the blessèd story
  Of the Gospel o'er the earth,
    Telling mortals
  Of our Lord and Saviour's birth.

4 Steadfast, then, in our endeavour,
  Heavenly Father, may we be;
And for ever, and for ever,
  We will give the praise to Thee;
    Hallelujah
  Singing, all eternity.

376

Moderate.

ALSTONE.
L. M.

We are but lit-tle chil-dren weak, Nor born in a-ny high es-tate;

What can we do for Je-sus' sake, Who is so high, and good, and great? A-MEN.

2 O, day by day each Christian child
Has much to do, without, within;
A death to die for Jesus' sake,
A weary war to wage with sin.

3 When deep within our swelling hearts
The thoughts of pride and anger rise,
When bitter words are on our tongues,
And tears of passion in our eyes;

4 Then we may stay the angry blow,
Then we may check the hasty word,
Give gentle answers back again,
And fight a battle for our Lord.

5 There's not a child so small and weak
But has his little cross to take,
His little work of love and praise
That he may do for Jesus' sake.

377 [402]

Joyous.

JERUSALEM.
C. M.

Je - ru - sa - lem, my hap-py home, Name e-ver dear to me,

When shall my la-bours have an end? In joy and peace, and thee? A-MEN.

2 When shall these eyes thy heaven-built
And pearly gates behold? [walls,
Thy bulwarks with salvation strong,
And streets of shining gold?

3 There happier bowers than Eden's bloom,
Nor sin nor sorrow know:
Blest seats! through rude and stormy
I onward press to you. [scenes

4 Why should I shrink from pain or woe,
Or feel at death dismay?

I've Canaan's goodly land in view,
And realms of endless day.

5 Apostles, martyrs, prophets, there
Around my Saviour stand:
And soon my friends in Christ below
Will join the glorious band.

6 Jerusalem, my happy home,
My soul still pants for thee;
Then shall my labours have an end,
When I thy joys shall see.

378

HEAVENLY CITY.
8s. 7s. *with Refrain.*

Joyous.

Dai - ly, dai - ly, sing the prais - es Of the Ci - ty God hath made;

In the beauteous fields of E - den Its foun - da - tion stones are laid.

a little slower.

Oh, that I might hear the An - gels, Sing - ing o'er the crys-tal sea,

And a-midst the fields of E - den, Find a home prepared for me! A - MEN.

ORG.

2 All the walls of that dear City
   Are of bright and burnished gold;
   It is matchless in its beauty,
   And its treasures are untold.
   Oh, that I might, &c.

3 There are sounds of many voices
   In the golden streets above,
   Filling all the air with gladness,
   Blended in eternal love.
   Oh, that I might, &c.

4 In those quiet resting places,
   Midst the pastures green and fair,
   Jesus gathers in the homeless,
   And He dwells among them there.
   Oh, that I might, &c.

5 Can we see the happy faces
   Of the dear ones gone before?
   They are ready now to greet us
   When we gain that blessèd shore.
   Oh, that I might, &c.

6 Then the pearly gates, unfolding,
   Never shall be closed again,
   We shall see within the City
   JESUS, 'mid His white-robed train.
   Oh, that I might, &c.

7 Oh, I would my ears were open
   Here to catch that happy strain!
   Oh, I would my eyes some vision
   Of that Eden could attain!
   Oh, that I might, &c.

379 [408]

Cheerful.

EWING.
7s. 6s. D.

Je - ru - sa - lem the gold - en, With milk and hon - ey blest,

Be - neath thy con - tem - pla - tion Sink heart and voice op - prest.

I know not, O I know not What joys a - wait us there,

What ra - dian - cy of glo - ry, What bliss be - yond compare. A-MEN.

2 They stand, those halls of Zion,
   All jubilant with song,
And bright with many an angel,
   And all the martyr throng.
The Prince is ever in them,
   The daylight is serene;
The pastures of the blessèd
   Are decked in glorious sheen.

3 There is the throne of David;
   And there, from care released,
The shout of them that triumph,
   The song of them that feast.
And they, who with their Leader,
   Have conquered in the fight,
For ever and for ever
   Are clad in robes of white.

4 O sweet and blessèd country,
   The home of God's elect!
O sweet and blessèd country,
   That eager hearts expect!
Jesus, in mercy bring us
   To that dear land of rest;
Who art, with God the Father,
   And Spirit, ever blest.

380 [407]

O BONA PATRIA.
7s. 6s. D.

Cheerful

For thee, O dear, dear coun-try, Mine eyes their vig-ils keep;

For ver-y love be-hold-ing Thy hap-py name, they weep,

The men-tion of thy glo-ry, Is unc-tion to the breast,

And med-i-cine In sick-ness, And love, and life, and rest. A-MEN.

2 O one, O only mansion;
    O Paradise of joy!
Where tears are ever banished,
    And smiles have no alloy;
The Lamb is all thy splendour,
    The Crucified thy praise;
His laud and benediction
    Thy ransomed people raise.

3 With jasper glow thy bulwarks,
    Thy streets with emeralds blaze;
The sardius and the topaz
    Unite in thee their rays:
Thine ageless walls are bonded
    With amethyst unpriced:
The saints build up its fabric,
    And the corner-stone is Christ.

4 Thou hast no shore, fair ocean!
    Thou hast no time, bright day!
Dear fountain of refreshment
    To pilgrims far away!
Upon the Rock of Ages
    They raise thy holy tower;
Thine is the victor's laurel,
    And thine the golden dower.

5 O sweet and blessèd country,
    The home of God's elect!
O sweet and blessèd country,
    That eager hearts expect!
Jesus, in mercy bring us
    To that dear land of rest;
Who art. with God the Father,
    And Spirit, ever blest.

381 [679]

S. MARGARET.
6s. D.

Moderate.

There is a bless-ed Home Be-yond this land of woe,

Where tri-als nev-er come, Nor tears of sor-row flow;

Where faith is lost in sight, And pa-tient hope is crown'd,

And ev-er-last-ing light Its glo-ry throws a-round. A-MEN.

2 There is a land of peace,
   Good angels know it well:
Glad songs that never cease
   Within its portals swell;
Around its glorious throne
   Ten thousand saints adore
Christ, with the Father One,
   And Spirit, evermore.

3 O joy all joys beyond,
   To see the Lamb who died,
And count each sacred wound
   In hands and feet and side:
To give to Him the praise
   Of every triumph won,
And sing through endless days
   The great things He hath done.

4 Look up, ye saints of God,
   Nor fear to tread below
The path your Saviour trod
   Of daily toil and woe;
Wait but a little while
   In uncomplaining love,
His own most gracious smile
   Shall welcome you above.

382 [553]

CHENIES.
7s. 6s. D.

Cheerful.

There's a Friend for lit - tle chil - dren, A - bove the bright blue sky,
A Friend who nev - er chan - ges, Whose love will nev - er die:
Un - like our friends by na - ture, Who change with chang-ing years,
This Friend is al - ways wor - thy The precious Name He bears. A-MEN.

2 There's a rest for little children,
   Above the bright blue sky,
Who love the blessèd Saviour,
   And to the Father cry,—
A rest from every trouble,
   From sin and danger free;
There every little pilgrim
   Shall rest eternally.

3 There's a home for little children,
   Above the bright blue sky,
Where Jesus reigns in glory,
   A home of peace and joy;
No home on earth is like it,
   Nor can with it compare,
For every one is happy,
   Nor can be happier there.

4 There are crowns for little children,
   Above the bright blue sky,
And all who look to Jesus
   Shall wear them by-and-by;
Yea, crowns of brightest glory
   Which He shall sure bestow,
On all who loved the Saviour,
   And walked with Him below.

5 There are songs for little children,
   Above the bright blue sky,
And harps of sweetest music
   For their hymn of victory:
And all above is pleasure,
   And found in Christ alone;
Lord, grant Thy little children,
   To know Thee as their own.

383

HUME.
L. M.

We give to God im-mor-tal praise, Mer-cy and truth are all His ways;

Won-ders of grace to God be-long, Re-peat His mer-cies in your song. A - MEN.

2 He built the earth, He spread the sky
And fixed the starry lights on high;
Wonders of grace to God belong,
Repeat His wonders in your song.

3 He fills the sun with morning light,
He bids the moon direct the night;
His mercies ever shall endure,
When sun and moon shall shine no more.

4 He sent His Son with power to save
From guilt and darkness and the grave
Wonders of grace to God belong,
Repeat His mercies in your song.

384

WRANISKY.
8s. 7s.

Chris-tian chil-dren, who would ev-er Tread the safe and nar-row way,

Je-sus' foot-steps long to fol-low, And His gen-tle voice o - bey. A-MEN.

2 As a rough road often trodden,
Smooth and easy doth become,
So the straight and narrow pathway,
Widens, brightens nearer Home.

3 Eye ne'er saw, nor ear hath heard it,
Neither can the heart conceive,
Of the joy which God prepareth,
For His children who believe.

4 Yet the Spirit doth reveal it
Here we have our bliss in part,
Since, our heritage for ever,
God abideth in our heart.

385 *Moderate.*

S. EDMUND.
6s. 4s.

We are but strangers here, Heaven is our Home; Earth is a des-ert drear,

Heaven is our Home. Danger and sorrow stand Round us on every hand, Heaven is our

Father-land, Heaven is our Home. A-MEN.

2 What though the tempests rage?
Heaven is our Home;
Short is our pilgrimage,
Heaven is our Home.
And Time's wild wintry blast
Soon shall be overpast,
We shall reach home at last;
Heaven is our Home.

3 There at our Saviour's side,
Heaven is our Home;
May we be glorified;
Heaven is our Home:
There are the good and blest,
Those we love most and best,
Grant us with them to rest;
Heaven is our Home.

4 Grant us to murmur not,
Heaven is our Home,
Whate'er our earthly lot,
Heaven is our Home.
Grant us at last to stand
There at Thine own Right Hand
Jesus, in Fatherland!
Heaven is our Home!

386 *Moderate.*

REALMS OF THE BLEST.
P. M.

We speak of the realms of the blest, Of that country so bright and so fair;

And oft are its glo-ries con-fess'd; But what must it be to be there? A-MEN.

2 We speak of its pathways of gold,
Of its walls deck'd with jewels most rare,
Its wonders and pleasures untold—
But what must it be to be there?

3 We speak of its freedom from sin,
From sorrow, temptation, and care,
From trials without and within. ·
But what must it be to be there?

4 We speak of its service of love,
The robes which the glorified wear
The Church of the First-born above—
But what must it be to be there?

5 Do Thou, Lord, 'midst pleasure or woe,
For heaven our spirits prepare;
Then soon shall we joyfully know
And feel what it is to be there

387 [398]

Hark! hark, my soul! An-gel-ic songs are swelling O'er earth's green fields and

Org. Ped.

o-cean's wave-beat shore : How sweet the truth those blessed strains are tell-ing

CHORUS.

Of that new life when sin shall be no more. An - gels of Je - sus,

An - gels of light, Sing-ing to welcome the pilgrims of the night. A-MEN.

2 Onward we go, for still we hear them singing,
   "Come, weary souls, for Jesus bids you come;"
  And through the dark, its echoes sweetly ringing,
   The music of the Gospel leads us home.
    Angels of Jesus, etc.

3 Far, far away, like bells at evening pealing,
   The voice of Jesus sounds o'er land and sea,
  And laden souls by thousands meekly stealing,
   Kind Shepherd, turn their weary steps to Thee.
    Angels of Jesus, etc.

4 Rest comes at length, though life be long and dreary,
   The day must dawn, and darksome night be past;
  Faith's journeys end in welcome to the weary,
   And heaven, the heart's true home, will come at last.
    Angels of Jesus, etc.

5 Angels, sing on! your faithful watches keeping;
   Sing us sweet fragments of the songs above;
  Till morning's joy shall end the night of weeping,
   And life's long shadows break in cloudless love.
    Angels of Jesus, etc.

PARADISE.
P. M.

Moderato.

O Par-a-dise! O Par-a-dise! Who doth not crave for rest?

Who would not seek the hap-py land, Where they that loved are blest?

Where loy-al hearts and true ... Stand ev-er in the light, ...

All rap-ture thro' and thro', In God's most ho-ly sight. A-MEN.

2 O Paradise, O Paradise,
  The world is growing old;
Who would not be at rest and free
Where love is never cold?
  Where loyal hearts and true, etc.

3 O Paradise, O Paradise,
  'T is weary waiting here;
I long to be where Jesus is,
To feel, to see Him near;
  Where loyal hearts and true, etc.

4 O Paradise, O Paradise,
  I want to sin no more,
I want to be as pure on earth
As on thy spotless shore;
  Where loyal hearts and true, etc.

5 O Paradise, O Paradise,
  I greatly long to see
The special place my dearest Lord
In love prepares for me;
  Where loyal hearts and true, etc.

6 Lord Jesus, King of Paradise,
  O keep me in Thy love,
And guide me to that happy land
  Of perfect rest above;
    Where loyal hearts and true,
    Stand ever in the light,
    All rapture through and through,
    In God's most holy sight.

389

PARRY.
8s. 7s. D.

Moderate.

to the wondrous

Listen to the won-drous sto-ry; Je - sus left His throne on high;

He. the Lord of life and glory,

He, the Lord of life and glo - ry, Came to dwell on earth and die. Prophets

thro' the long past a-ges, From Cre - a-tion's ear - ly dawn, Christ foretold in

sacred pages, Shadowing forth a glorious morn. A-MEN.

2 Like a vein of metal golden,
  Through the Holy books it ran ;
First obscured in language olden,
  Then a promise clear to man.
"Unto us a child is given,"
  Formed like us in mortal mould;
Sinless as the hosts of heaven,
  Jesus, Shepherd of the fold.

3 Seraphs bright on high adore Him
  In the crystal paven street;
Cast their glittering crowns before Him
  At the blessèd Saviour's feet.

He has closed hell's yawning portals,
  Opening wide the gates of heaven;
He has won for sinful mortals
  Peace, the peace of the forgiven.

390 [399]

REGENT SQUARE.
8s. 7s. Six lines.

Joyous.

Light's a - bode, ce - les - tial Sa - lem, Vis - ion whence true peace doth spring;

Bright-er than the heart can fan-cy, Man-sion of the high-est King:

O how glo-rious are the prais-es Which of thee the Prophets sing. A-MEN.

2 There for ever and for ever
Alleluia is outpoured;
For unending, for unbroken,
Is the feast-day of the Lord;
All is pure and all is holy
That within thy walls is stored.

3 There no cloud nor passing vapour
Dims the brightness of the air;
Endless noonday, glorious noonday,
From the Sun of suns is there;
There no night brings rest from labour,
There unknown are toil and care.

4 O how glorious and resplendent,
Fragile body, shalt thou be,
When endued with so much beauty,
Full of health, and strong and free;
Full of vigour, full of pleasure,
That shall last eternally.

5 Now with gladness, now with courage,
Bear the burden on thee laid,
That hereafter these thy labours
May with endless gifts be paid,
And in everlasting glory
Thou with brightness be arrayed.

391

Moderate.

CRUSADERS' HYMN.
P. M.

Beau-ti-ful Saviour, King of cre-a-tion, Son of God and Son of Man!

Tru-ly I'd love Thee, Tru-ly I'd serve Thee, Light of my soul, my Joy my Crown. AMEN.

2 Fair are the meadows,
Fairer the woodlands,
Robed in flowers of blooming spring;
Jesus is fairer,
Jesus is purer,
He makes our sorrowing spirits sing.

3 Fair is the sunshine,
Fairer the moonlight,
And the sparkling stars on high;

Jesus shines brighter,
Jesus shines purer,
Than all the angels in the sky.

4 Beautiful Saviour,
Lord of the nations,
Son of God and Son of man!
Glory and honour,
Praise, adoration,
Now and for evermore be Thine.

392 [561]

S. LUCY.
D. C. M.

Moderate.

When Je-sus left His Father's throne, He chose an humble birth; Like us, un-hon-our'd

and unknown, He came to dwell on earth, Like Him may we be found be-low, In wisdom's

path of peace; Like Him in grace and knowledge grow, As years and strength increase. A-MEN.

2 Sweet were His words and kind His look,
    When mothers round Him press'd;
  Their infants in His arms He took,
    And on His bosom bless'd.
  Safe from the world's alluring harms,
    Beneath His watchful eye,
  Thus in the circle of His arms
    May we for ever lie.

3 When Jesus into Salem rode,
    The children sang around;
  For joy they pluck'd the palms, and
    Their garments on the ground. [strow'd
  Hosanna our glad voices raise,
    Hosanna to our King!
  Should we forget our Saviour's praise,
    The stones themselves would sing.

393 [567]

MERIEL.
6s. 5s.

Quietly.

Je-sus, meek and gen-tle, Son of God Most High,

Pity-ing, lov-ing Sa-viour, Hear Thy children's cry. A-MEN.

2 Pardon our offences,
    Loose our captive chains,
  Break down every idol
    Which our soul detains.

3 Give us holy freedom,
    Fill our hearts with love;
  Draw us, Holy Jesus,
    To the realms above.

4 Lead us on our journey,
    Be Thyself the Way,
  Through terrestrial darkness,
    To celestial day.

5 Jesus, meek and gentle,
    Son of God Most High,
  Pitying, loving Saviour,
    Hear Thy children's cry.

394 [555]
Quietly.

S. AGATHA.
8s. 7s. SIX LINES.

Gra-cious Saviour, gentle Shepherd, Lit-tle ones are dear to Thee; Gathered with Thine

arms, and car-ried In Thy bos-om may we be; Sweetly, fond-ly, safely tend ed,

From all want and an-ger free. A-MEN.

2 Tender Shepherd, never leave us
From Thy fold to go astray;
By Thy look of love directed
May we walk the narrow way;
Thus direct us, and protect us,
Lest we fall an easy prey.

3 Let Thy holy Word instruct us;
Fill our minds with heavenly light;
Let Thy love and grace constrain us
To approve whate'er is right,
Take Thine easy yoke and wear it,
And to prove Thy burden light.

4 Taught to lisp the holy praises
Which on earth Thy children sing,
Both with lips and hearts unfeigned
May we our thank-offerings bring;
Then, with all the saints in glory,
Join to praise our Lord and King.

395 [569]
Moderate.

HOLYROOD.
S. M.

Fair waved the gold-en corn In Ca-naan's pleas-ant land,

When full of joy some shi-ning morn, Went forth the rea-per-band. A-MEN.

2 To God so good and great
Their cheerful thanks they pour;
Then carry to His temple-gate
The choicest of their store.

3 Like Israel, Lord, we give
Our earliest fruits to Thee,
And pray that, long as we shall live,
We may Thy children be.

4 Thine is our youthful prime,
And life and all its powers;
Be with us in our morning time,
And bless our evening hours.

5 In wisdom let us grow,
As years and strength are given,
That we may serve Thy Church below
And join Thy saints in heaven.

396 [425]

Moderate.

BEATITUDE.
C. M.

Thou art the Way; to Thee a - lone From sin and death we flee:

And he who would the Fa - ther seek, Must seek Him, Lord, by Thee. A - MEN.

2 Thou art the Truth; Thy word alone
True wisdom can impart;
Thou only canst inform the mind,
And purify the heart.

3 Thou art the Life; the rending tomb
Proclaims Thy conquering arm;
And those who put their trust in Thee
Nor death nor hell shall harm.

4 Thou art the Way, the Truth, the Life,
Grant us that Way to know,
That Truth to keep, that Life to win,
Whose joys eternal flow.

397 [565]

Moderate.

SILOAM.
C. M.

By cool Si - lo - am's sha - dy rill How fair the lil - y grows!

How sweet the breath, beneath the hill, Of Sha - ron's dew - y rose! A - MEN.

2 Lo! such a child, whose early feet
The paths of peace have trod,
Whose secret heart, with influence sweet,
Is upward drawn to God.

3 By cool Siloam's shady rill
The lily must decay;
The rose that blooms beneath the hill
Must shortly fade away.

4 And soon, too soon, the wintry hour
Of man's maturer age

Will shake the soul with sorrow's power,
And stormy passion's rage.

5 O Thou, whose infant feet were found
Within Thy Father's shrine,
Whose years, with changeless virtue
Were all alike divine: [crown'd,

6 Dependent on Thy bounteous breath,
We seek Thy grace alone,
In childhood, manhood, age, and death,
To keep us still Thine own.

398

FLOWERS.
P. M.

Quietly.

Up above the bright blue sky, Where the stars are peeping, Farther still than I can

see, Heav'nly watchers o - ver me, Night-ly care are keeping. A - MEN.

2 And, if like the Angels, I
  Could behold around me,
  I should see them come and go,
  Pass from Heaven to earth below;
  And their hosts surround me.

3 All day long, and all night too,
  While I'm safely sleeping,
  Busy on their task of love,
  They are sent from Heaven above
  Faithful vigil keeping.

4 And whilst us, from evil things
  Angels are defending,
  Little children robed in white

Sing before the throne of light,
  In daylight never ending.

5 Jesus took them for His own,
  Made them pure and holy,
  And on earth His gentle love
  Trained them for their Home above,
  Safe from sin and folly.

6 Blessèd Jesus take me too,
  Though I'm weak and lowly,
  Let Thy gentle grace within
  Make my garments white and clean,
  And my spirit holy.

399

GUARDIAN ANGELS.
L. M.

Quietly.

A - round the Throne of God a band Of glo - rious An - gels e - ver stand;

Bright things they see, sweet harps they hold, And on their heads are crowns of gold. A-MEN

2 Some wait around Him, ready still
  To sing His praise and do His will;
  And some, when He commands them, go
  To guard His servants here below.

3 Lord give Thy Angels every day
  Command to guide us on our way,

And bid them every evening keep
  Their watch around us while we sleep.

4 So shall no wicked thing draw near,
  To do us harm or cause us fear;
  And we shall dwell, when life is past,
  With Angels round Thy Throne at last.

400

Bost.
8s. 7s. D

Moderate.

All Thy works, O Heavenly Fa-ther, What Thou biddest them, ful - fil,

Shall not I, Thy child, much ra-ther Sing Thy praise and do Thy will?

Hith-er - to Thy hand hath led me, And hath brought me on my way;

Thou hast clothed me, Thou hast fed me, Thou hast blest me ev - cry day. A-MEN.

2 Lord, 'tis of Thy loving kindness
  That Thy Gospel I have known;
Else I might have sat in blindness,
  Bowing down to wood and stone.
To Thy Font my parents brought me,
  Ere Thy tender love I knew;
And Thy minister has taught me
  What to flee, and what to do.

3 Since my time is like an arrow,
  Hast'ning on without delay:
And Thy gate is straight and narrow,
  Very narrow is the way;
Thou who gav'st Thy Son to save me,
  Send Thy Holy Spirit down;
Make me do as Thou wouldst have me,
  Make me more and more Thine own.

401 [551]

ELEANOR.
7s.

Moderate.

God of mer - cy throned on high, Lis - ten from Thy lof - ty seat;

Hear, O hear our hum-ble cry, Guide, O guide our wan-d'ring feet. A-MEN.

2 Young and erring travellers, we
　All our dangers do not know;
　Scarcely fear the stormy sea,
　Hardly feel the tempest blow.

3 Jesus, Lover of the young,
　Cleanse us with Thy blood divine;
　Ere the tide of sin grow strong,
　Save us, keep us, make us Thine!

4 Let us ever hear Thy voice;
　Ask Thy counsel every day;
　Saints and angels will rejoice,
　If we walk in Wisdom's way.

5 Saviour, give us faith, and pour
　Hope and love on every soul:
　Hope, till time shall be no more;
　Love, while endless ages roll.

402 [304]

Moderate.　　　　　　　　　　　　　　　ANGEL VOICES.
　　　　　　　　　　　　　　　　　　　　　P. M.

An - gel voi - ces e - ver sing - ing Round Thy throne of light,

An - gel harps, for e - ver ring - ing, Rest not day nor night;

Thousands on - ly live to bless Thee, And confess Thee, Lord of might! A - MEN.

2 Thou, who art beyond the farthest
　Mental eye can scan,
　Can it be that Thou regardest
　Songs of sinful man?
　Can we feel that Thou art near us
　And wilt hear us? Yea, we can.

3 Yea, we know Thy love rejoices
　O'er each work of Thine!
　Thou didst ears and hands and voices
　For Thy praise combine!
　Craftsman's art and music's measure
　For Thy pleasure, didst design.

4 Here, Great God, to-day we offer
　Of Thine own to Thee:
　And for Thine acceptance proffer
　All unworthily,
　Hearts and minds, and hands and voices,
　In our choicest melody.

403 [562]

ROSSLYN.
P. M.

Moderate.

I think when I read that sweet sto - ry of old, When

Je - sus was here a - mong men, How He call'd lit - tle chil - dren as

lambs to His fold, I should like to have been with them then. A - MEN.

2 I wish that His hands had been placed on my head,
   That His arm had been thrown around me,
   And that I might have seen His kind look when He said.
   Let the little ones come unto Me.

3 Yet still to His footstool in prayer I may go,
   And ask for a share in His love;
   And if I thus earnestly seek Him below,
   I shall see Him and hear Him above.

4 In that beautiful place He has gone to prepare
   For all who are washed and forgiven;
   And many dear children shall be with Him there,
   For of such is the kingdom of heaven.

5 But thousands and thousands who wander and fall,
   Never heard of that heavenly home;
   I wish they could know there is room for them all,
   And that Jesus has bid them to come.

404

HOPKINS.
P. M.

Moderate.

God hath made the moon, whose beam Shimmers soft o'er hill and stream, Lighting with her sil - v'ry gleam All our lone-ly way; Glides she, with companions bright, Thro' the si-lent

hours of night; Then fades in o - ver-whelming light, Lost in per - fect day. A-MEN.

2 God hath made the glorious sun,
Through his daily course to run;
From the dawn till day is done
Brightly shineth he.
When his circling round is o'er,
And we see him here no more,
He rises on a brighter shore,
Far beyond the sea.

3 God hath sent me here below,
In my daily life to show,
Constant love to friend and foe,
As He showed for me.
When we here have closed our eyes,
Sunk where death's dark ocean lies,
To worlds of glory may we rise,
Lighted, Lord, by Thee!

405

Moderate.

WILFRED.
7s.

Gen - tle Je - sus, meek and mild, Look up - on a lit - tle child;

Pit - y my sim - plic - i - ty; Suf - fer me to come to Thee. A-MEN.

2 Hold me fast in Thine embrace;
Let me see Thy smiling face;
Give me, Lord, Thy blessing give;
· Pray for me, and I shall live.

3 Lamb of God, I look to Thee,
Thou shalt my example be;
Thou art gentle, meek, and mild;
Thou wast once a little child.

4 Let me, above all, fulfil
God my Heavenly Father's will;
Never His good Spirit grieve,
Only to His glory live.

5 Loving Jesus, gentle Lamb,
In Thy gracious hands I am;
Make me, Saviour, what Thou art,
Live Thyself within my heart.

6 I shall then show forth Thy praise,
Serve Thee all my happy days;
Then the world shall always see
Christ, the holy Child, in me.

406 [647]

Cheerful.

HOLY INNOCENTS.
8s. 7s. D.

Heaven-ly Fa - ther, send Thy bless-ing On Thy chil-dren gath-ered here,

May they all, Thy Name con - fess-ing, Be to Thee for e - ver dear:

May they be like Jo-seph, lov-ing, Du - ti - ful, and chaste, and pure;

And their faith like Da-vid, prov-ing, Steadfast un - to death en-dure. A-MEN.

2 Holy Saviour, who in meekness
  Didst vouchsafe a child to be,
Guide their steps and help their weakness,
  Bless and make them like to Thee;
Bear Thy lambs when they are weary
  In Thine arms and at Thy breast,
Through life's desert dry and dreary,
  Bring them to Thy heavenly rest.

3 Spread Thy golden pinions o'er them,
  Holy Spirit from above,
Guide them, lead them, go before them,
  Give them peace, and joy, and love:
Thy true temples, Holy Spirit,
  May they with Thy glory shine,
And immortal bliss inherit,
  And for evermore be Thine.

407

Moderate.

CECIL.
8s. 7s. 4.

Fa-ther, though Thy Name be ho - ly, High and lift - ed up Thy throne,

Still, Thou stoopest to the low-ly, And wilt such with fa-vour own.

Heav'nly Fa-ther, Heav'nly Fa-ther, Let us wor-ship Thee a-lone. A-MEN.

2 Heaven itself cannot contain Thee,
Bright and glorious as Thou art;
Yet a little child may claim Thee
As a dweller in his heart.
Heavenly Father,
Let me not from Thee depart.

3 With Thy gracious presence cheer me,
Keep me in Thy perfect love;
All my journey be Thou near me,
Bring me to Thy home above.
Heavenly Father,
May I all Thy fulness prove!

408

BREIDDEN.
7s. 6s.

* Joyous.

All things bright and beau-ti-ful, All creatures great and small,

*

All things wise and wonder-ful, The Lord God made them all. A-MEN.

* Omit in verse 1.

2 Each little flower that opens,
Each little bird that sings,
He made their glowing colours,
He made their tiny wings.

3 The rich man in his castle,
The poor man at his gate,
He made them, high and lowly,
And ordered their estate.

4 The purple-headed mountain,
The river running by,
The sunset, and the morning
That brightens up the sky.

5 The cold wind in the winter,
The pleasant summer sun,
The ripe fruits in the garden,
He made them every one.

6 The tall trees in the greenwood,
The meadows where we play,
The rushes by the water,
We gather every day;

7 He gave us eyes to see them,
And lips that we might tell
How great is God Almighty,
Who has made all things well.

409

Joyous.

DRESDEN.
7s. 6s. D. with *Chorus.*

We plough the fields, and scat - ter The good seed on the land, But it is fed and wa - tered By God's al-migh-ty hand; He sends the snow in win - ter, The warmth to swell the grain, The breezes, and the sunshine, And

CHORUS.

soft re-freshing rain. All good gifts a-round us Are sent from heaven above,

Then thank the Lord, Oh! thank the Lord, for all His love. A - MEN.

2 He only is the Maker
  Of all things near and far:
He paints the wayside flower,
  He lights the evening star;
The winds and waves obey Him,
  By Him the birds are fed;
Much more to us, His children,
  He gives our daily bread.
    Cho.—All good gifts, &c.

3 We thank Thee, then, O Father,
  For all things bright and good,
The seed-time and the harvest,
  Our life, our health, our food;
Accept the gifts we offer.
  For all Thy love imparts,
And, what Thou most desirest
  Our humble, thankful hearts.
    Cho.—All good gifts &c.

410 Moderate.

STAINER.
7s. 6s. D.

I love the Ho-ly An-gels, So beau-ti-ful and bright;

And though I can-not see them, They're with me day and night:

They watch a-round my bed-side. They see me at my play;

They know my eve-ry ac-tion, They hear the words I say. A-MEN.

2 'Tis God our Heavenly Father,
　Who doth the Angels send,
To guard His little children
　Until their life shall end.
When we are cross and naughty,
　The Holy Angels grieve.
For they are sad when children
　The way of goodness leave.

3 And when I die, the Angels
　Will bear my soul away,
While here my body resteth
　Until the Judgment Day.
They'll bear me gently, softly,
　With loving care most sweet,
And lay me down in safety
　At my Redeemer's feet.

4 There with the Holy Angels,
　And holy men of old,
And all good friends who loved me,
　Too many to be told,
Shall I be with the Angels,
　And all that people bright,
For ever and for ever,
　In God's most glorious light,

5 Among the flowers of Heaven
　That never die or fade,
And far more lovely music,
　Than here on earth is made,
For ever, ever happy
　Together we shall be,
For there our Lord and Saviour
　For ever we shall see.

411

S. HELIER.
7s. 6s. D.

Moderate.

The wise may bring their learn-ing, The rich may bring their wealth,

And some may bring their great-ness, And some bring strength and health;

We, too, would bring our treas-ures, To of-fer to the King;

We have no wealth or learn-ing, What shall we chil-dren bring? A-MEN.

2 We'll bring Him hearts that love Him,
  We'll bring Him thankful praise;
And young souls meekly striving
  To walk in holy ways.
And these shall be the treasures
  We offer to the King,
And these are gifts that ever
  The poorest child may bring.

3 We'll bring the little duties
  We have to do each day,
We'll try our best to please Him
  At home, at school, at play.
And better are these treasures
  To offer to our King,
Than richest gifts without them;
  Yet these a child may bring.

412

CALKIN.
6s. 5s. D.

Moderate.

Je-sus Christ, our Saviour, Once for us a child, In Thy whole be-ha-viour,

Meek, obedient, mild; In Thy footsteps treading We Thy lambs will be, Foe nor danger

dread - ing. While we follow Thee. A-MEN.

2 For all Thou bestowest,
All Thou dost withhold,
Whatsoe'er Thou knowest
Best for us, Thy fold.
For all gifts and graces
While we live below,
Till in heavenly places
We Thy face shall know.

3 We, Thy children, raising
Unto Thee our hearts,
In Thy constant praising
Bear our duteous parts.
As Thy love hath won us
From the world away,
Still Thy hands put on us;
Bless us day by day.

4 Let Thine Angels guide us;
Let Thine Arms enfold;
In Thy Bosom hide us,
Sheltered from the cold;
To Thyself us gather,
'Mid the ransomed host,
Praising Thee, the Father,
And the Holy Ghost.

413

S. MONICA.
7s.

Brightly.

Sweet it is for child like me, Bless - ed Lord, to think of Thee,

For our sake so low - ly made, And in Bethlehem's manger laid. A - MEN.

2 Of the Virgin Mary born,
Thou wilt not an infant scorn,
Wrapped in swaddling clothes wast Thou,
Throned in highest glory now.

3 Laid in helplessness to rest,
Pillowed upon Mary's breast,
Thou, whose everlasting Arms
Fold us all secure from harms.

4 What can little ones like me
Find to offer unto Thee ?
Only of Thy bounty fed,
Suppliants for our daily bread.

5 Saviour, from Thy Word I learn
There are gifts Thou wilt not spurn—
Gifts that little ones may bring
To their Brother and their King.

6 Childlike heart of truth shall be
Dearer gift than gold to Thee,
And its prayer and psalm shall rise
Like sweet incense to the skies.

7 Teach me then Thy steps to trace,
Jesus, full of truth and grace,
All Thy footsteps as a child,
Holy, harmless, undefiled.

414

Moderately quick.

HEAVENLY MESSENGERS.
6s. D.

The Ho - ly An - gels sing, Through all the end-less days,

One nev - er - end - ing song Of glad tri - um - phant praise.

The Ho - ly An - gels come To help us on our way;

Slow.

Ye bles-sed ones! for-bear, And close be - side us stay. A-MEN.

2 Forbear with all our sins,
  Our wayward selfish will;
Our penitence accept,
  And guide and bless us still.
"Heirs of Salvation" made
  Within His Holy Place,
The Angels now behold
  Our Heavenly Father's Face!

3 They worship, evermore
  On His Eternal Throne,
The perfect God and Man,
  The sole Begotten One.
Yet, day and night they guard
  His little ones from ill,
And by their works of love,
  They do His perfect will.

4 O gracious Father! grant
  That we, so loved and blest,
Like them, from praise and love
  May never, never rest.
Now to the Lamb, once slain,
  Blessing and thanks be given,
By Angels and by men,
  On earth, as, aye, in Heaven!

415 [540]

Joyful.

IRBY.
8s. 7s. 7.

Once in roy-al Da-vid's ci-ty Stood a low-ly cat-tle shed,

Where a moth-er laid her Ba-by, In a man-ger for His bed:

Ma-ry was that mother mild, Je-sus Christ her lit-tle Child. A-MEN.

2 He came down to earth from heaven,
  Who is God and Lord of all,
And His shelter was a stable,
  And His cradle was a stall;
With the poor, the mean, and lowly,
Lived on earth our Saviour Holy.

3 And, through all His wondrous childhood,
  He would honour, and obey,
Love, and watch the lowly maiden
  In whose gentle arms He lay;
Christian children all must be
Mild, obedient, good as He.

4 For He is our childhood's Pattern,
  Day by day like us He grew,
He was little, weak, and helpless,
  Tears and smiles like us He knew;
And He feeleth for our sadness,
And He shareth in our gladness.

5 And our eyes at last shall see Him,
  Through His own redeeming love,
For that Child so dear and gentle
  Is our Lord in heaven above;
And He leads His children on
To the place where He is gone.

6 Not in that poor lowly stable,
  With the oxen standing by,
We shall see Him; but in heaven,
  Set at God's right hand on high;
When like stars His children crowned
All in white shall wait around.

416

Moderate.

PURITAS.
L. M. D.

Bless - ed are the pure in heart; They have loved the bet - ter part;

When life's jour-ney they have trod, They shall go to see their God.

Till in glo - ry they ap-pear They shall oft - en see Him here;

And His grace shall learn to know In His glorious works be - low. A - MEN.

2 When the sun begins to rise,
Spreading brightness through the skies,
They will love to praise and bless,
Christ, the Sun of Righteousness.
In the watches of the night,
When the stars are clear and bright,
"Thus the just shall shine," they say,
"In the Resurrection-day."

3 When the leaves in Autumn die,
Falling fast and silently,   [dead,
"These," they think, "that now seem
Shall in Spring lift up their head."
God in everything they see;
First in all their thoughts is He:
They had loved the better part:—
Blessèd are the pure in heart.

417

Moderate.

ALLEN.
8s. 7s. 7.

Bless-ed Je - sus, wilt Thou hear us, Lit - tle children though we be?

Sa - viour, wilt Thou now be near us, While we try to sing to Thee?

Thou hast bid us not to fear;— "Bring the lit - tle children near." A-MEN.

2 We have often heard the story
    Of Thy great and wondrous love;
    How Thou left the world of glory,
    And Thy Father's house above,
    Here to suffer and to die
    For such little ones as I.

3 O how very meek and lowly
    Little children then should be,
    When the Son of God most holy
    Came a little child like me;—
    Thou didst suffer grief and shame
    Like a meek and quiet lamb.

4 May our sins be all forgiven,
    Take our naughty hearts away;
    Bring us all at last to heaven,
    Ever there with Thee to stay;
    There may we, Thy children, raise
    Hymns of joy and perfect praise.

418 Moderate.

VENABLES.
L. M.

With - in the tem - ple's hallowed walls, How meek-ly sat the Ho - ly Child,

And listened when the doctors taught, And meekly questioned soft and mild. A-MEN.

2 He did His Father's work betimes,
    He loved within His courts to stay,
    While three long days the Mother trod
    Alone her weary homeward way.

3 Oh! shame on any Christian child
    Who does not love the house of prayer;
    Who goes with cold, unwilling heart,
    To serve his Heavenly Father there:

4 Who takes no heed when holy words
    Are spoken to his listless ears,
    Nor ever questions in his heart,
    What mean the sacred things he hears.

5 Come let him learn what Jesus did,
    And love to trace, with wondering eyes,
    His perfect works, His holy ways,
    Who was in early years so wise.

6 And let him ask of God in heaven,
    A spirit teachable and mild,
    A simple heart to learn and love,
    Like Jesus, that sweet, Holy Child

419 THANET.

Moderate. *Voices in unison.* 7s. 6s. D.

We sing a lov-ing Je - sus Who left His throne a bove,

And came on earth to ran - som The chil - dren of His love;

It is an oft - told sto - ry, And yet we love to tell

ritard.

How Christ, the King of glo - ry, Once deigned with man to dwell. A-MEN.

2 We sing a holy Jesus;
   No taint of sin defiled
The Babe of David's city,
   The pure and stainless child:
O teach us, blessèd Saviour,
   Thy heavenly grace to seek,
And let our whole behaviour,
   Like Thine, be mild and meek.

3 We sing a lowly Jesus,
   No Kingly crown He had:
His heart was bowed with anguish,
   His face was marred and sad;
In deep humiliation
   He came, His work to do;
O Lord of our salvation,
   Let us be humble too.

4 We sing a mighty Jesus,
   Whose voice could raise the dead;
The sightless eyes He opened,
   The famished souls He fed.
Thou camest to deliver
   Mankind from sin and shame;
Redeemer and life giver,
   We praise Thy holy Name!

5 We sing a coming Jesus;
   The time is drawing near,
When Christ with all His Angels
   In glory shall appear;
Lord, save us, we entreat Thee,
   In this Thy day of grace,
That we may gladly meet Thee,
   And see Thee face to face.

420

Moderate.

Who is this, so weak and help-less, Child of low-ly He-brew maid?

Rude-ly in a sta-ble shel-ter'd, Cold-ly in a man-ger laid?

'Tis the Lord of all cre-a-tion, Who this won-drous path hath trod;

He is God from e-ver-last-ing, And to e-ver-last-ing, God. A-MEN.

2 Who is this, a Man of sorrows,
   Walking sadly life's hard way,
Homeless, weary, sighing, weeping
   Over sin and Satan's sway?
'Tis our God, our glorious Saviour,
   Who above the starry sky
Now prepares the many mansions,
   Where no tear can dim the eye.

3 Who is this—behold Him shedding
   Drops of blood upon the ground?
Who is this—despised, rejected,
   Mock'd, insulted, beaten, bound?
'Tis our God, who gifts and graces
   On His Church now poureth down;
Who shall smite in holy vengeance
   All His foes beneath His throne.

4 Who is this that hangeth dying,
   While the rude world scoffs and scorns,
On the cross with sinners number'd,
   Pierced by nails and crown'd with thorns?
'Tis the God who ever liveth
   'Mid the shining ones on high,
In the glorious golden city
   Reigning everlastingly.

421

Moderate.

CHEDDAR.
8s. 7s. D.

Lord, a lit-tle band and low-ly, We are come to sing to Thee,

Thou art great, and high, and ho-ly, Oh! how sol-emn we should be.

Fill our hearts with thoughts of Je-sus, And of heav'n where He is gone,

And let nothing e-ver please us, He would grieve to look up-on. A-MEN.

2 For we know the Lord of glory
   Always sees what children do,
And is writing now the story
   Of our thoughts and actions too.

Let our sins be all forgiven,
   Make us fear whate'er is wrong;
Lead us on our way to heaven,
   There to sing a nobler song.

422 [568]

Moderate.

SAMUEL.
6s. 8s.

Hushed was the eve-ning hymn, The tem-ple courts were dark,

The lamp was burn-ing dim, Be-fore the sa-cred ark:

When sud-den-ly a voice di-vine Rang thro' the si-lence of the shrine. A-MEN.

2 The old man, meek and mild,
   The priest of Israel, slept;
   His watch the temple-child,
   The little Levite, kept;
And what from Eli's sense was sealed,
The LORD to Hannah's son revealed.

3 Oh! give me Samuel's ear,
   The open ear, O Lord,
   Alive and quick to hear
   Each whisper of Thy word,
Like him to answer at Thy call,
And to obey Thee first of all.

4 Oh! give me Samuel's heart,
   A lowly heart, that waits
   Where in Thy House Thou art,
   Or watches at Thy gates.
By day and night, a heart that still
Moves at the breathing of Thy will.

5 Oh! give me Samuel's mind,
   A sweet, unmurmuring faith,
   Obedient and resigned
   To Thee in life and death.
That I may read with childlike eyes
Truths that are hidden from the wise.

423

Brightly.

HAPPY LAND.
P. M.

There is a hap-py land, Far, far a-way, { Oh, how they sweetly sing,
Where saints in glo-ry stand, Bright, bright as day: {

Worthy is our Saviour King; Loud let His praises ring; Praise, praise for aye. A-MEN.

2 Come to this happy land,
   Come, come away:
Why will ye doubting stand?
   Why still delay?
Oh, we shall happy be,
When from sin and sorrow free;
Lord, we shall live with Thee,
   Blest, blest for aye.

3 Bright in that happy land
   Beams every eye;
Kept by a Father's hand,
   Love cannot die.
On then to glory run.
Be a crown and kingdom won;
And bright above the sun
   Reign, reign for aye.

424   *Cheerful.*

RUGBY.
8s. 7s. D.

We are lit - tle Chris-tian chil-dren, We can run, and talk, and play;

The great God of earth and heav - en, Made and keeps us eve - ry day.

2. We are lit - tle Chris-tian chil-dren; Christ, the Son of God most high,

fz   *fz*

rall.

With His precious Blood redeem'd us, Dy - ing that we might not die. A-MEN.

rall.   *fz*

fz

3 We are little Christian children,
  God, the Holy Ghost, is here;
  Dwelling in our hearts, to make us
  Kind and holy, good and dear.

4 We are little Christian children,
  Sav'd by Him who lov'd us most,
  We believe in God Almighty,
  Father, Son, and Holy Ghost

425

WESTLAKE.
7s. D.

Cheerful.

In our work, and in our play, Je - sus, be Thou ev - er near;

Guard-ing, guid - ing all the day, Keep-ing in Thy ho - ly fear.

2. Thou didst toil, a low - ly Child, In the far off Ho - ly Land,

Bless-ing la - bour un - de - filed, Pure and hon - est of the hand. A -MEN.

3 Thou wilt bless our playhour too,
    If we ask Thy succour strong;
Watch o'er all we say and do,
    Hold us back from guilt and wrong.

4 Oh! how happy thus to spend,
    Work and playtime in His sight,
Till the Rest which shall not end,
    Till the Day which knows not night.

426

SILKSWORTH.
7s. 5s. 7.

Moderate.

Eve-ry morning the red sun Ris-es warm and bright; But the evening

com-eth on, And the dark, cold night: There's a bright land

far a-way, Where is nev-er end-ing day. A - MEN.

2 Every spring the sweet young flowers
   Open fresh and gay;
Till the chilly autumn hours
   Wither them away:
There's a land we have not seen
Where the trees are always green.

3 Little birds sing songs of praise
   All the summer long;
But in colder, shorter days
   They forget their song:
There's a place where Angels sing
Ceaseless praises to their King.

4 Christ our Lord is ever near
   Those who follow Him!
But we cannot see Him here,
   For our eyes are dim:
There is a most happy place,
Where men always see His Face.

5 Who shall go to that bright land?
   All who do the right:
Holy children there shall stand,
   In their robes of white,
For that Heaven so bright and blest,
Is our everlasting rest.

427 [573]

JESU, BONE PASTOR.
8s. 7s. 4.

Moderate.

Sa-viour, like a shep-herd lead us, Much we need Thy ten-der care;

In Thy pleas-ant pas-tures feed us; For our use Thy folds pre-pare:

Bless-ed Je-sus, Bless-ed Je-sus, Thou hast bought us, Thine we are. A-MEN.

2 Thou hast promised to receive us,
  Poor and sinful though we be;
Thou hast mercy to relieve us;
  Grace to cleanse and power to free:
    Blessèd Jesus!
  Let us early turn to Thee.

3 Early let us seek Thy favour,
  Early let us learn Thy will;
Do Thou, Lord, our only Saviour,
  With Thy love our bosoms fill:
    Blessèd Jesus!
  Thou hast loved us,—love us still.

428

Moderate.

BERNE.
7s. 6s.

Where is the Ho-ly Je-sus? He lives in Heav'n a-bove.

He looks up-on good chil-dren, With ten-der-ness and love. A-MEN.

2 Where is the Holy Jesus?
  His home is everywhere,
He loves that little children
  Should speak to Him in prayer.

3 Once He came down from Heaven;
  He came a little child;
He was so good and gentle,
  Obedient, meek, and mild.

4 He had no naughty temper,
  He said no angry word:
And all good little children
  Should be like Christ their Lord.

5 For He will make them holy,
  And teachable and mild,
And has sent His Blessèd Spirit
  To every Christian child.

6 Then every night and morning
  When I kneel down to pray,
I will ask the Holy Jesus,
  To help me day by day.

429 [409]

HERZOG.
C. M. D.

The ro-seate hues of ear-ly dawn, The brightness of the day;

The crim-son of the sun-set sky, How fast they fade a-way.

O for the pear-ly gates of Heaven, O for the gold-en floor,

O for the Sun of Righteousness, That set-teth ne-ver-more. A-MEN.

2 The highest hopes we cherish here,
  How fast they tire and faint;
How many a spot defiles the robe
  That wraps an earthly saint:
O for a heart that never sins;
  O for a soul wash'd white;
O for a voice to praise our King,
  Nor weary day or night.

3 Here faith is ours, and heavenly hope,
  And grace to lead us higher;
But there are perfectness and peace
  Beyond our best desire.
O by Thy love and anguish, Lord,
  O by Thy life laid down,
O that we fall not from Thy grace,
  Nor cast away our crown.

430

Cheerful.

What a strange and wondrous sto-ry From the book of God is read,

How the Lord of life and glo-ry Had not where to lay His head;

How He left His throne in heav-en, Here to suf-fer, bleed, and die,

That my soul might be for-gi-ven, And as-cend to God on high. A-MEN.

2 While I bless the Hand which gave me
    Life and health and all things here,
O may He who died to save me,
    To my soul be very dear.
Jesus Christ, my Lord, and Saviour,
    Let me not ungrateful be;
Let my words and my behaviour
    Prove I love and honour Thee.

3 Father, let Thy Holy Spirit
    Still reveal a Saviour's love,
And prepare me to inherit
    Glory, where He reigns above.
There with saints and Angels dwelling
    May I that great love proclaim,
And with them be ever telling
    All the wonders of His Name.

431

Joyously.

BONCHURCH.
7s. 6s. D.

'Twas God that made the o - cean, And laid its san - dy bed;

He gave the stars their mo - tion, And built the mountain's head;

He made the rol - ling thun - der, The light-ning's fork - ed flame;

His works are full of won - der, All glo-rious is His Name. A-MEN.

2 And must it not surprise us
   That One, so high and great,
Should see and not despise us,
   Poor sinners, at His feet?
Yet day by day He gives us
   Our raiment and our food;
In sickness He relieves us,
   And is in all things good.

3 But things that are far greater
   His mighty hand hath done;
And sent us blessings sweeter
   Through Christ His only Son;
Who, when He saw us dying
   In sin and sorrow's night,
On wings of mercy flying,
   Came down with life and light.

4 He gives His Word to teach us
   Our danger and our wants;
And kindly doth beseech us
   To take the life He grants.
His Holy Spirit frees us
   From Satan's deadly power;
Leads us by faith to Jesus,
   And makes His glory ours!

432

Moderate.

RUDSTONE.
C. M. D.

In the soft sea-son of thy youth, In nature's smiling bloom, Ere

age ar-rives, and, trembling, wait Its summons to the tomb. 2. Re-

mem-ber thy Cre-a-tor, God; For Him thy powers em-ploy. Make

Him thy fear, thy love, thy hope, Thy con-fi-dence, thy joy. A-MEN.

3 He shall defend and guide thy course
Through life's uncertain sea,
Till thou art landed on the shore
Of blest eternity.

4 Then seek the Lord betimes, and choose
The path of heavenly truth;
The earth affords no lovelier sight
Than a religious youth.

433 [572]

Moderate.

CANTERBURY.
Six 7s.

Lord, Thy chil-dren guide and keep, As with fee - ble steps they press

On the pathway, rough and steep, Through this wea-ry wil-der-ness.

Ho-ly Je-sus, day by day Lead us in the nar-row way. A-MEN.

2 There are stony ways to tread;
  Give the strength we sorely lack:
  There are tangled paths to thread;
  Light us, lest we miss the track.
  Holy Jesus, day by day
  Lead us in the narrow way.

3 There are sandy wastes that lie
  Cold and sunless, vast and drear,
  Where the feeble faint and die;
  Grant us grace to persevere.
  Holy Jesus, day by day
  Lead us in the narrow way.

4 There are soft and flowery glades
  Deck'd with golden-fruited trees;
  Sunny slopes and scented shades;
  Keep us, Lord, from slothful ease.
  Holy Jesus, day by day
  Lead us in the narrow way.

5 Upward still to purer heights,
  Onward yet to scenes more blest,
  Calmer regions, clearer lights,
  Till we reach the promised rest.
  Holy Jesus, day by day
  Lead us in the narrow way.

434 [571]

Moderate.

PASTORAL.
Six 6s.

Great Shepherd of the sheep, Who all Thy flock dost keep,

Lead - ing by wa - ters calm; Do Thou my foot-steps guide,

To follow by Thy side; Make me Thy little lamb, Make me Thy little lamb. A-MEN.

2 But when the road is long,
  Thy tender arm and strong
  The weary one will bear;
  And Thou wilt wash me clean,
  And lead to pastures green,
  Where all the flowers are fair.

3 Till from the soil of sin,
  Cleansed and made pure within,
  Dear Saviour, whose I am;
  Thou bringest me in love
  To Thy safe fold above,
  A little snow-white lamb.

435

FRANCES.
C. M.

Moderate.

I love to think, though I am young, My Saviour was a child;

That Je-sus walked this earth along, With feet all un - de - filed. A-MEN.

2 He kept His Father's word of truth,
  As I am taught to do;
  And while He walked the paths of youth,
  He walked in wisdom too.

3 I love to think that He who spake,
  And made the blind to see,
  And called the sleeping dead to wake,
  Was once a child like me.

4 That He who wore the thorny crown,
  And tasted death's despair,

Had a kind mother like my own,
  And knew her love and care.

5 I know 'twas all for love of me
  That He became a child,
  And left the heavens, so fair to see,
  And trod earth's pathway wild.

6 Then, Saviour, who wast once a child,
  A child may come to Thee;
  And oh! in all Thy mercy mild,
  Dear Saviour, come to me.

436

BETHLEHEM.
8s. 7s.

Moderate.

Youth-ful days are pass-ing o'er us, Childhood's years will soon be gone;

Cares and sorrows lie before us, Hidden dan-gers, snares unknown. A-MEN.

2 Oh! may He, who meek and lowly
Visited this world below,
Make us His, and make us holy,
Guard and guide us, where we go.

3 Hark! it is the Saviour calling,
"Come, ye children, come to Me."
Jesus, keep our feet from falling,
Teach us all to follow Thee.

4 Soon we part; it may be, never,
Never here to meet again;
May we meet in heaven for ever,
And the crown eternal gain.

437 *Moderate.*

FROME.
C. M.

There is a mo-ther's voice of love To hush her lit-tle child;

There is a fa-ther's voice of praise, So ear-nest and so mild. A-MEN.

2 But there is yet another voice,
That speaks in gentlest tone—
I think that we can hear it best
When we are quite alone.

3 It is a still, small, holy voice,
The voice of God most high,
That whispers always in our heart,
And says that He is by.

4 The voice will blame us when we're wrong,
And praise us when we're right;

We hear it in the light of day,
And in the quiet night.

5 And even they whose ears are deaf
To every other sound—
When they have listened in their hearts
The still small voice have found.

6 And they have felt that God is good,
And thanked Him for the voice
That told them what was right and true,
And made their hearts rejoice.

438

NORWOOD.
7s. 6s.

Joyous.

I hear the children's voi - ces In ten - der strains up - rise,

rall.

Their car - ols sweet-ly blend - ing With hymns be-yond the skies. A-MEN

2 Christ smiled on little children,
  And drew them to His breast;
  "Of such is Heaven's kingdom,"
  Of love, and joy, and rest.

3 They trust, and fear no evil,
  Confiding, gentle, kind;
  In simple faith, as children,
  We happiness may find.

4 They sing their joyous carols,
  With lips and hearts as free

As winds, and waves, and sunshine,
  Or birds upon the tree.

5 They love the fields and flowers,
  The fragrance, and the light;
  And all this world of ours
  For them is ever bright.

6 They love the name of Jesus,
  They trust His tender care,
  And all they know of Heaven,
  Is—Christ Himself is there.

439 *Moderate.*

HERBERT.
8s. 7s.

Lit - tle children, who would e - ver Tread the safe and nar - row way,

Je-sus' footsteps long to fol-low, And His gen-tle voice o - bey. A-MEN.

2 As a rough road often trodden,
  Smooth and easy doth become,
  So the straight and narrow pathway
  Widens, brightens nearer Home.

3 Eye ne'er saw, nor ear hath heard it,
  Neither can the heart conceive,
  Of the joy which God prepareth,
  For His children who believe.

4 Yet the Spirit doth reveal it,
  Here we have our bliss in part,
  Since, our heritage for ever,
  God abideth in our heart.

440 *Quietly.*

HEATHLANDS.
8s. 7. SIX LINES.

In the Name of Him who loves us With a love for e-ver true, Kind and patient

while He proves us, Noting what our hearts will do; We poor children, all un-wor-thy,

For our Father's blessing sue. A-MEN.

2 In the Name of Him who bought us
With His own atoning Blood,
To His fold in childhood brought us,
He our shelter, He our food;
We poor lambs upon the mountain
Gather round our Shepherd good.

3 In the Name of Him who gave us
All our childhood's guiding light,
Ready now to help and save us,
And to rule our lives aright;
We poor sinners, weak and helpless,
Here implore the Spirit's might.

4 Heavenly Father, bless Thy children;
Saviour, bind us fast to Thee;
Holy Spirit, teach us, save us,
Make us strong and truly free;
Lord of love, in truth and goodness
Thine for ever may we be.

441 *Cheerful.*

GOD IS GOOD.
6s. 5s.

See the shining dew-drops On the flow-ers strewed, Prov-ing as they spar-kle,

"God is e-ver good." A-MEN.

2 See the morning sunbeams
Lighting up the wood,
Silently proclaiming
"God is ever good."

3 Hear the mountain streamlet,
In its solitude,
With its ripple saying
"God is ever good."

4 In the leafy tree-tops,
Where no fears intrude,
Merry birds are singing
"God is ever good."

5 He who came to save us,
Shed His precious blood;

Better things it speaketh
"God is ever good."

6 Bring, my heart, thy tribute,
Songs of gratitude;
All things join to tell us
"God is ever good."

442 [319]

MARGARET.
P. M.

* Earnestly.

Thou didst leave Thy throne and Thy King-ly crown When Thou camest to earth for me; But in Beth-lehem's home was there found no room For Thy ho-ly na-tiv-i-ty. Oh, come to my heart, Lord Je-sus! There is room in my heart for Thee! AMEN.

* *The ties and slurs are to be used as the syllables require.*

2 Heaven's arches rang when the Angels sang,
  Proclaiming Thy Royal degree;
But in lowly birth didst Thou come to earth,
  And in great humility.
    Oh, come to my heart, Lord Jesus!
    There is room in my heart for Thee!

3 The foxes found rest, and the bird had its nest
  In the shade of the cedar tree;
But Thy couch was the sod, O Thou Son of God,
  In the desert of Galilee.
    Oh, come to my heart, Lord Jesus!
    There is room in my heart for Thee!

4 Thou camest, O Lord, with the living word
  That should set Thy people free;
But with mocking scorn, and with crown of thorn,
  They bore Thee to Calvary.
    Oh, come to my heart, Lord Jesus!
    There is room in my heart for Thee!

5 When the heavens shall ring and the Angels sing
  At Thy coming to victory,
Let Thy voice call me home saying " Yet there is room,
  There is room at My side for Thee."
    Oh, come to my heart, Lord Jesus!
    There is room in my heart for Thee!

443

ROTHERHAM.
C. M. D.

O Lord of all, we bring to Thee Our sac - ri - fice of praise,
To Thee with glad and thank - ful hearts Our joy - ous hymn we raise;
We are but chil - dren here on earth, And Thou art high a - bove,
But yet we dare to come to Thee, Be-cause Thy name is Love. A - MEN.

2 We praise Thee now for life, and health,
　And earthly happiness,
For all the sacred human love
　That still our lives doth bless;
For Thy dear Son whom Thou hast sent,
　Whose kind and tender voice
Bids the young children come to Thee,
　And in Thy love rejoice.

3 What shall we render Thee, O Lord?
　What tribute shall we bring?
O let us give our hearts, our lives,
　In thankful offering.
Although we are but children, yet
　Thou dost our service ask,
And each in Thy great work may find
　His own appointed task.

4 O make us watchful, lest by sin
　Our hearts be overborne;
O make us true in word and work,
　Though all the world should scorn;
O make us willing here to serve,
　In lowliness and love,
For Him who in a servant's form
　Came down from heaven above.

5 The night of sin must wane at last,
　The morn of joy begin,
When Christ in every human heart
　His royal throne must win;
O let us give Him now in youth
　Our ardour and our strength;
Work for His glorious kingdom here,
　And share His joy at length!

444

QUEST. *Earnestly.*

Whither are you go - ing, pilgrims of a day? Tar-ry but a mo-ment,

ANS.

rest you on the way; No, we can - not lin-ger here, day is wa-ning fast.

CHORUS.

We must reach the ha-ven, ere the light is past. Onward, ev - er on - ward,

tho' by tempest driven; O how sweet the prom-ise, we shall meet in Heaven. A-MEN.

QUEST. 2 You will soon be weary, pilgrims of a day,
    Trials are before you, dangers in your way;
  ANS. Still by faith we'll journey on, tho' our path be drear,
    If the Saviour lead us, what have we to fear?
      CHO:—Onward, ever onward, &c.

QUEST. 3 Pilgrims, are you going, where the Angels' song,
    O'er the fields of glory, gently flows along?
  ANS. Yes, we seek the better land, lovely, pure and fair,
    Where no grief can enter—will you meet us there?
      CHO:—Onward, ever onward, &c.

QUEST. 4 May we journey with you, pilgrims of a day?
    Will you help us onward in the heavenly way?
  ANS. Come, we gladly bid you come, day is waning fast,
    We must reach the haven, ere the light is past.
      CHO:—Onward, ever onward, &c.

445

Moderate.

ALSTONA.
L. M.

Yes, God is good: in earth and sky, From ocean's depths and spreading wood,

Ten thousand voi-ces seem to cry, God made us all, and God is good. A-MEN.

2 The sun that keeps his trackless way,
    And downward pours his golden flood,
Night's sparkling hosts, all seem to say,
    In accents clear, that God is good.

3 The merry birds prolong the strain,
    Their song with ev'ry spring renewed;
And balmy air, and falling rain,
    Each softly whispers, God is good.

4 Yes, God is good, all nature says,
    By God's own hand with speech endued:
And man, in louder notes of praise,
    Should sing for joy that God is good

5 For all Thy gifts we bless Thee, Lord,
    But chiefly for our heavenly food;
Thy pard'ning grace, Thy quick'ning word,
    These prompt our song that God is good.

446

Quietly.

AGNUS DEI.
7s. 6s.

O Lamb of God most low - ly! All free from spot and stain,

O help us now to serve Thee, And sing Thy praise a - gain. A - MEN.

2 O Lamb of God most holy!
    So great, and yet so meek;
May we, when pride allures us,
    Thy lowly spirit seek.

3 O Lamb of God most gentle!
    So kind, and good, and true,
May we, when passion tempts us,
    Thy gentleness pursue.

4 O Lamb of God most lovely!
    To Thee our faith would flee;
Reveal to us Thy beauty,
    And win our hearts to Thee.

447

Cheerful.

PEACE.
8s. 7s.

Shepherd of those sun-lit-moun-tains, Where e-ter-nal sum-mer reigns,

Where Thy love, like flow-ing fountains, Spreads bright glory o'er the plains! A-MEN.

2 In this wilderness of sorrow,
  May Thy crook now guide our feet;
Through Thy words, oh, feed and guide us
  To Thy truth most pure and sweet.

3 From Thy love like sheep we wander,
  We have erred from Thy way;
Let Thy loving voice reclaim us,
  Never let us from Thee stray.

4 Thou didst give Thy life to save us,
  Loving Shepherd of Thy sheep;
To Thy fold again restore us,
  All our hearts now claim and keep.

448

Moderate.

BAYSWATER.
7s.

When you're sleeping, chil-dren fair, An-gels keeping watch are there,

Through the night, till comes the light, And you say your morn-ing prayer. A-MEN.

2 When you're playing all the day,
  When you wander far away,
By your side an angel guide
  Watches, lest you go astray.

3 When, heart weary, each has trod
  Life's great journey all the road,
Angel hands, to other lands,
  Carry back the soul to God.

449

LUX.
P. M.

Moderate.

Sun - ny days of child-hood, Beau - ti - ful ye seem,

Fair as spring-tide flow - ers, Bright as sum - mer's beam.

Days with joy o'erflowing, Care nor sadness knowing, Must ye pass away? A-MEN.

2 Precious days of childhood!
  Days of promise fair;
If bedewed with wisdom,
  Rich the fruits ye bear.
Jesus' footsteps keeping,
Blest shall be our reaping
  In life's harvest day.

3 Happy days of childhood,
  Swiftly moving on;
Into manhood changing
  Ye will soon be gone,
Like a streamlet flowing,
Pause nor stillness knowing,
  Thus ye pass away!

4 Sunny days of childhood!
  We no tear will shed
When, like spring-tide flowers,
  Youth and health are fled.
Earthly scenes forsaking,
We shall hail the breaking
  Of an endless day.

450

BENISON.
Six 8s.

Moderate.

I praised the earth in beau-ty seen, With gar-lands gay of va-rious green;

I praised the sea whose am-ple field Shone glo-rious as a sil-ver shield;

And earth and ocean seemed to say, "Our beau-ties are but for a day." A-MEN.

2 I praised the sun, whose chariot rolled
On wheels of amber and of gold;
I praised the moon, whose softer eye
Gleamed sweetly through the summer sky;
And moon and sun in answer said,
"Our days of light are numbered."

3 O God! O Good beyond compare!
If thus Thy meaner works are fair,
If thus Thy bounties gild the span
Of ruined earth and sinful man,
How glorious must the mansion be,
Where Thy redeemed shall dwell with Thee!

451 *Moderate.*

CHILDHOOD.
L. M.

O Ho-ly Lord, con-tent to fill In low-ly home the low-liest place;

Thy childhood's law a mother's will, O-bedience meek Thy brightest grace. A-MEN.

2 Lead every child that bears Thy Name
To walk in Thine own guileless way,
To dread the touch of sin and shame,
And humbly, like Thyself, obey.

3 Oh! let not this world's scorching glow
Thy Spirit's quickening dew efface,
Nor blast of sin too rudely blow,
And quench the trembling flame of grace.

4 Gather Thy lambs within Thine arm,
And gently in Thy bosom bear;
Keep them, O Lord, from hurt and harm,
And bid them rest for ever there!

452

Quietly.

KEBLE.
7s.

Children, come and list to me, While I speak of GOD a-bove;

All the glorious things you see, Are His works of pow'r and love. A-MEN.

2 Wheresoe'er your feet have trod,
Scattered blessings round you lie,
All by GOD's kind love bestowed,
Who has made both earth and sky.

3 When you hear the loud winds howling,
Tearing by with sudden crash,
Or the thunder's fearful growling,
Mingled with the lightning's flash:

4 These are subject to the LORD,
All created by His will,
And with one Almighty word,
He can make the storm be still.

5 O dear children, you should try,
This Almighty GOD to love,
That when your frail bodies die,
Your may see His face above.

453

Cheerful.

CLARABELLA.
C. M.

There's not a tint that paints the rose, Or decks the li-ly fair,

Or streaks the humblest flower that blows, But God has placed it there. A-MEN.

2 At early dawn there's not a gale
Across the landscape driven,
And not a breeze that sweeps the vale,
That is not sent by Heaven.

3 There's not of grass a single blade,
Or leaf of loveliest green,
Where heavenly skill is not displayed,
And heavenly wisdom seen.

4 Around, beneath, below, above,
Wherever space extends,
There God displays His boundless love,
And power with mercy blends.

454 [395]

DAMASCUS.
6s. 5s. D.

Moderate.

Those e - ter - nal bow - ers Man has ne - ver trod,

Those un - fa - ding flow - ers Round the throne of God:

Who may hope to gain them Af - ter wea - ry fight?

Who at length at - tain them Clad in robes of white? A-MEN.

2 He who gladly barters
    All on earthly ground;
He who, like the martyrs,
    Says, "I will be crowned:"
He, whose one oblation
    Is a life of love;
Clinging to the nation
    Of the blest above.

3 Shame upon you, legions
    Of the heavenly King,
Citizens of regions
    Past imagining!
What! with pipe and tabor
    Dream away the light,
When He bids you labour—
    When He tells you, "Fight?"

4 Jesu, Lord of Glory,
    As we breast the tide,
Whisper Thou of beauty
    On the other side!
What though sad the story
    Of this life's distress;
Oh, the future glory!
    Oh, the loveliness!

455 VOICES IN UNISON.

PILGRIMAGE.
8s. 7s. D. WITH REFRAIN.

1. We, O
2. When we

Lord, are Christian pilgrims, Wending on our earth - ly way,
wak - en in the morn-ing, Give us strength that we may keep
Pressing onward, ev - er
In the ho - ly ways, till

on-ward, Hour by hour, and day by day. Great and ma - ny are the dangers, That up-
shadows Bring the hours of rest and sleep. Then, O Lord, our pray'rs as-cending, In Thy

on our road we see, But we pass them all un - heed-ed, For we put our trust in
realms of glo - ry hear, And, while night the earth o'er cov-ers, Watch a-bove us, Sa-viour

pp tempo.

Thee!   We, O Lord, are Chris-tian pil-grims, Bless our jour - ney, we im -
dear!

plore,   That, o'er-com-ing ev - 'ry dan-ger, We may reach the gold-en shore.   A - MEN.

456

1st Chorus. Whither, pil - grims, are you go - ing, Go - ing each with staff in

2d Chorus. hand? We are go - ing on a jour - ney, Go - ing at our King's com-

Both Choruses. mand. O - ver hills and plains and val - leys, We are go - ing to His

rall. pal - ace, Go - ing to the Bet - ter Land. A - men.

2 1st Cho. Fear ye not the way so lonely,
　　　　　You a little feeble band?
　2d Cho. No, for friends unseen are near us,
　　　　　Holy Angels round us stand.
Cho. Christ, our Leader, walks beside us,
　He will guard and He will guide us,
　Pilgrims to the Better Land.

3 1st Cho. Tell me, pilgrims, what you hope
　　　　　In that far-off better land?[for,
　2d Cho. Spotless robes and crowns of glory
　　　　　From a Saviour's loving Hand.
Cho. We shall drink of life's clear river,
　We shall dwell with God for ever
　In that bright and Better Land.

4 1st Cho. Pilgrims, may we travel with you
　　　　　To that bright, that better land?
　2d Cho. Come and welcome, come and welcome,
　　　　　Welcome to our pilgrim band.
　Cho. Come, oh, come, and do not leave us,
　　　Christ is waiting to receive us
　　　In that bright, that Better Land.

457

UNISON.

SAILING O'ER THE SEA.
P. M.

mf

We weigh the an-chor, spread the sail, To reach the promis'd shore; The

mf

cres.   *dim.*

wind springs up, we stand to sea, De - tain us here no more. . .

cres.   *dim.*

CHORUS.

p   *cres.*

Sail - ing, sail - ing o - ver the sea, In storm and sun-shine bright,

cres.

p

f   *dim.*

Bound for Par - a - dise are we, The land of true de - light. A - MEN.

dim.

f

2 Our brave ship is the Holy Church
  Which Jesus Christ commands;
And all the crew, both old and young,
  In His obedience stands.
    Sailing, etc.

3 The storm may break, the night may lower,
  The vessel toss and strain;
We fear no wreck, we steer right on,
  The sun will shine again.
    Sailing, etc.

4 Our Captain watches night and day,
  His Holy Ship to guide;
And safe we sail so long as we
  Within her walls abide.
    Sailing, etc.

5 Then keep us, Lord, when seas are smooth,
  And keep when storms o'erwhelm;
O may we ever hear Thy voice,
  And see Thee at the helm.
    Sailing, etc.

458 *Boldly.*

DARNTON.
6s. 7s. D.

Who is on the Lord's side? Who will serve the King? Who will be His help-ers?

Oth-er lives to bring! Who will leave the world's side? Who will face the foe?

cres.

Who is on the Lord's side? Who for Him will go? By Thy call of mer-cy,

p

By Thy grace divine, We are on the Lord's side: Saviour, we are Thine. A-MEN.

cres. *f rall.*

2 Not for weight of glory,
  Not for crown or palm,
Enter we the army,
  Raise the warrior psalm.
But for love that claimeth
  Lives for whom He died;
He whom Jesus nameth,
  Must be on His side.
    By Thy call of mercy, etc.

3 Jesus, Thou hast bought us,
  Not with gold or gem,
But with Thy own life-blood,
  For Thy diadem;
With Thy blessing filling,
  Each who comes to Thee,
Thou hast made us willing,
  Thou hast made us free.
    By Thy call of mercy, etc.

4 Fierce may be the conflict,
  Strong may be the foe.
But the King's own army
  None can overthrow.
Round His standard ranging,
  Victory is secure,
For His truth unchanging
  Makes the triumph sure.
    By Thy call of mercy, etc.

459

ASHBURTON.
7s. SIX LINES.

When our hearts are glad and light, When the path is fair and bright,

When from care and sor-row free, Help us, Lord, to cling to Thee:

Be our Com-fort-er and Friend, Guide and keep us to the end. A - MEN.

2 When the way is dark and drear,
When no loving friend is near;
When we suffer pain or loss,
When we bow beneath the cross,
Be our Comforter and Friend,
Guide and keep us to the end.

3 When we strive to do the right,
When we follow, serve, or fight,
When we seek to do Thy will,
When we hear Thee say, "Stand still,"
Be our Comforter and Friend,
Guide and keep us to the end.

4 When we near our endless home,
When the closing hour shall come,
When we cross death's chilling tide,
Lead us to the other side;
Be our Comforter and Friend,
Guide and keep us to the end.

5 When we reach that other land,
When before the Judge we stand,
When the books shall opened be,
Saviour, we would cling to Thee.
Living, dying, be our Friend;
Bless us, keep us to the end.

460

HARPER.
7s.

All things praise Thee, Lord most high, Heaven and earth, and sea and sky,

All were for Thy glo-ry made, That Thy great-ness thus dis-played,

Should all wor-ship bring to Thee; All things praise Thee: Lord, may we. A-MEN.

2 All things praise Thee — night to night
Sings in silent hymns of light:
All things praise Thee — day to day
Chants Thy power in burning ray;
Time and space are praising Thee,
All things praise Thee: Lord, may we.

3 All things praise Thee — high and low,
Rain, and dew, and seven-hued bow,
Crimson sunset, fleecy cloud,
Rippling stream, and tempest loud,
Summer, winter — all to Thee
Glory render: Lord, may we.

4 All things praise Thee — heaven's high
Rings with melody divine; [shrine
Lowly bending at Thy feet,
Seraph and archangel meet;
This their highest bliss — to be
Ever praising: Lord, may we.

5 All things praise Thee — gracious Lord,
Great Creator, powerful Word,
Omnipresent Spirit, now
At Thy feet we humbly bow;
Lift our hearts in praise to Thee;
All things praise Thee: Lord, may we.

461 [543]

MAITLAND.
8 s.

Lamb of God, for sin-ners slain; By Thy mer-cy born a-gain,

For Thy gui-dance still we pray, Lest from grace we fall a-way. A-MEN.

2 By the mystic, cleansing flood,
By the Water, and the Blood,
Washed and sanctified to Thee,
Holy may we ever be.

3 Aid us with Thy daily grace
Steadfastly to run our race;
Grant us victory in the strife,
And the prize of endless life.

4 Praise to Thee, from all on earth,
God, Who gavest us new birth;
Praise from all the heavenly host;
Father, Son, and Holy Ghost.

462

GOD IS LOVE.
7s. D.

UNISON.

Earth with her ten thousand flow'rs, Air with all its beams and showers,

O - cean's in - fi-nite ex-panse, Heaven's re - splen - dent coun - te-nance:

All a - round and all a-bove, Bear the re - cord "God is love,"

All a - round and all a-bove, Bear the re-cord "God is love." A - MEN.

2 Sounds among the vales and hills,
In the woods and by the rills,
Of the breeze and of the bird,
By the gentle summer stirred:
All these sounds, beneath, above,
Have one burden "God is love."

3 All the hopes and fears that start
From the fountain of the heart;
All the quiet bliss that lies
In our human sympathies:
These are voices from above,
Sweetly whispering, "God is love."

4 But the great Redeemer's birth,
All He did and said on earth,
All His agonies and woes,
All the gifts His hand bestows,
All His pleadings now above,
Loudly publish, "God is love."

463

Brisk.

SERVICE.
8s, 7s. D.

If you can-not on the o-cean, Sail a-mong the swift-est fleet,

Rock-ing on the high-est bil-lows, Laugh-ing at the storms you meet:

Voices in Unison.

You can stand a-mong the sai-lors, An-chor'd yet with-in the bay,

In Harmony.

poco rall.

You can lend a hand to help them, As they launch their boats a-way.   A-MEN.

poco rall.

2 If you are too weak to journey
  Up the mountain steep and high,
You can stand within the valley,
  While the multitudes go by;
You can chant in happy measure,
  As they slowly pass along;
Though they may forget the singer,
  They will not forget the song.

3 If you cannot in the conflict
  Prove yourself a soldier true,
If where fire and smoke are thickest
  There's no work for you to do;
When the battle-field is silent,
  You can go with careful tread,
You can bear away the wounded,
  You can cover up the dead.

4 Do not, then, stand idly waiting
  For some greater work to do;
O! improve each passing moment,
  For these moments may be few;
Go, and toil in any vineyard,
  Do not fear to do or dare;
If you want a field of labour
  You can find it anywhere.

464 [582]

WEBB.
7s, 6s. D.

Stand up, stand up for Je - sus, Ye sol-diers of the Cross,

Lift high His roy - al ban - ner, It must not suf - fer loss;

From vic - tory un - to vic - tory, His ar - my He shall lead,

Till ev - 'ry foe is van-quish'd, And Christ is Lord in - deed. A - MEN.

2 Stand up, stand up for Jesus!
   The trumpet call obey!
   Forth to the mighty conflict
   In this His glorious day!
   Ye that are men now serve Him
   Against unnumbered foes!
   Let courage rise with danger,
   And strength to strength oppose.

3 Stand up, stand up for Jesus!
   Stand in His strength alone!
   The arm of flesh will fail you,
   Ye dare not trust your own;
   Put on the gospel armour,
   And watching unto prayer,
   When duty calls, or danger,
   Be never wanting there!

4 Stand up, stand up for Jesus,
   The strife will not be long:
   This day, the noise of battle;
   The next, the victor's song.
   To him that overcometh
   A crown of life shall be;
   He with the King of glory
   Shall reign eternally.

465

CENSORINUS.
8s, 7s. D.

All things bless Thee, God most ho - ly, To Thy feet their wor - ship bring;

Thou art wor - thy of all prai - ses, Ev - er bless - ed, glo - rious King.

Earth, and air, and o- cean's ful-ness, All Thy power and love de - clare;

And in this ex - ult-ant cho - rus, May not we, Thy chil-dren, share? A-MEN.

2 Childhood's treasures are Thy giving,
  Sunny days and laughing hours,
Daisied meadows in the spring time,
  Roses in the summer bowers ; —
Food and raiment, home and shelter,
  Sleep for wearied eye and limb,
Dawning day and happy waking
  To the birds' sweet morning hymn.

3 And when old and young had wandered
  Into faults and follies wild,
Surely Thou didst think of children,
  Sending forth Thy Son a child.
Lord, forgive our many errors,
  And restore us when we fall,
Thy loved Child is our Redeemer—
  By His mercy save us all.

4 Help us now to be as He was,
  Pure and gentle, good and kind,
Give us of His peaceful Spirit,
  And His meek and lowly mind.
Teach our hearts to feel Thy mercy,
  Turn our eyes to look to Thee;
May we trust in Thee, our Father,
  And Thy loving children be.

5 And when youth's brief morn is over,
  Still be Thou our constant Guide;
Through the hot day's dusty travel,
  Set of sun, and eventide.
And when death's dark night has fallen,
  Lead us through the "open door;"
Satisfy us with Thy presence,
  Be our joy for evermore.

466 [656]

WALSINGHAM.
P. M.

Breast the wave, Christian, When it is strong-est; Watch for day, Chris-tian,

When the night's long-est; On-ward and on-ward still Be thine en - dea-vour;

The rest that re - main-eth Will be . . for ev - er. A - MEN.

2 Fight the fight, Christian,
　　Jesus is o'er thee;
　Run the race, Christian,
　　Heaven is before thee;
　He who hath promisèd
　　Faltereth never;
　He who hath loved so well,
　　Loveth for ever.

3 Lift thine eye, Christian,
　　Just as it closeth;
　Raise thy heart, Christian,
　　Ere it reposeth;
　Thee from the love of Christ
　　Nothing shall sever;
　And, when thy work is done,
　　Praise Him for ever.

467 UNISON.

BEACON LIGHT.
8s, 7s. D.

We are sail-ing o'er an o - cean To a far and for-eign shore,

And the waves are dash-ing round us, And we hear the break-ers roar;

8ves . . . .

But we look a-bove the bil-lows, In the dark-ness of the night,

cres - - - - - *cen* - - - *do.*

And we see the stead-y gleam-ing Of our change-less bea-con light.

O the light is flash-ing bright-ly From a calm and stormless shore,

Where we hope to cast our an-chor When the voyage of life is o'er. A-MEN.

8ves ....

2 Though the skies are dark above us,
  And the waves are dashing high,
Let us look toward the beacon;
  We shall reach it by and by.
'T is the light of God's great mercy,
  And He holds it up in view,
As a guide-star to His children,
  As a guide to me and you.
    O the light is flashing brightly, etc.

3 Rising high on mountain billow,
  Sinking low beneath the wave;
Clouds may oft obscure our vision,
  Fear extort the cry, Lord, save!
Let the tempest rage around us,
  Lightning flash and thunder roar,
Firm as rock our beacon standeth,
  Shining from yon heavenly shore.
    O the light is flashing brightly, etc.

4 He will keep it ever burning
  From the lighthouse of His love;
And it always shines the brightest
  When the skies are dark above.
If we keep our eyes upon it,
  And we steer our course aright,
We shall reach the harbour safely,
  By the blessèd beacon light.
    O the light is flashing brightly, etc.

468

CARTER'S GATE.
8s, 6s.

Dolce.

And dost Thou ask me, dearest Lord, With tender voice and gentle word, In faith to

follow Thee? Close to Thyself, where'er Thou art, With child-like trust, and loving heart,

Thy guiding hand to see.   A - MEN.

2 Yes, 'tis Thy voice, Thou dearest Lord!
Gladly I'll listen to Thy word —
   "Come, soul, and follow Me;"
And be the way, Lord, rough or plain;
Be it all joy, or be it pain,
   I still will follow Thee.

3 If Thou should'st keep me for awhile,
Without the sunshine of Thy smile,
   Yet in Thy love I'll hide:
Remem'bring always that Thy way, [day
Sometimes thro' night, sometimes thro'
   Will lead me to Thy side.

4 If Thou should'st summon me to leave
My home and friends, I will not grieve,
   I'll do it for Thy sake;
Knowing that Thou wilt make amends,
For all I loved: home, riches, friends,
   Whatever I forsake.

5 Then let me, Lord, in poverty,
Obedience, and chastity,
   Count it all joy to be;
Then when my trial days are past,
I at Thy feet my crown may cast,
   And ever worship Thee.

469 [532]

ROCKLANDS.
6s, 5s.

With glad-some hearts we come,   With - in our ho - ly home,   Our

Saviour's Name to sing. O well His House we love! O joy all joys a-

bove To praise the children's King! AMEN.

And still Thy glory show
By deeds of love below,
  To praise the children's King.

4 And may our hearts aspire
To join the heavenly choir,
  Whose strains for ever ring;
And learn on earth their hymn,
The song of seraphim,
  To praise the children's King.

2 The angels sing on high
Thy glory through the sky,
  And then to earth they wing;
To guard us while we sleep
And, as their watch they keep
  To praise the children's King.

3 Oh, may we while we live
Such willing service give,
  A holy offering.

5 O Light of Light, to Thee
Let earth and sky and sea
  Eternal homage bring;
And grant us through Thy love
Before Thy throne above
  To praise the children's King.

CAMBORNE.
P. M.

470

mf Trust-ing-ly, trust-ing-ly, Je-sus to Thee Come I; Lord, lov-ing-ly

Come Thou to me: Then shall I lov-ing-ly, Then shall I joy-ful-ly,

Walk here with Thee. A - MEN.

Peace Thou hast left to us,
Thy peace hast given us:
  So let it be.

3 Happily, happily, pass I along,
Eager to work for Thee, earnest and
Life is for service true,   [strong.
Life is for battle too,
  Life is for song.

4 Hopefully, hopefully, onward I go;
Cheerfully, cheerfully, meet I the foe;
Crowns are awaiting us,
Glory prepared for us,
  Joys overflow.

2 Peacefully, peacefully, walk I with Thee;
Jesus, my Lord, Thou art all, all to me;

471 [531]

WAKEFIELD.
6s, 5s. D.

Je-sus King of glo - ry Throned a-bove the sky, Je - sus, ten-der Sav - iour, Hear Thy children cry. Par - don our trans-gress - ions, Cleanse us from our sin; By Thy Spir - it help us Heav'n-ly life to win.

REFRAIN.

Je-sus, King of glo - ry, Throned a-bove the sky, Je-sus, ten-der Sav - iour, Hear Thy children cry. A-MEN.

2 On this day of gladness,
Bending low the knee
In Thine earthly temple,
Lord, we worship Thee;
Celebrate Thy goodness,
Mercy, grace, and truth,
All Thy loving guidance
Of our heedless youth.
Jesus, etc.

3 For the little children,
Who have come to Thee;
For the glad, bright spirits
Who Thy glory see;
For the loved ones resting
In Thy dear embrace;
For the pure and holy
Who behold Thy face.
Jesus, etc.

4 For Thy faithful servants
Who have entered in;
For Thy fearless soldiers
Who have conquered sin;
For the countless legions
Who have followed Thee,
Heedless of the danger,
On to victory.

5 When the shadows lengthen,
Show us, Lord, Thy way;
Through the darkness lead us
To the heavenly day.
When our course is finished,
Ended all the strife,
Grant us with the faithful
Palms and crowns of life.
Jesus, etc.

472

ELLWOOD.
6s. 5s. D.

Shep-herd, good and gra-cious, Je-sus, Lord of all, . .
Lead-ing though we lin-ger, Hear-ing when we call;
Thee we love to fol-low, Joy-ful all the way; . .
As in ear-ly morn-ing, So in clos-ing day. . . A-MEN.

2 Shepherd good, defend us
Through the garish day,
When the flowery pathway
Lures our feet astray;
Then, Thyself revealing,
Bring that better joy
Earth could never promise,
Death can ne'er destroy.

3 Shepherd good, be near us
Through the gloomy night,
When the foes we see not
Most our hearts affright;
Round the home of sorrow,
O'er the couch of pain,
Breathe, oh, pitying Saviour,
Peace and health again!

4 Shepherd good, recall us
If we fall away;
Plead for us in mercy
When we cannot pray;
When our wasted bodies
Yield their latest breath,
Bear our life to glory
Through the gate of death.

473

MARION.
P. M.

The beau - ti - ful bright sun - shine, That smiles on all be - low, . .

The wav - ing trees, the cool, soft breeze, The rippling streams that flow,

SOLO.

The sha - dows on the hill - side, The ma - ny - tint -ed flowers,

FULL.

O God! how fair Thy lov - ing care Has made this earth of ours. A - MEN.

2 The beautiful affections
   That gather round our way,
   The joys that rise from household ties
   And deepen day by day;
   The tender love that guards us
   Whenever danger lowers,
   O God! how fair thy loving care
   Has made this earth of ours.

3 But brighter is the shining,
   And tenderer is the love,
   And purer still, the joys which fill
   The unseen home above,—
   The home where all His children
   Shall sing with fuller powers,
   "O God! how fair Thy loving care
   Has made this Heaven of ours."

474

Joyfully.

We come with songs of glad - ness, To praise our God and King, And

for His love and mer - cy Our grate - ful tri - bute bring. The blessings of His

boun - ty Have crown'd with joy our days; Then sing we Al - le - lu - ia,

CHORUS.

And thank - ful voi - ces raise. Sing the songs of glad - ness, Lift the shout of

praise! "Glo - ry in the high - est," Un - to God we raise. A - MEN.

2 We praise Thee for earth's beauty,
　And for the sky's blue dome;
　We praise Thee for our country;
　We praise Thee for our home;
　We praise Thee for Thy Gospel,
　And for a Saviour's love;
　We praise Thee for the promise
　Of endless life above. CHORUS.

3 The angels lift their anthems
　Of heavenly joy on high,
　And fill Thy courts with music
　In songs that never die.
　And when beyond the river
　We reach the City fair,
　We'll sing the songs of gladness
　With sweeter rapture there. CHORUS.

475

WARFARE.
P. M.

We are sol-diers of the Cross, Ours the old, old sto-ry;

Count-ing all our gains as loss But the gain for glo-ry.

In the path our fa-thers trod, With their faith un-swerv-ing;

He-roes of the Church of God, So would we be serv-ing. A-MEN.

2 As we raise our martial song,
Courage ne'er abating,
Angel bands, a holy throng,
On our steps are waiting.
Soon the journey will be o'er,
Passed each dark affliction;
Let us think how Jesus bore
Scourge and crucifixion.

3 See the heavenly mansions bright
Faithful hope adorning!
Far behind us looms the night,
But before, the morning:
Onward, onward to the goal,
Jesus goes before us;
Come, O come! each ransomed soul
Sound on high the chorus.

476

SANDON.
P. M.

Je - sus, who call-edst lit -tle ones to Thee, To Thee I come; O take my hand in Thine, and speak to me, And lead me home; Lest from the path of life my feet should stray, And Sa - tan prow-ling make Thy child his prey. A-MEN.

2 I love to think that Thou with holy feet
    My path hast trod,
Along life's common lane and dusty street
    Hast walked with God,
On Mary's bosom drawn a baby's breath,
And served Thy parents dear at Nazareth.

3 O gentle Jesus, make this heart of mine
    (So full of sin)
As holy, harmless, undefiled, as Thine,
    And dwell therein:
Then, God my Father, I like Thee shall know,
And grow in wisdom as in strength I grow.

4 To Thee, my Saviour, then, with morning light
    Glad songs I'll raise,
My saddest hours and darkest shall be bright
    With silent praise;
And should my work or play my thoughts employ,
Thy will shall be my law, Thy love my joy.

477

GLOUCESTER.
7s. D.

When the morning paints the skies, And the birds their songs re - new,

Let me from my slum-bers rise, Say - ing "What would Je - sus do?"

Count - less mer - cies from a - bove Day by day my path-way strew;

Is it much to bless Thy love? "Fa - ther, what would Je - sus do?" A - MEN.

2 When I ply my daily task,
  And the round of toil pursue,
Let me often brightly ask,
  " What, my soul, would Jesus do?'
Would the foe my heart beguile,
  Whispering thoughts and words untrue;
Let me to his subtlest wile
  Answer, "What would Jesus do?"

3 When the clouds of sorrow hide
  Mirth and sunshine from my view,
Let me, clinging to Thy side,
  Ponder, "What would Jesus do?"
Only let Thy love, O God,
  Fill my spirit through and through,
Treading where my Saviour trod,
  Breathing, " What would Jesus do?"

478 [65]

WESTWOOD.
7s, 6s. D.

O one with God the Fa - ther, In ma - jes - ty and might,

The bright-ness of His glo - ry, E - ter - nal light of light;

O'er this our home of dark - ness Thy rays are stream-ing now;

The sha-dows flee be - fore Thee, The world's true light art Thou. A-MEN.

2 Yet, Lord, we see but darkly :
  O heavenly Light, arise!
Dispel these mists that shroud us,
  And hide Thee from our eyes!
We long to track the footprints
  That Thou Thyself hast trod :
We long to see the pathway
  That leads to Thee our God.

3 O Jesu, shine around us
  With radiance of Thy grace :
O Jesu, turn upon us
  The brightness of Thy face.
We need no star to guide us,
  As on our way we press,
If Thou Thy light vouchsafest,
  O Sun of Righteousness.

479

BRAINE.
8s, 7s. D.

There is joy a-mong the Angels As they gath-er in the skies, Whispering some

REFRAIN.
VOICES IN UNISON.

hap-py se-cret Thro' the fields of Par-a-dise. They are sing-ing sweet

HARMONY.

songs of joy, They are sing-ing sweet songs for me, I can but

fall at Thy feet, dear Lord, And of-fer my tears to Thee. A-MEN.

2 There is joy among the blessed
    As they catch the Angels' strain,
And they echo back the tidings,
    " Lost awhile — but found again!"
    They are singing sweet songs of joy, etc.

3 There is joy in highest Heaven,
    From the very throne above,
For the tender heart of Jesus
    Beats with an eternal love!
    They are singing sweet songs of joy, etc.

480 [678]

BROOKS.
C. M.

There is a land of pure delight, Where Saints im-mor-tal reign; E-
cres.

ter-nal day ex-cludes the night, And pleas-ures ban-ish pain. A - MEN.
dim.

2 There everlasting spring abides,
  And never-fading flowers;
Death, like a narrow sea, divides
  This heavenly land from ours.

3 Bright fields beyond the swelling flood
  Stand dress'd in living green;
So, to the Jews fair Canaan stood,
  While Jordan roll'd between.

4 But timorous mortals start and shrink
  To cross the narrow sea;

And linger, trembling on the brink,
  And fear to launch away.

5 O could we make our doubts remove
  Those gloomy doubts that rise,
And see the Canaan that we love,
  With faith's illumin'd eyes:—

6 Could we but climb where Moses stood,
  And view the landscape o'er,
Not Jordan's stream, nor death's cold flood,
  Should fright us from the shore.

481

HOME.
P. M.

Home! Home! for the night is past, And the shad-ows flee a - way, And the

mists of earth are melt-ing fast, In the light of end - less day. A -MEN.

2 Home! Home! to the happy fold,
  To the pastures green and fair,
To the shining city paved with gold,
  And the dear ones wandering there.

3 Home! Home! for the weary feet,
  For the broken-hearted — rest,
For the aching head — a pillow sweet,
  On the Saviour's loving breast,

4 Home! Home! to the Land of love,
  For the winter days are o'er,

And the flowers are bright that bloom a-
  It is Spring for evermore!   [bove;

5 Home! Home! to the Land of peace,
  In the first faint light of dawn,
I can hear the songs that never cease,
  And the dark clouds all are gone!

6 Home! Home! for the night is past,
  And the shadows flee away,
And the wanderer finds his rest at last
  In the light of endless day!

482 [403]

THE HOLY CITY.
C. M. D.

mf

O moth-er dear, Je-ru-sa-lem! When shall I come to thee? . .

When shall my sor-rows have an end? Thy joys when shall I see? . .

mf

O hap-py har-bour of God's saints! O sweet and pleas-ant soil! . .

mf

In thee no sor-row can be found, Nor grief, nor care, nor toil. A-MEN.

2 No murky cloud o'ershadows thee,
  Nor gloom, nor darksome night;
But every soul shines as the sun:
  For God Himself gives light.
O my sweet home, Jerusalem!
  Thy joys when shall I see?
The King that sitteth on thy throne
  In His felicity?

3 Thy gardens and thy goodly walks
  Continually are green, [flowers
Where grow such sweet and pleasant
  As nowhere else are seen. [sound,
Right through thy streets, with silver
  The living waters flow,
And on the banks on either side,
  The trees of life do grow.

4 Those trees for evermore bear fruit;
  And ever more do spring,
There evermore the angels are
  And evermore do sing.
Jerusalem, my happy home,
  Would God I were in Thee,
Would God my woes were at an end,
  Thy joys that I might see.

483

LITTLEWOOD.
P. M.

Far, far a - way, there's a many-mansioned dwelling, Where the Saviour waits to

wel- come the dear souls for whom He died, All a - cross the dark - some

val - ley I can hear their an - thems swell-ing, And a - mid the gold - en

glo-ry I can see them by His side, In the Home so far a-way! A-MEN.

2 Far, far away, there 's a haven deep and quiet,
    Where the noiseless waves lie sleeping on the mountain-sheltered shore,
    Where the surges never enter, where no stormy tempests riot,
    Where the sails are furled for ever, and the ship goes out no more,
        From the Haven far away!

3 So thitherward I travel, in gladness or in sorrow,
    Across these trackless waters, with His love to cheer me through.
    And as every sunset closes, I can fancy that the morrow
    Will fire the heavenly mountains, with the Haven full in view
        And no longer far away!

484 (TEACHERS.)

WELLS.
Six 7s

Je - sus, Mas - ter, whom I serve, Though so fee - bly and so ill,

Strengthen hand and heart and nerve, All Thy bid - ding to ful - fil;

O- pen Thou mine eyes to see All the work Thou hast for me. A - MEN.

2 Jesus, Master, wilt Thou use
One who owes Thee more than all?
As Thou wilt, I would not choose,
Only let me hear Thy call;
Jesus, let me always be
In Thy service, glad and free.

485 (FOR A FLOWER SERVICE).

CLARE MARKET.
11s. 10s.

Here, Lord, we of - fer Thee all that is fair - est, Bloom from the gar - den, and

flowers from the field; Gifts for the strick- en ones, know- ing Thou car - est

More for the love than the wealth that we yield. A - MEN.

2 Send, Lord, by these to the sick and the dying,
  Speak to their hearts with a message of peace.
  Comfort the sad, who in weakness are lying,
  Grant the departing a gentle release.

3 Raise, Lord, to health again those who have sickened,
  Fair be their lives as the roses in bloom;
  Give of Thy grace to the souls Thou hast quickened,
  Gladness for sorrow, and brightness for gloom.

4 We, Lord, like flowers, must bloom and must wither;
  We, like these blossoms, must fade and must die;
  Gather us, Lord, to Thy Bosom for ever,
  Grant us a place in Thy House in the sky.

486

(*TEMPERANCE.*)

"SOLDIERS TRUE."
6s. 5s. D.

Unison, with spirit.

Soldiers true and faith - ful, Hear the trumpet's call, 'Neath your Captain's banner

Range ye, one and all. Not against the dev - il, Not against the world, Must the red-cross

poco rall.

ban - ner On - ly be unfurled. A-MEN.

2 Subtle foes are lurking,
    Deep your hearts within,
  There first wage the battle
    With the power of sin.
  O'er the sight and hearing,
    Touch, and taste, and smell,
  Set a watch, good Christians,
    Guard those portals well.

3 Satan, through the senses,
    Seeks your souls to slay,
  Let no secret traitor
    Jesus' cause betray.
  If to lusts enticing
    Ye betray your heart,
  Can ye bid the devil,
    And the world depart?

4 By the sign upon you,
    By Christ's life within,
  Close in deadly conflict
    With each pleasant sin.
  Jesus' eye is on you,
    Keep your solemn vow,
  Then a crown immortal
    Shall adorn your brow.

487 [278]

TEMPERANCE.

WALTHAM ABBEY
7s, 6s. D.

O Lord, our strength in weak - ness, We pray to Thee for grace;

For power to fight the bat - tle, For speed to run the race:

When Thy bap - tis - mal wa - ters Were poured up - on our brow,

We then were made Thy chil-dren, And pledged our ear - liest vow. A - MEN.

2 We then were sealed and hallowed
  By Thy life-giving word;
  Were made the Spirit's temples,
  And members of the Lord;
  With His own blood He bought us,
  And made the purchase sure;
  His are we: may He keep us
  Sober, and chaste, and pure.

3 Conformed to His own likeness
  May we so live and die,
  That in the grave our bodies
  In holy peace may lie;
  And at the resurrection
  Forth from those graves may spring,
  Like to the glorious body
  Of Christ, our Lord and King.

4 The pure in heart are blessèd,
  For they shall see the Lord
  For ever and for ever
  By seraphim adored;
  And they shall drink the pleasures,
  Such as no tongue can tell,
  From the clear crystal river,
  And life's eternal well.

488 (CHORISTERS.)

SOLITUDE.
6s. D.

How can we serve Thee, Lord, How sing a-right Thy praise

To Whom An-gel-ic Hosts, Their songs of tri-umph raise?

How can our fee-ble tongues, The Heav'n-ly An-them swell?

And in Thy Church on earth Thy joys and glo-ries tell? A-MEN.

2 Dear Lord! we know not how,
   But Thou Thyself hast said
That, " out of infants' lips,"
   Thy praise is perfected;
So now accept the gift
   Of heart and voice we bring,
And teach us, Gracious Lord,
   To love Thee while we sing!

3 Teach us to cast ourselves
   In worship at Thy Feet,
And, for our holy work,
   O Jesu! make us meet;
Daily increase us, Lord,
   With faith, and hope, and love,
That we at last may join
   The Angel-Choirs above!

Litanies.

[These Litanies may be sung by the clergyman, or any other person, the school singing the Response to every verse: or the verses may be taken alternately by the boys and girls, all joining in the Response. They should be sung kneeling.]

489
LITANY OF THE HOLY CHILD JESUS.

VERSE.

God's dear child, re - turn - ing home, Suf - fer, in Thy

RESPONSE.

love, to come, Ho - ly Child,...... to THEE. A - MEN.

2 And Thy gentle hands to bless,
Lay in brotherly caress,
Holy Child, on me.

3 Let my joy be in the thought
That I was in childhood brought
Holy Child, to Thee:

4 Let my hope be in the grace
That will never turn Thy face,
Holy Child, from me.

5 All my work, with all my might,
Let me do as in Thy sight,
Holy Child, for Thee;

6 And before the Father's throne,
O, present it as Thine own,
Holy Child, for me.

7 In my pleasant hours of play
Be not ever far away,
Holy Child, from me.

8 Let me, all the happy while,
Have the comfort of a smile,
Holy Child, from Thee.

9 All my sins, repented sore,
Let them be a grief no more,
Holy Child, to Thee.

10 Put the pure and seamless dress
Of Thy perfect righteousness,
Holy Child, on me.

11 Turn my heart, when sins surprise,
And temptations in me rise,
Holy Child, to Thee;

12 And with Thy dear Word of might
Satan put again to flight,
Holy Child, from me.

13 Fix my thoughts, and rest my heart,
(Choosing thus the better part,)
Holy Child, on Thee.

14 Never let my footsteps stray,
Nor Thy Spirit take away,
Holy Child, from me.

15 Thy dear will my will control,
Be the sunshine of my soul,
Holy Child, in Thee;

16 And my only shade or night,
When Thou dost not shed Thy light,
Holy Child, on me.

17 By Thy Father's love divine,
Fill with love this soul of mine,
Holy Child, for Thee.

18 By Thy Mother's tears and grief,
In my sorrows bring relief,
Holy Child, to me.

19 For the blessing of the Dove
That hath settled from above,
Holy Child, on me.

20 To the Father laud and praise,
Offered be, through all my days,
Holy Child, by Thee.

490 VERSE. LITANY OF THE HOLY CHILDHOOD, No. I.

Ho - ly Je - su, Child Di - vine, By the glo - ries that are Thine,

RESPONSE.

Veil'd within so poor a shrine: *Hear us, Ho - ly Je - su.* AMEN.

2 By Thy form so weak and small,
By Thy plaintive infant call,
By Thy childish tears that fall:
Hear us, Holy Jesu.

3 By the Angels' holy song,
As around they wondering throng,
Owning Thee Their Ruler strong:
Hear us, Holy Jesu.

4 By the lowly cattle shed,
. By the narrow manger-bed,
By the rough clothes o'er Thee spread:
Hear us, Holy Jesu.

5 By the solemn praise and prayer,
By the gifts and offerings rare
Laid in lowly manger there:
Hear us, Holy Jesu.

6 By Thy blessèd mother's woes,
By Thy fleeing from Thy foes,
By Thy grief that no man knows:
Hear us, Holy Jesu.

7 By Thy growing, day by day,
By Thy zeal in wisdom's way,
Quick to learn and to obey:
Hear us, Holy Jesu.

8 By Thy life, so lone and still,
By Thy waiting to fulfil
In its time Thy Father's will:
Hear us, Holy Jesu.

9 By the care that weighed on Thee,
By Thy toil and poverty,
By Thy sorrows yet to be:
Hear us, Holy Jesu.

10 Jesu, Holy Child Divine,
On our darkened nature shine,
Give us virtues like to Thine:
Hear us, Holy Jesu.

11 Make us pure and undefiled,
Gentle, patient, loving, mild,
Trustful as a little child:
Hear us, Holy Jesu.

12 Make us ever long to know
Where our God would have us go,
Shrinking not from toil or woe:
Hear us, Holy Jesu.

13 May we mark the pattern fair
Of Thy life of work and prayer,
And for truth all perils dare:
Hear us, Holy Jesu.

14 May we calmly suffer blame,
Bear the cross, despise the shame,
In Thy strength and in Thy Name.
Hear us, Holy Jesu.

15 As we live, from year to year,
Jesu, be Thou ever near;
Make us like Thee, Saviour dear;
Hear us, Holy Jesu.

16 Bid us come at last to Thee,
And for ever perfect be,
When Thy glory we shall see:
Hear us, Holy Jesu.

491 Music for Parts I and III.
VERSE.

God the Fa-ther, God the Son, God the Spir-it, Three in One,

Hear us from Thy heavenly Throne. Spare us, Ho-ly Trin-i-ty. A-MEN.

2 Jesu, Saviour ever mild,
Born for us a little Child
Of the Virgin undefiled:
  Hear us, Holy Jesu.

3 Jesu, by the Mother-Maid
In Thy swaddling-clothes arrayed,
And within a manger laid:
  Hear us, Holy Jesu.

4 Jesu, at whose infant feet
Shepherds, coming Thee to greet,
Knelt to pay their worship meet:
  Hear us, Holy Jesu.

5 Jesu, unto whom of yore
Wise men, hastening to adore,
Gold and myrrh and incense bore:
  Hear us, Holy Jesu.

6 Jesu, to Thy temple brought,
Whom, by Thy good Spirit taught,
Simeon and Anna sought:
  Hear us, Holy Jesu.

7 Jesu, who didst deign to flee
From King Herod's cruelty
In Thy earliest infancy:
  Hear us, Holy Jesu.

8 Jesu, whom Thy Mother found,
'Midst the doctors sitting round,
Marvelling at Thy words profound:
  Hear us, Holy Jesu.

Part II. VERSE.

From all pride and vain con-ceit, From all spite and an-gry heat,

From all ly-ing and de-ceit, Save us, Ho-ly Je-su. D.C.

2 From all sloth and idleness,
From not caring for distress,
From all lust and greediness:
  Save us, Holy Jesu.

3 From refusing to obey,
From the love of our own way,
From forgetfulness to pray:
  Save us, Holy Jesu.

LITANIES.

Part III.   (For Tune, see preceding page.

1 By Thy Birth and early years,
By Thine Infant wants and fears,
By Thy sorrows and Thy tears;
Save us, Holy Jesu.

2 By Thy Pattern bright and pure,
By the pains Thou didst endure
Our salvation to procure.
Save us, Holy Jesu.

3 By Thy wounds and thorn-crowned head.
By Thy blood for sinners shed,
By Thy rising from the dead:
Save us, Holy Jesu.

4 By the Name we bow before,
Human Name, which evermore
All the hosts of heaven adore,
Save us, Holy Jesu.

5 By Thine own unconquered might,
By Thy glory in the height,
By Thy mercies infinite:
Save us, Holy Jesu.

492 VERSE.   LITANY OF THE CHURCH.

God the Fa-ther, God the Son, God the Spir-it, Three in One,

RESPONSE.

Hear us from Thy heav'nly Throne; Spare us, Ho-ly Trin-i-ty. A-MEN.

2 Jesus, with Thy Church abide.
Be her Saviour, Lord, and Guide,
While on earth her faith is tried;
We beseech Thee, hear us.

3 Arms of love around her throw,
Shield her safe from every foe,
Comfort her in time of woe:
We beseech Thee, hear us.

4 Keep her life and doctrine pure,
Grant her patience to endure.
Trusting in Thy promise sure:
We beseech Thee, hear us.

5 May she one in doctrine be,
One in truth and charity.
Winning all to faith in Thee:
We beseech Thee, hear us.

6 May she guide the poor and blind,
Seek the lost until she find,
And the broken-hearted bind
We beseech Thee, hear us

7 May her lamp of truth be bright,
Bid her bear aloft its light
Through the realms of heathen night:
We beseech Thee, hear us.

8 May her scattered children be
From reproach of evil free,
Blameless witnesses for Thee:
We beseech Thee, hear us.

9 May she soon all glorious be,
Spotless and from wrinkle free,
Pure, and bright, and worthy Thee:
We beseech Thee, hear us

10 Fit her all Thy joy to share
In the home Thou dost prepare,
And be ever blessèd there:
We beseech Thee, hear us.

493 [514]   **Processionals.**   BARNBY.
P. M.

With spirit.

We march, we march to vic - to - ry, With the Cross of the Lord be-fore us, With His

lov-ing Eye looking down from the sky, And His Holy Arm spread o'er us, His Ho-ly Arm spread

o'er us. We come in the might of the Lord of Light In marshall'd train to meet Him;

And we put to flight the armies of night, That the sons of the day may greet Him,

The sons of the day may greet Him. We march, we march to vic - to - ry, With the

Cross of the Lord be-fore us, With His lov-ing Eye looking down from the sky, And His

All verses except last. | Last verse only.

2d verse.

Ho - ly Arm spread o'er us, His Ho-ly arm spread o'er us. The o'er us, AMEN.

2 The bands of the Alien flee away
When our chant goes up like thunder,
And the van of the Lord in serried array,
Cleaves Satan's ranks asunder.
We march, we march, &c.

3 Our sword is the Spirit of God on High,
Our helmet His Salvation;
Our banner the Cross of Calvary,
Our watchword—THE IN-CAR-NA-TION.
We march, we march, &c.

4 He marches in front of His banner unfurl'd,
Which He raised that His own might find
Him;
And the Holy Church throughout all the world
Fall into rank behind Him.
We march, we march, &c,

5 And the choir of Angels with songs awaits
Our march to the golden Sion;
For our Captain has broken the brazen gates,
And burst the bars of iron.
We march, we march, &c.

6 Then onward we march, our arms to prove,
With the banner of Christ before us,
With His eye of love looking down from above,
And His Holy Arm spread o'er us.
We march, we march, &c.

494

Joyous.

LICHFIELD.
7s.

Palms of glo - ry, rai - ment bright, Crowns that nev - er fade a - way,

Gird and deck the Saints in light, Priests, and kings, and conquerors they. AMEN.

2 Yet the conquerors bring their palms
To the LAMB amidst the Throne,
And proclaim in joyful psalms
Victory through His Cross alone.

3 Kings their crowns for harps resign,
Crying as they strike the chords,
"Take the Kingdom, it is Thine,
King of kings, and LORD of lords."

4 Round the Altar Priests confess,
If their robes are white as snow,
'Twas the Saviour's Righteousness,
And His Blood, that made them so.

5 They were mortal too like us;
O, when we like them must die,
May our souls translated thus
Triumph, reign, and shine on high.

495 [519]

Moderate.

EDINA.
6s. 5s. D.

1. Sa - viour, Bless - ed Sa - viour, Lis - ten whilst we sing,
2. Near - er, e - ver near - er, Christ, we draw to Thee,

Hearts and voi - ces rais - ing Prais - es to our King.
Deep in a - do - ra - tion Bend - ing low the knee.

All we have to of - fer, All we hope to be,....
Thou for our re - demp - tion Cam'st on earth to die,....

Bo - dy, soul, and spir - it, All we yield to Thee.
Thou, that we might fol - low, Hast gone up on high. A-MEN.

3 Great and ever greater
　　Are Thy mercies here,
　True and everlasting
　　Are the glories there.
　Where no pain or sorrow,
　　Toil, or care is known,
　Where the Angel-legions
　　Circle round Thy Throne.

4 Brighter still and brighter
　　Glows the western sun,
　Shedding all its gladness
　　O'er our work that's done;
　Time will soon be over,
　　Toil and sorrows past,
　May we, Blessèd Saviour,
　　Find a rest at last.

5 Onward, ever onward,
　　Journeying o'er the road,
　Worn by saints before us,
　　Journeying on to God:
　Leaving all behind us,
　　May we hasten on,
　Backward never looking
　　Till the prize is won.

6 Bliss, all bliss excelling,
　　When the ransomed soul
　Earthly toil forgetting
　　Finds its promise goal;
　Where in joys unheard of
　　Saints with angels sing,
　Never weary raising
　　Praises to their King.

496 [396]

Earnestly.

ALFORD.
P. M.

Ten thou-sand times ten thou-sand, In spark-ling rai-ment bright,

The ar-mies of the ransomed saints Throng up the steeps of light.

'Tis fin-ished! all is fin-ished, Their fight with death and sin;

Fling o-pen wide the gold-en gates, And let the vic-tors in. A-MEN.

2 What rush of Alleluias
  Fills all the earth and sky!
What ringing of a thousand harps
  Bespeaks the triumph nigh!
O day, for which creation
  And all its tribes were made!
O joy for all its former woes
  A thousand-fold repaid.

3 Oh, then what raptured greetings
  On Canaan's happy shore,
What knitting severed friendships up,
  Where partings are no more!
Then eyes with joy shall sparkle
  That brimmed with tears of late;
Orphans no longer fatherless,
  Nor widows desolate.

4 Bring near the great salvation,
    Thou Lamb for sinners slain,
  Fill up the roll of Thine elect;
    Then take Thy power and reign:
  Appear, Desire of nations,
    Thine exiles long for home:
  Show in the heavens Thy promised sign;
    Thou Prince and Saviour, come.

497 [522]

Joyous.

HERMAS.
11s.
with Chorus.

On our way re - joic - ing as we homeward move, Hearken to our prais- es,

O Thou God of love! Is there grief or sad-ness? Thine it can-not be!

CHORUS.

Is our sky be-cloud-ed? Clouds are not from Thee! On our way re - joic- ing

as we homeward move, Hearken to our prais-es, O Thou God of love! AMEN.

2 If with honest-hearted love for God and man,
Day by day Thou find us doing what we can,
Thou who giv'st the seed-time wilt give large increase,
Crown the head with blessings, fill the heart with peace.
    CHO:— On our way rejoicing, &c.

3 On our way rejoicing gladly let us go;
Conquered hath our Leader, vanquished is our foe!
Christ without, our safety, Christ within, our joy;
Who, if we be faithful, can our hope destroy?
    CHO:— On our way rejoicing, &c.

4 Unto God the Father joyful songs we sing;
Unto God the Saviour thankful hearts we bring;
Unto God the Spirit bow we and adore,
On our way rejoicing now and evermore!
    CHO:— On our way rejoicing, &c.

498 [515]

With spirit.

S. ALBAN.
6s. 5s. D. *with Refrain.*

Brightly gleams our banner, Pointing to the sky, Waving wanderers onward To their home on high. Journey-ing o'er the des-ert. Glad - ly thus we pray, And with hearts u - ni - ted Take our heavenward way. Brightly gleams our banner, Pointing to the sky, Waving wanderers on-ward To their home on high. A-MEN.

2 Jesus, Lord and Master,
   At Thy sacred feet.
   Here with hearts rejoicing
   See Thy children meet;
   Often have we left Thee,
   Often gone astray,
   Keep us mighty Saviour,
   In the narrow way.
      Brightly gleams, &c.

3 All our days direct us
   In the way we go,
   Lead us on victorious
   Over every foe;
   Bid Thine angels shield us
   When the storm-clouds lour,
   Pardon Thou and save us
   In the last dread hour.
      Brightly gleams, &c.

4 Then with Saints and Angels
   May we join above,
   Offering prayers and praises
   At Thy Throne of love;
   When the toil is over,
   Then comes rest and peace,
   Jesus, in His Beauty,
   Songs that never cease.
      Brightly gleams, &c.

498 [515] [SECOND TUNE.]

S. THERESA.
6s, 5s. 12 lines.

1. Brightly gleams our banner, Pointing to the sky, . Waving wand'rers onward
2.   Jesus, Lord and Mas-ter, At Thy sa-cred feet, Here with hearts rejoicing
3.   All our days di-rect us In the way we go, . Lead us on vic-to-rious
4. Then with Saints and angels May we join a-bove, Off'ring prayers and prai-ses

To their home on high. Journeying o'er the des-ert Glad-ly thus we pray,
See Thy chil-dren meet: Of-ten have we left Thee, Of-ten gone a-stray;
O-ver ev-'ry foe; Bid Thine an-gels shield us When the storm clouds lower,
At Thy throne of love; When the toil is o-ver, Then come rest and peace,

CHORUS.

And with hearts u-ni-ted, Take our heav'nward way.
Keep us, migh-ty Saviour, In the narrow way. Brightly gleams our banner,
Par-don, Thou, and save us In the last dread hour.
Je-sus in His beau-ty, Songs that never cease.

UNISON.

Pointing to the sky, Waving wand'rers onward To their home on high. A-MEN.

499 [516]

With spirit.

S. GERTRUDE.
6s. 5s. D. *with Refrain.*

Onward, Christian soldiers, Marching as to war, With the Cross of Je - sus
Go - ing on be-fore. Christ, the Roy-al Mas - ter, Leads against the foe,
Forward in - to bat-tle See, His banners go. Onward, Christian sol - diers,
Marching as to war, With the Cross of Je - sus Go - ing on be - fore. A - MEN.

2 At the sign of triumph
  Satan's host doth flee;
On, then, Christian soldiers,
  On to victory.
Hell's foundations quiver,
  At the shout of praise;
Brothers, lift your voices,
  Loud your anthems raise.
    Onward, Christian soldiers, &c.

3 Like a mighty army
  Moves the Church of God;
Brothers, we are treading
  Where the Saints have trod;
We are not divided,
  All one body we,
One in hope and doctrine,
  One in charity.
    Onward, Christian soldiers, &c.

4 Crowns and thrones may perish,
  Kingdoms rise and wane,
But the Church of Jesus
  Constant will remain;
Gates of hell can never
  'Gainst that Church prevail;
We have Christ's own promise,
  And that cannot fail.
    Onward, Christian soldiers, &c.

5 Onward, then, ye people,
  Join our happy throng,
Blend with ours your voices,
  In the triumph song—
Glory, laud and honour,
  Unto Christ the King,
This through countless ages
  Men and Angels sing.
    Onward, Christian soldiers, &c.

499 [SECOND TUNE.]

VICTORY.
6s. 5s. D.

On-ward, Christian sol-diers, Marching as to war, With the cross of Je - sus
With the cross . . .
Go - ing on be - fore. Christ, the roy-al Mas - ter, Leads a-gainst the foe;
Christ, the roy - al . . .
ORGAN OR 1ST TREBLES. Onward, Chris - - - tian soldiers, Marching,
Forward in - to bat - tle, See His banners go. On-ward, Christian sol - diers,
march - ing to war,
Marching as to war, . . . With the cross, the cross of Jesus, Go - ing on be - fore. A-MEN.

2 At the sign of triumph
  Satan's host doth flee;
On, then, Christian soldiers,
  On to victory.
Hell's foundations quiver,
  At the shout of praise;
Brothers, lift your voices,
  Loud your anthems raise.
    Onward, Christian soldiers, etc.

3 Like a mighty army
  Moves the Church of God;
Brothers, we are treading
  Where the Saints have trod;
We are not divided,
  All one body we,
One in hope and doctrine,
  One in charity.
    Onward, Christian soldiers, etc.

4 Crowns and thrones may perish,
  Kingdoms rise and wane,
But the Church of Jesus
  Constant will remain;
Gates of hell can never
  'Gainst that Church prevail;
We have Christ's own promise,
  And that cannot fail.
    Onward, Christian soldiers, etc.

5 Onward, then, ye people,
  Join our happy throng,
Blend with ours your voices,
  In the triumph song —
Glory, laud, and honour,
  Unto Christ the King,
This through countless ages
  Men and Angels sing.
    Onward, Christian soldiers, etc.

500

Boldly.

FESTIVAL.
7s. 6s. *with Refrain.*

Forth to the fight, ye ran-som'd, Migh-ty in God's own might,

Stem-ming the tide of bat-tle, Rout-ing the hosts of night.

FULL.

Lift ye the Blood-red Ban-ner, Wield ye the vic-tor's sword,

Raise ye the Christian's war-cry— "The Cross of Christ the Lord." A - MEN.

Full Swell.

Large notes on Great Organ Reed.

SW. *to* PED. *dopp.*

2 Fear not the din of battle,
    Follow where He has trod
Perfecting strength in weakness—
    JESUS, INCARNATE GOD.
      Lift ye, &c.

Trebles and Altos in Unison.

3 Angels around us hover,
    Succour in time of need,
Ever at hand to strengthen,
    Guardians they indeed.
      Lift ye, &c.

Tenors and Basses in Unison.

4 Arm ye against the battle,
    Watch ye, and fast, and pray,
Peace shall succeed the warfare,
    Night shall be changed to day.
      Lift ye, &c.

5 Fight, for the Lord is o'er you,
    Fight, for He bids you fight;
There where the fray is thickest
    Close with the hosts of night.
      Lift ye, &c.

501 [523]

S. BOTOLPH
6s. 5s. Twelve lines

Boldly.

Forward! be our watchword, Step and voices joined, Seek the things before us,

Not a look be-hind; Burns the fier-y pil-lar At our ar-my's head;

Who shall dream of shrinking, By our Captain led? Forward thro' the des-ert,

Thro' the toil and fight, Jordan flows be-fore us. Si-on beams with light. A-MEN.

2 Forward when in childhood
  Buds the infant mind;
All through youth and manhood,
  Not a thought behind:
Speed through realms of nature,
  Climb the steps of grace;
Faint not, till in glory
  Gleams our Father's face.
Forward, all the life-time
  Climb from height to height:
Till the head be hoary,
  Till the eve be light!

3 Forward, flock of Jesus,
  Salt of all the earth,
Till each yearning purpose
  Spring to glorious birth;
Sick, they ask for healing,
  Blind, they grope for day;

Pour upon the nations
  Wisdom's loving ray.
Forward, out of error,
  Leave behind the night;
Forward through the darkness,
  Forward into light.

4 Glories upon glories,
  Hath our God prepared,
By the souls that love Him
  One day to be shared;
Eye hath not beheld them,
  Ear hath never heard;
Nor of these hath uttered
  Thought or speech or word.
Forward, marching eastward
  Where the heaven is bright,
Till the veil be lifted,
  Till our faith be sight!

502

Earnestly.

S. BONIFACE.
6s. 5s. Twelve lines.

Far o'er yon hor - i - zon Rise the cit - y towers; Where our God a - bid - eth;

That fair Home is ours: Flash the streets with jas-per, Shine the gates with gold;

Flows the gladdening riv - er, Shedding joys un - told. Thither, on-ward thith-er,

In the Spi - rit's might; Pilgrims to your coun-try, For-ward in - to light. A-MEN.

2 Into God's high temple
  Onward as we press,
Beauty spreads around us,
  Born of holiness;
Arch, and vault, and carving,
  Lights of varied tone,
Softened words and holy,
  Prayer and praise alone:
Every thought upraising
  To our city bright,
Where the tribes assemble
  Round the Throne of light.

3 Nought that city needeth
  Of these aisles of stone:
Where the GODHEAD dwelleth,
  Temple there is none;
All the Saints, that ever
  In these courts have stood.

Are but babes, and feeding
  On the children's food.
On through sign and token,
  Stars amid the night.
Forward through the darkness,
  Forward into light.

4 To the eternal FATHER
  Loudest anthems raise;
To the SON and SPIRIT
  Echo songs of praise;
To the Lord of glory,
  Blessed THREE in ONE,
Be by men and Angels
  Endless honours done:
Weak are earthly praises;
  Dull the songs of night;
Forward into triumph,
  Forward into light!

503

CONQUEST.
6s. 5s. D. *with refrain.*

With spirit.

Sol-diers of the Captain! Stand, for Him, and fight, Hardness glad en - dur - ing,

Armour'd in His might! He is that great Vic-tor Praised in Angels' songs,

Glo - ry of each sol - dier Who to Him be - longs. Sol - diers of the Cap-tain!

Last time.

Stand, for Him, and fight, Hardness glad en-dur-ing, Armour'd in His might! Might! A - MEN.

2 Leader never vanquished—
   More than conquerors too,
Through Himself, He maketh
   All His soldiers true;
O'er the foe, triumphant,
   He must still prevail—
So, His soldiers faithful,
   With Him cannot fail.
      Soldiers of the Captain! &c.

3 Take ye, then, the Helmet,
   Breastplate, Shield, and Sword—
Thus equipped, for battle
   Ready at His word:
Fierce though be the warfare,
   Sure is the renown—
And, though dark the conflict,
   Bright the promised crown.
      Soldiers of the Captain! &c.

4 Jesus! Captain! help us
   Soldiers good to be—
Living, dying, ever,
   Fighting Lord, for Thee:
Eager to march forward,
   In those ranks of Thine—
Waiting but the order
   From Thy voice divine!
      Soldiers of the Captain! &c.

504 *Boldly.*

S. EDWARD, CONFESSOR.
P. M.

Advance! advance! the day is come To sing our Ma-ker's prai-ses;

Each thankful heart in faith and hope, The strain of joy up - rai - ses:

In robes all pure and white We chase the shades of night, The gloom shall pass a-

way Be-fore the dawn of day; The Lord of Hosts is with us. A-MEN.

2 Advance! Advance! though sore the strife,
Though timid hearts are quailing,
The Lord of Hosts doth lead our van,
And He is all availing:
With His blest Presence near,
No mortal foe we fear;
Our Captain goes before.
'Mid strife of battle sore;
The Lord of Hosts is with us.

3 Advance! Advance! nor gaze behind,
Nor deem the pathway weary;
The Leader's footsteps print the track,
Through all that region dreary:
In faith we follow on,
We tread where He has gone;
The stormy wind may rave,
The stormy wind we brave;
The Lord of Hosts is with us.

4 Advance! Advance! lift up your hearts;
The sky above doth lighten:
Most dark around the shadows fall,
Ere rays of dawn may brighten:
The night is dark and chill,
The dawn is on the hill,
We reck not of the night,
'Twill soon be warm and bright;
The Lord of Hosts is with us.

5 Advance! Advance! ah, dearest Lord,
'Tis Thou, 'tis Thou dost lead us;
'Tis Thou dost point the narrow way,
'Tis Thou dost tend, dost feed us:
No power, no might have we,
Our strength is all of Thee;
At morn, at eventide,
Our aid, our hope, our guide.
Great Lord of Hosts be with us.

505

ELMENDORF.
P. M.

Small notes for organ only.

1. March, march, on-ward,
3. See, see, yon-der

sol - diers true, Take thro' cloud and mist your way. Yon-der flows the fount of life,
shines your home; Gates of pearl and walls of gold. Joy that heart hath nev - er known,

Yon-der dwells e - ter-nal day; March, tho' myr-iad foes are nigh, For-ward till ye
Bliss that tongue hath never told. Vic - tors then thro' Christ your Lord, Gath-ered round His

reach the shore; Then when all the strife is done, Rest in peace for ev - er-more.
glo-rious throne, Be it yours to sing His praise, Praise that He your King shall own.

2. Hark, hark, loud the trum-pet sounds; Wake, ye chil-dren of the light, Time is past for
4. Praise, praise Him who reigns on high; Praise the co - e - ter - nal Son, Praise the Spir-it,

sloth and sleep; Wake, and arm you for the fight. Spear and sword each war - rior needs;
Lord of life; Praise the bless-ed Three in One. Praise Him, ye who toil and fight;

Foes are round you, friends are few; Faint not, tho' the way be long, Fainting still your
Praise Him, ye who bear the palm, As the sound of mighty seas Pour your ev - er

way pur - sue, Faint-ing still your way pur - sue. ORG.
last-ing psalm, Pour your ev - er - last-ing psalm.

506

CŒLIUM.
8s, 5s.

An - gel voi - ces sweet-ly sing - ing, Ech-oes thro' the blue dome ring-ing,

News of wondrous glad-ness bring-ing; Ah! 'tis Heaven at last. A-MEN.

2 Now, beneath us all the grieving,
All the wounded spirit's heaving,
All the woe of hopes deceiving:
Ah, 't is Heaven at last!

3 On the jasper threshold standing,
Like a pilgrim safely landing,
See, the strange bright scene expanding!
Ah, 't is Heaven at last!

4 What a city! what a glory!
Far beyond the brightest story
Of the ages old and hoary:
Ah, 't is Heaven at last!

5 Not a tear-drop ever falleth,
Not a pleasure ever palleth;
Song to song for ever calleth;
Ah, 't is Heaven at last!

6 Christ Himself, the living splendour,
Christ, the sunlight mild and tender;
Praises to the Lamb we render;
Ah, 't is Heaven at last!

7 Broken death's dread bands that bound us,
Life and victory around us;
Christ the King Himself hath crowned us;
Ah, 't is Heaven at last!

507

LLOYD.
P. M.

Hark! the sound of the fight hath gone forth, And we must not tar ry at home;

For our Lord, from the South and the North Has commanded His sol-diers to come.

We must on with our ban-ner un-furl'd: We must on: it is Je-sus who leads;

We must has-ten to conquer the world With the sign of the Lamb who bleeds. AMEN.

2 We must stand to our colors like men;
Our Lord is a leader to love;
For the wounded He heals, and the slain
He crowns in His city above.
We must march to the battle with speed,
Upon earth our one duty is strife;
O blest are the soldiers who bleed
For the Saviour who died to give life!

3 There is Jesus in heaven above,
There is Jesus on earth below,
And His the one standard we love,
And His the one watchword we know.
Let us sing the new song of the Lamb;
Let us sing round our banner so brave;
Let us sing of that life-giving Blood
That was shed to redeem and to save.

508 *With spirit.* *mf*

FORWARD.
P. M.

"Forward!" said the Proph - et, Point-ing to the sea, "March, ye roy-al

peo - ple, Thro' it fear-less-ly! What tho' foes are gath'ring, Dark'ning all the plain,

f CHORUS.

God's right arm extend - ed, Shall their force restrain. Roll back, rushing wa - ters!

Stay thy waves, O sea! That I may gain the blessed land My God has promis'd me. AMEN.

2 What though broad before you
　Spreads a tossing tide?
　God is strong and mighty
　　Waters to divide.
　With my rod uplifted,
　　Forward see me go;
　Back! ye hungry billows,
　　Let the people through.
　　Roll back, etc.

3 Dread not threatening billows
　Which like walls uprear;
　Dread not hosts pursuing,
　　Armed with sword and spear.
　Wherefore now faint-hearted?
　　Trust ye in your God!
　Look on me, your leader,
　　With uplifted rod.
　　Roll back, etc.

4 Soon shall all be gathered
　Safe on yonder Shore;
　Foes who long have daunted,
　　Ye shall see no more.
　Looking back, shall wonder
　　What ye had to fear;
　Marvel how ye doubted
　　When your help was near.
　　Roll back, etc.

509 [520]

MARION.
S. M.

Re-joice, ye pure in heart; Re-joice, give thanks and sing — Your

glo-rious ban-ner wave on high; The Cross of Christ your King.

Tutti.

Re-joice, Re-joice, Re-joice, give thanks and sing. A-men.

Re-joice, Re-joice,

2 Bright youth and snow-crowned age,
Strong men and maidens meek,
Raise high your free exulting song,
God's wondrous praises speak.
Rejoice, etc.

3 With all the angel choirs,
With all the saints of earth,
Pour out the strains of joy and bliss,
True rapture, noblest mirth.
Rejoice, etc.

4 Your clear Hosannas raise
And Alleluias loud;
While answering echoes upward float,
Like wreaths of incense cloud.
Rejoice, etc.

5 Still lift your standard high,
Still march in firm array,
As warriors through the darkness toil,
Till dawns the golden day.
Rejoice, etc.

6 At last the march shall end,
The wearied ones shall rest,
The pilgrims find their Father's House,
Jerusalem, the blest.
Rejoice, etc.

7 Then on, ye pure in heart,
Rejoice, give thanks, and sing;
Your festal banner wave on high,
The Cross of Christ, your King.
Rejoice, etc.

510

A-wake! for the trumpet is sounding a - far; Then let us, like soldiers, en-

gage in the war; The stan-dard of Je - sus with vig - our de-fend, And

ne - ver give up till the con - flict shall end. On to the field! let us

on to the field! Fear-less and faith-ful, lead on to the field! We'll

die in the battle, but never will yield; Then fearless and faithful, lead on to the field! Amen.

2 The foe may surround us, but why should
we fear?   [near;
To shield and protect us, our Captain is
He bids us remember this truth in the
fight —   [bright.
By watching and praying our arms we keep
On to the field, etc.

3 Then let us be valiant our foes to subdue;
How cheering the prospect, our crown is in
view;
A crown never-fading our Saviour will
give,   [shall live.
And they who have conquered, in glory
On to the field, etc.

511

SOLDIERS OF THE CHURCH.
8s, 7s. WITH CHORUS.

With spirit.

Sons of Je - sus, gal - lant sol-diers, Brace your sin - ews for the fight,

In your sil - ver ar - mour har-ness'd For the Truth and Right.

CHORUS.

Al - le - lu - ia! Al - le - lu - ia! Sol-diers of the Church are ye,

Al - le - lu - ia! Al - le - lu - ia! March to vic - to - ry. A - MEN.

2 Draw the sword to blast of trumpet,
  Charge the shrinking hosts of Hell!
  Keep the tread! the Church united
    Is invincible.
      Alleluia! etc.

3 Follow where the fiery pillar
  Leadeth, ever-present guide;
  Feed upon the falling manna
    And be satisfied.
      Alleluia! etc.

4 Lo! the golden ark attends us!
  Lo! the tables traced by God!
  Lo! the everlasting priesthood,
    Ever budding rod.
      Alleluia! etc.

5 Lo! upon the holy mountain
  Jesus, more than Moses stands,
  Interceding, with uplifted
    And extended hands.
      Alleluia! etc.

6 What though stung by fiery serpents?
  To the Cross we look, and live!
  Marah's wells by wood are sweetened
    And refreshment give!
      Alleluia! etc.

7 Lo! before us shines our country,
  Lit by an eternal sun;
  Flows with milk, and streams with honey,
    Ours the battle won.
      Alleluia! etc.

512

In martial style.

CHURCH ARMY.
P. M.

mf The ban-ners are wav-ing, the trum-pet sounds, The sol-diers are gird-ing for war; The summons is sound-ed to form in rank, And gath-er from near and far. The shield of the Faith on the arm made fast, The sword of the Lord in hand! We march in the glo-rious Host of God, We fight at the King's com-mand. A-MEN.

2 The man and the maiden, the old, the young,
   Are all in the Church of God ;
And all have to fight in the self-same fight,
   And tread where the Saints have trod.
The Captain above us is Jesus Christ,
   His Banner the Cross so red.
We march in the glorious Host of God,
   We follow our King and Head.

3 But One is the army that Christ commands,
   In ages that pass, but One;
But One is the warfare wherever waged,
   In the self-same way begun.
The Faith of the army of Christ is One,
   The strength of its Hope the same.
We march in the glorious Host of God,
   In the great Commander's Name.

4 Then who will be found from the Host to stray?
   And who from the Faith to fall?
As Satan of old from the ranks above,
   From Jesus the All-in-all?
With shoulder to shoulder, and firm as flint,
   We swerve not to left or right,
We march in the glorious Host of God,
   The soldiers and sons of Light.

513

Pro Deo et Ecclesia.

Briskly.

Forward! Forward Christians, Forward to the fight! For the Cross of Je - sus,

For the Gos - pel light; 'Tis no time to dal - ly, 'Tis no time to wait,

CHORUS.

When the host of e - vil Thun-ders at the gate, Forward! Forward, Christians,

Forward! to the fight, For the Cross of Je - sus, For the Gos-pel light. A-men.

2 Come, let us adore Him,
Let us bow the knee;
King, He claims our worship,
Who hath made us free.
He that gift has given
Which we love so well,
God with us for ever,
Christ, Emmanuel.
Forward! etc.

3 Shall we slight His Presence?
Shall we Christ deny?
Shall we stint our worship
When He draweth nigh?
God in Heaven forbid it!
God attest our word,
We will worship Jesus,
We will serve the Lord.
Forward! etc.

4 Hark! the sound of battle
Swells upon the breeze;
Do we shun the conflict?
Do we dwell at ease?
They are coward Christians
Who the summons slight,
"Forward Christian soldiers,
Forward to the fight!"
Forward! etc.

514

SONG OF COURAGE.
6s, 5s. D. WITH CHORUS.

Hear the roy - al sum-mons, Gird you for the fight,'Gainst the pow'rs of dark-ness,

March the sons of Light. Fear not you the con - flict, On to vic-t'ry go,

CHORUS.

You, with Christ as hel - per, No de - feat can know. Dare to do your du - ty

Standing for the right; Dare obey the Mas - ter, Walking in His light. A-MEN.

2 When the hosts are rallied,
  Dare your Lord confess;
Dare to bear your witness
  Other hearts to bless.
When your Captain calls you,
  Forward dare to go;
When the Tempter tries you,
  Dare to answer, "No."
    Dare to do your duty, etc.

3 Armed with Christ's own spirit,
  Strike at every wrong;
Think not of your weakness,
  He will make you strong.
Shrink not then from danger,
  Bravely bear the cross;
Christ will turn to blessing
  All your seeming loss.
    Dare to do your duty, etc ·

4 Hear the royal promise,
  Victory is sure;
Wrong shall be defeated,
  Right shall reign secure.
March we on with courage;
  Help to save the world;
Be this conquering banner
  O'er all lands unfurled.
    Dare to do your duty, etc.

515 [518]

EVELYNS.
11s.

At the Name of Je - sus ev-'ry knee shall bow, Ev-'ry tongue confess Him King of glo - ry now; 'Tis the Father's pleas-ure
we should call Him Lord, Who from the be-gin-ning was the Mighty Word. AMEN.

2 At His voice creation sprang at once to sight,
  All the angel faces, all the hosts of light,
  Thrones and dominations, stars upon their way,
  All the heavenly orders, in their great array.

3 Humbled for a season, to receive a name
  From the lips of sinners unto whom He came,
  Faithfully He bore it spotless to the last,
  Brought it back victorious, when from death He passed;

4 Bore it up triumphant with its human light,
  Through all ranks of creatures, to the central height:
  To the throne of Godhead, to the Father's breast;
  Filled it with the glory of that perfect rest.

5 In your hearts enthrone Him; there let Him subdue
  All that is not holy, all that is not true:
  Crown Him as your Captain in temptation's hour;
  Let His will enfold you in its light and power.

6 Brothers, this Lord Jesus shall return again,
  With His Father's glory, with His angel train;
  For all wreaths of empire meet upon His brow,
  And our hearts confess Him King of glory now.

516 [397]

O QUANTA QUALIA.
Ancient Plain-song.

O what the joy and the glo-ry must be, . . Those end-less Sab-baths the
bless-ed ones see; . . . Crown for the val-iant, to wea-ry ones
rest; God shall be All and in all ev-er blest. A-MEN.

2 What are the Monarch, His court, and His throne?
What are the peace and the joy that they own?
O, that the blest ones who in it have share,
All that they feel could as fully declare!

3 Truly, Jerusalem name we that shore,
Vision of peace, that brings joy evermore;
Wish and fulfilment can severed be ne'er,
Nor the thing prayed for come short of the prayer.

4 There, where no troubles distraction can bring,
We the sweet anthems of Sion shall sing,
While for Thy grace, Lord, their voices of praise
Thy blessèd people eternally raise.

5 There dawns no Sabbath, no Sabbath is o'er,
Those Sabbath-keepers have one evermore:
One and unending is that triumph-song
Which to the angels and us shall belong.

6 Now in the meanwhile, with hearts raised on high,
We for that country must yearn and must sigh;
Seeking Jerusalem, dear native land,
Through our long exile on Babylon's strand.

7 Low before Him with our praises we fall
Of Whom, and in Whom, and through Whom are all;
Of Whom, the Father; in Whom, the Son;
Through Whom, the Spirit, with Them ever One.

517

1. On - ward! On-ward! March to glo - ry, Tread each foot-print of the Lord.
2. Though for sin our hearts must sor - row, Though tempta-tions round us throng,

Who hath taught in Gos - pel sto - ry How to gain the great re - ward.
Hymns of an - gels let us bor - row, Je - sus, Sav - iour, be our song.

Here we pass through des - ert drear - y. Here are realms of star - less night,
And while loud our an - thems ring-ing, One har - mo - nious strain up - raise,

Yet though weak our limbs, and wea - ry, We may win the Ci - ty bright.
Let our lives be like our sing - ing. Let no dis - cord mar our praise.

After each verse.

On-ward! On-ward! March to glo - ry, Tread each foot - print of the Lord,

Who hath taught in Gos - pel sto - ry How to gain the great re - ward. A - MEN.

3 Let us march to take our station
  With the white-robed choirs on high,
  Out of every age and nation
  Who to God's high Throne are nigh;
  We on earth like worship leading,
  Lives like theirs must strive to live,
  And, His merits always pleading,
  Unto Christ our being give.
    Onward, etc.

4 Onward then, nor faint, nor falter,
  Onward to the rest above;
  Christ, His promise will not alter,
  But will meet us in His love.
  Now with voice and understanding,
  Psalms and hymns of joy upraise,
  And with choirs of Angels banding,
  Father, Son, and Spirit praise.
    Onward, etc.

518

ALL ANGELS.
P. M.

Massive.

Ye ho-ly an-gels bright, Who wait at God's right hand, Or

thro' the realms of light Fly at your Lord's com-mand, As-sist our song, For

Sw.Org. *Gt. Org.*

Ped.

else the theme Too high doth seem For mor-tal tongue. A-MEN.

2 Ye blessed souls at rest,
  Who run this earthly race,
  And now from sin released
  Behold the Saviour's face.
    God's praises sound,
    As in His light,
    With sweet delight,
  Ye do abound.

3 Ye saints who toil below,
  Adore your heavenly King.
  And onward as ye go
  Some joyful anthem sing.
    Take what He gives
    And praise Him still,
    Through good or ill,
  Who ever lives.

4 My soul, bear thou thy part,
  Triumph in God above.
  And with a well-tuned heart,
  Sing thou the songs of love
    Let all thy days
    Till life shall end,
    Whate'er He send,
  Be filled with praise.

5 To God the Father, Son,
  And Spirit ever blest,
  Eternal Three in One.
  All worship be addressed;
    God's mighty power
    Shall be enrolled
    Now, as of old,
  And evermore.

519

ONWARD.
8s, 5s. WITH REFRAIN.

With spirit.

Press-ing for-ward, reach-ing for-ward, To the things be - fore, See! the Church of God moves on-ward Ev - er more and more, Rough the road and stern the tri - al, But the end is sure; Faith can smile thro' self - de - ni - al, Cour - age can en - dure.

Press-ing for-ward, Press-ing for-ward, Press-ing for-ward, Press-ing for-ward, Press-ing for-ward, to the things before, See the Church of God moves onward, onward, onward, Ever more and more. A-MEN.

2 Angels at our side attend us,
  Missioned from above;
Spirit-hosts unseen befriend us —
  Ministries of love;
God, our Father, still protects us;
  Jesus is our stay;
God, the Holy Ghost, directs us,
  Through the lifelong way.
    Pressing forward, etc.

3 Saints of old have trod before us
  All the same hard road;
Saints, who now are watching o'er us
  From their blest abode,
Once they passed through tribulation:
  Now their labours cease,
Now they see the Great Salvation,
  Now they rest in peace.
    Pressing forward, etc.

4 Oh, how grand will be the meeting
  When the race is run;
Oh, how sweet will be the greeting,
  "Faithful one, well done!"
Oh, the thought of clearly seeing
  What we dimly see;
Oh, the joy, our God, of being
  Evermore with Thee!
    Pressing forward, etc.

520

(EASTER.)

EASTER.
P. M.

Andante.

O the gold-en, glowing morn-ing, All the wait-ing earth a - dorn-ing For this

Eas - ter Day! To the King in all His splendour, Lord of life and death, we

Highest lauds . . . .

ren - der Highest lauds this day. Let the ban-ners float be - fore us, While we

He is ris - en! High est lauds this day!

raise th'exulting chorus, Christ is ris - en! He is ris-en! This is Easter Day! A-MEN.

2 Hark! the highest heavens ringing,
   Hark! the quivering angels singing
     "This is Easter Day!
  No more grieving! no more sighing!
  No more weeping! no more dying!
     Christ is King this day!"
  With the blessed ones before us,
  We will swell the heavenly chorus —
     Christ is risen! He is risen!
     This is Easter Day!

3 Shout aloud the wondrous story,
   For the King in all His glory
     Draweth nigh this day!
  Vernal benediction giving —
  Christ, the Life — the Ever-living!
     On this Easter Day!
  Let the banners float before us
  Send along the angel chorus —
     Christ is risen! He is risen!
     This is Easter Day!

4 On the Festal Altar glowing
   Lo! the Paschal Emblems — showing
     Forth this Easter Day!
  Come with garlands, come with treasure,
  Come with anthem's raptest measure
     For this Easter Day!
  How the bells are chiming o'er us
  While we join the heavenly chorus!
     Christ is risen! He is risen!
     This is Easter Day!

5 O that longed-for day of union,
   When Thine own, in Thy communion,
     Lord of Easter Day —
  Into life eternal waking,
  Celebrate — Thy love partaking —
     Endless Easter Day!
  For the joy that waits before us,
  We will swell the angel chorus
     Christ is risen! He is risen!
     This is Easter Day.

521 [109]

(EASTER.)

WELCOME, HAPPY MORNING.
11s. WITH REFRAIN.

Wel - come, hap - py morn - ing! age to age shall say:

Hell to - day is vanquish'd, heav'n is won to - day;

Lo, the Dead is liv - ing, God for ev - er - more!

poco rit.

Him, their true Cre - a - tor, all His works a - dore.

ff REFRAIN, IN UNISON.

Wel - come, hap - py morn - ing! age to age shall say:

Hell to-day is vanquished, heav'n is won to-day!

Lo! the Dead is liv - ing, Lord for - ev - er - more!

Him, their true Cre - a - tor, all His works a - dore. A - MEN.

2 Earth her joy confesses, clothing her for spring,
   All fresh gifts returned with her returning King:
   Bloom in every meadow, leaves on every bough,
   Speak His sorrow ended, hail His triumph now.
   Hell to-day is vanquished, heaven is won to-day.

3 Months in due succession, days of lengthening light,
   Hours and passing moments praise Thee in their flight;
   Brightness of the morning, sky and fields and sea,
   Vanquisher of darkness, bring their praise to Thee!
   " Welcome, happy morning! " age to age shall say.

4 Maker and Redeemer, life and health of all,
   Thou from heaven beholding human nature's fall,
   Of the Father's Godhead true and only Son,
   Manhood to deliver, manhood didst put on.
   Hell to-day is vanquished, heaven is won to-day.

5 Thou, of life the author, death didst undergo,
   Tread the path of darkness, saving strength to show;
   Come then, true and faithful, now fulfil Thy word;
   'T is Thine own third morning, rise, O buried Lord!
   " Welcome, happy morning! " age to age shall say.

6 Loose the souls long prisoned, bound with Satan's chain;
   All that now is fallen raise to life again;
   Show Thy face in brightness, bid the nations see:
   Bring again our daylight: day returns with Thee!
   Hell to-day is vanquished, heaven is won to-day!

Carols.

Christmas and Epiphany.

Sleep, Holy Babe!

522

Tenderly.

pp — *cres.* — *mf*

Sleep, Ho - ly Babe! up - on Thy Mo - ther's breast; Great

Lord of earth and sea and sky, How sweet it is to see Thee lie

dim. — *pp*

In such a place of rest, In such a place of rest....... *Accomp.*

2 Sleep! Holy Babe! Thine Angels watch around,
   All bending low with folded wings,
   Before the Incarnate King of kings,
In reverent awe profound.

3 Sleep! Holy Babe! while I with Mary gaze
   In joy upon that Face awhile,
   Upon the loving infant smile
Which there Divinely plays.

4 Sleep! Holy Babe! ah! take Thy brief repose;
   Too quickly will Thy slumbers break,
   And Thou to lengthened pains awake
That Death alone shall close.

523 Once again, O blessed time.

Smoothly.

Once again, O bless-ed time, Thankful hearts em - brace thee; If we lost thy festal chime, What could e'er re-place........ thee? What could e'er...... re-place thee? Change will darken many a day, Many a bond dis - sev - er; Many a joy shall pass away, But the "Great Joy" nev - er! But the "Great Joy" nev - - er........ But the "Great Joy" nev - - - er!

2 Once again the Holy Night
  Breathes its blessing tender;
Once again the Manger Light
  Sheds its gentle splendour;
O could tongues by Angels taught
  Speak our exultation
In the Virgin's Child that brought
  All mankind Salvation !

3 Welcome Thou to souls athirst,
  Fount of endless pleasure;
Gates of Hell may do their worst,
  While we clasp our Treasure;
Welcome, though an age like this
  Puts Thy Name on trial,
And the Truth that makes our bliss
  Pleads against denial!

4 Yea, if others stand apart,
  We will press the nearer:
Yea, O best fraternal Heart,
  We will hold Thee dearer:
Faithful lips shall answer thus
  To all faithless scorning,
" Jesus Christ is God with us,
  Born on Christmas morning."

5 So we yield Thee all we can,
  Worship, thanks, and blessing:
Thee true God, and Thee true Man,
  On our knees confessing:
While Thy Birth-day morn we greet
  With our best devotion,
Bathe us, O most true and sweet!
  In Thy Mercy's ocean.

524 **Stars all bright are beaming.**

Brightly. VERSE.

Stars all bright are beaming, From the skies a - bove, Nature's face all

gleam-ing, Shines with Heav'n's own love. Wake and sing, good Christians,

CHORUS.

On this Birth-day Morn, Heaven and Earth are telling God for man is born.

2 Here for us abiding,
  Cradled in a Stall,
  All His glory hiding,
  See the Lord of all! CHO.

3 Born that He might lead us,
  From this desert home,
  Guide our way, and feed us,
  Till the end shall come. CHO.

4 Thousand thousand blessings
  Sing we for His Love,
  Choral Hymns addressing
  To our Lord above. CHO.

5 Glory in the Highest,
  For this wondrous Birth;
  Choir of Heaven! thou criest
  Peace to all the Earth! CHO.

525 **Sleep, my Saviour, sleep.**

Softly.

1. Sleep, my Saviour, sleep, On Thy bed of hay, An-gels in the spangled Heaven
2. Sleep, my Saviour, sleep, On Thy bed of hay, Ere the mourning An-gel com-eth

Sing their glad-some Christmas car - ols, Till the dawn of day,
To the moon-lit o - live gar-den, Wip-ing tears a - way.

3 Sleep, my Saviour, sleep,
  Sweet on Mary's breast.
Now the shepherds kneel adoring,
Now the mother's heart is joyous,
  Take a happy rest.

4 Sleep, my Saviour, sleep,
  Sweet on Mary's breast:
Crucified, with wounds and bruises,
Bleeding, purple, stained, disfigured,
  One day Thou wilt rest.

526

All this night bright angels sing.

Moderate.

1. All this night bright angels sing, Nev-er was such car-ol-ling, Hark! a voice which
2. Wake, O earth, wake eve-ry thing, Wake and hear the joy I bring: Wake and joy; for

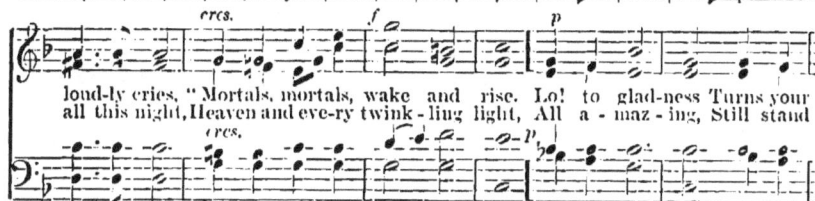

loud-ly cries, "Mortals, mortals, wake and rise. Lo! to glad-ness Turns your
all this night, Heaven and eve-ry twink-ling light, All a-maz-ing, Still stand

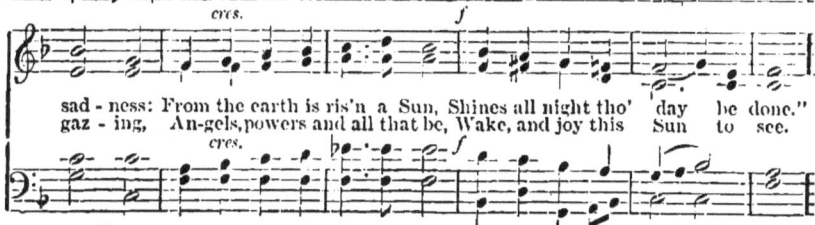

sad-ness: From the earth is ris'n a Sun, Shines all night tho' day be done."
gaz-ing, An-gels, powers and all that be, Wake, and joy this Sun to see.

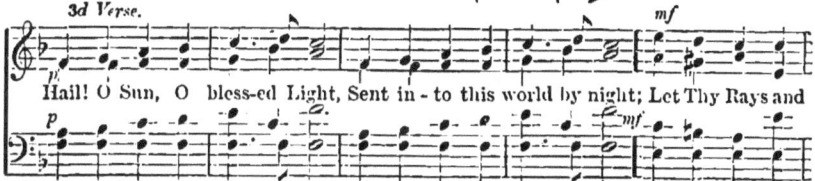

3d Verse.

Hail! O Sun, O bless-ed Light, Sent in-to this world by night; Let Thy Rays and

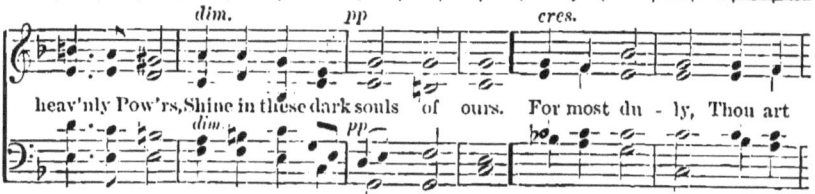

heav'nly Pow'rs, Shine in these dark souls of ours. For most du-ly, Thou art

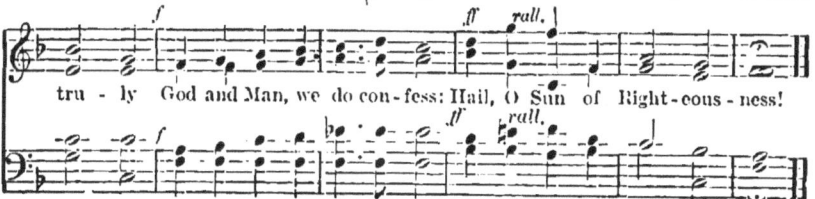

tru-ly God and Man, we do con-fess: Hail, O Sun of Right-cous-ness!

527 Carol, sweetly carol.

Brightly.

Words by F. J. Crosby.
Music by T. E. Perkins.
Copyrighted, 1860.

1. Ca - rol, sweetly ca - rol, A Saviour born to - day; Bear the joy - ful
2. Ca - rol, sweetly ca - rol, As when the An-gel throng O'er the vales of
3. Ca - rol, sweetly ca - rol, The hap-py Christmas time; Hark! the bells are

tid-ings, Oh, bear them far a - way. Ca - rol, sweet-ly ca - rol, Till
Ju - dah, A - woke the heavenly song. Ca - rol, sweet-ly ca - rol, Good
peal-ing Their mer-ry. mer - ry chime; Ca - rol, sweet-ly ca - rol, Ye

earth's re - mot-est bound Shall hear the mighty chorus, And echo back the sound.
will, with peace and love, Glo - ry in the highest, To God who reigns above.
shin - ing ones a - bove, Sing in loudest numbers, Oh, sing redeeming love.

CHORUS.

Ca - rol, sweet-ly ca - rol, Ca - rol, sweet-ly to - day;
Ca - rol, Ca - rol, Ca - rol,

Ca - rol sweetly, Ca - rol sweet - ly to - day.

Bear the joy - ful tid - ings, Oh, bear them far a - way.

528 *With spirit.* **Sing ye the songs of praise.**

1. Sing ye the songs of praise; Je - sus is come! High your glad
2. This day in Beth-le - hem, Je - sus was born! King of Je -

voi - ces raise; Je - sus is come Cast world - ly cares a - way,
ru - sa - lem, Je - sus was born! Sun of all right-eous-ness,

Wor-ship and homage pay, Wel-come the blessed day, Je - sus is come!
Shin-ing with blessed - ness, Heal-ing our wretchedness, Je - sus was born!

3 Cleanse us from all our sin,
  Saviour Divine!
Make our thoughts pure within,
  Saviour Divine!
Lo! now the herald sound
Carols the love profound,
Telling of Jesus found,
  Saviour Divine!

4 Save through Thy merit,
  Great Prince of Peace!
Give Thy good Spirit,
  Great Prince of Peace!
Let not Thy love depart,
But holy gifts impart,
Born into every heart,
  Great Prince of Peace!

529 *Moderate.* **Christ is born of maiden fair.**

Christ is born of maid - en fair; Hark the her-alds in the air, Thus a-

dor - ing des - cant there, "In ex - cel - sis glo - ri - a."

2 Shepherds saw those Angels bright,
  Carolling in glorious light;
"God, His Son is born to-night,
  In excelsis gloria."

3 Christ is come to save mankind,
  As in holy page we find,
Therefore this song bear in mind,
  "*In excelsis gloria.*"

530 From far away we come to you.

Moderate.

From far a-way we come to yon; The snow un-der foot and the
moon in the sky, To tell of great ti-dings, strange and true, Christian men all, sal-
va-tion is nigh! Sal-ra-tion is nigh. From far a-way we
come to you; To tell of great ti-dings, strange and true; From far away we
come to you, To tell of great ti-dings strange . . . . and true. . . . .

2 Out on a field where the night was deep,
   The snow under foot, &c.   [sheep,
  There lay three shepherds tending their
   Christian men all, &c.

3 "O ye shepherds what did you see?
   The snow under foot, &c.
  To make you so full of joy and glee?"
   Christian men all, &c.

4 "In an oxstall this night we saw,
   The snow under foot, &c.
  A Babe in a manger, laid on straw,
   Christian men all, &c.

5 And as we gazed this sight upon,
   The snow under foot, &c.
  The angels called Him, the Holy ONE,
   Christian men all, &c.

6 And a marvellous song we straight heard
   The snow under foot, &c.   [then,
  Of Peace on Earth, Good will towards
   Christian men all, &c.   [men,"

7 News of a fair and marvellous thing!
   The snow under foot, &c.
  Nowell, Nowell, Nowell, we sing!
   Christian men all, &c.

N. B.—In the 2nd, 3rd, 4th and 9th verses, the melody in the first bar will need a slight modification, in order to fit it to the accent of the words.
And a corresponding change must be made in the subsequent parts of the melody where the same words recur.

Carol, brothers, Carol.

531 CHORUS. *Cheerfully.*

Car-ol, brothers car-ol, Car-ol joy-ful-ly, Car-ol the good tidings, Car-ol mer-ri-ly,

And pray a gladsome Christmas, For all good Christian men ; Car-ol brothers, car-ol, Christmas-Day a-gain. *Fine.*

DUETT.

Car-ol, but with gladness, Not in songs of earth; On the Saviour's birthday Hallowed be our mirth;

While a thousand blessings Fill our hearts with glee, Christmas-day we'll keep, The Feast of Chari-ty. *D.C.*

2 At the merry table,
    Think of those who've none,
  The orphan and the widow,
    Hungry and alone.
  Bountiful your offerings
    To the altar bring;
  Let the poor and needy
    Christmas carols sing.
CHORUS. Carol, brothers, carol, &c.

3 Listening angel music,
    Discord sure must cease—
  Who dare hate his brother
    On this day of peace ?
  While the heavens are telling
    To mankind good will,
  Only love and kindness
    Every bosom fill.
CHORUS. Carol, brothers, carol, &c.

4 Let our hearts responding
    To the seraph band.
  With this morning's sunshine
    Bright in every land :
  Word, and deed, and prayer
    Speak the grateful sound,
  Telling " Merry Christmas "
    All the world around,
CHORUS. Carol, brothers, carol, &c.

532 Gather around the Christmas Tree.

Brightly. [I. *To be sung before the Distribution of Gifts.*]

‖; Gather around the Christmas tree! :‖ Ever green Have its branches been, It is king of all the

woodland scene; For Christ, our King, is born to-day! His reign shall nev-er pass a-way,

CHORUS.

Ho - san - na, Ho - san - na, Ho - san-na in the high - est!

[II. *To be sung after the Distribution of gifts.*]

2 ‖: Gather around the Christmas tree! :‖
 Once the pride
 Of the mountain side,
Now cut down to grace our Christmas-tide:
For Christ from heaven to earth came down,
To gain, through death, a nobler crown.
   Hosanna, &c.

3 ‖: Gather around the Christmas tree! :‖
 Every bough
 Bears a burden now,—
They are gifts of love for us, we trow:
For Christ is born, His love to show,
And give good gifts to men below.
   Hosanna, &c.

4 ‖: Farewell to Thee, O Christmas tree! :‖
 Thy part is done,
 And Thy gifts are gone,
And thy lights are dying one by one:
For earthly pleasures die to-day,
But heavenly joys shall last alway.
   Hosanna, &c.

5 ‖: Farewell to thee, O Christmas tree! :‖
 Twelve months o'er,
 We shall meet once more,
Merry welcome singing, as of yore:
For Christ now reigns, our Saviour dear,
And gives us Christmas every year!
   Hosanna, &c.

533 *Moderate.* Good Christian men rejoice.

Good Christian men, re - joice With heart and soul and voice, Give ye heed to what we say; news! news! Jesus Christ is born to-day: Ox and ass before Him bow, And

He is in the manger now, Christ is born to - day! Christ is born to - day!

2 Good Christian men, rejoice
With heart, and soul, and voice;
Now ye hear of endless bliss:
Joy! Joy!
Jesus Christ was born for this!
He hath oped the heav'nly door,
And man is blessèd evermore.
Christ was born for this!

3 Good Christian men, rejoice
With heart, and soul, and voice;
Now ye need not fear the grave;
Peace! Peace!
Jesus Christ was born to save!
Calls you one and calls you all,
To gain His everlasting hall:
Christ was born to save.

Hark! what sounds.

534 *Moderate.*

Hark! what sounds are sweet-ly steal - ing, Soft thro' Beth-lehem's midnight air?

Loud - er yet, and loud - er peal-ing, An - gel ac - cents sure are there.

2 See! a light from heaven is streaming,
  Night and darkness quit the plain;
See! an angel brightly beaming,
  Followed by a radiant train.

3 "Fear not, shepherds! glad my story,
  Tidings of the greatest joy:

Christ is born, the Lord of glory!
  I proclaim a Saviour nigh."

4 Thus the angel, then ascending,
  Seeks again the realms of light;
Now the chorus faintly ending,
  All is silence, all is night.

Now lift the Carol.

535 *Moderate.* VERSE.

Now lift the car-ol, men and maids, Now wake ex-ult-ant sing-ing; This day the Well of Life first sprang, Who shall declare His springing? It is the Birth-day of our Peace; This day for man the wea-ry, The E-ver-lasting Son of God Was born of bless-ed Ma-ry.

CHORUS.

No-el! No-el! Proclaim the Saviour's Birth; He rais-es us to Heaven, O hail His com-ing down to earth.

2 He was not born in such sweet days,
   As we of yore remember;
  'Twas not the sunny summer time,
   Oh! 'twas the cold December:
  As shines the sun above the snows,
   When nature's life is lying
  Fast bound in winter's icy chain,
   So came He to the dying.
  CHO.— Noel, Noel, &c.

3 There were poor shepherds in the field,
   Their flocks at midnight tending:
  Then Heaven came down and brought the
   A rapture never ending: [news,
  So they went swift to Bethlehem,
   And saw—and told the story
  Of Christ the Lord, a little Child,
   And Angels singing "Glory."
  CHO.— Noel, Noel, &c.

4 Not in the manger lies He now;
   Far o'er the sapphire portal
  At God's right Hand of power He sits
   Who was this day made mortal:
  All in the highest, holiest place,
   Where there may dwell none other,
  There our own Manhood sits enthroned,
   There is our Elder Brother.
  CHO.— Noel, Noel, &c.

5 The Birthday of our God and King—
   Lo! we are called to greet Him;
  The Everlasting Bridegroom comes,
   Oh, go ye out to meet Him.
  This is the end of all below,
   The crown of Love's best story;
  Christ stands and knocks—oh, happy souls,
   Receive the King of Glory.
  CHO.— Noel, Noel, &c.

536 See amid the winter's snow.

Moderate.

Solo. (Treble or Tenor alternately.)

See a-mid the win-ter's snow, Born for us on earth be-low,

See the ten-der Lamb ap-pears, Prom-ised from e-ter-nal years.

CHORUS. *ff*

Hail! Thou ev-er-bless-ed morn! Hail, Re-demp-tion's hap-py dawn!

Sing through all Je-ru-sa-lem, Christ is born in Beth-le-hem.

2 Lo, within a manger lies
He who built the starry skies;
He, who throned in height sublime,
Sits amid the Cherubim!
Cho.— Hail! Thou ever-blessed, &c.

3 Say, ye holy shepherds, say,
What your joyful news to-day;
Wherefore have ye left your sheep
On the lonely mountain steep?
Cho.— Hail! Thou ever-blessed, &c.

4 "As we watched at dead of night,
Lo, we saw a wondrous light;
Angels singing peace on earth,
Told us of the Saviour's Birth."
Cho.— Hail! Thou ever-blessed, &c.

5 Sacred Infant, all Divine,
What a tender love was Thine;
Thus to come from highest bliss
Down to such a world as this!
Cho.— Hail! Thou ever-blessed, &c.

6 Teach, O teach us, Holy Child,
By Thy Face so meek and mild,
Teach us to resemble Thee,
In Thy sweet humility!
Cho.— Hail! Thou ever-blessed, &c.

In the early morning.

537 *Joyously.*

In the ear-ly morn-ing, ear-ly, Ere the dawn was e-ven nigh—

Glo-ri-a in ex-cel-sis De-o! Glo-ry be to God on high.

When the crown-like stars were lus-trous; When the dew was on the sod,

Sang the An-gels to the shepherds, Sang the chor-is-ters of God.

2 To the humble Bethlehem shepherds,
　On the first glad Christmas morn,
Sang the choir of God Angelic,—
　Christ the Son of God is born!
When the dew was white and pearly,
　Flashed a light across the sky,
In the early morning, early,
　Glory be to God on high.

3 Glory in the heavens eternal,
　Upon earth be glory, too,
For the day of grace hath broken,
　And a King is born to you.
In the early morning, early,
　Glory be to God on high;
Rang the sound of Angels harping,
　Through the stilly list'ning sky.

538 What Child is this.

Moderate.

What Child is this, who, laid to rest, On Ma-ry's lap is sleeping;

Whom an-gels greet with anthems sweet,While shepherds watch are keep-ing?

This, this is Christ, the King,Whom shepherds guard,and an-gels sing:

Haste, haste to bring Him laud,The Babe, the Son of Ma-ry!

2 Why lies He in such mean estate,
  Where ox and ass are feeding?
Good Christian, fear: for sinners here
  The silent Word is pleading:
Nails, spear, shall pierce Him through,
  The Cross be borne, for me, for you;
Hail! Hail! the Word made flesh,
  The Babe, the Son of Mary!

3 So bring Him incense, gold and myrrh,
  Come peasant, King, to own Him;
The King of kings salvation brings;
  Let loving hearts enthrone Him.
Raise, raise the song on high,
  The Virgin sings her lullaby:
Joy! joy! for Christ is born,
  The Babe, the Son of Mary!

539 Holy night! peaceful night!

Moderate.

Ho - ly night! peace-ful night! All is dark, save the light,

Yon-der where they sweet vi - gil keep O'er the Babe who in si - lent sleep,

Rests in hea - ven - ly peace, Rests in hea - ven - ly peace.

2 Holy night! peaceful night!
Only for shepherds' sight,
Came blest visions of Angel throngs,
With their loud Alleluia songs,
 Saying, JESUS is come,
 Saying, JESUS is come.

3 Holy night! peaceful night!
Child of heav'n! O! how bright [born
Thou didst smile on us when Thou was
Blest indeed was that happy morn,
 Full of heavenly joy,
 Full of heavenly joy.

540. Waken, Christian children.

Brightly.

Waken, Christian children, Up, and let us sing, With glad hearts and voi-ces,

Of our new-born King. Up! 'tis meet to wel - come With a joyous lay

Christ, the King of Glo - ry, Born for us to - day.

2 In a manger lowly
  Sleeps the heavenly Child,
  O'er Him fondly bendeth
  Mary, Mother mild.
  Far above that stable,
  Up in heaven so high,
  One bright star outshineth,
  Watching silently.

3 Fear not, then, to enter,
  Though we cannot bring
  Gold, or myrrh, or incense,
  Fitting for a King.

Gifts He asketh richer,
  Offerings costlier still,
  Yet may Christian children
  Bring them if they will.

4 Brighter than all jewels
  Shines the modest eye;
  Best of gifts, He loveth
  Infant purity.
  Haste we, then, to welcome
  With a joyous lay
  Christ, the King of Glory,
  Born for us to-day.

541 *Moderate.* **Christians, Carol sweetly.**

Christians, car - ol sweet-ly, Up to-day and sing! 'Tis the hap - py birth - day

Of our Ho - ly King: Haste we then to greet Him, Hum - bly fall - ing down,

While our hands entwine Him, Dearest Babe, a crown.

2 Crowds of snow-white Angels
  Throng the golden stair;
  All things are resplendent,
  All things passing fair:
  Bells, clear music making,
  Peal the news o'er earth;
  Chimes within make answer,
  All is glee and mirth.

3 Michael, at the manger,
  Bows his royal face;
  Gabriel, with lily,
  Hides transcendent Grace;
  For, dear friends, the glory
  Of that lowly bed
  Overpowers the beauty
  On Archangels shed.

4 Shall I tell of Joseph,
  Who, with rapt surprise,
  Sees the light from Godhead
  Fill those infant eyes?
  Shall I sing of Mary,
  Who, upon her breast,
  Cradles her Creator,
  Soothes Him to His rest?

5 Angels, Mary, Joseph,
  Yes, I greet you all!
  Falling down in worship
  At the manger stall!
  For you hail our Monarch
  Born a Child to-day;
  So, with you I worship,
  And my homage pay.

542. In the field with their flocks.

Moderate. Unison.

2 "To you in the City of David,
   A Saviour is born to-day!"
And sudden a host of the heav'nly ones
   Flash'd forth to join the lay!
O never hath sweeter message
   Thrill'd home to the souls of men,
And the Heav'ns themselves had never
   A gladder choir till then.— [heard
For they sang that Christmas Carol,
   That never on earth shall cease, &c.

3 And the shepherds came to the Manger,
   And gaz'd on the Holy Child;
And calmly o'er that rude cradle
   The Virgin Mother smil'd;
And the sky, in the star-lit silence,
   Seem'd full of the angel lay;
"To you in the City of David
   A Saviour is born to-day;"
Oh they sang—and I ween that never
   The carol on earth shall cease, &c.

543 Silent night! peaceful night!

Softly.

Si - lent night! peaceful night! Through the darkness beams a light;

Si - lent night! peace-ful night; Through the darkness beams a light.

Through the dark-ness beams a light! Yonder, where they sweet vig - ils keep

Rallentando.

O'er the Babe, who, in si - lent sleep, Rests in heavenly peace, Rests in heavenly peace.

2 Silent night! holiest night!
  Darkness flies and all is light!
Shepherds hear the angels sing—
"Hallelujah! hail the King!
  Jesus Christ is here!"

3 Silent night! peaceful night!
  Child of heaven! O how bright
Thou didst smile when Thou wast born;
Blessèd was that happy morn,
  Full of heavenly joy.

4 Silent night! holiest night!
  Guiding Star, O, lend thy light!
See the eastern wise men bring
Gifts and homage to our King!
  Jesus Christ is here!

5 Silent night! holiest night!
  Wondrous Star! O, lend thy light!
With the angels let us sing
Hallelujah to our King!
  Jesus Christ is here!

544

Deep the gloom.

Deep the gloom, and still the night, Cold and damp the weather, When the chill night air de-spite, Met three kings to-geth-er. One was old with snow-white hair, One the prime of manhood bare, And the third, a youth, stood there With them on the heath-er.

2 Looking for the promised King,
   Who, in Eastern quarters,
Soon should spring to life, to rule
   O'er earth's sons and daughters,
Them this eve, while rapt in sleep,
One had roused in accents deep,
" Haste ye; watch ye; vigil keep
   By Euphrates' waters!"

3 Up they spring, and quickly hie,
   Each his pathway bending,
Through the chilly mist and gloom,
   O'er the earth depending.
How the world in darkness lay,
Till the Day-Star shed Its ray,
Nature thus would fain display;
   Mystic emblems lending.

4 Then the kings with solemn gaze
   Looked on high beholding;
For the marvel yet to come,
   Heav'n their spirits moulding,
When behold, with silent awe,
Suddenly the clouds they saw
Like a darkened veil withdraw,
   Wonders more unfolding.

5 In a trice a star shone forth,
   O! so brightly shining!—
Nearer, nearer yet it came,
   Still towards earth inclining!
And 'twas shaped—O wondrous sight!
Like a child enthroned in light,
Crown'd, though yet, with sceptre bright
   Victor—cross combining! *

6 Then one cried, " Behold the star
   Of which seers have spoken,
Beaming on the land afar,
   And of life the token!
Haste we, brothers! let us speed;
See, it moves! It comes to lead
To the Christ, of Judah's seed
   Born of line unbroken!"

7 Up they rise, and bend their way,
   Toil nor labour sparing,
Over mountain, hill, and plain,
   Costly treasures bearing.—
So do ye your off'rings make,
Fear no pain for Jesu's sake,
Ever strive heaven's road to take.
   For your Lord preparing!

* An allusion to a legend, preserved in an ancient Commentary on St. Matthew, that the star, on its first appearance to the Magi, had the form of a radiant child, bearing a sceptre or cross.

545 Ring the Bells.

CAROL.

Ring the bells, the Christmas bells; Chime out the wondrous sto-ry; First in song on An-gel tongues It came from realms of glo-ry; Peace on earth, good-will to men, An-gel-ic voi-ces ringing—Christ the Lord to earth has come, His glorious message bring-ing.

Chorus.

Ring the mer-ry Christmas bells; Chime out the wondrous sto-ry; Glo-ry be to God on high, For ev-er-more be glo-ry.

Wise men hastened from the East
To bring their richest treasures—
Gold, and myrrh, and frankincense,
And jewels without measure.
Him they sought, although a King,
They found in birthplace lowly
There within a manger lay
The Babe so pure and holy.
CHO.— Ring the merry Christmas bells, &c.

Earthly crowns were not for Him;
He came God's love revealing;
On the Cross He died for us,
His blood forgiveness sealing.
'Tis the Saviour promised long,
Ring out your loudest praises;
Every heart this happy day
Its grateful anthems raises.
CHO.— Ring the merry Christmas bells, &c.

546 The Stars are shining bright.

CAROL.

The stars are shining bright and clear, The hills are white with snow;

Our Christ-mas eve has come a-gain, Our hearts with joy o'er-flow;

The Christmas car-ols, sweet and glad, Are sound-ing on the air;

And Christmas wreaths, in glist'ning show, Make bright the house of prayer. A-MEN.

2 Not here across the snow was heard
  The first sweet Christmas song;
But where the crimson lilies bloom,
  Judæa's hills among:
Those hills where David long before
  His father's sheep had kept;
And where, o'er Rachel's lonely tomb,
  The mourning Jacob wept.

3 And not by earthly choristers
  Was that first carol sung;
Not through the temple's shining courts
  Its faultless music rung;
No listening crowds had gathered there,
  That wondrous chant to hear;
Save watchful shepherds on the hills,
  No human soul was near.

4 'Twas sung by countless multitudes
  Of Angels pure and bright,
And o'er the bare and silent hills
  There shone a glorious light;
Such heavenly music ne'er was heard
  Before by sons of men,
And never more shall song like that
  Be heard on earth again.

5 We know the tidings which they brought
  Of Christ our Saviour's birth,
Their song of "Glory be to God,
  Good will and peace on earth;"
And so the Christmas carol, sung
  By Angels long ago,
Is sweeter than all other songs
  Which Christians sing below.

547 Ring out the merry bells.

Allegretto.

Ring out the mer-ry, mer-ry bells, The mer-ry Christmas bells, Their

mu-sic bears the an-gel-song, And joy-ful news it tells; "Fear not: the Sav-iour

of the world In Beth-le-hem is born!" Then let our hearts sing out their joy,

Chorus.

And fill with praise the morn. Ring out the mer-ry, mer-ry bells, The

merry Christmas bells; Good news of God's great love to men Their joyful music tells.

2 Ring out the merry, merry bells
    In pealing tones of praise;
  We'll echo back the angel-song
    As hymns of joy we raise;
  "All glory be to God most high,"
    Who reigns in light above;
  "Peace on the earth, good-will to men,"
    Shall mark His reign of love.—Cho.

3 Ring out the merry, merry bells;
    For in the Saviour's birth
  Our Father in His mercy gave
    His choicest gift to earth.
  And we will give our gifts of love
    To those around us here,   [world.
  Till Christ's "good-will" shall rule the
    And life is full of cheer.—Cho.

548 There dwelt in old Judea.

S. VOICE.

1. There dwelt in old Ju - de - a, A maid-en fair to see, The
2. And as the in-fant Je - sus, Lay on His low - ly bed, A
3. The shepherds bow'd be - fore Him, While an-gels swift did fly, On
4. For this was Prince Em-man - uel, Who laid a - side His crown, And

p

colla voce.

moth - er mild and un - de - filed, Of a bless-ed babe was she.
cir - cle bright of heaven-ly light Shone round a - bout His head.
blest em-ploy, with songs of joy, To fill the star - ry sky.
all to win our souls from sin, Un - to the earth came down.

CHORUS. *After each verse.*

p

Oh! No - ël, sing No - ël, And mer-ry be al - way, For

f   *ff*

Christ was born in the ear - ly morn, Christ was born in the ear - ly morn,

SOLO.   FULL.

All on a Christ-mas day. . . . All on a Christ-mas day.

549 Christ was born on Christmas day.

Christ was born on Christmas day; Wreathe the holly, twine the bay; *Christus natus ho-di-e* ;The

Babe, the Son, the Ho-ly One of Ma-ry.

Ex Maria Virgine:
The God, the Lord, by all adored for ever.

2 He is born to set us free,
He is born our Lord to be,

3 Let the bright red berries glow,
Everywhere in goodly show;
Christus natus hodie:
The Babe, the Son, the Holy One of Mary.

4 Christian men, rejoice and sing;
'Tis the birthday of a King,
Ex Maria Virgine;
The God, the Lord, by all adored for ever.

5. Night of sadness ; morn of gladness, Evermore :Ever, ev-er; Af- ter many troubles sore,

Morn of glad-ness, ev - ermore and ev - ermore. 6. Midnight scarcely pass'd and over, Drawing to this

ho - ly morn, Ve - ry ear - ly, ve-ry ear-ly, Christ was born. 7. Sing out with bliss, His

Name is this: Em-man- u - el: As was fore-told in days of old by Ga - bri - el.

550 Ring out, ring out, O Christmas bells.

Ring out, ring out, O Christmas bells! A tale of joy your mu - sic tells;

A Saviour King was born to-day To rule the hearts of men for aye.

CHORUS.

For this we join to swell the strain The an-gels sang o'er Ju-dah's plain!

Glo - ry to God, good will to men, Shall rise and fill the heav'ns a - gain.

2 O Lord of lords, and King of kings,
   Sweet peace and joy Thy presence brings;
   We know the Father loves us well
   To rescue thus our souls from hell.
       For this we join, etc.

3 But who can measure all the love
   That brought Thee from Thy throne
   With us to live, for us to die,   [above,
   That we might reign with Thee on high.
       For this we join, etc.

4 Dear Saviour, elder Brother, Friend,
   Abide with us till life shall end;
   And then, when death shall set us free,
   Within the kingdom won by Thee,
       Earth's ransomed ones shall swell the strain,
       "All worthy was the Lamb once slain,
       Honour and glory to receive
       From all created things that breathe."

551 Joyously, joyously, silvery clear.

Joy - ous - ly, joy - ous - ly sil - ver - y clear, Christ-mas bells fall on each lis-t'ning ear, Gai - ly they e-cho o'er land and o'er sea, Mu-si-cal peals full of mu - si - cal glee. E - choes of strains sung by An - gels on high, E - choes re - e-choed be-yond the blue sky, E - choes of strains sung by An - gels on high, E - choes re - e-choed be - yond the blue sky.

2 Hopefully, hopefully swells out the strain,
Telling Christ's birth again, and again,
Sweetly the harps tuned in Christ's home
  above
Take up the song and repeat it in love;
Echoes of strains sung by Angels on high,
Echoes re-echoed beyond the blue sky.

3 Tenderly, tenderly die now the chimes,
Passing away as they passed in old times,
Hushed now the music while grateful
  hearts share
In offerings gladly of song and of prayer;
Silent the bells, but in heart and with voice,
We hail the Lord's birth and for it rejoice.

552 Child Jesus lay on Mary's knee.

SOLO. *Andante.*

1. Child Je - sus lay on Ma - ry's knee, And o - pen'd wide were His sad
2. Child Je - sus' eyes were clos'd in sleep, And as He slept His moth - er
3. Child Je - sus woke from sleep a - gain, And His glad eyes were o - pen'd

eyes; Oh! sleep, my lit - tle King, said she, Oh! sleep, the stars are in the
mild Did bend her head and watch-ing keep With tears a - bove the Heavenly
wide; Oh! Ma - ry's heart was joy - ous then, And all of Ma - ry's tears were

rit.   *accel.*

skies. Then round a - bout that won-drous pair, An - gel - ic voi - ces fill'd the air.
Child, And still a - round that won-drous pair, An - gel - ic voi - ces fill'd the air.
dried, And still a - round that won-drous pair, An - gel - ic voi - ces fill'd the air.

CHORUS. *Allegro animato.*

Sing we the sto - ry of the Sa - viour's birth, Peace and good will to all on earth,

1. Peace for the wea - ry and the worn, Since Christ is born.
2. Par - don for sins re - pent - ant sigh, Since Christ shall die.
3. New hope for life be - yond the skies, Since Christ shall rise.

553 Joyfully, joyfully angels are singing.

mf

1. Joy - ful - ly, joy - ful - ly an - gels are sing - ing, O'er Bethlehem's plains of light;
2. Peace - ful - ly, peace - ful - ly light is now beaming, Sa - ges have come from a - far;
3. Wist - ful - ly, wist - ful - ly wise men are seeking "The Christ in the House of Bread;"

mf

Won - der - ful, won - der - ful message now bringing To wel - come the Christmas night.
Beau - ti - ful, beau - ti - ful brightly now gleaming Bethlehem's wonder - ful Star.
Ten - der - ly, ten - der - ly Ma - ry is keep - ing Her watch o'er that low - ly Bed.

CHORUS.

ff

pp

"Glo - ry to God in the high - est, all glo - ry! Peace on the earth and good - will;"

f

ritard.

a tempo.

An - gels are tell - ing the mar - vell - ous sto - ry, Shepherds are list - 'ning still.

554 Ring out, sweet bells.

Not too fast.

1. Ring out, sweet bells, your Christmas chime, Your chime of wel-come,
2. A babe, in rus-tic man-ger laid, And low-ly guise, our
3. Ring out, sweet bells, ring out, ring out, To ev-'ry crea-ture

p *cres.*

clear and brave; This night there came with us to dwell Our Jesus, came to dwell and
Saviour came; "Eman-u-el" of prophets told, "The Holy Babe of Beth-le-
glad, for-lorn, The message of "Goodwill to man," And "Peace on earth" with Jesus

cres.

f *pp* *mf* *rall.*

save.. Ring out, sweet bells, Ring out, sweet bells, Our Jesus came to dwell and save.
hem." Ring out, sweet bells, Ring out, sweet bells, "The Holy Babe of Bethlehem."
born. Ring out, sweet bells, Ring out, sweet bells, "Goodwill" and "Peace" with Jesus born.

555 The Christmas stars are shining.

The Christmas stars are shin-ing, The winds are wailing low; And o'er the earth is

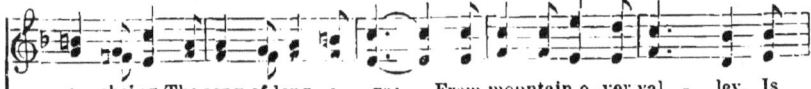

e-choing The song of long a-go; . From mountain o-ver val-ley, Is

heard the glorious cry, "O com-fort ye my peo-ple, The Prince of Peace draws nigh."

2 Sing of the Christ-Child's coming
   In lowliest estate;
When long-time kings and prophets
   With eager hearts did wait.
Where'er His footsteps linger
   Shall blossom forth the rose;
And peace shall be abounding
   Where'er His spirit goes.

3 O Babe in humble manger,
   Amongst the poor of earth,
Kings brought myrrh, gold, frankincense,
   To offer at Thy birth,
The host of heaven triumphant
   A glorious strain did sing.
"Peace and good will for ever
   Through Christ, the new-born King."

4 Awake, awake, O Sion,
   And put on all thy strength;
Filled is the throne of David,
   Thy King hath come at length.
His star hath shone in heaven,
   And angels at His birth,
Have brought the fair evangel
   "Peace and good will on earth."

556   Hark! how the bells.

Briskly.

Hark! how the bells at mid-night hour, Tell-ing their tale from tower to tower,

Bring-ing glad ti - dings to the morn, Mer-ri-ly are ring-ing. "Christ is born."

2 Hark to the songs of heavenly love
Angels are hymning from above;
Hark! as again we hear them sing
"Glory in the highest; Christ is King!"

3 Hail to the King! who comes so meek,
Hail to the Child! so poor, so weak,
Hail to the Son! our God, the Word,
Alleluia! praise ye Christ, the Lord.

4 Come, Christians, come and joyous greet
Jesus, the Child; with welcome meet;
Bringing salvation, born for you,—
Laud Him then with hearts and voices true.

CAROLS.

557 In a manger lies the Child.

Moderato. SOPRANOS IN UNISON.

In a man-ger lies the child, Lord of heav'n and earth, . .

Hark! the sweet an-gel-ic choir Now pro-claim His birth. . .

CHORUS. *Joyful.*

Ring the joy-ful Christ-mas bells, And loud an-thems sing;

rall. last verse only.

With the an-gels in the sky . . Wel-come Christ the King.

2 He from highest heaven above,
Hath come down below:
Peace on earth, good will to men,
And God's love to show.
Ring the joyful, etc.

3 To the shepherds in the fields
Was His birth made known;
And with wondering looks they kneel
At the manger throne.
Ring the joyful, etc.

4 Let us then the angels join
In their Christmas strain;
And with thankfulness and joy
Tell His love again.
Ring the joyful, etc.

558 Away! with loyal hearts.

Briskly.

A-way! with loy-al hearts and true, O'er hill and dale they pressed, Full four-score wea-ry miles to do The Cæ-sar's high be-hest; And Ma-ry sang "Magni-fi-cat," Her own, her ancient song, For well wist she that God's de-cree Was bear-ing her a-long. Was bear-ing her a-long.

2 Away through fields and meadows green,
  O'er purple heather-bed,
By mountain pass, or deep ravine,
  The faithful couple sped.
And soft and sweet, where'er they went,
  To glad the weary way,
Sang Mary that "Magnificat,"
  Her own, her ancient lay.

3 O'erhead the storm-clouds often wept,
  And tempests o'er them passed,
And cold around them often swept
  The bleak December blast.
But still she sang "Magnificat"
  Through weather foul or fair;
For all was rest within her breast,
  'Twas always sunshine there.

4 And when the pilgrimage was o'er,
  And of their royal kin,
Not one would open wide his door,
  And bid them enter in;

Still Mary sang "Magnificat"
  With ever joyful tone;
"Whate'er betide, the Lord," she cried,
  "Is mindful of His own."

5 Worn out at last, and ill bestead,
  Right glad were they to find
Within a sorry cattle-shed
  A shelter from the wind.
And Mary sang "Magnificat"
  Right through that wondrous night,
And ere the birth of morn on earth
  Was born the Light of Light.

6 Then let us all with one accord
  Join Mary's song, and say,
"My soul doth magnify the Lord
  For ever and for aye."
Loud let us sing "Magnificat,"
  That dear and ancient lay,
For God's own Son with us is one,
  And He is born to-day.

561 **O'er the hill and o'er the vale.**

Joyfully.

O'er the hill and o'er the vale Came three kings to-geth-er,

Car-ing nought for snow and hail, Cold, and wind, and weath-er:

Now on Per-sia's sand-y plains, Now where Ti-gris swells with rains,

They their cam-els teth-er; Now thro' Sy-rian lands they go,

Now thro' Mo-ab faint and slow, Now thro' E-dom's heath-er.

2 O'er the hill and o'er the vale,
   Each king bears a present;
Wise men go a Child to hail,
   Monarchs seek a peasant:
And a star in front proceeds,
Over rocks and rivers leads,
   Shines with beams incessant.
Therefore onward, onward still!
Ford the stream and climb the hills:
   Love makes all things pleasant.

3 He is God ye go to meet;
   Therefore incense proffer.
He is King ye go to greet:
   Gold is in your coffer.
Also Man He comes to share
Every woe that man can bear.
   Tempter, Railer, Scoffer,
Therefore now against the day,
In the grave where Him they lay,
   Myrrh ye also offer.

Easter.

562 The Easter Sunshine breaks again.

With spirit.

The Eas - ter sun-shine breaks a - gain On all the sin - ful earth,

More glo-rious than the star - lit morn, We've sang at Je - sus' Birth!

rall.

We've watch'd be-side our Sa-viour's Cross, We've sorrowed at His Grave;

First two verses. *Third verse.**

But now He's broken Death's dark bands, Our Jesus, strong to save! Way! Sing

Last verse only.

cres.

on ye hap - py Chris - tian hearts, The Lord is risen to - day!

* The last two lines of verse 3 are repeated.

2 Fair blossoms on the Easter morn
  Fling forth their fragrance sweet,
And tell of Resurrection-joy,
  And Jesus' work complete!
But fairer still the offering
  Each loving heart should bring,
Of faith and love and penitence,
  To Christ, its risen King.

3 So on this glorious Easter-day
  Our gladsome songs we raise,
And echo e'en to Heaven's own gates
  Our happy notes of praise!
For He who died is risen again,
  "The Life, the Truth, the Way!"
Sing on, ye happy Christian hearts,
  The Lord is risen to-day.

563 Bright Easter skies.

Joyous.

1. Bright Eas-ter skies! Fair Eas-ter skies! Our Lord is risen, We, too, shall rise.
2. Green Easter fields! Fair Easter fields! Heaven's first ripe fruit, Death, conquer'd, yields.
3. Sweet Easter flowers! White Easter flowers! From Heaven descend Life-giving showers.
4. O Christian child! O Christian men! Our Vic-tor Lord, Shall come a-gain.

Nor walls of stone, hewn firm and cold, Nor Ro-man sol-diers, brave and bold;
In church-yards wide the seed we sow, Beneath the cross the wheat shall grow;
Each plant that bloomed at E-den's birth, Shall blow a-gain o'er ransomed earth.
Wake we our hearts at His com-mand; Lift we our love to His right hand.

dim.

Nor Satan's marshalled hosts could keep The pierced hands in death-ly sleep:
One Eas-ter-Day death's reign shall end, And golden sheaves shall heav'nward send.
Pluck lil-ies rare and ro-ses sweet, And strew the path of Je-sus' feet.
With warmest hopes, to Eas-ter skies, Stretch we our arms, and fix our eyes:

cres. *f*

Just as the Easter day-beams dawn, Our bur-ied Lord is risen and gone.
Hail the blest morn, by whose glad light, An-gels shall reap the har-vest white.
Throw fragrant palms be-fore our King, And wreathe the crown the saved shall bring.
Till in the clouds His sign we see, And quick and dead shout "Ju-bi-lee!"

AFTER EACH VERSE.

mf *cres.* *f*

Bright Eas-ter skies! Fair Eas-ter skies! Our Lord is risen, We, too, shall rise.

564

God hath sent His Angels.

Lively.

God hath sent His An-gels to the earth a-gain, Bringing joyful tid-ings to the sons of men.

TREBLES.

They who first at Christ-mas, throng'd the heav'nly way, Now be-side the tomb-door, sit on Eas-ter Day.

CHORUS.

An-gels sing His tri-umph, as you sang His birth, "Christ the Lord is ris-en," "Peace, good-will on earth."

Slower,

2 In the dreadful desert, where the Lord was tried,
There the faithful Angels gathered at His side.
And when in the garden, grief and pain and care
Bowed Him down with anguish, they were with Him there.
CHO.—Angels, sing, &c.

3 Yet the Christ they honour, is the same Christ still,
Who, in light and darkness, did His Father's will.
And the tomb deserted, shineth like the sky,
Since He passed out from it, into victory.
CHO.—Angels, sing, &c.

4 God has still His Angels, helping, at His word,
All His faithful children, like their faithful Lord;
Soothing them in sorrow, arming them in strife,
Opening wide the tomb-doors, leading into Life.
CHO.—Angels, sing, &c.

5 Father, send Thine Angels unto us, we pray;
Leave us not to wander, all along our way.
Let them guard and guide us, wheresoe'er we be,
Till our resurrection brings us home to Thee.
CHO.—Angels, sing, &c.

The world itself keeps Easter Day.

565 *Moderate.*

The world it-self keeps Eas-ter Day, And Eas-ter larks are sing-ing:

And Eas-ter flowers are blooming gay, And Eas-ter buds are springing:

Al-le-lu-ia! Al-le-lu-ia! The Lord of all things lives a-new, And

all His works are ri-sing too. Al-le-lu-ia! Al-le-lu-ia! Al-le-lu-ia!

2 There stood three Maries by the tomb
   On Easter morning early,
When day had scarcely chased the gloom,
   And dew was white and pearly;
      Alleluia! Alleluia!
With loving but with erring mind
They came the Prince of Life to find:
      Alleluia! Alleluia! Alleluia!

3 But earlier still the Angel sped
   His news of comfort giving;
And "why," he said, "among the dead
   "Thus seek ye for the living?"
      Alleluia! Alleluia!
"Go tell them all and make them blest,
"Tell Peter first, and then the rest."
      Alleluia! Alleluia! Alleluia!

4 But one, and one alone, remained
   With love that could not vary;
And thus a joy past joy she gained,
   That sometime sinner Mary:
      Alleluia! Alleluia!
The first the dear, dear form to see
Of Him who hung upon the tree:
      Alleluia! Alleluia! Alleluia!

5 The Church is keeping Easter Day,
   And Easter hymns are sounding,
And Easter flowers are blooming gay,
   The holy Font surrounding;
      Alleluia! Alleluia!
The Lord hath risen, as all things tell,
Good Christians, see ye rise as well:
      Alleluia! Alleluia! Alleluia!

566 Ye happy bells of Easter Day.

With spirit. ORGAN.

Ye hap-py bells of Eas-ter Day!

Ring, ring your joy.... Thro' earth and sky.... Ye ring a

glo-rious word. The notes that swell in glad-ness tell.... The ris-ing

ORGAN.

of the Lord.

2 Ye carol-bells of Easter Day!
 The teeming earth,
 That saw His birth
When lying 'neath the sword,
Upspringeth now in joy, to show
 The rising of the Lord!

3 Ye glory-bells of Easter Day!
 The hills that rise
 Against the skies,
 Re-echo with the word—
The victor-breath that conquers death—
 The rising of the Lord!

4 Ye passion-bells of Easter Day!
 The bitter cup
 He lifted up,
 Salvation to afford.
Ye saintly bells! your passion tells
 The rising of the Lord!

5 Ye mercy-bells of Easter Day!
 His tender side
 Was riven wide,
Where floods of mercy poured:
Redeemed clay doth sing to-day
 The rising of the Lord!

6 Ye victor-bells of Easter Day!
 The thorny crown
 He layeth down:
Ring! ring! with strong accord—
The mighty strain of love and pain,
 The rising of the Lord!

567 Shine, O Sun, in splendour bright.

Brightly.

Shine, O Sun, in splendour bright, Em-blem of the Lord of light,

Who this day rose from the dead, And cap-tiv'-ty cap-tive led.

CHORUS.

Sing joy-ous-ly, ye mor-tals, For Christ hath op'd the por-tals Of

life to all a-gain. Al-le-lu-ia, Al-le-lu-ia, Al-le-lu-ia, A-

men! Al-le-lu-ia! Al-le-lu-ia, Al-le-lu-ia! A-men!

2 Now the flowers budding sweet,
In the soil beneath our feet,
Raise themselves from sleep like death,
Praising God with fragrant breath.
CHO.—Sing joyously, &c.

3 All the trees and plants in spring
To the Resurrection bring
Signal offerings, and declare
Christ is ris'n, ev'ry where.
CHO.—Sing joyously, &c.

568 *Fast.* **Now all the bells are ringing.**

Al - le - lu - ia! Al - le - lu - ia! Al - le - lu - ia!

Now all the bells are ring - ing To welcome Eas-ter Day, And we with joy are

sing-ing Our ca-rol sweet and gay; For Jesus hath a - ri - sen From Joseph's rocky

cave, Hath burst His three days' pri - son, And tri-umph'd o'er the Grave.

Al - le - lu - ia! Al - le - lu - ia! Al - le - lu - ia! A-MEN.

2 Alleluia! Alleluia! Alleluia!
 O hasten we to meet Him,
 With our companions dear,
With love and awe to greet Him,
 As He is drawing near;
Of old His friends were bidden
 To haste to Galilee:
Still in His Church, all glorious,
 Our risen Lord will be.
 Alleluia! Alleluia! Alleluia!

3 Alleluia! Alleluia! Alleluia!
 Still, Jesus! we adore Thee
 With faith which may not fail;
Still, as we kneel before Thee,
 We hear Thee say "All hail"!
Thou, who art now descending
 To raise us up to Thee,
An Easter-tide unending
 Grant us in Heaven to see.
 Alleluia! Alleluia! Alleluia!

569 [113]
Christ is risen!

With spirit.

1. Christ is ris-en! Christ is ris-en! He hath burst His bonds in twain! Christ is ris-en!
2. Lo, the chains of death are broken! Earth below, and heaven above! Joy a-new in
3. An-gel legions, downward thronging, Hail the Lord of earth and skies! Ye who watch'd with

Christ is ris-en! Earth and Heav'n prolong the strain! He who suffered pain and loss,
eve-ry to-ken Of Thy triumph, Lord of love! He o'er earth and heav'n shall reign,
ho-ly long-ing Till your sun a-gain should rise: He is ris-en! Earth, re-joice!

In His love to us, Dy-ing on the bit-ter Cross, Lives vic-to-ri-
At His Father's side, Till He com-eth once a-gain, Bridegroom to His
Sing, ye star-ry train! All things living, find a voice! Je-sus lives a-

ous! Christ is ris-en! Christ is ris-en! He hath burst His bonds in twain!
Bride. Christ is ris-en! Christ is ris-en! He hath burst His bonds in twain!
gain! Christ is ris-en! Christ is ris-en! He hath burst His bonds in twain!

Christ is ris-en! Christ is ris-en! Earth and Heav'n, pro-long the strain!
Christ is ris-en! Christ is ris-en! Earth and Heav'n, pro-long the strain!
Christ is ris-en! Christ is ris-en! Earth and Heav'n, pro-long the strain!

570 The bells are ringing joyfully.

Joyfully.

VERSE, OR SEMI-CHORUS.

The bells are ringing joyfully, Their music fills the air, While from the world our

CHORUS. UNISON.

steps we turn, And seek the house of prayer. O   Eas-ter bells, glad Eas-ter bells, Our

HARMONY.

purest gifts we bring, And while our hearts with rapture swell, Arisen Lord we sing.

2 The bells are ringing joyfully,
   And, as we walk to-day,
Behold the loving Saviour comes,
To meet us on the way.
   O Easter bells, etc.

3 The bells are ringing joyfully,
   They ring from year to year,
But, as the Easter time comes round,
They seem to us most dear.
   O Easter bells, etc.

4 The bells are ringing joyfully.
   The earth is filled with flowers,
The risen Lord in mercy crowns
These sinful hearts of ours.
   O Easter bells, etc.

571 Have you heard the wondrous story?

BOYS.　　　　　　　　　　　　　　　　　　　　　　　　GIRLS.

1. Have you heard the wondrous sto-ry Of this glo - rious Eas-ter day? Yes, the
2. How shall we show forth our gladness On this bless - ed Eas-ter day? Praise the
3. But can words show forth the measure Of the debt of love we'd pay? No! in

BOTH.

Lord of life is ris - en, Hear what earth and heaven say: Christ is ris - en, Al-le-
Lord of life and glo - ry, And with all His peo-ple say: Christ is ris - en, Al-le-
ho - ly deed and lov - ing, Let our lives for ev - er say: Christ is ris - en, Al-le-

lu - ia! He hath won the vic - to - ry; He hath burst the grave's dark por - tals, And hath set ... His peo - ple free; .. He hath

burst the grave's dark por - tals, And hath set His peo- ple free. ...

572 Christ the Lord is risen to-day.

1. "Christ the Lord is ris'n to - day;" List - en while the An - gels say:
2. "Christ the Lord is ris'n to - day;" List - en while the Sol - diers say:
3. "Christ the Lord is ris'n to - day;" List - en while the Proph - ets say:
4. "Christ the Lord is ris'n to - day;" List - en while His bless'd lips say:

From His tomb the stone we roll'd, Eas - ter skies were cloth'd in gold;
Arms up - lift from rest and sleep, Sword nor spear the Lord could keep;
Where lay bound His sa - cred Head, Death and hell must loose their dead;
Graves and seas shall hear My word, Saints shall wake and hail Me Lord;

Forth in tri - umph Je - sus pass'd, Death's torn bands be - hind Him cast.
Cal - vary's mount did rock and reel; Burst the guard of stone and seal.
Preach it to a cap - tive world, Eas - ter ban - ners are un - furled.
Where He soars lift we our heart, Christ from us Death can - not part.

573 Beyond the starry skies.

Moderato.

Be - yond the star - ry skies, Far as the eter - nal hills, There in the boundless world of light Our great Re - deem - er dwells. A - round Him au - gels fair ... In count-less ar - mies shine; And ev - er in ex - alt - ed lays, They of - fer songs di - vine, And ev - er in ex - alt - ed lays, They of - fer songs di - vine.

" Hail, Prince of life!" they cry,
" Whose unexampled love,
Moved Thee to quit these glorious realms
And royalties above."
And when He stooped to earth,
And suffered rude disdain,
They cast their honours at His feet,
And waited in His train.

3 They saw Him on the cross,
While darkness veiled the skies,
And when He burst the gates of death,
They saw the conqueror rise.
They thronged His chariot wheels,
And bore Him to His throne;
Then swept their golden harps and sung,
" The glorious work is done."

574 The morning purples all the sky.

VERSE.

The morning purples all the sky, The air with praises rings: De-feated hell stands

sul-len-ly, The world ex-ult-ing sings: While He,the King,all strong to save,

Rends the dark doors away, And thro' the breaches of the grave Strides forth into the day.

CHORUS.

ff Glo-ry to God! our glad lips cry, All glo-ry be to God most High!

Glo-ry to God! our glad lips cry, All glo-ry be to God, to . .

rall.

God most High! God most High!

2 Death's captive, in his gloomy prison
Fast fettered He has lain;
But He has mastered death, is risen,
And death wears now the chain.
The shining angels cry, "Away
With grief; no spices bring;
Not tears, but songs, this joyful day,
Should greet the rising King!"
Glory to God, etc.

575 O joyous Easter morning.

O joy-ous Eas-ter morn-ing, That saw the Lord a-rise! O
bright and hap-py morn-ing! The clouds have left the skies. The
night of grief is end-ed. The day has come a-gain. And
dim.   *ril.*
Christ has won the vic-t'ry, For all the sons of men.

2 O gladsome Easter morning!
    Our hearts rejoice to-day,
The grave and death are conquered
    He is of Life the Way.
The hosts of sin are vanquished
    He is the Victor King!
Then let us all with gladness
    Our thankful praises sing.

3 O blessed Easter morning!
    What day so bright as this,
When, through His mighty triumph,
    He won the courts of bliss!
The doors of Heaven are open,
    The grave no more has dread;
For risen is our Saviour,
    The first fruits of the dead.

576 Near the Tomb where Jesus slept.

Con spirito.

Near the Tomb where Je - sus slept, Ro - man guards their night-watch kept,

Pac - ing to and fro a - lone, By the close - ly seal - ed stone.

CHORUS.

f

Christ! Thou Con - quer - or! All hail! Guard and stone can nought a - vail!

f

Death is slain in mor - tal strife; Hail the Prince and Lord of Life!

2 In the darksome midnight, lo!
Hark! an earthquake rolls below!
Sign of deadly conflict o'er,
Death despoiled for evermore!
Christ! Thou Conqueror! etc.

3 That which by the cave-mouth lay,
Angel hands have rolled away;
And the Lord, His three days sped,
Comes triumphant from the dead!
Christ! Thou Conqueror! etc.

4 O! the breathless fear which fell
On the guards no tongue may tell;
Prostrate all, in sore dismay,
As He rose, and passed away!
Christ! Thou Conqueror! etc.

5 Christ! Thou Victor o'er the tomb,
Take us in the Day of Doom,
Take us to Thine own dear side,
At the last great Easter-tide.

Chorus after last verse.
Christ! Thou Conqueror! all hail!
Let not Death o'er us prevail;
Help us in our mortal strife,
Bring us to the Land of Life!

577 Roman Soldier, tell us true.

CHILDREN. *Moderate.*

1. Ro-man Sol - dier, tell us true, What sort of a watch on guard are you?
2. Ro-man Sol - dier, tell us then, Why slew you not those thieving men?

The sep-ul-chre, sealed safe at night, How came it emp-ty at morn-ing light?
Were a few un-arm-ed Jews too hard, For a vet-e-ran mail-clad, Roman guard?

ROMAN SOLDIER. *

Why, Pe-ter and An - drew, James and John, They came by night, re-moved the stone,
O no! you Jews we nev - er fear; But we had no chance for sword or spear,

And long be-fore the break of day, They stole His Bod - y far a - way.
For up so soft-ly they did creep, While we were all of us fast a - sleep.

CHILDREN. *rall.* CHORUS.

Fie, Old Roman, why tell a lie? For Christ is ris-en, Christ is ris-en in-deed.
Fie, Old Roman, etc.

rall.

* NOTE.—The Roman Soldier's part is set in the G-clef for the convenience of children; but it is much better when sung by a man, an octave below.

Hal-le - lu - jah! Hal-le - lu - jah! Hal-le - lu - jah! A - MEN.

Child. 3 Roman Soldier, if you were
　　　All fast asleep, as you declare,
　　　How could you know, or see, or say,
　　　Who 'twas that stole the Lord away?

Sol. Old Annas and Caiphas told me so:
　　The truth they wished that none
　　　should know;
　　They gave me, therefore, silver and
　　　gold,
　　To tell the story I have told.

Child. Fie, old Roman, why tell a lie! For
　　Cho.—Christ is risen, &c.

Child. 4 Roman Soldier, tell no more
　　　The stories you have told before—
　　　Too foolish to deceive our youth;
　　　But tell us now the simple truth.

Sol. An earthquake rolled the stone away;
　　Half dead with fear we Romans lay;
　　While, like full sunrise at midnight,
　　Christ rose, and glided from our sight.

Child. Aye, Old Roman, why tell a lie! For
　　Cho.—Christ is risen, &c.

Child. 5 Roman Soldier, your own eyes
　　　Have seen our Lord and God arise;
　　　How can you, now that He is known,
　　　Still worship gods of wood and stone?

Sol. We Romans conquer where we come,
　　But Christ hath power to vanquish
　　　Rome;
　　My idols all I cast away,
　　Christ's soldier till my dying day.

Child. Right, Old Roman, fight for the Light.
　　Cho.—Christ is risen, &c. [For

578 　　　'Twas at the matin hour.

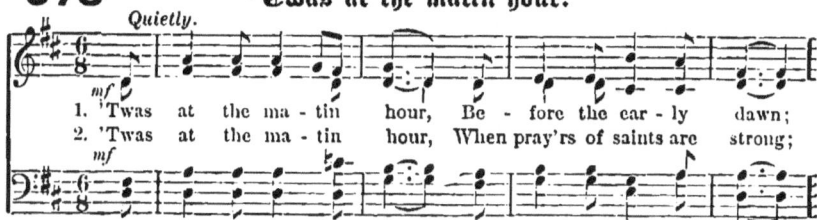

Quietly.

mf

1. 'Twas at the ma - tin hour, Be - fore the ear - ly dawn.
2. 'Twas at the ma - tin hour, When pray'rs of saints are strong;

mf

The pris - on doors flew o - pen, The bolts of death were drawn.
When two short days a - go He bore The spit - ting, wounds, and wrong.

3 From realms unseen, an unseen way,
　Th' Almighty Saviour came,
　And following on His silent steps,
　An Angel armed in flame.

4 The stone is rolled away,
　The keepers fainting fall,
　Satan and Pilate's watchmen,
　The day has scared them all.

5 The Angel came full early,
　But Christ had gone before,
　Not for Himself, but for His Saints,
　Is burst the prison door.

6 When all His Saints assemble,
　Make haste ere twilight cease,
　His Easter blessing to receive,
　And so lie down in peace.

579 Let the merry Church bells ring!

Fast.

Let the mer-ry Church bells ring! Hence with tears and sighing! Frost and cold have

fled from Spring, Life hath con-quered dy - ing. Flow'rs are smil-ing,

fields are gay, Sun - ny is the weath-er; With our ris - ing Lord to - day,

All things rise to-geth - er. Let the mer-ry Church bells ring! Ring! Ring!

Ring! Let the mer-ry Church bells ring! Ring! Ring! Ring!

2 Let the birds sing out again
  From their leafy chapel.
Praising Him, with whom in vain
  Satan sought to grapple;
Sounds of joy come fast and thick,
  As the breezes flutter;
Resurrexit, non est hic,
  Is the strain they utter.
    Let the merry, &c.

3 Let the past of grief be past;
  This our comfort giveth,
He was slain on Friday last,
  But to-day He liveth:
Mourning heart must needs be gay,
  Nor let sorrow vex it,
Since the very grave can say,
  Christus Resurrexit.
    Let the merry, &c.

Whitsuntide.

580   Sing your carols to-day.

Earnestly.

Sing your car - ols to - day, And your glad - som - est lay,
To the PA - RA - CLETE pay— Now to mor - tals giv - en;
Now sent down from heav - en, Sing, of joy, joy, joy; And to - day,
raise the lay, TE DE - UM LAU - DA - MUS, DOM - I - NUM.

2 Death and hell overcome,
Easter morn. from the tomb
Jesus chased all the gloom,—
Ope'd the prison portals—
Freedom brought to mortals.
Sing, of life. life, life,
And the strain. raise again,
TE DEUM LAUDAMUS, DOMINUM.

3 Forty days more with men
Did the Lord live again,
Blessed rites to ordain.
And His Kingdom founded
By the round world bounded.
Sing of joy, joy, joy,
Till it rise to the skies,
TE DEUM LAUDAMUS, DOMINUM.

4 Risen, never to die,
Having gone up on high
To His Throne in the sky,
He sent His Spirit Holy.
To bless His people solely.
Sing of joy, joy, joy,
Praise His Name with acclaim,
TE DEUM LAUDAMUS, DOMINUM.

5 With bright tongues as of flame,
Then the Comforter came,
In the Blessed One's Name
Dissipating sadness,—
Bringing joy and gladness,—
Sing of joy, life, and peace:
Him adore, ever more,
TE DEUM LAUDAMUS, DOMINUM.

Index of First Lines.

438

Carols.

www.ingramcontent.com/pod-product-compliance
Lightning Source LLC
Chambersburg PA
CBHW032301280326
41932CB00009B/658